The Constitution for Europe and an Enlarging Union: Unity in Diversity?

Europa Law Publishing, Groningen 2005

The Constitution for Europe and an Enlarging Union: Unity in Diversity?

Edited by Dr. Kirstyn Inglis & Dr. Andrea Ott

Europa Law Publishing is a publishing company specializing in European Union Law and international public law.
For further information please contact Europa Law Publishing via email: info@europalawpublishing.com or visit our website at: www.europalawpublishing.com.

Typeset in Scala and Scala Sans, Graphic design by G2K Designers, Groningen/Amsterdam

NUR 828; ISBN 90-76871-38-8

British Library Cataloguing-in-Publication Data
A catalogue record for this book is available from the British Library

Acknowledgements

This book publication is the end result of the research project 'The EU's Future in an enlarged Europe' which was supported by the European Commission under the Jean Monnet grant A-3022 from July 2003 to August 2004.

This edited volume contains selected contributions presented at a three-day young scholars seminar 'Enlargement and the Future of the European Union: Parallel Paths or Crossroads?' which was held in Warsaw (Poland) from 1 to 4 July 2004. We set out to explore current themes arising in law and political science in the context of constitutionalisation and differentiation in an enlarging Union as well as the conditionality applied to countries acceding to the Union. It was this methodology that imposed the choice of contributions from the many presented during the July 2004 seminar in Warsaw.

The Editors wish to thank all the authors and all those who delivered papers during the seminar; their input in terms of research and their active participation in the debates made a success of the event. The level and commitment of the contributions in particular is to be congratulated. Among those who delivered papers which we were unable to include, we want to thank: Vitalie Diaconu, Martin-John Doris, Nikolai Kaveshnikov, Andrea Keesen, Allard Knook, Dimitry Kochenov, Denys Kuzmin, Dr. Adam Lazowski, Alessio Lo Guidice, Dr. Veronika Lörincz, Vanessa Mak, Marcin Ozog, Jacek Sokolowski, Kyriaki Topidi and Dr. Vadim Voynikov.

We also would like to thank Jeroen Boender (First Secretary to the Royal Netherlands Embassy in Warsaw) for his presentation at the seminar, Professor Eugeniusz Piontek, University of Warsaw, for his support and chairmanship and, of course, Dr. Frank Hoffmeister from the European Commission for his full attendance and lively participation throughout the seminar, and indeed for his encouragement and support for the entire project. Adam Lazowski, deserves special thanks, having provided invaluable help in opening doors and facilitating the implementation of the project in Warsaw. In addition, the editors wish to thank Dr. Youri Devuyst from the European Commission for his support in implementing this project.

Dr. Andrea Ott would like to thank the European University Institute (Italy) for enabling her with a Jean Monnet scholarship to research the matters explored in her article. She also would like to mention the administrative support of Maastricht University, especially for budget matters Joof Schöpping and during the editing process Urszula Karkowska. Kirstyn Inglis would like to thank the Flemish Scientific Research Fund (Fonds voor Wetenschappelijk Onderzoek) for their support.

Introduction

Since the editing of this volume was finalised in the spring of 2005, the road to the Constitution for Europe seems to have come to a dead end. While the Spanish approved the Constitutional Treaty by a 76.73% majority in February 2005, the French turned down the Constitutional Treaty in a referendum on 29 May 2005 by a 55% majority and the Dutch followed in a consultative referendum on 1 June 2005 with a 61.8% majority against. As a consequence, the ratification process has come to a halt and subsequent positive referendums in Cyprus and Luxembourg have not kick- started the process. Of the remaining Member States, Austria, Belgium, Germany, Greece, Hungary, Italy, Latvia, Lithuania, Luxembourg, Malta, Slovakia, Slovenia and Spain have all ratified the Constitutional Treaty in accordance with their national constitutional procedures. But the French and Dutch votes have rendered the entire process, in the words of the Member States' governments, untenable. At their Council meeting on 16 June 2005, the Member States decided to postpone the ratification process. The Council intends to take some decision on how to proceed in June 2006. We have entered instead a serious period of reflection – a lay-by or a passing place – in the road to the future of an enlarged and enlarging European Union.

History is known for repeating itself. The ratification of the Maastricht Treaty in 1992 also suffered initial defeats. It seems appropriate to ask; 'Is the Constitutional Treaty now truly at a dead-end?' After all, this time around the stakes are higher and the situation is infinitely more complicated in an enlarged European Union of twenty-five Member States. The Constitutional Treaty was intended to consolidate and simplify the existing Treaties and Protocols of the two European Communities and the European Union to enable the Union to work in the expanded system.

Yet again, even after reforms introduced by the Maastricht Treaty, a new public discussion about the prospects and chances of the European Union have started. The majority of French and Dutch supporters for the Constitutional Treaty were aged 55 and older. It would seem that for the younger generation, prosperity and stability are taken for granted in Europe of the Twenty-first Century and Europe's long past of bloody wars and divisions have been forgotten.

More insightful, however, and patently more sophisticated than such interpretations of the negative French and Dutch referendums, is the more balanced, independent public opinion survey commissioned by the European Commission. The Eurobarometer Flash survey[1] published subsequent to the French and Dutch rejections of the Constitutional Treaty provides a greater understanding of these votes. This survey establishes that these were not in fact votes against

1 See 'Le "non" à la Constitution n'est pas un "non" à l'Europe', 15 June 2005, to be found at http://europa.eu.int/comm/public_opinion/index_fr.htm.

membership of the Union. The support in France for membership of the EU still amounts to 88% of the population and in the Netherlands it stands at 82% of the population. Moreover, among the 'no' votes, 83% of the population in France and 78% of the population in the Netherlands remain supporters of their EU membership! In the same survey the reasons for the negative votes are outlined. They were motivated by dissatisfaction with socio-economic concerns and the actual results achieved by the EU in the case of the French. For the Dutch the reasons were primarily the lack of information and fears over the loss of national sovereignty.

Most certainly, however, it is fair to say that the European Union has a communication problem towards its citizens; neither the Union nor its Member States have proved able to convince their citizens of the value of the achievements of the Union, particularly of the integration project and what it stands for.

The relatively harmless exercise of simplification of the existing treaty texts by the Constitutional Treaty has been overshadowed. The Constitutional Treaty is perceived as a far more radical instrument than it is in reality. The Constitutional Treaty is now paying for the failures of past years to win the hearts and minds of the Union's citizens for the European integration project. And failure to ratify the Constitutional Treaty has not only put a question mark over the entire integration project; it has even called into question the very legitimacy of the European Union. Enlargement and the EURO currency are of more concern to the average citizen than the long overdue simplification and consolidation process we urgently need for the existing treaties.

The Union's motto 'Unity in Diversity' is proclaimed in Article I-8 of the Constitutional Treaty. The Constitutional Treaty was intended to enable the Member States to function in a Union of twenty-five and more members. How much unity can now be achieved in such a diversity of Member States for the purposes of managing the political and legal affairs of the European Union? The enlarged Union is confronted with slow and cumbersome decision-making in the absence of the Constitutional Treaty. It will now be very difficult to introduce in palatable form any amendments proposed by the Constitutional Treaty given these stumbling blocks. These stumbling blocks are not going to go away. They will certainly come back to haunt the Union. Current financial contributions are at stake with discussions about cutting back on the expensive agricultural budget and renegotiation of the contribution of net contributors.

Finally, the diversity in a Union of twenty-five or more members also highlights the necessity of defining legally which unifying principles hold the Union together. Is the Union built upon the fundamental principles of equality and solidarity? Is the Union to be characterised as a mere customs union with special characteristics of an internal market? Or is the European Union integrated by law and a common constitutional system?

Ghent/Maastricht, July 2005

Foreword by Frank Hoffmeister

One of the key aspects of the European Union's success may be found in its design and operation as a Community of Law. The EU traditionally attached great attention to the uniform application of its law throughout the Member States and their equality before the law. Do these cornerstones of European integration stand after 1 May 2004 as solid as before? Or are Member States in an ever widening Europe more and more in need of special treatment? If so, are we witnessing a temporary era of 'opt-ins/opt-outs' / 'transitional arrangements' or will diversity of applicable EU rules in an EU 25 replace the traditional concept of unity? In this volume, young and promising scholars from both old and new Member States approach this intriguing question in three parts, building on a research seminar held in Warsaw in July 2004.

In the first part, highly analytical studies about the current shape of constitutionalisation are presented. *Michiel Brand* deals with theoretical objections against the idea that European Union law today not only operates as the common law of Member States, but as European constitutional law. He convincingly concludes that the Constitutional Treaty must be neither seen as foundation, nor completion or finalisation of European polity, but rather as maturation. The democratic challenge of the European Union is the subject of *Fabian Amtenbrink*'s enlightening study, who does not seem to expect many changes from the democratic innovations of the Constitutional Treaty. *Peter van Elsuwege* and *An Vermeersch* travel through the difficult issue of institutional reforms. They present a good overview about the complicated balancing act between old/new as well as big/small Member States as well as about the institutional balance between the EU institutions. An important comparative law contribution stems from *Phillip Kiiver* who aptly deals with the different levels of influence that national Parliaments, including in the new Member States, exercise over their governments on EU issues.

The second part deals with several areas of differentiation in EU Law and Policy. *Andrea Ott* shows that "enhanced cooperation", as introduced by the Treaty of Amsterdam, remained a dead letter so far in EU practice. Her plea that some core EU principles impose limits on the EU treaty-making powers of the Member States, may be seen as a central piece of this book, erecting legal barriers against too much of 'diversity' in EU primary law. However, that concept does not come into play, when Member States expressly adopt a "stages" approach to primary rights and obligations, as is the case with the European Monetary Union. Here, as *Beata Dcziechciarz* points out, different statuses are expressly aimed at. It will therefore largely depend on the political will of the new Member States, whether the Eurozone will rather grow or remain a "minority club". *Nikolaos Skoutaris* examines thoroughly the unique status of Turkish Cypriots who are living in the northern areas outside the control of the Cyprus government. As citizens of the Republic of Cyprus they are EU citizens, but they cannot exercise EU citizen rights on that very territory. Whereas this required a special rule for Cyprus in the Accession Treaty (Protocol 10), the Treaty introduced distinct rules in the agricultural sector for all new Member States. *Sandra Marco Colino* demonstrates in detail that this inequality before the law was closely connected with the discussions on reforming the Common Agricultural Policy as a whole. Hence, it is not improbable that agricultural law in the EU will have been changed, before even full equality is achieved for the new Member States. Finally, *Przemysław Zysk* tackles the other most sensitive issues in the last enlargement round, namely internal security. He conceives the new justice and home affairs safeguard as "double standard" and observers that true EU cooperation in these areas presuppose a high level of mutual trust between the security institutions of the Member States.

The EU policy tool of conditionality is the focal point of part Three. *Kirstyn Inglis* skilfully outlines the relevant instruments of the enlargement process. Indeed, it seems that more and more "sticks" have been applied for States to join the European Union, and the bigger the European Union grows, the more difficult it will become to adapt internally. One of the biggest challenges in the new Member States and may be one of the clearest examples of successful conditionality was minority protection, as *Peter van Elsuwege* argues. Again, the repercussions on the European Union itself are less evident. There may be only limited spill-over for an EU wide *internal* monitoring mechanism. From a country perspective, Turkey is the most breathtaking example of EU conditionality. *Ahmet Sözen* demonstrates how closely reform steps in Turkey are linked with the incentive to get closer to the European Union. His distinguished contribution may be a point of reference for any broader debate on EU-Turkey relations.

In sum, the book assembles highly stimulating scholarly insights in a number of important EU topics. I am deeply impressed by the high quality of the contributions. The editors managed to gain skilful young authors who will surely make their academic and/or professional way. I can only congratulate both the editors and the authors for this exercise and hope that many readers will be as inspired as me by 'Unity in Diversity'.

Brussels, September 2005

List of Contributors

Amtenbrink, Dr., Fabian
Senior lecturer in European Law, Fellow at the Centre for Law, Administration and Society (CRBS), University of Groningen, Netherlands

Brand, Michiel
Research Assistant, Tilburg University, The Netherlands

Dziechciarz, Beata
Ph.D. Candidate, Viadrina University Frankfurt/Oder, Germany

Inglis, Kirstyn,
Senior Researcher, European Institute, University of Ghent Belgium

Kiiver, Dr. Philipp
Lecturer in European and Comparative Public Law, Maastricht University, The Netherlands

Marco Colino, Sandra
Ph.D. Candidate, European University Institute, Italy

Ott, Dr., Andrea
Lecturer in European Law, University of Maastricht, The Netherlands

Skoutaris, Nikolaos
PhD candidate, European University Institute, Florence

Sözen, Prof. Dr. Ahmet
Eastern Mediterranean University, Northern Cyprus

van Elsuwege, Peter
Academic Assistant, European Institute, University of Ghent,

Vermeersch, An
Academic Assistant, European Institute, University of Ghent

Zysk, Przemysław
Ph.D. Candidate, European University Institute, Italy

CHAPTER 5 The 'Principle' of Differentiation in an Enlarged European Union; Unity in Diversity?

Andrea Ott

CHAPTER 6 Impact of European Union Enlargement on EMU; Monetary Split-up into 'Ins' and 'Outs' as a Temporary or Permanent Phenomenon?

Beata Dziechciarz

PART I – CONSTITUTIONALISATION AND INTEGRATION

CHAPTER I

Formalising European Constitutionalism

Potential Added Value or 'Death by Constitution'[1]

Michiel Brand

1 Introduction

1.1 The debate on the future of Europe

Whereas the functional Monnet method of 'piece-meal engineering' and 'result-based masterminding'[2] has always sustained a near absence, at least on the political level,[3] of grand and constructive debates on the future of Europe, more recent times have altered this situation. The start of a wide-ranging debate was marked by the speech of Germany's Foreign Minister Joschka Fischer on 12 May 2000 to the Humboldt University, where he presented his own view on the future shape of Europe.[4] Subsequent events took us from the Nice[5] and Laeken[6] declarations to the Convention on the future of Europe which discussed reforms to the Union's Treaty structure.

1.2 A European constitution

Due to the fact that issues of a fundamental and constitutional nature were put on the reform agenda,[7] the idea of a European constitution rapidly gained centre stage in the debate. Many political statements were made favouring a European constitution[8] and quite remarkably even the more eurosceptic forces known for having 'engaged in a symbolic practice of 'consti-

---

1 J. Klabbers and P. Leino, 'Death by Constitution? The Draft Treaty Establishing a Constitution for Europe', 4:12 *German Law Journal* (2003) p. 1293, www.germanlawjournal.com.

2 K. Lenaerts and M. Desomer, 'New Models of Constitution-Making in Europe: The Quest for Legitimacy', 39 *CMLRev.* (2002) p. 1217, at p. 1224.

3 The European Parliament must be mentioned here as the exception to this observation: see ibid., p. 1223 and n. 28 there.

4 J. Fischer, 'Speech by Joschka Fischer at the Humboldt University in Berlin, 12 May 2000; From Confederacy to Federation: Thoughts on the Finality of European Integration', in C. Joerges, Y. Mény and J.H.H. Weiler, eds., *What Kind of Constitution for What Kind of Polity? Responses to Joschka Fischer* (Florence, European University Institute 2000), p. 19.

5 Declaration 23 to the Final Act of the Treaty of Nice.

6 Laeken Declaration on the Future of the European Union, Annex I to the Presidency Conclusions of the Laeken European Council of 14 and 15 December 2001.

7 The Nice declaration mentions four core issues, *i.e.* the delimitation of powers between the EU and the Member States; the status of the Charter of Fundamental Rights; simplification of the Treaties and the role of the national parliaments in the European architecture.

8 E.g. Fischer, op. cit. n. 4; J. Chirac, 'Our Europe, speech by M. Jacques Chirac, President of the Republic, to the Bundestag, 27 June 2000', www.yem.org.uk/files/speech_chirac.pdf; J. Rau, 'Plädoyer für eine Europäische Verfassung: Rede von Bundespräsident Johannes Rau vor dem Europäischen Parlament am 4. April 2001 in Straßburg', *Die Welt*, 5 April 2001; L. Jospin, 'Lionel Jospin on the Future of an Enlarged Europe' (2001), www.europa.eu.int/futurum/documents/speech/sp280501_en.htm.

tutional denial'[9] became reconciled to the idea of a European constitution and participated in the constitutional debate,[10] mostly perhaps because of the potentially restrictive rather than expansionary function of a constitution.

The careful stance taken by the Laeken declaration, which asked whether the intended simplification and reorganisation of the Treaties 'might not lead *in the long run* to the adoption of a constitutional text in the Union',[11] was soon overtaken by the Convention that transformed itself into a constitutional Convention from the very beginning.[12] In less than a year and a half the Convention produced a 'Draft Treaty establishing a Constitution for Europe'[13] that was presented to the European Council in Rome on 18 July 2003.[14] Subsequently, an Intergovernmental Conference was initiated on 4 October 2003 to discuss the fate of the Convention draft. Whereas disagreement in the IGC on the *content* of the constitution soon emerged, it was notable that the constitutional terminology itself was virtually uncontested. After the initial failure to reach agreement at the summit in December 2003, eventually the constitutional package – with some important substantive revisions in comparison with the Convention draft – was accepted at the Brussels European Council of 17 and 18 June 2004. The 'Treaty establishing a Constitution for Europe'[15] was then signed on 29 October 2004 in Rome and now awaits the final phase of ratification by all the Member States of the European Union (hereinafter 'EU').

But how must this explicit adoption of the language of constitutionalism on the EU plane be judged? Reactions range from the politically rhetorical, characterising the Constitutional Treaty as 'an historic step forward in the process of integration and co-operation in Europe',[16] to the (moderately) enthusiastic, such as Convention President Giscard d'Estaing who said that the result is 'not perfect, yet unexpected', to the outright apocalyptic, employing phrases like 'death by Constitution' and referring to the Constitutional Treaty as 'the end of European integration as we know it'.[17] This contribution portrays a vision of

9 N. Walker, 'The Idea of Constitutional Pluralism', 65 *MLR* (2002) p. 317 at p. 332.

10 See, e.g., J. Straw, 'Strength in Europe Begins at Home, Speech by Jack Straw, Edinburgh, 27.08. 2002', europa.eu.int/futurum.

11 Emphasis added.

12 Before the start of the Convention, its President, Valéry Giscard d'Estaing, compared the body to the Philadelphia Convention that wrote the US constitution in 1787; see 'Giscard wants to be Europe's Benjamin Franklin', *EUobserver*, www.euobserver.com, visited on 7 February 2002.

13 CONV 850/03 and *OJ* 2003 C 169/1.

14 See also 'Report from the Presidency of the Convention to the President of the European Council of 18 July 2003', CONV 851/03 and V. Giscard d'Estaing, 'Rome Declaration, 18 July 2003', european-convention.eu.int/docs/Treaty/Rome_EN.pdf.

15 Denoted in the footnotes by 'Constitutional Treaty'.

16 Presidency Conclusions of the June 2004, Brussels European Council.

17 Klabbers and Leino, op. cit. n. 1.

positive realism, arguing that the Constitutional Treaty has a potential added value for the integration process, whereas on the other hand it should certainly not be considered as the 'magical' or 'final' solution for Europe. The main focus will be on the theoretical and formal aspects of Europe's 'constitutional question', rather than on the content of the Constitutional Treaty. The substantive elements of Europe's Constitution must thus be regarded as being somehow *separate* from the 'terminological' question, even though the two are of course strongly intertwined. In other words, the prospective establishment of a European Treaty explicitly framed in constitutional terms, is an issue that can also be defended or contested regardless of the content of that document.

In this contribution, I will argue, as do many others,[18] that the present Union already is endowed with its own constitution. The constitutional process must thus be understood not as aiming to create a constitution for Europe but as intending to bring about a modified and more explicit form of constitution for Europe. It will, moreover, be asserted that this process towards the elaboration of a European constitution is a useful and desirable exercise, signifying an affirmation and refinement of already existing European constitutionalism.

It is obvious that this argument is subject to much and heavy criticism. These critical positions will be closely looked at in this paper and I will try to provide convincing counter arguments against them. The fiercest and most well-known of those critical positions is the no demos thesis, with which we shall start the discussion.

2 The no demos thesis

2.1 A short summary of the no demos thesis

The no demos thesis constitutes a fundamental challenge to the contention that Europe is already endowed with its own constitution. Moreover, the thesis holds that Europe should not, and in principle also is not *able* to, have a constitution. The no demos thesis finds its origin in German constitutional thinking and has been put forward most notably by Dieter Grimm[19] and by the (in)famous Maastricht judgment of Germany's Federal Constitutional

---

18 See, e.g., W. Van Gerven, 'Toward a Coherent Constitutional System within the European Union', 2 *EPL* (1996) p. 81; M. Zuleeg, 'The European Constitution under Constitutional Constraints: The German Scenario', 22 *ELRev.* (1997) p. 19; J.H.H. Weiler, *The Constitution of Europe; 'Do the New Clothes Have an Emperor?' and Other Essays on European Integration* (Cambridge University Press 1999); A. Føllesdal, 'Drafting a European Constitution – Challenges and Opportunities', Constitutionalism Web-Papers, ConWEB No. 4/2002, les1.man.ac.uk/conweb.

19 D. Grimm, 'Does Europe need a Constitution?', 1 *ELJ* (1995) p. 282.

Court, the *Bundesverfassungsgericht*.[20] As the thesis is relatively well-known, a short summary of the argument suffices here.[21]

The no demos thesis conceives of a demos as an ethno-cultural, organic and static concept, characterised by a certain degree of homogeneity.[22] This view of a demos is an extremely rigid and indivisible one, setting high and demanding criteria for the existence of a people. It is obvious that this extreme conception of demos is exclusively linked to the state rather than to a non-state polity such as the EU where the strong criteria can hardly be met. Since, however, 'it is inherent in a constitution in the full sense of the term that it goes back to an act taken by or at least attributed to the people, in which they attribute political capacity to themselves',[23] the EU does not have a constitution. The ethno-cultural and organic demos is conflated with the concepts of state, democracy and constitution. The European Union lacks a demos, is not an independent democratic source and does not have a constitution. If the EU were to have a constitution based on a single European demos, however unlikely[24] and undesirable that may be, it would transform automatically into a European state thereby replacing the national states and demoi.

2.2 The critique

The no demos thesis has been the subject of severe criticism. Below, I will offer some lines of response to the no demos view to show that it is fundamentally flawed in certain respects.

---

20 *Brunner v. The European Union Treaty* [1994] 1 *CMLRep.* 57.

21 It should be emphasised that this is but one interpretation, since the no demos argument has been used in different variants. In the same way, it is to be noted that the critique of the no demos thesis I will present below is not necessarily directed against all variations, 'soft' or 'hard', of that thesis. For a 'composite version of the No Demos thesis culled from the [Maastricht judgment] and some of the principal exponents of this thesis', see J.H.H. Weiler, 'Does Europe Need a Constitution? Demos, Telos and the German Maastricht Decision', 1 *ELJ* (1995) p. 219, at p. 224 et seq.

22 See further ibid., pp. 225-226.

23 Ibid., p. 290.

24 Grimm does keep the possibility of the future existence of a European people open, as he speaks of the fact that 'there is *as yet* no European people', Grimm, op. cit. n. 19, at p. 297 [emphasis added]. However, his insistence on a common European language, impeding the existence of European communication systems as well as his statement that the democracy deficit is 'structurally determined', indicate his scepticism as to the idea that a real European democracy based on one European people might ever be realised. Noteworthy is that also the *Bundesverfassungsgericht* seems to keep the possibility of a future European demos open; see *Brunner judgment*, *supra* n. 20, para. 41-42.

2.2.1 The concepts of demos and identity

When observed from the viewpoint of law-making and, more specifically, self-legislation, the notion of identity may be conceived of in two different ways.[25] First of all, there is the static view on identity as expounded by the *Bundesverfassungsgericht* in its Maastricht decision. Taking up the classic distinction between *pouvoir constituant* and *pouvoir constitué*, valuing the former over the latter, the court holds that the people is 'the starting point for a state power relating to that people' and that the 'process of political will-formation' gives 'legal expression to what binds the people together'.[26] In other words: the identity of a people is the prior normative closure preceding the enactment of legal norms that express that identity. Law-making in this view is no more than a *reproduction* or *imitation* of identity in the form of a pre-given and directly accessible set of characteristics.

This is complemented by the second view on identity in the form of constructivism[27] according to which legal norms may also produce identity and the opposite conceptual sequence to that of the *Bundesverfassungsgericht* may also be the case: first a state/constitution, then a people. This second conception is more dynamic and open in that identity is at stake in every step of the integration process, formed in and modified by every act of the Union. The dynamic view is aptly illustrated by the process of enlargement – most notably where it includes a country like Turkey that could be considered the 'least European' of the current and prospective Member States on several counts – which allows us to acknowledge that neither European identity nor the borders of the Union as a legal and political entity, are pre-fixed.[28]

It is the static and descriptive view that prevents European identity from being a substantively vacuous notion, albeit that the dynamics involved in the enactment of legal norms entails that identity is in constant flux and that any substantiation must be considered, to a greater or lesser extent, provisional.[29]

---

25 See also M. Brand and L. Corrias, 'Editorial: The Enlarging Europe and Its Implications for the Concept of European Identity: The Case of Turkey', 12 *Tilburg Foreign Law Review* (2005) p. 103; A. lo Giudice, 'The European Self: A Reflexive Approach towards European Identity', 12 *Tilburg Foreign Law Review* (2005), p. 145; H. Lindahl, 'European Integration: Popular Sovereignty and a Politics of Boundaries', 6 *ELJ* (2000) p. 239; H. Lindahl, 'Acquiring a Community: The Acquis and the Institution of European Legal Order', 9 *ELJ* (2003) p. 433.

26 See the *Brunner judgment, supra* n. 20, para. 44.

27 See e.g. J. Habermas, 'Why Europe needs a Constitution', 11 *New Left Review* (September- October 2001) p. 5, pointing to 'the voluntaristic character of a civic nation, the collective identity of which exists *neither independent of nor prior to the democratic process from which it springs*', at p. 15 (Emphasis added).

28 Brand and Corrias, op. cit. n.25.

29 A more radical view on this is put forward by Lindahl 2003, op. cit. n.25, who notes that: 'If constituent power claims to represent the common good, the inverse holds as well: there is no direct access to the

It seems clear, however, that the aforementioned substantiation of identity made by the no demos thesis, is to be used with great care and in any case is an *incomplete* one. First of all, when we have regard to our present Western, multicultural societies, we should realise that the 'thick' and homogeneous demos, as advanced by the no demos thesis, should be used in a relative rather than absolute sense.[30] Secondly, Weiler has convincingly challenged the view that the concept of demos be understood exclusively in organic, cultural and homogeneous terms but, conversely, we should also understand the concept of demos (and the European demos in particular):

> *'in non-organic civic terms, a coming together on the basis not of shared ethnos and/or organic culture, but a coming together on the basis of shared values, a shared understanding of rights and societal duties and shared rational intellectual culture which transcend organic-national differences'.*[31]

The concept of a civic demos thus requires that nationality (in the organic, national-cultural sense) be decoupled from citizenship and *Volk* from demos, something that is inconceivable in accordance with the no demos thesis. One can belong simultaneously to two, co-existing demoi: a 'thick', national demos and a 'thin', civic, European demos. The latter does not replace the former but rather complements it.

2.2.2 Some erroneous conflations

The no demos thesis tends to conflate the concepts of state, constitution, demos and democracy.[32] The thick demos, characterised by a certain degree of spiritual, social and political homogeneity and (often) characterised by the use of a common language, is linked almost inextricably to the state and to the constitution on which it is founded. Remarkable is the enslavement to the notion of state, which is considered the only viable framework for constitutional democracy.

---

common good; it is only accessible mediately, by way of its representations. Deprived of representations which concretise it, the common good is but an empty normative signifier which provides no normative orientation whatsoever', at p. 447.

30 See T. Koopmans, 'Rechter, D-Mark en Democratie: Het *Bundesverfassungsgericht* en de Europese Unie' [Judge, D-Mark and Democracy: The *Bundesverfassungsgericht* and the European Union], 69 *Nederlands Juristenblad* (1994) p. 245.

31 See Weiler, op. cit. n.18, at pp. 243-244.

32 Again, it needs to be borne in mind that not every version of the no demos thesis would make the same extreme conflations; e.g. the *Brunner* judgment, *supra* n. 20 at para. 40 hints at the possibility of post-State democracy. Also, as we will see in Chapter IV, Joseph Weiler, even though being a fierce opponent of the no demos view, nevertheless subscribes to certain parts of this cluster of conflations.

However, such conflation is ill-founded. First of all, the 'thick demos' is often but certainly not exclusively linked to the democratic state as shown by reality.[33] Next, Paul Craig explains that constitutions, as Grimm asserts, do not necessarily have to go back to an act taken by or attributed to the people as the empirical and normative foundation for that claim is not readily apparent.[34] Also, the alleged indissoluble relation between constitution and state, especially when having regard to our post-Westphalian world, is unjustified. After all:

'[T]he notion of 'Constitution' is older than the notion of 'State', and [...] a constitution is not necessarily reserved to the 'sovereign state' as defined in the modern age. [...] A prerequisite for a constitution is the existence of a political community: a state as such is not required. In other words, the shape of the political system depends upon the provisions of the constitution. With the notion of 'constitution' thus understood in a wider sense, notably as the basic legal order of a political system, there is no obstacle for the capacity of the European Union, being not a state but a supranational entity sui generis, to have a constitution. Moreover, the term 'constitution' has already been applied to the foundation charters of other international organizations.'[35]

A European constitution does not inevitably lead to a European state.[36] Whereas the changes that would be needed in order to create a European state (such as full EU sovereignty in all external matters, a European army and police force, a common European fiscal policy, etc.) could of course be included in a constitution, there is no necessary reason why this should be so. However, it has to be accepted that there remains a strong link between the two concepts, as constitutions are often traditionally defined as the basic law of a state. Adopting a broad view of a constitution requires us to cut 'the umbilical cord connecting the Constitution and the nation-state',[37] something not everyone considers as acceptable.

---

33 Mancini points, amongst others, to states like South Africa and India, which are comprised of several nations, or thick demoi, but which are nevertheless democracies. See G.F. Mancini, 'Europe: The Case for Statehood', 4 *ELJ* (1998) p. 29 at pp. 36-37.

34 See P. Craig, 'Constitutions, Constitutionalism and the European Union', 7 *ELJ* (2001) p. 125, at pp. 137-138.

35 See C. Dorau and P. Jacobi, 'The Debate over a 'European Constitution': Is it Solely a German Concern?', 6 *EPL* (2000) p. 413 at pp. 417-418.

36 See Craig, op. cit. n. 34, at p. 138. Also politicians advocating a European constitution have continuously stressed that they do not thereby envisage the creation of a European superstate. See, e.g., Chirac, op. cit. n. 8, Jospin, op. cit. n. 8 and Rau, op. cit. n. 8.

37 B. de Witte, 'The Closest Thing to a Constitutional Conversation in Europe: The Semi-Permanent Treaty Revision Process', in P. Beaumont, C. Lyons and N. Walker, eds., *Convergence and Divergence in European Public Law* (Oxford, Hart Publishing 2002), p. 39, at p. 39 - n. 1.

The no demos thesis conceives of the relationship between Europe and its Member States in 'either-or' terms. This is precisely the big danger and fallacy of the thesis. Proponents of the thesis hold that, currently, the only legitimate source of democracy is the Nation-State and that if we were to create a European demos, as construed in their conception of it, it would necessarily mean the destruction of the separate national demoi thereby creating a European state. It is thus a zero-sum game, the existence of national demoi alongside a European demos is simply excluded. In the European context, such a view is particularly difficult. The thick conception of demos simply denies the existence of a European democracy and puts all weight solely on national democracies. This surely cannot be so.[38] The Union is already based on a demos, has its own democratic source and is capable of having a constitution. This is not to deny that the national democracies are not valuable, on the contrary. But it must lead us to the conclusion that national states surely are not the only framework in which the democratic constitutional state can be adequately realised as Grimm suggests. Both the Member States and the EU constitute a source of democracy and their relationship is complementary rather than exclusionary.

3 The current EU Constitution

3.1 A gradualising approach towards constitutionalism[39]

Taking Joseph Raz's[40] notion of 'thin' and 'thick' constitutions as a starting point, one must observe that a constitution is not a very precisely definable concept. This opens up the way of perceiving differing degrees of constitutionalism. Concrete conceptualisations of a constitution strongly diverge and range from an approach of 'trivial minimalism' – as adopted for example by Jack Straw who stated that even 'Golf Clubs have constitutions'[41] – to 'extreme maximalism' – looking at constitutions with the presupposition of a thick demos and inextricably linking the concept to states. Trivial minimalism, however, may

---

38 Cf. Weiler, op. cit. n. 18, at p. 231-232; 'Whether or not there is a European demos, it is hard to see how in the already *existing* stage of European integration both pre- and post-Maastricht, statal structures, processes and institutions alone, including the German Federal Constitutional Court itself, can possibly provide adequate democratic guarantees for the European construct.'

39 Constitutionalism can be defined as 'the set of beliefs associated with constitutional government', N. Walker, 'European Constitutionalism and European Integration', *Public Law* (1996) p. 266 at p. 267 or as: 'the normative discourse through which constitutions are justified, defended, criticised, denounced or otherwise engaged with', Walker, op. cit. n. 9, at p. 318.

40 J. Raz, 'On the Authority and Interpretation of Constitutions: Some Preliminaries', in L. Alexander, ed., *Constitutionalism: Philosophical Foundations* (Cambridge University Press 1998) p. 152, at pp. 153-154.

41 Straw, op. cit. n. 10.

be too weak[42] and extreme maximalism, as already suggested, too strong. Adopting a gradualising approach towards constitutionalism, one could imagine a certain threshold beyond which it is appropriate to speak of a constitution. It will be argued in the following section that the EU finds itself beyond this threshold and that it can thus rightly be described in constitutional terms.

3.2 The constitutionalisation thesis

The 'constitutionalisation' or 'transformation' thesis holds that the EC/EU has developed from a creature of international law to a federal-type, constitutional legal order, conferring judicially enforceable rights and obligations on public as well as private parties.[43] The European Court of Justice has done most to fuel the constitutionalisation claim. Most prominent are the ECJ's notorious doctrines of direct effect and supremacy, which have generally been accepted by the national courts.[44] Also relevant to mention here are the doctrine of implied powers, pre-emption, and the ECJ's jurisprudence on fundamental rights. Crucial has also been the specific language used by the Court, such as in the famous 1986 *Les Verts* judgment, in which it referred to the EEC Treaty as the 'basic constitutional charter' of the Community.[45]

The Treaties display the minimal content of a constitution: they contain the Union's foundational values; they refer to rights that are also found in many national constitutions,[46] and; they contain organisational provisions on the institutions. It is evident that the Treaties 'go far beyond classic international treaties, and they do indeed contain some important elements which are mentioned by law dictionaries as defining what a Constitution is'.[47] It should again be stressed

---

42 Neil Walker ironically remarks on Straw's statement: 'This attitude fails to acknowledge that the European Union, unlike any golf club with which I am acquainted, is an active geo-political player, implicated like all such active players in the competition for scarce symbolic resources.', N. Walker, 'Postnational Constitutionalism and the Problem of Translation', Institute for International Law and Justice, NYU School of Law - Working Paper IILJ 2003/03, www.nyuiilj.org/governance/workingpapger_2003_03.pdf, at n. xii.

43 See, e.g., E. Stein, 'Lawyers, Judges and the Making of a Transnational Constitution', 75 *AJIL* (1981) p. 1; J-C Piris (1999), 'Does the European Union have a Constitution? Does it need one?', 24 *ELRev.* (1999) p. 557, at pp. 559-565, Weiler, op. cit. n. 18, Chapter 2 and Craig, op. cit. n. 34, pp. 128-130.

44 The acceptance of absolute supremacy, *i.e.* supremacy of Community law over provisions of the national constitutions, has proven difficult however. Cf for example *Brunner, supra* n. 20.

45 ECJ, Case 294/83, *Les Verts*, [1986] *ECR* 1339, para. 23. See also ECJ, Case C-2/88, *Zwartveld*, [1990] *ECR* I-3365, para. 16; *Opinion 1/91*, [1991] *ECR* I-6079, para. 1; and Case C-314/91, *Weber*, [1993] *ECR* I-1093, para. 8.

46 E.g. the provisions on the prohibition of discrimination (Arts. 12, 13, 141 EC) and the citizenship provisions of Arts. 17-22 EC. Also relevant to mention are Art. 6 (1) and (2) and Art. 7 EU.

47 Piris, op. cit. n. 43, p. 559.

that this does not equal a stately constitution. The fact that the Union can be said to be endowed with a constitution is by no means to say that it *is* a state nor that it is, or should be, in the process of becoming one.[48] As already indicated above, constitutions and states are strongly related but far from being conflated.

The Union clearly cannot be viewed anymore as a traditional international organisation. After all, it has strong supranational features, such as an independent Commission, a directly elected Parliament, qualified majority voting in the Council and an independent Court with the power of binding decision-making. The EU also unfolds its activities into a vast range of policy areas, which even led Koen Lenaerts to conclude that '[t]here simply is no nucleus of sovereignty that the Member States can invoke, as such, against the Community'.[49] The foregoing analysis strongly supports the argument that the EC/EU has transformed into an autonomous, supranational and constitutional legal order with federal characteristics.[50]

The constitutionalisation thesis, however, is contested by a sizeable group of scholars taking the approach of 'defensive internationalism',[51] which 'seeks to grasp and contain all the transformations of authoritative structures and processes beyond the state [thus also the EU] within the traditional paradigm of international law' [author's additional clarification in brackets].[52] Without going into the argument here,[53] I believe that the position of defensive internationalism cannot undermine the cogent constitutionalisation thesis. Borrowing some useful metaphors, to persist in describing the EU in purely internationalist terms is much like trying 'to push the toothpaste back in the tube'[54] or

---

48 The idea of creating a centralised European state completely subsuming the Member States is unrealistic and undesirable. For a rare plea in favour of such development, however, see Mancini, op. cit. n. 33 and the response by J.H.H. Weiler, 'Europe: The Case Against the Case for Statehood', 4 *ELJ* (1998) p. 43.

49 K. Lenaerts, 'Constitutionalism and the Many Faces of Federalism', 38 *AJCL* (1990) p. 205 at p. 220. See, however, Walker, op. cit. n. 9, at p. 346, n. 107.

50 It is significant that Art. 1 of an earlier Convention draft, CONV 528/03, stated that the EU 'shall administer certain common competences on a federal basis'. The 'F-word', however, sparked much controversy, most notably in the UK, which eventually led to its removal from the Convention's final Draft Constitution.

51 See, e.g., D. Wyatt, 'New Legal Order, or Old?', 7 *ELRev* (1982) p. 147; T. Schilling, 'The Autonomy of the Community Legal Order: An Analysis of Possible Foundations', 37 *Harv. ILJ* (1996) p. 389; T. Schilling, 'Rejoinder: The Autonomy of the Community Legal Order', *Jean Monnet Working Paper 10/96*, www.jeanmonnetprogram.org; and J. Allain, 'The European Court of Justice Is an International Court', 68 *NorJIL* (1999) p. 249.

52 Walker, op. cit. n. 9, at p. 322.

53 For a more elaborate analysis, see M. Brand, 'Affirming and Refining European Constitutionalism: Towards the Establishment of the First Constitution for the European Union', *EUI Working Paper Law*, No. 2004/2, pp. 22 et seq.

54 Weiler, op. cit. n. 18, at p. 298.

'to force square pegs into round holes'.[55] It should be borne in mind, however, that defensive internationalism must primarily be understood as an argument that contests the description of the present Union in constitutionalist terms. This does not mean, however, that defensive internationalism – though, as the approach seems to be driven by a fear of post-state entities such as the EU eroding national sovereignty and transforming the traditional intergovernmental view of international law – also necessarily rejects the possibility or even the desirability of a future European constitution.[56]

4 The case against a European Constitutional Treaty

Notwithstanding the fact that the 'declining years of the 20th century have been described as [...] the global hour of the constitutional state'[57] and notwithstanding the Union's process of constitutionalisation, it has been observed that the ideas of constitutionality and constitutionalism have been 'subject to a perhaps unprecedented range and intensity of attack'.[58]

Apart from the already sketched critical position of the no demos thesis, there are indeed quite some scholars who are opposed to the idea of creating a European constitution. In this chapter, I will take a closer look at four critical opinions that make the case against a further constitutionalisation of the Union. Interestingly enough, they all proceed from the assumption that there is some kind of problematic relation between the enactment of a constitution and the European identity/demos. It is held either that the constitution will do too little for European identity or that it will do too much in this respect.

4.1 A 'constitution' will do too little

Ian Ward[59] argues that 'the 'new' Europe has been too easily distracted by the temptations of constitutionalism'[60] as it 'chooses to press on, from Treaty to Treaty, Directive to Directive, immersed in a legalistic twilight that means nothing to the overwhelming majority of its alienated citizenry'.[61]

---

55 Walker, op. cit. n. 9, at p. 337.

56 See for example Schilling. op. cit. n. 51, who, though contesting the constitutionalisation thesis, nevertheless pleads for a European constitution to be adopted.

57 Walker, op. cit. n. 9, at p. 317, quoting Häberle.

58 Ibid., p. 318.

59 I. Ward, 'Beyond Constitutionalism: The Search for a European Political Imagination', 7 *ELJ* (2001) p. 24.

60 Ibid.

61 Ibid., p. 39.

Instead, Ward claims that 'what Europe really needs is a 'universal' public philosophy',[62] for which he seeks inspiration mainly in Leibniz's universal jurisprudence.[63] Such a public philosophy is a 'state of mind' and cannot be found in some parchment constitutional declaration. According to Ward, Europe needs a strong identity but a constitution will simply achieve too little in this regard. Ward at one point even indicates that constitutionalism can go against a European public philosophy: 'For the temptations of constitutionalism do not necessarily serve the interests of a European public philosophy. Indeed, it can be argued that the very opposite is true.'[64] This claim, I believe, surely goes too far. Nonetheless, Ward's critique of 'constitutional fetishism'[65] is useful in the sense that it points to the intrinsic limits of European constitutionalism. Indeed, it is wrong to assert that a European constitution would be the magic solution to all of Europe's problems. However, this does not also mean that, as will be further elaborated in the subsequent chapter, a constitution lacks any added value.

Klabbers and Leino,[66] on the other hand, took the Convention's Draft Constitution as the focus of their critique, albeit that an important theoretical concern about the constitutionalisation process *per se* lies also at the basis of their argument. They contend that the Constitution effectively takes an intergovernmental approach by shifting the focus of power to the Member States. This implies that the Constitution does too little for the Union's citizens. They state that:

> *'the Draft constitution barely speaks to Europe's residents, or even its citizens. Instead, it dodges the issue of whether it wants a European political community of individuals. And for a treaty (sorry, we mean constitution, of course) that was drafted under the explicit instruction to bring the Union closer to its citizens, that is simply not good enough: one cannot bring Europe closer to its citizens while keeping the [Member States] as an intermediate layer, indeed, strengthening the position of this intermediate layer.'*[67]

This leads them to the conclusion that 'the Draft Constitution spells the end of European integration and marks the final passage of the transition from integration to intergovernmental co-operation'.[68] For sure, this conclusion is exaggerated. The Constitution also includes some integrationist and supranational elements – something that also Klabbers and Leino themselves acknowledge – and on balance it is questionable whether intergovernmentalism wins the day.

---

[62] Ibid., p. 26.

[63] Ibid., p. 32 et seq.

[64] Ibid., p. 26.

[65] Walker, op. cit. n. 9, at p. 324 et seq.

[66] Klabbers and Leino, op. cit. n. 1.

[67] Ibid., p. 1303.

[68] Ibid.

However, for an idealistic federalist striving for a statist Europe, which seems to be the approach Klabbers and Leino support,[69] the Constitution must be disappointing. It is a chimera, however, to plead for full constitutional federalisation and supranationalisation.

On a theoretical level, the opinion of Klabbers and Leino seems to be based on a more fundamental concern, namely the view that the Constitutional Treaty will bring about the finality of European integration. It is this presumption that makes them worry so much about the intergovernmental elements in the Constitutional Treaty, as they hold that 'the more the position of the [Member States] is carved in stone by being constitutionalised, the more difficult it will be to upgrade the position of citizens where doing so would be difficult to reconcile with the position of [Member States]'.[70] As will be further elaborated in the following chapter, it is, however, false to assume that the Constitutional Treaty forms the final brick of the integration process.

4.2 A 'constitution' will do too much

Joseph Weiler[71] points out that Europe, in its choice to preserve the distinct peoplehood of its component Member States, rightfully rejected the federal state model, which predicates instead the existence of a single constitutional demos. Europe's constitutional architecture, which 'has never been validated by a process of constitutional adoption by a European constitutional demos',[72] encapsulates what Weiler calls 'the Principle of Constitutional Tolerance'. This principle – which is according to Weiler 'one of Europe's most important constitutional innovations'[73] – means that we acknowledge and maintain the identity of the other (the alien) but at the same time, whilst preserving the boundaries, we reach over that boundary and accept the other as ourselves. These points are justified. Weiler, however, goes further and makes a distinc-

69 Completely missing the mark (but correct for the ones advocating the relegation of the Member State level to a subordinate status in a European statist construct) is their statement that '[t]he mere fact, incidentally, that the draft constitution can unhesitatingly accept the existence of national constitutions [Art. IV-8 Convention Draft/Art. IV-447 Constitutional Treaty referring to Treaty ratification by the Member States 'in accordance with their respective constitutional requirements'] already suggests that Europe's constitution cannot be very constitutional', ibid., p. 1304, at n. 40.

70 Ibid., p. 1303.

71 See J.H.H. Weiler, 'Epilogue; Fischer: The Dark Side', in C. Joerges, Y. Mény and J.H.H. Weiler, Eds., *What Kind of Constitution for What Kind of Polity? Responses to Joschka Fischer* (Florence, European University Institute 2000) p. 235; J.H.H. Weiler, 'Federalism and Constitutionalism: Europe's Sonderweg', *Jean Monnet Working Paper* 10/00, www.jeanmonnetprogram.org; and J.H.H. Weiler, 'A Constitution for Europe? Some Hard Choices', 40 *JCMS* (2002) p. 563.

72 Weiler, *Jean Monnet Working Paper* 10/00, op. cit., n. 71.

73 Ibid.

tion between the current constitution of the EU and a 'formal constitution'. He fears that such a formal constitution would violate the principle of constitutional tolerance, since '[t]olerance is bred by the very fact that constitutional discipline is asked for, not demanded with the authority of a formal constitution backed up by a constitutional demos.'[74] A formal constitution in Weiler's view would probably be a 'statist-type constitution', such as typically exists in federal states:

'Whether one could have a Europe which would respect the current constitutional acquis, would embed it in a formal constitution adopted through a European constituent power, but which would not, at the same time, become a federal state in all but name is very doubtful [...]. I think this view is a chimera'.[75]

Thus, when it comes down to it, Weiler also tends to an approach of 'extreme maximalism' and to a conflation of the concepts of constitution, people and state. He adheres to the constitutionalisation thesis and believes in the existence of a European constitution which is based on a thin, civic demos but nevertheless is against a formal constitution as this would, in all probability, contradict the principle of constitutional tolerance by suggesting demos-unity and statism rather than demos-diversity and post-statism.

His argument, however, is rather weak. There is absolutely no reason to believe that a formal European constitution would necessarily violate the principle of constitutional tolerance. Just as much as the present constitution is based on this principle, also the future formal constitution could, and should, explicitly recognise the importance of the diversity of the European peoples.[76] Similarly, just as the present constitution does not imply the existence of a state, also a future formal constitution would not, and should not, signal the creation of a state. Also, Weiler himself realises that this specific objection could be raised and, softening his argument, he acknowledges that a formal European constitution could perhaps (although the chances appear small in his view) be drafted in a way that would fully recognise the principle of constitutional tolerance.[77] But his final answer is simple: there is no need for such a formal constitution because 'Europe has charted its own brand of constitutional federalism. It works. Why fix it?'[78] In my view, however, from a number of perspectives there certainly *is* a potential added value in formalising European constitutionalism. I will further elaborate this argument in chapter 6.

---

[74] Weiler 2002, op. cit. n. 71, p. 569.

[75] Weiler, 'Epilogue; Fischer: The Dark Side', op. cit. n. 71, p. 238.

[76] Also Føllesdal, op. cit. n. 18, p. 8: '[A] European constitution could still include in its preamble precisely what Weiler seeks, namely expressions to the effect that the political order was one of peoples rather than one of the people of Europe.'

[77] Weiler, *Jean Monnet Working Paper* 10/00, op. cit., n. 71.

[78] Ibid.

Ulrich Haltern[79] on the other hand, believes that a European constitution would overstretch the, in his view, weakly developed European political community. The Union texts constitute no more than a common market and EU law merely 'embodies the fluid surface of consumer identity'.[80] Europe's 'ceaseless political action'[81] provokes the citizens' distrust, which the Union tries to soothe by initiating 'counter-measures' that are meant to compensate for the lack of real European history, like the Charter of Fundamental Rights[82] and the constitution-to-be. The Union in this sense tries to create pathos and patina for itself. This is not necessarily a bad thing. But the problem is that the Union actually believes that a counter-measure like the Charter 'really is a step towards shared European identity'.[83] Even though Haltern agrees with the argument made by the constitutionalisation thesis,[84] he believes that we do not need a more formal constitution or 'constitutional pathos' because it simply does not accord with the rational, consumerist project that European integration is. But Haltern seems to go further, apparently advancing the opinion that adopting a European constitution is not only an unnecessary and undesirable exercise but a dangerous one, since the consequent 'political perspective of the will' – which is so characteristic of the Nation State and which has led to disastrous events in the Twentieth Century in the form of extreme nationalism – could induce the same negative and far-reaching consequences on the Union level.[85] Although Haltern does not tend to conflate, he certainly does make a strong link between an EU constitution and a state.

But this is not all that is problematic in Haltern's argument. It is, in my opinion, ill-founded to view the present Union as merely constituting a common market. Whereas economic integration was one of the primary reasons for starting the integration process, this was obviously part of the broader agenda of achieving (internal and external) security and stability on the European continent, an agenda which is still relevant today – be it to a far more limited extent thanks to that very same process of integration. European integration has moved beyond purely consumerist and economic forms of integration and has extended its policy activities into more political areas like a common foreign and security policy and justice and home affairs. Also, other areas such as the environment,

79 U. Haltern, 'Europe Goes Camper; The EU Charter of Fundamental Rights From a Consumerist Perspective', *Constitutionalism Web-Papers*, ConWEB No. 3/2001, les1.man.ac.uk/conweb and U. Haltern, 'Pathos and Patina: The Failure and Promise of Constitutionalism in the European Imagination', 9 *ELJ* (2003) p. 14.

80 Haltern 2003, op. cit. n. 79, p. 14.

81 *Ibid.*, p. 18.

82 On the Charter, see especially Haltern 2001, op. cit. n. 79.

83 Haltern 2003, op. cit. n. 79, p. 38.

84 Ibid., pp. 14-16.

85 Ibid., p. 44.

social policy and the protection of human rights (and, in this context, I also do not share Haltern's sceptical view of the value of the Charter) have gained an important place in the European enterprise. European integration simply *is* more than just a common market and shallow consumerism, in the context of which the adoption of a European constitution, as a confirmation of the EU's status as a constitutional polity, is a logical and legitimate step. In this respect also, Haltern's argument that the European citizens are merely consumers who are not interested in and in any case do not need the Union to move beyond the limited perspective he paints of the EU, seems very much ill-founded. After all, this would not explain the fact that Europe's citizens want the Union to tackle all kinds of transnational issues which cannot be dealt with sufficiently on the national level alone; that they want the Union to be actively involved on the world stage through more European involvement in the areas of foreign affairs and defence[86], and; finally and importantly, that they, as eurobarometer polls indicate, support with a clear majority the adoption of the very European constitution that Haltern claims they do not need.[87]

5 EU constitutionalisation as a danger-free exercise

5.1 A European constitutional treaty will not have any inherent negative consequences

It is to be realised that, as has become clear in the previous chapters, there are no grave dangers inherent to creating a European constitution. Such a constitution will not be a useless tool in constructing European political community, nor will it, on the other hand, overstretch a mistakenly alleged weak and consumerist form of European identity. The mere enactment of a European constitution will not automatically lead to the presupposition of a thicker, single constitutional demos thereby threatening demos diversity and violating the principle of constitutional tolerance. Nor will it present a Trojan horse for introducing European statehood. The European constitution will not, and should not, be a document that signals a constitutional rupture, an inescapable move away from the current constitutional architecture. Instead, it must be understood as a concretisation and amelioration of the extant constitutional structure that is currently 'buried' and not clearly recognisable as such. The European constitution will not be a revolution, in the sense of a dramatic reshuffle of the relationship between the Union and its Member States.

Another important concern that has been voiced with regard to the establishment of a European constitution is its potential realisation of 'the finality

86 See the Laeken Declaration, *supra* n. 6, pp. 20-21 under the heading 'The expectations of Europe's citizens'.

87 Eurobarometer reports are accessible at europa.eu.int/comm/public_opinion.

of European integration'[88] – which is understood as the definitive settlement of certain core constitutional questions – thereby acting to the detriment of required flexibility and openness in the European construct. However, Neil Walker[89] has rightly observed that, given the contestation over those finality issues,[90] it would not only be undesirable but also unfeasible to 'freeze' them in a settled constitutional form.

The potential for finalisation involved in the constitutionalisation process, even though it is considered a relatively minimal potential, must in any case be taken into account and constrained as far as possible. Turning now to the Constitution, it is submitted that it does not form a true realisation of finality, considering both its substance and the revision procedure it puts forward. To begin with the latter, it must be pointed out that the current treaty amendment procedure of Article 48 EU is already one of the most rigid procedures conceivable.[91] Whereas in principle this procedure could have been made even more rigid, leading to a further entrenchment and finalisation of European primary law,[92] this has not happened.[93] Also as far as substance is concerned, the Constitution does not mark the finality or end-stage of the integration process by definitively setting in stone issues such as the division of competences between the EU and the Member States.[94] Thus, it is concluded that the dynamic nature

---

88 Which even was the, perhaps a bit unfortunately chosen, *leitmotiv* in Fischer's Humboldt speech, Fischer, op. cit. n. 4.

89 N. Walker, 'The Idea of a European Constitution and the Finalité of Integration', *Francisco Lucas Pires Working Paper Series on European Constitutionalism*, no. 2002/01, www.fd.unl.pt/je/wpflp05a.doc.

90 Walker, ibid., distinguishes seven different ways in which we might conceive of finality, namely: territorial finality, political finality, institutional finality, finality of purpose, social finality, legal finality and constitutional finality.

91 As it requires an IGC to determine 'by common accord' the amendments to be made to the Treaties, which then have to be ratified by all Member States 'in accordance with their respective constitutional requirements' (in practice involving the approval by national parliaments or the holding of a referendum).

92 As Walker, op. cit. n. 89, points out, the amendment procedure of Art. 48 TEU could have been further compounded (and indeed, there have been discussions in the Convention whether or not to do so) by adding more dimensions to it, for example by requiring the findings of the Convention to be ratified in a Europe-wide referendum or by turning the European Parliament into an additional voting, and thus vetoing, party.

93 Arts. IV-443 to IV-445 Constitutional Treaty.

94 This is, however, a specific 'finality-concern' put forward by S. Weatherill, 'Is constitutional finality feasible or desirable? On the cases for European constitutionalism and a European Constitution', *Constitutionalism Web-Papers*, ConWEB No. 7/2002, les1.man.ac.uk/conweb, who regards the 'quest to devise a formula for dividing up State and Community competences [...] as one example of a wider alluring but mistaken attempt to 'find answers'.', at p. 3. See also S. Weatherill, 'Competence', in B. de Witte, ed., *Ten Reflections on the Constitutional Treaty for Europe* www.iue.it/RSCAS/e-texts/200304-10RefConsTreaty.pdf (2003) p. 45.

of the Union, with its 'semi-permanent Treaty revision process',[95] will not be undesirably and negatively affected by any imposed finality and rigidity through the promulgation of a European constitution.[96]

5.2 An approach of constitutional pluralism

Following from all this, it can in general be stated that European constitutionalism must not be viewed as posing a threat to national constitutionalism. Instead of adhering to constitutional monism, which regards states as the only possible sites of constitutional authority, we must adopt an approach of constitutional pluralism, which recognises the European order as a constitutional setting alongside the national constitutional settings and characterises the relationship between those two levels as heterachical rather than hierarchical. This means that 'the doctrine of supremacy of Community law should by no means be confused with any kind of all-purpose subordination of [Member State law] to Community law'.[97]

There is, in my view, also no reason to believe that the enactment of a European constitution and, more specifically, the explicit codification of the supremacy principle therein (Art. I-6, Constitutional Treaty[98]) would contradict and be

[95] De Witte, op. cit. n. 37.

[96] Cf. also B. de Witte, 'Entry into Force and Revision', in B. de Witte, ed., *Ten Reflections on the Constitutional Treaty for Europe* www.iue.it/RSCAS/e-texts/200304-10RefConsTreaty.pdf (2003) p. 203, at p. 214: 'The Constitutional Treaty may well mark an important new stage of the European integration process, but not its end-stage.'

[97] N. MacCormick, *Questioning Sovereignty: Law, State and Nation in the European Commonwealth* (Oxford University Press 1999), at pp. 117-118. Thus, the Bundesverfassungsgericht's *Brunner* judgment (*supra* n. 20), which contradicts the ECJ's claim to judicial *Kompetenz-Kompetenz* (Case 314/85, *Foto-Frost*, [1987] *ECR* 4199), is very much explainable from the viewpoint of constitutional pluralism that presents both the European and the national level as distinct and partially independent systems in which the respective highest decision-making authorities have ultimate interpretative power. This pluralist system, characterised by the occurrence of contestation and the absence of an ultimate arbiter of constitutionality, naturally begs the question how to deal with the possibility of normative collisions between the two levels. In practice, however, concrete collisions are avoided and contestation rather leads to healthy conversation. In this context, one can point to the alleged link between the case of *Solange I*, [1974] 2 *CMLRep.* 540 and the development by the ECJ of its human rights jurisprudence as well as to the alleged link between the *Brunner* case (*supra* n. 20) and the ECJ's *Tobacco Advertising* judgment (Case C-376/98, *Germany v. Parliament and Council*, [2000] *ECR* I-8419), which showed the ECJ taking more seriously its task of policing the limits of Community competence. Supremacy is thus 'a process that involves a greater degree of inter-court dialogue than one might expect', Weatherill 2002, op. cit. n. 94, p. 13.

[98] 'The Constitution and law adopted by the institutions of the Union in exercising competences conferred on it shall have primacy over the law of the Member States.'

detrimental to the idea of constitutional pluralism in the European context.[99] A constitution does not lead to the realisation of a European monist approach where the Member State level would be relegated to the mere status of a subordinate subsystem of the Union level. Even though it could perhaps be contended that the room for contestation from the part of the national legal orders will be slightly lessened by a European constitution that strengthens the Union's constitutional claim, ultimately the pluralist conception is not eradicated by further constitutionalisation since the Union remains a bottom-up, interactive and heterarchical construct, not a top-down, hierarchical one. The dialogic nature of the pluralist system will not perish with a constitution and the inclusion of the supremacy principle therein must 'merely' be seen as a codification of *acquis judiciaire* that already applies.[100] It must not be seen as giving the Union level all-purpose legal and judicial superiority over the national level.[101] The European framework in the post-constitution context retains its pluralist character, as the Union will remain heavily dependent on the national level for the implementation of, and acceptance of the supremacy of, European law.[102]

5.3 Concluding remarks

It is argued here that the drafting of a European constitution *as such* must essentially be seen as a danger-free exercise. Thus, it is concluded that the earlier mentioned criticisms and concerns with regard to the drafting of a European constitution are not convincing enough to refute the usefulness and desirability of the constitutionalisation process. However, it has to be admitted that the concerns as to possible dangers of detracting from the principle of constitutional tolerance in a European constitution, the negative possibility of

---

99 Thus, I do not agree with Weatherill 2002, op. cit. 94, who assumes exactly so. In his view, a constitution could be a finality in the sense of providing the definitive solution to the question of the true site of political and legal authority in Europe, thus undesirably eradicating contestation and dialogue. This negative development would be achieved, in his view, by the inclusion of the supremacy principle in the European constitution.

100 This is also expressly stipulated by the IGC in its declaration on the constitutional primacy clause: 'The Conference notes that Article I-6 reflects existing case law of the Court of Justice of the European Communities and of the Court of First Instance', CIG 87/04 ADD 2 REV 2.

101 Cf. also P. Craig, 'What Constitution does Europe Need? The House that Giscard Built: Constitutional Rooms with a View', *Federal Trust Constitutional Online Essay 26/03*, www.fedtrust.co.uk/Media/Craig.pdf, pp. 8-9.

102 The Constitutional Treaty in fact provides a strong affirmation of a pluralist conception, as it indicates the prime importance and distinct nature of the State level by including a new provision giving Member States the possibility of voluntary withdrawal from the Union: Art. I-60 Constitutional Treaty. See on this matter: H. de Waele, 'The European Union on the Road to a New Legal Order – the Changing Legality of Member State Withdrawal', 12 *Tilburg Foreign Law Review* (2005) p. 169.

a constitution creating a European state generally speaking and the concerns with regard to the potential realisation of the finality of European integration, are valid in the sense that they portray a correct normative vision of how the European framework should be structured. But then again whereas the substance of any European constitution can obviously bring about these undesirable consequences, it is false to assume that the constitutionalisation of Europe will generate such negative consequences and to the extent that the mentioned criticisms and concerns do assume so, they should be strongly resisted. Moreover, the substantive changes introduced by the Constitutional Treaty do not attend to any of the anxieties that have been expressed.

6 The case for a European Constitution

6.1 A pragmatic argument of substance, form and process

On the basis of a pragmatic argument of substance, form and process, it is held that the text that has been prepared by the Convention can appropriately be labelled a constitution. The Nice reform agenda is very much a constitutional agenda. Especially three of the issues that are mentioned by the Nice declaration are important in this respect; the delimitation of powers between the EU and the Member States, the status of the Charter of Fundamental Rights and the simplification of the Treaties. Even though the Nice declaration itself avoided referring to the drafting of a constitution, it is clear that that is exactly what was on the cards.[103]

The link between the reform agenda and the creation of a constitution is visible on the point of substance, since the division of competences between the different levels of governance is an issue that is normally addressed by a constitution and also fundamental rights usually take a prominent place within a constitution. But also the simplification of the Treaties in the sense of changing the form of primary law (a single document merging the European Treaties), is germane to the drafting of a constitution.[104] Finally, the pragmatic argument is also one of process. The Constitutional Treaty was prepared by a Convention, which was characterised by a high degree of transparency and legitimacy. The new and revolutionary Convention method, which performs a supplementary

[103] E.M.H. Hirsch Ballin, 'Een Wezenlijke Maatstaf voor Alle Actoren in de Gemeenschap; De Voorlopige Juridische Status van het Handvest van de Grondrechten van de Europese Unie' [An Essential Yardstick for All Actors in the Community; The Provisional Legal Status of the Charter of Fundamental Rights of the European Union], 49 *Sociaal-economische Wetgeving* (2001) p. 330, at p. 331.

[104] This is shown clearly by the Laeken declaration, *supra* n. 6, which states: 'The question ultimately arises as to whether this simplification and reorganisation might not lead in the long run to the adoption of a constitutional text in the Union.'

role in the procedure for Treaty reform next to the old IGC method, signals an inclusionary and constitutional process.

The EU has, as argued before, a constitution already. This constitution, however, has been implicit and not clearly recognisable as such. This situation has changed since the constitutional reform process has brought to the fore the EU's constitutional character. The Constitutional Treaty merges the European Treaties in a single text, incorporates the Charter of Fundamental Rights, addresses the issue of competence division and has been prepared by a novel procedure securing high input from various actors including the European people(s). How can such a document not appropriately be called a constitution?

Moreover, it is argued that the creation of Europe's first Constitution is a useful and desirable development having regard to the mentioned substantive, procedural and form-related changes that have culminated in the Constitutional Treaty. Whereas space precludes a thorough discussion, some brief remarks can be made here. Firstly, the Constitutional Treaty approach towards the division of competences, though obviously not in any way providing a definitive 'solution' to the issue of competence division in a pluralist and multi-level governance system such as the EU, must be regarded as a further improvement of the current system. Without departing too much from the existing situation, the Constitutional Treaty provides a useful clarification through its new categorisation and definition of the different types of competences.[105] Also the *ex ante* and *ex post* monitoring of compliance with subsidiarity has been improved by giving national parliaments, as well as the Committee of the Regions, a role in this respect.[106] Secondly, the incorporation of the Charter in Part II of the Constitutional Treaty serves the Charter's goals of increasing legitimacy, visibility and legal certainty and is in accordance with the widespread support to do so. Thirdly, the single constitutional text simplifies, reorganises and replaces the previous European Treaties and abandons the awkward pillar structure leaving a single entity intact, called the Union, which is given legal personality.[107] This will increase transparency and may also strengthen popular support for the process of European integration.[108] Finally, in contrast with the traditional

[105] See Title III 'Union Competences' of Part I Constitutional Treaty.

[106] See the 'Protocol on the application of the principles of subsidiarity and proportionality' Constitutional Treaty.

[107] Art. I-7 Constitutional Treaty.

[108] As B. de Witte, 'Simplification and Reorganization of the European Treaties', 39 *CMLRev.* (2002) p. 1255, at p. 1265, remarks: '[I]t is now generally accepted that public disaffection with the European Union might be cured, in part at least, by drafting a new Treaty text that would be easier to understand and explain. A legible document, particularly if reduced in length, would arguably enhance the legitimacy of the European Union's operation in the eyes of its citizens. However, these are still unproved assumptions and a clearer Treaty text may well also provide a better focus for opposition to European integration.'

IGC format the Convention method – now formalised in paragraph two of the Constitutional Treaty revision clause, Article IV-443 – introduces a much wider participation in the Treaty revision process, has a higher degree of transparency, provides for more effectiveness and has a potential community-strengthening effect.[109]

It follows that the post-Nice reform process is not primarily about the creation of a European constitution, rather it is about making the necessary and desirable changes with regard to substance, procedure and form that in effect make up such a constitution. But there must be more than that. It is one thing to pursue and give effect to a reform process that is in essence constitutional in nature, it is a whole different matter to explicitly label the document that results from that reform process a constitution. Such a label may be, as argued, appropriate and logical, but what kind of impact does it have and is it also desirable given the present circumstances?

6.2 Adopting the language of constitutionalism

Andreas Føllesdal has argued that, 'the central issue is not whether the EU should have a constitution, because for most intents and purposes it already has one. Instead, the crucial issues concern the substantial content such a constitution should have, and how to best obtain it.'[110] Indeed, it has to be accepted that the process and substance of the Constitutional Treaty are of primary importance. However, I do not believe that one should draw the conclusion that the question of terminology is not that relevant. The 'constitutional question' should not be treated, as Føllesdal treats it, with a large degree of indifference, since this question *does* matter very much. After all, even though '[t]he choice of words would not make a direct legal difference', it has to be said that 'the use of the word 'constitutional' would arguably be meaningful in symbolic, political and therefore also indirectly in legal terms'.[111] Indeed, the impact of the explicit adoption of the language of constitutionalism in the EU context must not be underestimated, as fierce resistance to the adoption of a European constitution serves to illustrate.

In my view, the use of the term constitution for the future Treaty is useful in several respects. First of all, it serves to affirm the fact that the European construct has developed from an internationalist and mainly economic frame-

---

109 For some critical notes on the Convention method, see C. Closa, 'Improving EU Constitutional Politics? A Preliminary Assessment of the Convention', *Constitutionalism Web-Papers*, ConWEB No. 1/2003, les1.man.ac.uk/conweb; J. Scott, 'The culture of constitution-making? 'Listening' at the Convention on the Future of Europe', 3:9 *German Law Journal* (2002), www.germanlawjournal.com; and J. Shaw, 'Process, Responsibility and Inclusion in EU Constitutionalism', 9 *ELJ* (2003) p. 45.

110 Føllesdal, op. cit. n. 18, p. 1.

111 De Witte, op. cit. n. 108, at p. 1282.

work into a constitutional architecture that stands in a heterarchical relation to the constitutional level of the Member States.

Secondly, the symbolic and powerful language of constitutionalism desirably increases the normative force of European law. European law has a tremendous impact on national legal systems and this makes it justifiable and useful to 'back it up' with a constitutional language that underpins the concept of a limited and constitutional polity founded on the rule of law, democracy, fundamental rights and constitutional adjudication.

Thirdly, it can be argued that a European constitution also serves to refine, improve and 'mature' European constitutionalism by adding and ameliorating constitutional elements within primary law, for example by incorporating the Charter of Fundamental Rights. This is, obviously, again an argument related more to substance. However, it should be pointed out that the adoption of constitutional language serves as a *vehicle* for making such substantive changes, which might otherwise not have been carried through.

Fourthly, and finally, a constitution has a certain community-strengthening potential. A constitution can bring Europe closer to its citizens and increase Europe's legitimacy in that it can strengthen European political community and help in further constructing the European demos. This is again strongly interwoven with the participatory, dialogic process of adopting a European constitution. However, even though the Convention could also have been used as a method to construct an 'ordinary' Treaty, the community-strengthening effect of such a process is arguably higher when the process is explicitly framed in constitutional terms. A constitutional, rather than a non-constitutional, reform process 'raises the stakes' and, because of the increased importance of the text that results from such a constitutional process, it enhances discussion and dialogue within that process, making it a useful tool for strengthening European identity. As Habermas has termed it, the constitutionalisation process forms a 'self-fulfilling prophecy' with regard to building a sense of political community.[112] Also the outcome of that constitutional process – which must be seen not only as a more legitimate assertion of common European values given the participatory process that preceded it but also as a document that, framed in powerful constitutional terms, has a higher symbolic value and a stronger community-constructivist effect than an ordinary Treaty – has a positive impact on European identity.

[112] Habermas, op. cit. n. 27. As Walker, op. cit. n. 89, aptly remarks: '[I]n order to generate the forms and levels of dialogic, solidary and infrastructural goods conducive to a legitimate conception of continental political community, however modestly or ambitiously defined, it is important for Europe to engage in the kind of inclusive political conversation which a constitutional process – and at this stage of specific development of the vast and heterogeneous Euro-polity and in this era of general disaffection with traditional political forms, perhaps *only* a constitutional process – can offer.'

Two final points need to be made with regard to the community-enhancing function of a European constitution(al process). Firstly, it should be stressed that the community-strengthening effect of a constitution should not be overestimated since actual results will, arguably, be modest. A European constitution and the process that produces it will certainly contribute to enhancing European identity but its limited effects make it unrealistic to assume that it will construct an advanced, mature form of political community that is capable of completely bridging the presumed social legitimacy gap. Secondly, it should be pointed out that the community-strengthening effect of European constitutionalisation will not go as far as generating a thicker, ethno-cultural form of European identity.[113] As argued above, the Union already is based on a thin, civic demos that is characterised by the existence of shared values. An inclusive constitutional process is an ideal way to articulate these shared values and subsequently to embed them in a normatively strong constitutional framework. This is aptly reflected by the Habermasian term 'constitutional patriotism'.[114] European constitutionalisation thus forms an ideal way to enhance Europe's thin, civic demos rather than that it, conversely, will lead to any undesirable thickening of identity.

6.3 Conclusion

The document that is the outcome of the IGC can appropriately be called a constitution on the basis of a pragmatic argument of substance, form and process. The changes made in the latter areas moreover signify a useful and desirable development within the integration process, making the adoption of a constitution also a legitimate exercise. However, even though the usefulness of the adoption of a European constitution is strongly interwoven with the need for the realisation of certain substantive, procedural and form-related changes, it would be going too far to completely conflate these two. There must thus be a justification for the use of the language of constitutionalism that cuts deeper. This question of terminology, contrary to how some might have it, has indeed a high degree of relevance.

It has been argued that the explicit adoption of the language of constitutionalism for the future Treaty to be adopted is useful in a number of respects, namely: it serves as a confirmation of already existing constitutionalism; it increases the normative force of European law; it serves to refine, improve and 'mature' European constitutionalism; and it has a certain community-strengthening potential.

---

113 Cf. also Walker, ibid.

114 J. Lacroix, 'For a European Constitutional Patriotism', 50 *Political Studies* (2002) p. 944.

7 Concluding remarks

7.1 Summary

In this paper it has been argued that the no demos thesis – which holds that the EU currently does not have a constitution and moreover should not, or is in principle not able to, have one – is an untenable position. Also the connected position of defensive internationalism, which denies Europe's constitutional format, is not a satisfactory approach. Finally, also the position of those scholars, who adhere to the constitutionalisation thesis but who nevertheless believe that the enactment of a European constitution is either a useless or a negative development, is to be resisted. Instead, this paper advances the argument that the European Union has a constitution already and that it is useful and desirable to bring this better to the fore in a more explicit constitution. Such an explicit constitutionalisation will not bear any inherent negative (stately) consequences, as some might have it. The creation of an EU constitution is desirable on the basis of a pragmatic argument of substance (fundamental rights, competences), form (simplification in terms of merger and reorganisation) and process (Convention), as well as for more symbolic and normative reasons.

The Constitutional Treaty must be seen as a logical and useful step in the Union's steady constitutional development. Thus, the Constitutional Treaty must be seen neither as the foundation[115] nor as the completion or finalisation of the European polity, but rather as its maturation.

7.2 The way forward

Even though the Constitutional Treaty must not be seen as a dramatic revolution in the sense of a constitutional rupture with the current state of affairs, it does form an important and significant step in the integration process. The Union now embraces the symbolic and powerful language of

[115] Interesting to mention in this respect is the *refoundation* or *constitutional rupture* theory that has emerged on the scene (see De Witte, op. cit. n. 96, p. 208 et seq.). In this approach, the constitution is seen as a refoundation, rather than a continuation and revision of the Treaties. More specifically, this means that the *existing* revision rules of Art. 48 TEU can be circumvented by posing that the Constitution will come into force *without* the unanimous backing of the Member States. This approach is taken in Art. 77 of the Draft Constitution proposed by the European Policy Centre (www.theepc.net/Word/EUconst.doc) and by the Commission's Draft Constitution 'Penelope', available at europa.eu.int/futurm/documents/offtexts/const051202_en.pdf. Such strategy is meant to secure the smooth entry into force of the constitution, or, more pejoratively, to 'kick awkward members out of the European Union', see Charlemagne, The Perils of Penelope, *The Economist*, 14 December 2002. This constitutional rupture approach, however, is legally not acceptable: De Witte, op. cit. n. 96, pp. 211-212.

constitutionalism in the most explicit way, but also many significant substantive changes are introduced, which might not have been carried through with such swift determination by way of the ordinary IGC procedure.

Now that the IGC has given it the green light, the Constitutional Treaty faces a ratification phase that will undoubtedly prove to be more difficult than previous Treaty ratifications. Not only will the fiat be required of no less than 25 Member States, the Constitution has also inspired successful calls for more popular involvement meaning that a considerable number of Member States will hold referenda on the issue. The road to Europe's first constitution is long and full of risks, but, given its potential added value, it is to be hoped that we will get there in the end.

CHAPTER 2

Towards a More Democratic Union?

Comments on the Treaty establishing a Constitution for Europe

Fabian Amtenbrink

1 Prologue

The Declaration of the Laeken European Council of December 2001 observed the existence of a 'democratic challenge facing Europe' and referred to a European Union (hereinafter 'EU') that '... needs to become more democratic, more transparent and more efficient'.[1] Some may have felt reminded of the debates at the time of the coming into existence of the Treaty on European Union in 1992 (EU Treaty) or of the Treaty of Amsterdam in 1997 or of the Treaty of Nice in 2001. Indeed, already in 1994 *Piris* wondered whether the Community institutions had become more efficacious, more democratic and more transparent.[2] Little seems to have changed in the course of almost a decade. The Laeken Declaration can be read as a clear admittance of the fact that despite several attempts to remedy the shortcomings the EU has not lost the stigma of being somewhat remote from its citizens and essentially undemocratic. The initial 'No' by the Irish people in the referendum on the Treaty of Nice and the rejection by the Swedish electorate to allow Sweden to join the Euro area provide more recent proof of the deep mistrust held by many citizens of anything coming from Brussels.

The Laeken Declaration described a research agenda, asking -among other things- how the democratic legitimacy of the EU could be increased and which initiatives could be taken to bring the 'European institutions' closer to EU citizens. Against the background of the mixed record of past Intergovernmental Conferences (hereinafter IGC's), this time around the Laeken European Council decided to depart from the traditional path by setting up a Convention on the Future of Europe to study these questions and to make proposals. The well known result of these efforts where put together in a Draft Treaty establishing a Constitution for Europe which was presented to the President of the European Council on 18 July 2003. Finally, on 29 October 2004, after considerable amendments to the original draft, the Treaty establishing a Constitution for Europe (hereinafter 'Constitutional Treaty') was signed in Rome by all twenty-five Member States.[3]

While it is far from certain at the time of the writing of this contribution, whether the Constitutional Treaty will ever come into force, it seems nevertheless appropriate to explore whether and to what extent it would alter the present

1 Laeken Declaration on the Future of the European Union of 15 December 2001 (hereafter: Laeken Declaration) section II paragraph 1.

2 J.-C. Piris, 'After Maastricht, are the Community Institutions More Efficacious, More Democratic and More Transparent?', 19 *ELRev.* 1994 p. 449. Also the question whether Europe needs a constitution was raised, see e.g. D. G. Grimm, 'Braucht Europa eine Verfassung?,' *JZ*, vol. 50, no. 12 (1994) p. 581. Due to the limited space available, despite their relevance, reflections on transparency and efficiency cannot be included in this contribution.

3 See *OJ* 2004, C 310/1.

patterns of democratic legitimacy and whether and to what extent the European institutions would indeed be brought closer to their citizens. In doing so, considering the limited space available, this contribution follows a straight forward institutional approach by examining the most important institutional arrangements at the European level.[4]

2 Democratic legitimacy in today's system of multi-level governance

The Laeken Declaration states that '[T]he European Union derives its legitimacy from the democratic values it projects, the aims it pursues and the powers and instruments it possesses.' According to this '[...] the European project also derives its legitimacy from democratic, transparent and efficient institutions' and 'the national parliaments also contribute towards the legitimacy of the European project.'

Reference is made to two interwoven concepts: democracy and legitimacy. In the conventional approach democracy as a form of government stands for the notion of the government by the people. The people are the holder of the *pouvoir constituant,* the holders of the sovereign power. Yet, in a democratic system the people do not only hold, but moreover also exercise power: government by the people. Democracy may thus be summarized as an organizational principle for the holding and exercise of state power.[5] It is inherent to such a system that all state power has to be founded on the sovereign power of the people. Any political power has to be authorized through the people. All state power must be legitimized.[6] Arguably, the patterns of democratic legitimacy depend upon the chosen form of democracy. In a direct or participatory democracy the people take all the necessary decisions themselves by means of plebiscites; they thus exercise sovereign power themselves without the need for further legitimacy. On the contrary, representative democracies are characterized by the delegation of the sovereign power of the people to a group of representatives entrusted with the exercise of the state power, the latter being primarily expressed through the creation of laws, the exclusive power of legitimate force (*Gewaltmonopol*) and – one may add – the right of taxation.

---

4 For a broader approach to the notion of (democratic) legitimacy see e.g. J. Steffek, Sources of Legitimacy Beyond the State: A View from International Relations', in Ch. Joerges et. al., eds., *Transnational Governance and Constitutionalism* (Oxford and Portland, Oregon, Hart Publishing 2004), p. 81; A. J. Menéndez, 'No Legitimacy without Politics: Comments on Jens Steffek, in Ch. Joerges et. al., op. cit., p. 103.

5 E.W. Böckenförde, Demokratie als Verfassungsprinzip, in J.Isensee and P. Kirchhof, eds., *Handbuch des Staatsrechts Vol. I* (Heidelberg, F. Müller Juristischer Verlag 1987), §22, sidenote 9.

6 F. Amtenbrink, *The democratic accountability of central banks- A comparative study of the European Central Bank* (Oxford and Portland, Oregon, Hart Publishing 1999), at p. 35, with further references.

In a parliamentary democracy, the representatives are united in a parliamentary assembly. Legitimacy is renewed in regular intervals through fair and free elections, which may or may not result in the withdrawal of confidence of the people in the previously chosen representatives. Representative democracy then amounts to the legitimacy of rule.[7] Yet, elections may be considered to constitute more than just a repeating justification of state power. They are at the same time a mechanism by which the representatives are held accountable for their past performance.[8] This latter point has to be emphasized, as many political scientists would point out that the somewhat romanticized view of representative democracy as government of the people, by the people and for the people hardly reflects political realities anymore. Indeed, representative democracy is understood as a system of limitation and control of power.[9]

At the same time democracy arguably also relates to decision-making processes. On the one hand, this includes rules on how decisions are taken and by whom. Common grounds in this respect are that Parliament makes the laws and decisions are taken at least by a majority (the so-called majority rule).[10] On the other hand, it describes the extent to which the people are involved in the decision-formation and thus also the extent to which decisions actually reflect the preferences of the people (electorate). Democratic legitimacy is not only an issue of legally binding rules but also an issue of perception. It is the perception of the people that their preferences are reflected by the policies formulated and decisions which are taken on their behalf. The patterns of decision-making play a vital role in the assessment of democratic structures.

The challenge of identifying patterns of democratic legitimacy in the context of European integration has been identified for some time.[11] It is rooted in the uncharacteristic structure of the EU. Despite the impressions that those not dealing with the issue on a daily basis may gain in particular from publicly made statements by euro critics who at times draw a somewhat distorted picture of Europe as a sort of 'super state', the EU is far from constituting a state in the

7 P. Hirst, *Representative Democracy and its Limits* (Oxford, Polity Press 1990) at p. 29.

8 Amtenbrink, op. cit. n. 6, at p. 28 also with regard to the term 'accountability'.

9 G. Sartori, *The theory of democracy revisited* (Chatham, NJ, Chatham House Publishers 1987) at p. 280; I. Harden, 'Democracy and the European Union', in P. Hirst and S. Khilnani, *Reinventing Democracy* (Oxford, Blackwell Publishers 1996) p. 132, at p. 134.

10 R. Bellamy and D. Castiglione, *The Uses of Democracy; Reflections on the European Democratic Deficit*, in E.O. Eriksen et al., eds, *Democracy in the European Union: Integration Through Deliberation* (Routledge, London 2000) 65 – 84, at p. 70.

11 See e.g. K. Featherstone, 'Jean Monnet and the 'Democratic Deficit' in the European Union', *JCMS* (1994) p. 149; N. MacCormick, 'Democracy, Subsidiarity, and Citizenship in the "European Commonwealth" ', 16 *Law and Philosophy* (1997) pp. 331 – 356; E. O. Eriksen and J. E. Fossum, 'The European Union and Post-national Integration', *ARENA Working Papers*, WP 99/9, online at www.arena.uio.no/publications/wp99_9.htm, visited on 15 February 2005.

classical sense, be it of a centralistic or federalist nature. While the Member States have transferred powers to a newly established supranational organization where these powers are exercised on its behalf by institutions established for that purpose, the powers of the EU are limited to those specifically conferred on it by the Member States.[12] Already early on in the history of European integration the European Court of Justice (hereinafter 'the ECJ') emphasized that the Member States had created a Community of unlimited duration.[13] Yet, the corresponding limitation of sovereignty is arguably not indefinite as Member States could theoretically agree collectively to reclaim sovereignty by means of a new Treaty.[14] The Member States remain the 'Masters of the Treaties' through their right to change the Treaty, as is highlighted by the signing of the Treaty establishing a Constitution for Europe.

At the same time it also becomes evident from these observations that this supranational organization is much more than a confederation of sovereign states. The difficulties in labeling this new legal order was underscored by the attempts of the German Constitutional Court (*Bundesverfassungsgericht*) in its decision on a constitutional complaint against the Treaty on the European Union, where the court refers to a *'Staatenverbund'*, a sort of hybrid between a confederation and a federation.[15] While the introduction of such new categories can be explained by the desire to give the EU a clear label, they can hardly comprehend the complex structure of the EU. European integration combines the co-operation of sovereign states in certain policy areas with the exercise of competencies by supranational institutions on behalf of the supranational organization and the Member States belonging to the latter. The EU has not replaced the governmental systems of the Member States. Rather, it has added an additional layer of governance, which does not simply stand in competition to or above the national systems but, rather, is intertwined with them.[16] It resem-

---

[12] The so-called principle of attributed powers laid down in Art. 5 EC. See also more recently ECJ, Case C-376/98 *Germany* v. *European Parliament and Council* [2000] *ECR* I-8419. Thus, Member States maintain sovereignty in important areas, such as taxation.

[13] ECJ, Case 6/64 *Costa* v. *E.N.E.L.* [1964] *ECR* 585.

[14] Whether individual Member States can do so de jure even against the expressed will of the other Member States is debatable given the lack of an explicit exit provision in the EC and EU Treaty. However, de facto little could be done to prevent a Member State from denunciating the founding treaties if that state was willing to bear the mainly economic consequence resulting from such a decision. But see P. J.G. Kapteyn and P. VerLoren van Themaat, *Introduction to the Law of the European Communities*, 3rd edn. (edited by L.W. Gormley) (London, The Hague, Boston, Kluwer Law International 1998) at p. 81, which refer to an 'irreversible nature'.

[15] BVerfGE 89, 155.

[16] See e.g. I. Pernice, *Rethinking the Methods of Dividing and Controlling the Competencies in the Union*, Walter-Hallenstein-Institut, Paper 6/01, online at www.whi-berlin.de, visited on 15 February 2005, refers in this context to 'multilevel constitutionalism'.

bles a system of multi-level governance, where Member States do not only retain competencies in important areas but, moreover, play an important role in the implementation and enforcement of European rules in the domestic legal order including in areas where the Community has been given exclusive competences.

If democracy (in a formal legal sense) basically amounts to providing mechanisms to ensure the legitimacy of power, much depends upon how these powers are divided across the different levels of governance, that is to say between the Member States and the EU, on the composition of and relationship between the institutions exercising these competencies on the EU level and the extent to which these institutions can be held accountable for their performance on the European and/or national level.[17] Leaving aside the question of the distribution of competences which is dealt with extensively elsewhere[18], the current institutional arrangements at the EU level substantiate the description of the EU as a system of multi-level governance in that democratic legitimacy is facilitated both by the Member States and the Community institutions.[19]

The Council of the European Union (hereinafter 'the Council') and the European Parliament (hereinafter 'the EP') which, together with the European Commission (hereinafter 'the Commission'), are central to the exercise of power reflect this division and highlight where the centre of gravity lies in legitimizing the EU. While competences in a considerable number of areas are exercised directly on the supranational level, democratic legitimacy to a large extent has remained intergovernmental in the sense that it is facilitated through the Member States even in areas where the Member States have vested exclusive competencies in the EU. One important reason for this is to be found in the Council, consisting of the representatives of the governments of the Member States at ministerial level, which takes central stage in the decision-making process at the European level.[20] In areas where the co-decision procedure applies

---

17 Issues which are regularly also addressed under the heading 'institutional balance', see e.g. more recently J.-P- Jacqué, 'The Principle of Institutional Balance', 41 *CMLRev.* (2004) pp. 383-391; L. W. Gormley, 'Disturbing or Rebalancing Powers Within the European Union?, in J. de Zwaan, J. H. Jans, F. A. Nelissen and S. Blockmans, eds., *The European Union: An Ongoing Process of Integration: Liber Amicorum Alfred E. Kellermann* (The Hague, T.M.C. Asser Instituut 2004), p. 35. See also P. van Elsuwege and A. Vermeersch in chap. 3 of this volume.

18 See e.g. I. Pernice, 'The Framework Revisited: Constitutional, Federal and Subsidiarity Issues, 2 *Columbia Journal of European Law* (1996) p. 403; G. de Búrca and B. de Witte, 'The Delimitation of Powers Between the EU and its Member States, in A. Arnull and D. Wincott, eds., *Accountability and Legitimacy in the European Union* (Oxford, Oxford University Press 2002), p. 201; G. Davies, 'The post-Laeken division of competences', 28 *ELRev.* (2003) p. 686, with further references.

19 U. di Fabio, 'Mehrebenendemokratie in Europa, Auf dem Weg in die komplementäre Ordnung', Vortrag an der Humboldt-Universität zu Berlin am 15. November 2001, FCE 10/01, online at www.whi-berlin.de visited on 15 February 2005 refers to a 'multilevel democracy'.

20 Art. 202 EC.

it shares this responsibility with the EP.[21] However, in other decision-making procedures in the context of the EC Treaty and even more so in the context of the second and third pillar of the EU, the justification of power exercised on the EU level derives almost exclusively from the democratic legitimacy of the governments of the Member States and thus ultimately derives from the national parliamentary systems. Whether and to what extent national parliaments are actually actively involved in legitimizing the position of the national government in the Council differs, as the government may have a general mandate to act whereby it is required to defend its position ex post and/or it may be required to seek a parliamentary mandate for negotiations ex ante.[22] The EC Treaty does not formally recognize this vital role of the national parliaments as one of the primary source of democratic legitimacy.[23]

The significance of the Member States as a source of legitimacy is further highlighted by the role of the European Council, comprising the Heads of State or Government and the Commission President, which are supported by the Ministers for Foreign Affairs of the Member States and another member of the Commission.[24] Despite the fact that until now it does not *de jure* have the status of a Community institution, the European Council has gained importance in the Community decision-making process not only by defining the general policy guidelines of the EU as a whole but by increasingly acting as a mediator and quasi higher authority in circumstances when the Council proves incapable of coming to an agreement.[25]

As a body, arguably neither the European Council nor the Council are effectively accountable for their actions vis-à-vis other Community institutions, let alone national parliaments.[26] Accountability in this area follows the patterns of democratic legitimacy. National parliaments can hold their respective governments accountable for their position in the Council and ultimately the national electorate may decide not to extent the term of office of government.[27] Yet, this

---

[21] Art. 251 EC.

[22] The latter is the case in Denmark with regard to decisions of a wider scope, see The European Affairs Committee of the Folketing, *Parliamentary control of government policy in the EU*, Copenhagen, Folketing, online at www.eu-oplysningen.dk/upload/application/pdf/e45978e6/euu_engelsk.pdf visited on 15 February 2005.

[23] See also the contribution by P. Kiiver in Chap. 4 of this volume.

[24] Art. 4 EU.

[25] On the increasing role of the European Council in the history of European integration see generally J. Werts, *The European Council* (Amsterdam et al., North Holland 1992).

[26] However, acts by the Council of the European Union can be challenged pursuant to Art. 230 EC or can become the basis for a non-contractual liability of the Community.

[27] It is among others in this context that transparency in the decision-making process and access to information plays a vital role, see e.g. A. Peters, 'European Democracy After The 2003 Convention', 41 *CMLRev.* (2004) pp. 37 – 85, at p. 63 et seq.

mechanism arguably runs empty to some extent in areas of (qualified-) majority voting in the Council if the government in question has not supported the decision that is questioned by the national parliament.[28] It is this form of decision-making, that has been continuously extended to new policy areas in the EC Treaty.

Given that the EP constitutes the only Community institution whose members are directly elected by the electorate of the Member States it seems predestined to function as the primary source of democratic legitimacy both with regard to Community acts as well as other Community institutions. Yet, apart from the question whether and to what extent the current composition of the EP actually supports this view[29], it can in any event only function as a source of legitimacy of Community action to the extent that it can impose its view on the Council and the Commission in the decision-making procedure and depends on its position in the overall institutional structure.

With regard to the decision-making procedures, despite the fact that the profile of the EP in primary Community law has been raised continuously since the Single European Act 1986, it still does not hold the same central role in the European system of governance that national parliaments hold. The EP has practically no formal right to propose Community legislation, a role that is assigned to the Commission.[30] In the field of application of the EC Treaty, with regard to influencing the contents and the decision on the adoption of Community law, the position of the EP is arguably the strongest in the co-decision procedure. Here the EP does not only has a right to propose amendments to legislative proposals, thereby actively shaping Community legislation, but also has the power to effectively block the Council from passing legislation. This role is arguably more constructive than that in the so-called assent procedure.[31] While any Council action requires the assent of the EP, the influence of the latter is in principle limited to a 'take it or leave it' decision.[32] The right of the EP to veto legislation in the co-decision procedure forms an important element in what may be described as an inter-institutional system of checks and balances. The role of the EP in the budgetary procedure, namely with regard to the so-called non-compulsory expenditure, adds weight to its position in the institutional balance. Yet, until now the influence of the EP extents only to about half of the annual budget, as its role in the area of compulsory expenditure is in principle limited to submitting proposals for modifications to the draft budget.[33]

---

28 See also Piris, op. cit., n. 2. Critically on the relevance of this argument Peters, op. cit., n. 27, p. 55 et seq.

29 This point will be further explored in section 4.

30 An exception is to be found in Art. 190 EC. According to Art. 192 EC, the EP can only request the Commission to submit a proposal.

31 See e.g. Art. 49 EC.

32 See however Piris, op. cit., at n. 2, according to which the assent procedure is 'an even clearer form of co-decision'.

33 Art. 272 EC. See F. Amtenbrink and H.H.B. Vedder, *Het Recht van de Europese Unie* (The Hague, Boom Juridische uitgevers 2005) at p. 125 et seq.

Moreover, in the second and third pillars of the EU, as well as with regard to treaty amendments the role of the EP can be described as marginal.[34]

While the role of the EP in the legislative process is still circumscribed compared to that of national parliaments, it fulfills an important function in legitimizing the Commission.[35] Under the present system both the nomination of the Commission President and, thereafter, the Commission as a body requires the approval by the EP before the Council can appoint it. While the EP's power in this regard may be diminished by the fact that, apart from the nomination for Commission President, it cannot *de jure* reject individual nominations for the post of Commissioners, the events of October 2004 surrounding the appointment of the Barroso Commission clearly show the actual influence of the EP.[36] Moreover, the EP can hold the Commission responsible for its performance, in particular by means of the discharge of the Commission in respect of the implementation of the budget and, more generally through its right of parliamentary inquiry and the motion of censure.[37] A similar role of the EP vis-à-vis other central Community institutions and organs, such as the Court of Auditors and the European Central Bank, is missing.

The Commission is the third institution that takes on a central role in the Community system of governance. Rather than the EP it is the Commission that takes centre stage in setting the legislative agenda through its right of initiative.[38] Moreover, the Commission exercises its own partly original and partly delegated decision-making powers.[39] In terms of democratic legitimacy the position of the Commission may be the most vulnerable one for potential criticism given that it is neither directly elected nor composed of government representatives.[40] However, with the increasing influence of the EP in the election of the

---

[34] According to Arts. 21 and 39 EU the EP has to be regularly informed and is consulted. See Amtenbrink and Vedder, op. cit., n. 34, at p. 75. It is for this reason that the legitimacy of any treaty amendments in accordance with Art. 48 EU can only derive from the level of the Member States.

[35] Critical with regard to an extension of the role of the EP D. Tsatsos and P. Schiffauer, 'Das Europäische Parlament als Verfassungsgeber? Legitimation und Grenzen der parlamentarischen Mitwirkung an der Entwicklung der Unionsgrundordnung', Symposium Europäisches Verfassungsrecht "Entwicklungsperspektiven der europäischen Verfassung im Lichte des Vertrags von Amsterdam", Humboldt University, 12 and 13 November 1998, www.whi-berlin.de, visited on 15 February 2005.

[36] See Amtenbrink and Vedder, op. cit., n. 33, at p. 57 et seq.

[37] Art. 197(3) EC and Art. 201 EC.

[38] In the second and third pillar of the EU, the Commission shares this right with the Member States.

[39] Art. 211 EC.

[40] See e.g. N. Moussis, ' For a drastic reform of European institutions', 28 *ELRev.* (2003), p. 250, p. 251 et seq.; Featherstone, op. cit., n. 11.

Commissioners and in holding it to account for its performance it is arguable also the democratic legitimacy of the Commission has improved somewhat.[41]

3 The institutional structure in the future Union: towards new patterns of democratic legitimacy?

The contribution which the Constitutional Treaty makes in altering the above described patterns of democratic legitimacy is modest. Indeed, it can be argued that it cements the existing construction rather than to provide for new channels of legitimacy.

Despite the prominent reference in its name, the Treaty establishing a Constitution for Europe is just that, a Treaty between - in this regard – sovereign states. It does not replace the above-described system of multi-level governance and legitimacy by some new structure. The utilization of the term 'constitution' may be misleading at least to the extent that it is loaded with a national notion of a written or unwritten body of law and practices laying down the organizational system of a state. The Constitutional Treaty does not define the constitutional system of a European state.[42] The term 'constitution' appears ill chosen as it may trigger undesired reactions outside expert circles both from advocates and opponents of further European integration. While the former may find their high hopes based on the terminology shattered in the light of the contents of the Constitutional Treaty, the latter may oppose the Constitutional Treaty merely because it implies the creation of (the constitutional basis of) a European state. It is only once the notion of constitution is separated from the notion of state and thus, once a post-national notion of constitution is applied that the significance of the Constitutional Treaty can be correctly classified.[43]

The Constitutional Treaty undoubtedly describes fundamental rules by which the Union is supposed to be bound in the exercise of its competences. It creates a legal framework within which the institutions and organs of the Union can act both vis-à-vis Member States and their citizens, and describes rights and obligations not only for Member States but expressly also for individuals.[44]

---

41 On the democratic legitimacy of the Commission, see J. Temple Lang, 'How Much Do The Smaller Member States Need The Commission? The Role Of The Commission In A Changing Europe', 39 *CMLRev.* (2002): pp. 315 – 335, p. 325 et seq.

42 See e.g. J. Kokott and A. Rüth, 'The European Convention and its Draft Treaty establishing a Constitution for Europe: Appropriate Answers to the Laeken Questions?', 40 *CMLRev.* (2003) pp. 1315-1345, at p. 1321, brackets added.

43 See e.g. A. Albi, 'The EU Constitution, National Constitutions and Souvereignity: An Assessment of a European Constitutional Order', 29 *ELRev.* (2004) p. 741, at p. 747 et seq.

44 I. Pernice, 'European and National Constitutions', 1 *EuConst* (2005) p. 99, at p. 99 et seq. This includes in particular fundamental rights, as included in Part II of the Constitutional Treaty.

It has rightly been pointed out that in principle the function of the Constitutional Treaty will hardly be any different from today's founding treaties and the EC Treaty in particular, which for a long time has been described as the 'basic constitutional charter'.[45] Indeed, as Kokott and Rüth state: 'The establishment of the Constitutional Treaty [...] was therefore not an exercise of constitutionalization, but of constitutional rewriting and formalization.'[46] If ratified by all twenty-five Member States, the Constitutional Treaty will become the constitutional basis for a Union which enjoys legal personality.[47]

Article I-2 of the Constitutional Treaty refers to democracy as one of the values on which the Union is build.[48] According to Article I-46 of the Constitutional Treaty, the functioning of the Union is founded on representative democracy whereby citizens are directly represented at Union level in the EP, while Member States are represented in the European Council by their Heads of State or Government and in the Council by their governments, themselves democratically accountable either to their national Parliaments or to their citizens.[49] For the first time the system of multi-level legitimacy characteristic of the system of multi-level governance in today's EU is explicitly recognized. Still, what also becomes plain from this provision is that the Constitutional Treaty does not, in principle, envisage changing this system.

Indeed, to the extent that legitimacy continues to derive from the level of the Member States, the Constitutional Treaty explicitly leaves it to the Member States to provide sufficient channels of democratic legitimacy and accountability. The only ray of hope in this regard would be the future obligation for the Council to meet in public when considering and voting on a draft legislative act. This way it may become more difficult for national governments to disguise their own position in the Council vis-à-vis the national parliament and electorate.[50] While with the above stated reference the Constitutional Treaty gives the impression of increasing the importance of the Member States in providing the democratic legitimation of the Union, it does not include any details on the principles that Member States should observe in ensuring the democratic backcoupling of the European with the national level of governance. Given the interdependence

---

45 ECJ, Case 295/83 *Parti écologiste 'Les Verts'* v. *European Parliament* [1986] *ECR* 1339; recently ECJ, Case C-15/00 *Commission* v. *European Investment Bank* [2003] *ECR* I-7281.

46 Kokott and Rüth, op. cit., n. 42, at p. 1320.

47 Art. I-7 Constitutional Treaty.

48 This corresponds with Art. 6 EU.

49 With regard to the role of the citizens see section 5.

50 Art. I-24(6) Constitutional Treaty. Whether and to what extent this requirement will really substantially enhance the transparency in the decision-making process may however be questionable given the role of COREPER and the subordinated expert committees and working groups in the preparation of Council decisions.

of these two levels it seems at least questionable whether the Member States should continue be left to their own devices in this regard.

With the coming into force of the Constitutional Treaty, the European Council will have come a long way from constituting an ad-hoc forum for discussions of the Heads of State or Government in the 1960s, its acknowledgment in the Single European Act 1986, and its formal recognition outside the Community framework by the Treaty on European Union 1992. It will enjoy the status of a Union institution on a par with the Council, the Commission, the EP and the ECJ as part of a single institutional framework. The fact that the Constitutional Treaty explicitly excludes the exercise of legislative functions by the European Council should not be mistaken as evidence that its role in the future Union will be restricted to defining the general political directions and the priorities of the EU.[51] Indeed, the inclusion of the European Council in the institutional framework is more than just a symbolically important development as it is accompanied by functions which it does not as such fulfill in the context of the EC Treaty.[52] In some instances the European Council takes over functions assigned in the current system to the Council meeting in the composition of Heads of State or Government, as is the case with regard to the nomination of the Commission President for example, or in the case of the Council with regard to the future treaty revision procedure.[53] In other instances the European Council will be empowered to take decisions of far reaching importance, such as in relation to the functioning of other Union institutions.[54] The European Council will be indirectly provided with a role in the legislative procedure. Firstly, Article IV-444 of the Constitutional Treaty includes a passerelle clause, empowering the European Council to authorize the Council to act by a qualified-majority in areas where under the Constitutional Treaty unanimity is required. Interest-

---

51 The European Council will e.g. retain its strong role in the area of the common foreign and security policy (Art. III-295 Constitutional Treaty) and will define the strategic guidelines for legislative and operational planning within the area of freedom, security and justice (Art. III-258 Constitutional Treaty).

52 A. Dashwood and A. Johnston, 'The Institutions of the Enlarged EU under the Regime of the Constitution Treaty', 41 *CMLRev.* (2004) 1481-1518, at p. 1490, who refer to symbolic gesture while at the time recognizing the new role of the European Council under the Constitutional Treaty.

53 Art. I-27 and III-443 Constitutional Treaty. See also Art. I-59 Constitutional Treaty, which will replace Art. 7 EU concerning the suspension of membership rights. Interestingly, it does not become clear whether the Presidents of the European Council and of the Commission will be excluded from this decision, as according to Art. I-25(4) Constitutional Treaty the Commission President is only excluded from qualified majority decisions, whereas Art. I-59(2) Constitutional Treaty requires a unanimous decision.

54 Such as with regard to the composition of the EP (Art. I-20 Constitutional Treaty), the number of Commissioners (Art. I-26 Constitutional Treaty) and the authorization of the Council to act by qualified majority rather than unanimity (Arts. I-55(4) and III-300(3) Constitutional Treaty). The European Council acts by means of a European decision as defined in Article I-33(1) Constitutional Treaty.

ingly, such an amendment of the Constitutional Treaty outside the regular treaty amendment procedure cannot take place against the express opposition of the parliaments of the Member States.[55] Moreover, according to Article III-136 of the Constitutional Treaty on measures in the field of social security, Member States that consider a proposal to affect fundamental aspects of its social security system may request that the matter be referred to the European Council, thereby suspending the legislative procedure as foreseen in Article III-396 of the Constitutional Treaty. If the European Council requests the Commission to submit a new proposal, the original proposal is deemed not to have been adopted.[56]

The Constitutional Treaty establishes a permanent presidency for the European Council, replacing the current six-monthly rotation system.[57] While it may be observed that the enlargement of the EU to twenty-five Member States renders a rotating presidency held by an acting Head of State or Government of one of the Member States unpractical,[58] it does tilt the institutional balance in favour of the Member States. The future President of the European Council will hold a key position as he or she will chair the meeting of the European Council, is supposed to drive forward its work, will ensure the preparation and continuity of the work of the European Council in co-operation with the Commission President and on the basis of the work of the General Affairs Council, and is supposed to endeavor to facilitate cohesion and consensus within the European Council. Moreover, the President in his or her capacity is supposed to ensure the external representation of the Union on issues concerning its common foreign and security policy.[59]

For the European Council as a body, democratic legitimacy is split between the Member States and the Union. Whereas the President of the Commission derives its legitimacy partly from the Member States and partly from the EP, for the Heads of State or Government the same mechanisms of legitimacy and accountability apply as for the Council.[60] Yet, the President of the European Council who is explicitly excluded from holding national office falls outside these schemes.[61] Suggestions to directly elect the President by the citizens of

55 See Art. IV-444(3) Constitutional Treaty. This provision is somewhat vague, given that it does not include any details as to exactly how many parliaments must oppose such a decision by the European Council.

56 See also Art. III-270(3) Constitutional Treaty in the area of judicial cooperation in criminal matters.

57 This should not be confused with the Presidency of the Council that, with the exception of the Foreign Affairs Council, will continue to exist under the conditions laid down in Art. I-23(6) Constitutional Treaty.

58 See Dashwood and Johnston, op. cit., n. 52, p. 1491 et seq.

59 Art. I-22 (1) Constitutional Treaty.

60 However, different to the current situation, the action or inaction of the European Council can under certain circumstances become subject of legal proceedings (see Arts. III-365(1) and III-367 Constitutional Treaty; see also Art. III-371 Constitutional Treaty.

61 Art. I-22(3) Constitutional Treaty.

the Member States, thereby strengthening the democratic legitimacy of the new post, have not been taken up in the body of the Constitutional Treaty. The candidate will be elected by the European Council by qualified majority for a period of two and a half years.[62] The officeholder can only be removed by the European Council in the event of an impediment or serious misconduct. The phrase 'impediment' applied in Article I-22(1) of the Constitutional Treaty is nowhere defined; it is likely to refer to any legal obstructions rather than to the performance of the President of the European Council. In analogy with similar arrangements for the dismissal of Commissioners and of members of the Executive Board of the European Central Bank, 'serious misconduct' is also likely to be interpreted as referring to punishable behavior and thus, also not to related to the performance of the officeholder.[63]

More evidence that the position of the Member States is consolidated and thus, that the democratic legitimacy also in the future will have to be facilitated to large extent by the Member States, can be found in the creation of the Union Minister for Foreign Affairs (Union Minister). In conducting the Union's common foreign and security policy and common security and defense policy, the Union Minister has to serve two masters.[64] On the one hand the Union Minister carries out his tasks as mandated by the Council. In this function he presides over the Foreign Affairs Council. However, at the same time the Union Minister holds the position of Vice-President of the Commission. In this function and to the extent that this does not conflict with his mandate by the Council, the Union Minister is bound by Commission procedures.[65]

This accumulation of functions may result in conflicts not only between the Council and the Commission, but also between the Union Minister and the President of the European Council.[66] Notable in this context are the provisions concerning the appointment and dismissal of the Union Minister, which show some inconsistencies. The Union Minister is appointed by the European Council by qualified majority with the agreement of the Commission President. As is the case with regard to the President of the European Council, the EP is not even consulted on this important appointment. Yet, in his position as Vice-President of the Commission, the Union Minister has to be approved by the EP together with the President and the other members of the Commission as a collective

---

62 Art. I-22 Constitutional Treaty. With regard to the definition of qualified majority the same definition applies both for the European Council and the Council, see Art. I-25 Constitutional Treaty. As to the problem of proportionate representation see section 4.

63 Amtenbrink, op. cit., n. 6, 271-272.

64 Gormley, op. cit., n. 17, refers to a 'strange animal'.

65 Art. I- 28(4) Constitutional Treaty.

66 More optimistic Dashwood and Johnston, op. cit., n. 53, at p. 1504. See also J. Schwarze, 'Guest Editorial: The Convention's Draft Treaty Establishing A Constitution For Europe', 40 *CMLRev.* (2003) pp. 1037 – 1045, at p. 1039.

body.[67] One may wonder whether one appointment takes precedence over the other or whether the EP could really block the taking up of office of the Union Minister. What is more, it is doubtful whether and to what extent the Union Minister, in his function as Vice-President of the Commission becomes subject to the dismissal procedures applicable to the latter. Article I-27(3), in conjunction with Article I-28(1), of the Constitutional Treaty suggests that only the European Council can end the term of office of the Union Minister by qualified-majority vote. Yet it is unclear, whether a request by the Commission President in accordance with Articles I-27(3) of the Constitutional Treaty would impose a legal obligation on the European Council to dismiss the Union Minister. With regard to a motion of censure by the EP the legal situation is clearer, as Article III-340 of the Constitutional Treaty states unequivocally that while the members of the Commission resign as a body, the Union Minister for Foreign Affairs resigns from duties that he or she carries out in the Commission.[68]

The role of the Commission in the institutional structure and in particular its position vis-à-vis the Council and the EP in the legislative procedure, remains basically unchanged. The Commission will continue to be the promotor of the general interest of the Union and the main initiator of legislative acts.[69] If anything, given the introduction of a permanent European Council Presidency and a Union Minister who is only partly attached to the Commission, it may be argued that the political weight of the latter, and in particular of the Commission President, diminishes somewhat. A further loss of political influence vis-à-vis the Council is feared as a result of the restriction in the future of number of Commissioners to two-thirds of the number of Member States.[70] With regard to the future appointment procedures, according to the Article I-27 of the Constitutional Treaty the European Council has the right to propose to the EP a candidate for Commission President whom must then be elected by the latter. The provision states that the European Council has to take into account the elections to the EP. Whether this is a substantive improvement of the current arrangements is questionable. It is presently suggested that the role of the EP has been pepped up in terms of usage of terminology rather than by changing the substance of the procedure.[71] Even the general invitation to the European Coun-

[67] Another channel for the EP could be to hold the Commission President accountable for his approval of the Union Minister.

[68] Supposedly, in order to ensure the affectivity of the function of Union Minister the European Council would be under some pressure to replace a Union Minister, which has come under fire for its conduct in the Commission.

[69] Art. I-26(1) - (2) Constitutional Treaty.

[70] See Temple Lang, op. cit., n. 41, at 318 et seq.; Schwarze, op. cit., n. 66, at p. 1039. For the first Commission appointed under the provisions of the Constitutional Treaty, the principle of one Commissioner per Member State is upheld.

[71] The phrase 'elected' rather than 'approved' is applied.

cil in making its nomination for the office of Commission President to take into account the political composition of the EP cannot disguise the fact that the EP does not gain a right of nomination.

While Article I-20(1) of the Constitutional Treaty states that the EP shall exercise legislative functions jointly with the Council, its role in the different legislative procedures remains basically unchanged.[72] While the Constitutional Treaty in general also does not foresee a general right of initiative for the EP, different from Article 48 EC, Article IV-443 of the Constitutional Treaty gives the EP the right to submit to the Council proposals for an amendment of the Constitutional Treaty. However, even under the new regime, the EP will not play any role in the final decision to amend the Constitutional Treaty, which is reserved to the Member States.[73] Nevertheless, it may be argued that overall the profile of the EP in the legislative procedure is raised in as much as the field of application of the co-decision procedure is further broadened in the Constitutional Treaty. According to Article I-34(1), as a rule, the future European laws and framework laws as defined in Article I-33 of the Constitutional Treaty are adopted on the basis of proposals from the Commission, jointly by the European Parliament and the Council under the ordinary legislative procedure set out in Article III-396. The co-decision procedure thus becomes the standard legislative procedure, although exceptions apply.[74] Moreover, the co-operation procedure, which is still utilized in Title VII of the EC Treaty on Economic and Monetary Union, will cease to exist. This is not to say that the role of the EP in this context will be strengthened in all instances. Indeed, while in the future the co-decision procedure will apply for the adoption of detailed rules for the multilateral surveillance procedure[75], in other areas the influence of the EP will be reduced to a right for being consulted.[76]

In the highly relevant area of powers delegated by the Council to the Commission, the power of the EP is enhanced. European laws and framework laws delegating to the Commission the power to adopt delegated European regulations to supplement or amend certain non-essential elements of the law or framework law can also provide the EP with a right to object to the entry into force of such an act or, otherwise, to provide the EP with a right to revoke

[72] Peters, op. cit., n. 27, p. 48 et seq., however highlights a number of simplifications in the co-decision procedure under Art. II-396 Constitutional Treaty, which indeed is phrased in a much more comprehensible way than today's Art. 251 EC.

[73] With regard to this procedure see also section 4.

[74] Art. I-34(2) – (3) Constitutional Treaty.

[75] See Art. III-179(6) Constitutional Treaty (now: Art. 99(5) EC).

[76] See Art. III- 183(2) Constitutional Treaty (now: Art. 103(2) EC) and Art. 186(2) (now: Art. 106(2) EC). According to Art. 252 EC, in case of a rejection of the Council's common position by the EP, a unanimity decision is required in the Council in order to act. Such a requirement does not exist in case that the EP is only consulted.

the delegation of such powers to the Commission under certain conditions.[77] If applied, these rights could certainly enhance the democratic legitimacy of the delegation of powers to the Commission. Another notable extension of the power of the EP relates to the budgetary procedure, as Article III-404 of the Constitutional Treaty no longer differentiates between compulsory and non-compulsory expenditure and puts the EP on an equal footing with the Council in establishing the Union's annual budget as a whole. However, despite these improvements in favor of the EP and despite the fact that the Union will stand for a uniform structure, this is not to say that the integration of today's largely intergovernmental second and third pillars will be fully supranationalized and made subject to the Community method. Instead special rules have been included in the Constitutional Treaty, among others relating to the common foreign and security policy and the common security and defense policy. The EP rights in these areas are restricted to those of being regularly consulted and informed.[78]

Rather than substantially redefining the role of the EP in the legislative process, a closer link is built with national parliaments. This is not realized by a direct participation of the latter in the decision-making process on the European level side-by-side with the EP.[79]. Instead, national parliaments are put in charge of ensuring the observance of the subsidiarity principle referred to in Article I-11(3) of the Constitutional Treaty and in the Protocol on the application of the principles of subsidiarity and proportionality (the Protocol).[80] Seemingly with this arrangement two birds are killed with one stone. Firstly, in addition to the categorization of competences introduced by the Constitutional Treaty, by adding more substance to the subsidiarity principle, longstanding concerns about a creeping loss of competences at the expense of the national legislator are met. Moreover, by involving national parliaments, the democratic legitimacy of Union activities and the accountability of the Council, the Commission and the EP could be enhanced. Given that the arrangement surrounding this mechanism is dealt with extensively elsewhere in this volume,[81] it suffices to observe that it is doubtful whether the procedure foreseen in the Constitutional Treaty will be able to meet these high expectations. Apart from the question of whether

---

77 Art. I-36(2) Constitutional Treaty.

78 Art. I-40(8) and Art. I-41(8) Constitutional Treaty.

79 Such as by a double mandate whereby a MEP also has to be a member of a national parliament. See e.g. suggestions by the German Foreign Minister Joschka Fischer in his much recognized speech on the future of Europe, see J. Fischer, 'Vom Staatenverbund zur Förderation – Gedanken über die Finalität der europäischen Integration', Forum Constitutionis Europae, *FCE Spezial* 2/00, online at www.whi-berlin.de visited on 15 February 2005.

80 Currently Art. 5 EC. See also Protocol on the role of national Parliaments in the European Union annexed to the Constitutional Treaty.

81 See the contribution by P. Kiiver.

the national parliaments, or rather the respective national parliamentary committees, will be able to deal with all legislative proposals within the short time frame prescribed by the Protocol, a negative opinion by the national parliaments will at least *de jure* have relatively little impact on the decision-making process itself. The reason for this is that the Union institutions are only invited to take these opinions into account. At most the Commission is required to reconsider its proposal. National parliaments cannot block Union legislation but, in the first instance, will have to rely on putting enough pressure on their own governments to reject the legislative proposal in the Council. Arguably the real baptism of fire will be the challenge of Union legislation before the ECJ based on the subsidiarity principle, a possibility explicitly foreseen in the Protocol.[82] Interestingly, this right to appeal is also given to the Committee of the Regions to the extent that it has a right to be consulted in the regular legislative process. Thus, in the future also regional governments and parliaments/assemblies are indirectly involved in legitimizing of Union legislation to the extent that they can review its compatibility with the subsidiarity principle.

Yet, limiting the involvement of the national parliaments to the review of the compliance with the subsidiarity principle may backfire on the Union. National parliaments, which do not restrain their activities in this regard, will have to be told that they are effectively exceeding their competences. The growing awareness of the national parliaments of the limits to their influence may become a growing bone of contention. Moreover, it is far from certain that opinion formation in the national parliaments will be based on the merits of the respective legislative proposal rather than domestic political considerations.

4 Representative democracy in the future Union; bringing European institutions closer to its citizens?

Given the governance structures described earlier, the question arises as to the extent that the Constitutional Treaty can succeed in bringing the Union institutions closer to its citizens, as envisaged by the Laeken Declaration.

Despite the fact that the somewhat ill chosen reference to the Athenian democracy preceding the preamble of the Draft Treaty establishing a Constitution for Europe has not found its way in the final version of the Constitutional Treaty, this reference may still be symptomatic of the approach taken in the Constitutional Treaty.[83] Indeed, while Article I-45 of the Constitutional Treaty

82 This may result in interesting legal situations in Member States with a two-chamber parliamentary system if the opposition holds a majority in one of the two chambers, as in accordance with Art. 8 Protocol Member States have to bring an action on behalf of their parliament or chamber. The Convention working group on subsidiarity had suggested giving national parliaments the right to appeal directly.

83 Draft Treaty of 18 July 2003: 'Our Constitution ... is called a democracy because power is not in the hands of a minority but for the greatest number vested.'

declares that the Union in all its activities has to observe the principle of the equality of its citizens and that the latter have to receive equal attention from its institutions, bodies, offices and agencies, arguably this principle is not fully observed in the representation of citizens of the Member States in the Union institutions. Indeed, despite the recognition of representative democracy as one of the foundations of the Union[84], the latter will rely more on the principle of equality of states than on the equality of its citizens.

In the case of the European Council and the Council, representation of the citizens is mediated through the Member States' governments, which represent their respective national constituencies. Where decisions are taken by unanimity, it relies entirely on the principle of equality of Member States. Where decisions are taken by qualified-majority, under the present arrangements each Member State is assigned a certain number of votes that are linked to its share in the overall population of the Union.[85] With more policy areas being moved into qualified-majority voting over time, the dispute among the Member States on the allocation of voting rights has become more fierce. Smaller Member States fear the dominance of the larger Member States, whereas the latter are concerned that the increasing number of smaller Member States resulting from enlargement will outvote them. Member States are more concerned about their position vis-à-vis other Member States than about a proportionate representation of the citizens of the Union as a whole. Simply assigning more or less votes to the different Member States arguably cannot solve this conflict. With the Treaty of Nice a safeguard clause in form of a double-majority requirement has been introduced into the EC Treaty. Currently, a Member State can request verification that the Member States constituting the qualified majority represent at least 62 per cent of the total population of the Union. Where this is not the case the decision in question is not adopted.[86]

This introduction of population as an element in the qualified majority procedure in the Council has been followed through in the Constitutional Treaty while at the same time also upholding the principle of equality of Member States.[87] The system of weighted votes has been entirely replaced. Based on Article I-25 of the Constitutional Treaty, a qualified majority will be defined in case of an act based on a proposal from the Commission or the Union Minister as at least 55 per cent of the Member States, comprising at least fifteen of them and representing Member States comprising at least 65 per cent of the popula-

---

84 Art. I-46(1) Constitutional Treaty. See also section 3.

85 To be sure, this only refers to persons holding the nationality of a Member State and does not include EU foreigners and third-country nationals.

86 Art. 205(4) EC.

87 For a detailed overview over the qualified majority provisions applicable and population figures see Appendices 1 - 3 of Dashwood and Johnston, op. cit., n. 52.

tion of the Union.[88] The latter requirement has been described illustratively by Peters as a 'demographic safety net'.[89] Yet, by providing that a blocking minority in the Council must include at least four Member States (regardless of their size in terms of population) or else the qualified majority will be deemed attained, it seems that overall the state element gains the upper hand in the procedure.[90]

While being used in different places throughout the Constitutional Treaty, the term 'population' is nowhere defined. Indeed, elsewhere the Constitutional Treaty also refers to nationals of the Member States and citizens of the Union.[91] Under the current Article 205(2) EC the practice is to translate this phrase into nationals of a Member State. This reading is likely to have been the intention of the drafters of the Constitutional Treaty. However, it would have added to the clarity of the Constitutional Treaty if the provision were to have referred to Union citizens, as the term 'population' in a more generic interpretation may also refer to inhabitants occupying a Member State, which would not only comprise the nationals of that Member State or the Union citizens residing in that Member State but even third-country nationals.

The EP has long been criticized for not representing the citizens of the Member States proportionately as a result of which it lacks democratic legitimacy to some extent. Indeed, under the present arrangements the nationals of smaller Member States are over-represented compared to nationals of larger Member States. The fact that ninety-nine MEPs from Germany represent approximately 82.5 million citizens, whereas six MEPs from Luxembourg represent only approximately 0.4 million citizens highlights the limitations of the present system.[92] The requirement stated in Article 190(2) EC that the number of representatives elected must ensure appropriate representation of the people of the states is not met. The drafters of the Constitutional Treaty seem to have resigned themselves to this reality, firstly by no longer including this requirement and, secondly, by stating that the representation of European citizens is 'degressively proportional'. This term is not defined anywhere in the Constitu-

---

88 The original thresholds proposed in the Draft Constitution became one of the stumbling blocks at the European Council meeting in December 2003 when the Member States failed to reach consensus on the TCE. In all other cases the qualified majority is defined as at least 72 per cent of the members of the Council, representing Member States comprising at least 65 per cent of the population of the Union.

89 Peters, op. cit., n. 27, at p. 57.

90 The blocking minority requirement is redefined in areas where not all Member States vote in the Council, see Art. I-44(3) Constitutional Treaty. Interestingly also this requirement is somewhat qualified by the reintroduction of the *Ioannina Compromise* regarding blocking minorities in the Council, see Editorial Comments, 'A Constitution for Europe', 41 *CMLRev.* (2004) 899 – 907, at p. 905.

91 See e.g. Art. I-8 and Art. I-19(2) Constitutional Treaty.

92 It could be argued that the system is further distorted by the fact that seats for the EP are not allocated on the basis of the actual number of EU residents in a Member State, which can participate in the elections to the EP.

tional Treaty. While the actual composition of the EP will have to be established by European Council decision, given that the total number of MEPs is restricted to 750, the minimum threshold is set at six members per Member State and the maximum number of members per Member State is set at ninety-six, it becomes clear that the ratio between the number of seats assigned to a Member State and the share in the population size (in terms of EU citizens) of the Union will be progressively more favorable towards Member States with fewer nationals.[93] 'Degressively proportional' is, therefore, just an elegant way of stating that the EP will continue to be based on a disproportionate representation of the citizens of the Union.

The function of the EP as a source of democratic legitimacy may also have its limitations when observing the opinion formation process. In the parliamentary systems of the Member States political parties offer a channel for public opinion to enter the decision-making process. The presence of parties across the political spectrum should, in principle, ensure that a broad range of opinions is taken into account. The role that political parties play in this context in the Member States in many instances is institutionalized and even given a constitutional status.[94] In the European context, since the coming into force of the EU Treaty, political parties are explicitly mentioned in the EC Treaty.[95] Yet, despite general elections to the EP since 1979 and the introduction of a European citizenship under the EU Treaty, the much sought after European awareness or rather identity is missing, as are European political parties which could function as intermediaries between the EU citizens as the electorate and the EP and indeed other Community institutions.[96] National parties, which nominate candidates for the elections to the EP prevail. The lack of a uniform electoral system and the allocation of seats to Member States rather than European constituencies facilitate a system whereby MEPs are elected on the basis of domestic issues rather than European ones. What is more, once elected often relatively little is heard or seen in the national constituencies of MEPs. Public scrutiny of their performance seems to be largely lacking.[97] Yet, by what means is the EP then held accountable for its conduct? The Constitutional Treaty offers little in this regard, as Article I-46 only declares that citizens shall have the right to participate in the democratic life of the Union and restates, in a somewhat unsubstantiated way, that political parties at European level contribute to forming European political

---

93 Art. I-20(2) Constitutional Treaty. See also Part 2 of the House of Lords, Select Committee on European Union, Twenty – First Report, Session 2002-2003, where an explanation of this term is demanded.

94 See e.g. Art. 21 German Basic Law and Art. 4 of the French Constitution of 1958.

95 Art. 191 EC.

96 Until now the EP is organized in political groups which are given certain procedural right under the Rules of Procedure, but do not constitute political parties.

97 To be sure, this is likely to be part of a more structural problem which can already be found in national parliamentary systems.

awareness and express the will of citizens of the Union.[98] For the time being, these remain empty words.

While the drafters of the Constitutional Treaty still seem to put their hopes in the sudden emergence of European political parties, they also introduce what could be interpreted as a plebiscitary element into the Constitutional Treaty. According to Article I-47(4) at least one million citizens who are nationals of a significant number of Member States are required in order to take the initiative of inviting the Commission, within the framework of its powers, to submit any appropriate proposal on matters where citizens consider that a legal act of the Union is required for the purpose of implementing the Constitutional Treaty.[99] A closer reading of this provision reveals however that this citizen's right amounts to little more than a petition to the Commission, which, as the choice of the word 'invite' suggests, is under no obligation to act.[100] Moreover, the requirement of a million signatures from a significant number of Member States may prove to be too high a hurdle to give this provision any real meaning. A somewhat more upbeat assessment may be that this will promote the emergence of social and/or political movements on a European level, which have been missing until now. Non governmental organizations (NGOs), such as Greenpeace, may already have the necessary network and experience to successfully launch such a procedure.

Suggestions for a greater participation of the Union citizens in the appointment of key figures at Union level, such as the new President of the European Council or the Commission President, have not found their way into the Constitutional Treaty.

5 The Convention process as a source of democratic legitimacy in the future Union?

While the content of the Constitutional Treaty arguably does not alter the patterns of democratic legitimacy dramatically as the latter continues to rely substantially on the national rather than the Union level, one may wonder whether the real significance of the Constitutional Treaty is to be found in the reform process itself.

Different from the purely intergovernmental negotiations of the past, the Laeken Declaration called for a broader and more open preparation of the next IGC. To this end, the Laeken European Council chose to convene a Convention to consider, as it was stated, the key issues arising for the Union's future

98 See also Art. III-331 Constitutional Treaty.

99 Details including the minimum number of Member States will have to be determined by a European law.

100 In this regard the citizen's initiative ironically will share the faith of a request to the Commission by the EP as foreseen in Art. III-332 Constitutional Treaty.

development and try to identify the various possible responses. To be sure, this approach was not entirely new as the convention approach had been applied successfully before in establishing the Charter of Fundamental Rights of the European Union, which itself has found its way into Part II of the Constitutional Treaty.[101]

Similar to the Convention established by the Cologne European Council in 1999 for the Charter of Fundamental Rights, the so-called Convention on the Future of Europe brought together representatives of the Member States and candidate state governments, members of all national parliaments and of the EP, two representatives of the Commission as well as numerous representatives from other Community bodies with an observers status.[102] It was lead by a Praesidium consisting of representatives of Council Presidencies, of the national parliaments and the EP and the Commission. The Praesidium was headed by a troika of a chairman and two vice-chairmen and was supported by a Secretariat.[103] This basic composition of the Convention was already laid down in the Laeken Declaration itself.

The Chairman of the Convention, Valérie Giscard d'Estaing, and the two vice-chairmen, Giuliano Amato and Jean-Luc Dehaene, were elected by the Laeken European Council rather than by the members of the Convention. The modus of selection of representatives from the Member States governments and parliaments was left to the Member States. Given the fact that an equal number of participants were assigned to all Member States and national parliaments, the composition of the Convention reflected a proportionate representation of Member States rather than of Union citizens. The representatives from the MEP on the other hand reflected the political composition of the elected EP at the time.

Together with the national parliamentarians, the MEPs formed the strongest group in the Convention and outnumbered the government representatives. Yet, this is not to say that the Convention method was primarily that of a constitutional convent dominated by national parliaments and/or the EP. Indeed, the chairman of the Convent and the Praesidium in many regards became the dominant forces in the Convention process, a role that was already foreseen in the Laeken Declaration.[104] Moreover, the composition of the eleven

---

[101] Despite of not being legally binding, the Presidents of the EP, the Council and the Commission signed and proclaimed the Charter on behalf of their institutions on 7 December 2000. See Kokott and Rüth, op. cit. n. 42, p. 1327 et seq.

[102] According to the Laeken Declaration, while taking fully part in the proceedings, representatives from candidate countries could not prevent any consensus emerging.

[103] For a list of all the members including their alternates see Report from the Presidency of the Convention to the President of the European Council of 18 July 2003 (CONV 851/03), Annex I.

[104] For an interesting account of the works of the Convention see e.g. P. Norman, *The Accidental Constitution* (Brussels, EuroComment 2003); also P. Craig, 'Constitutional Process and Reform in the EU: Nice, Laeken, the Convention and the IGC', 10:4 *EPL* (2004) p. 653.

working groups and three so-called discussion circles , set up in the course of the Convention to develop proposals, were also not staffed representatively.[105] In fact, while the Laeken Declaration lacks any detail on this, the self-imposed Convention's Working Methods only states in broad terms that the Chairman or a significant number of the members of the Convention could recommend that the Praesidium set up working groups and it was for the Praesidium to determine the mandate, working arrangements and composition, taking into account the specific expertise of members, alternates and observers in relation to the subject under discussion. In principle every member of the Convention had a right to attend all such meetings.

One of the aims expressed in the Laeken Declaration was to stimulate a broad-based debate in the Convention involving all citizens. To this end a Forum was opened which was supposed to form the basis for an exchange between so-called civil society and the Convention. Organizations such as the social partners, the business representatives, NGOs and academia, where supposed to be heard or consulted on specific topics. However, some comments by observers of the Convention process suggest that this Forum lacked the broad participation that a reference to civil society would suggest.[106] The working documents of the working groups show some civil society input, albeit arguably not in a structural manner and with a clear dominance of European and national government officials and academics.

The Convention had the task of drawing up a final document to comprise either different options or recommendations if consensus was achieved. Together with the outcome of national debates on the future of the Union, the final document was to provide a starting point for discussions in the IGC. In this regard the Draft Treaty establishing a Constitution for Europe presented in the end was possibly more than most had either hoped or wished for. This draft was not put to the vote in the Convention nor would such a vote have added any real legitimacy, given the unrepresentative character of the Convention and the fact that the decision on the final text remained with the Member States in any event. Despite its limitations, the Convention method has found its way into the Constitutional Treaty. According to Article IV-443 of the Constitutional Treaty, if the European Council, having consulted the EP and the Commission, adopts by simple majority a decision in favour of examining amendments that have been proposed, the President of the European Council has to convene a Convention unless the EP consents to abstain from this procedure. The composition of the Convention has to be similar to that used in drafting the Constitutional Treaty, whereby any recommendations require consensus. While the role of the EP and

[105] Critically Norman, op. cit., n. 104, at p. 129. Interestingly, the final reports of the working groups lack any reference to their composition.

[106] Norman, op. cit. n. 104, at p. 50 refers to a participation that was 'heavily tilted towards organizations from inside the Brussels ring road.

also of the national parliaments in the treaty amendment process is enhanced, the final decision remains firmly with the Member States acting by unanimity. Given the experience with the Draft Constitutional Treaty and the subsequent amendments inserted by the Member States this is more than just a formality.

Ultimately, the Constitutional Treaty will derive its (initial) democratic legitimacy from the same source as the founding treaties of the European Communities and all the subsequent treaties have; that is through its ratification by the Member States. The idea of a Europe-wide referendum on the Constitutional Treaty was met with resistance by those Member States whose constitutional systems do not allow for referenda. Thus, while in many Member States the participation of the electorate is channeled by the national parliaments, the fact that at the time of the writing of this contribution referenda have already and still have to be held in some Member States could suggest that the degree of democratic legitimacy of the Constitutional Treaty may vary.[107] Yet, even if the Constitutional Treaty is characterized as a constitutional document, it may be argued that history teaches us that the legitimacy of constitutions can hardly ever be based on their method of establishment but rather on the extent to which they succeed over time to provide the legal and institutional basis for safeguarding and enforcing fundamental values underlying society, such as freedom and equality.

6 Epilogue

Europe at the crossroads, indeed! This description about the current state of affairs of the EU, which has found its way into the title of the research seminar is a truism.[108] Europe has been at crossroads ever since six states decided to join in the journey towards a united Europe. When Robert Schuman articulated Jean Monnet's vision of a united Europe he envisaged a process rather than a particular end result.[109] With each new state that joined, with each new step in the integration process that was taken, another crossroads was met and another path was chosen, the final destination of which was and possibly still is open. The Constitutional Treaty is no different in this regard. It does not signify the finality of European integration but, at best, describes yet another crossroad.

---

[107] In Lithuania the TCE was approved by Parliament on 11 November 2004, in Hungary on 20 December 2004 and in Slovenia on 1 February. Generally on referenda in the Member States A. Peters, 'Citizen's Voices via Referendum?', Conference Paper, *The EU Constitution: The Best Way Forward?* (34th Session Asser Institute Colloquium on European Law, 13-16 October 2004, The Hague).

[108] The Research seminar 'Enlargement and the Future of the European Union: Parallel Paths or Crossroads?' in which this contribution was first presented was held in Warsaw from 1 July until 4 July 2004.

[109] Robert Schuman, Declaration of 9 May 1950, online at europa.eu.int visited on 15 February 2005.

Even in the present construction, the EU no longer only receives its legitimacy from the Member States but, to a certain extent, also from the EU citizens.[110] Yet, the division between the national and supranational exercise of power and the splits in democratic legitimacy and accountability resulting from that is here to stay even if the Constitutional Treaty is ratified by all twenty-five Member States. Despite its many good intentions, for the time being Europe to a large extent remains a project of the Member States rather than its citizens. Labels cannot substitute contents. It may therefore be necessary in the future not only to refer to a democratic deficit in the Union but instead to analyse more carefully whether and to what extent democratic legitimacy and accountability might also be enhanced at national level. As has been pointed out, the involvement of the national parliaments as foreseen in the Constitutional Treaty does not provide an adequate answer in this regard.

The discussion on the democratic credentials of European integration will continue. As Eriksen and Fossum have put it: 'The question of the democratic deficit has direct bearings on what type of polity the EU is, what it aspires to be, and what we want it to be.'[111] It seems that the answer to some of these questions is still at large.

---

[110] For a somewhat optimistic assessment of the current situations see A. Moravcsik, 'In Defense of the "Democratic Deficit": Reassessing Legitimacy in the European Union', 40:4 *JCMS (2002)* p. 603.

[111] Eriksen and Fossum, op. cit., n. 11.

CHAPTER 3

Institutional Reform in the European Union

A Difficult Balancing Act

Peter Van Elsuwege and An Vermeersch

1 Introduction

The Copenhagen European Council of 21-22 June 1993 is generally regarded as the starting point for the European Union's historic fifth enlargement wave. On this occasion, the Heads of State or Government discussed the applications of Malta and Cyprus[1] and explicitly acknowledged the membership perspectives of the associated countries from Central and Eastern Europe. Moreover, the Presidency Conclusions laid down the conditions for accession. Apart from the three well-know Copenhagen pre-accession criteria,[2] to be fulfilled by the applicant countries, the members of the European Council also imposed a condition on themselves when they mentioned 'the Union's capacity to absorb new members while maintaining the momentum of European integration ... [as] ... an important consideration in the general interest of both the Union and the candidate countries'.[3] The latter precondition can be reformulated as a requirement to give every Member State in an enlarged EU an appropriate place in the various EU institutions without undermining the Union's decision-making capacity.[4] This paper analyses how the EU has dealt with this challenge and explores the characteristics of the institutional reform process. In particular, specific attention will be devoted to the concept of 'balance' within the European Union.

The European integration process has always been characterised by a search for compromise and balance between divergent actors with divergent interests. The constant widening and deepening has put the original solutions under increasing strain as the EU's institutional framework had to take into account an

1 The Presidency Conclusions confirmed that the applications of Malta and Cyprus (submitted in 1990) would be considered on their own merits and stated that the enlargement to include the EFTA countries would be without prejudice to the situation of other applicants. Moreover, the European Council welcomed the Commission's intention to present its opinions on both countries and promised that the Council would act rapidly once it had received the Commission's views. Presidency Conclusions, June 1993 Copenhagen European Council, 6 *Bull. EC*, 1993, I.11.

2 These 'Copenhagen criteria' require 'stability of institutions guaranteeing democracy, the rule of law, human rights and respect for and protection minorities'; the existence of a functioning and competitive market economy and the 'candidate's ability to take on the obligations of membership including adherence to the aims of political, economic and monetary union'. Ibid., I.13.

3 Ibid.

4 The term 'decision-making capacity' refers to 'the probability that a political system, given the diversity of interests to which it is exposed, will be able to take decisions'. B. de Witte, 'The Impact of Enlargement on the Constitution of the European Union', in M. Cremona, ed., *The Enlargement of the European Union*, (Oxford, Oxford University Press 2003) p. 212. See also: B. Kerremans, 'The Political and Institutional Consequences of Widening: Capacity and Control in an Enlarged Council', in P. H. Laurent and M. Maresceau, eds., *The State of the European Union (Vol.4): Deepening and Widening*, (Boulder, Riener 1998) p. 87.

increasing geographical and political diversity. The fifth enlargement wave and the accompanying reform of the institutions has revealed clearly the tensions among big and small Member States and those countries defending either a supranational or more intergovernmental vision on the future of the Union. The adoption of the 'Treaty establishing a Constitution for Europe' (hereafter 'the Constitutional Treaty') on 18 June 2004 marked the provisional closure of the institutional debates.[5] At the earliest, the Constitutional Treaty will enter into force in November 2006 on condition that the process of national ratifications has been finalised in time.[6] Before analysing the consequences of these new institutional provisions, this paper gives an overview of the complex institutional compromises that determine the current and future composition of the institutions. To begin with, it analyses the complexity of the institutional reform process and the interrelationship between the widening and deepening of European integration.

2 EU enlargement and the complexity of institutional reform

The original institutional framework of the European Economic Community (EEC) was designed for six Member States and provided a pragmatic, political functional balance between three large and three smaller States. The distribution of votes within the Council illustrated this equilibrium. In cases of qualified majority voting (QMV), the three large Member States (France, Germany and Italy) had four votes, Belgium and the Netherlands two, and Luxemburg only one. It was agreed that a decision could be blocked by a coalition of one large and one small Member State (Belgium or the Netherlands). However, a coalition of one large and one very small (Luxembourg) could not hinder the decision-making.[7] The qualified majority vote (12 votes out of 17) corresponded to 70 per cent of the population. This system of weighted votes in the Council combined with an independent Commission and a rotating Council Presidency proved to be a fair mixture of intergovernmental and supranational elements.[8] In practice, it also reflected a compromise between two contradictory

5 The official signing ceremony took place in Rome on 29 October 2004. See *OJ* 2004 C310/1.

6 According to Article IV-447 Constitutional Treaty, 'this Treaty shall enter info force on 1 November 2006, provided that all the instruments of ratification have been deposited, or, failing that, on the first day of the second month following the deposit of the instrument of ratification by the last signatory State to take this step. '

7 B. Bobay, *Political Economy of the Nice Treaty: Rebalancing the EU Council*, Policy Paper B 28, (Bonn, Center for European Integration Studies 2001) pp. 3-4.

8 P. Magnette and K. Nicolaidis, 'Large and small Member States in the European Union: reinventing the balance', *Research and European* Issues, N 25, Groupement d'études et de recherches, Notre Europe, (June 2003) p. 5.

but at the same time two essential principles of the European integration process: equality between States and equality between citizens.

This balance proved to be very delicate. Any proposal to change one component necessarily put the entire framework under strain. The creation of the European Council, for instance, raised a lot of questions. The principal concern was that the meeting of Heads of State or Government would result in a further step towards growing intergovernmentalism, especially feared by the small Member States. To win their support, the Paris Summit (1974) agreed to introduce direct elections of the European Parliament.[9]

Both the deepening and widening of the integration process challenged the original institutional arrangements. For instance, French resistance to the introduction of QMV in the field of agriculture, resulting in the 1966 Luxembourg compromise,[10] significantly increased the importance and influence of the Council of Ministers. Only in 1987, when the Single European Act entered into force, was this practice for the adoption of legislation brought to an end. As this Treaty considerably increased the number of articles prescribing a qualified majority vote it became crucial to stop the *de facto* unanimity voting within the Council.[11] The growing importance of QMV also fuelled the debate on the weighting of votes in the Council. Successive enlargement waves resulted in a majority of smaller Member States and further highlighted the need for change. The new Member States were integrated in the scheme by means of calculating their votes based on a comparison with the six original Member States. The enlargement from twelve to fifteen Members (with the accession of Austria, Finland and Sweden in 1995) highlighted the delicate balance of power between large and small Member States. As a consequence of the new division of votes and the required threshold of 62 votes to reach QMV out of a total of 87 votes, a blocking minority could no longer be achieved by a 'traditional' coalition of two large States and one small.[12] To restore the original balance, the Member States

---

9 P. Stirk, *A History of European Integration since 1914*, (London, Pinter 1996) p. 187; S. Bulmer, and W. Wessels, *The European Council*, (London, Macmillan 1987) p. 45.

10 *Bull. EC* 1966/3, p. 10. The Member States declared that 'Where, in case of decisions which may be taken by a majority vote on a proposal of the Commission, very important interests of one or more partners are at stake, the Members of the Council will endeavour, within a reasonable time, to reach solutions which can be adopted by all the Members of the Council.'

11 K. Lenaerts, and P. Van Nuffel, *Constitutional Law of the European Union*, 2nd edn. (London, Sweet & Maxwell 2005) pp. 420. In practice this was realized by an amendment of the Council's Rules of Procedure, introducing a new rule according to which voting proceedings had to be opened on the invitation of a member of the Council or of the Commission, provided that a majority of the Member States agreed to do so. See 87/508/Euratom, ECSC, EEC: Amendment of the Council' s Rules of Procedure adopted by the Council on 20 July 1987, on the basis of Article 5 of the Treaty of 8 April 1965 establishing a Single Council and a Single Commission of the European Communities, *OJ* 1987 L 291/27.

12 Number of votes was as follows: Germany, France, Italy and United Kingdom: 10; Spain: 8; Belgium, Greece, Netherlands and Portugal: 5; Austria and Sweden: 4; Denmark, Ireland and Finland: 3; Luxembourg: 2.

adopted the 'Ioannina Compromise',[13] providing the big Member States with an additional safeguard of their blocking ability.

Apart from these political and rather modest modifications during the first four decades of the European integration process, the original institutional framework had never been subject to a comprehensive reform. Only in the 1990s did institutional reform become a precondition for further enlargement(s) of the Union. It was no longer seen as a consequence of enlargement requiring a few technical adaptations of the existing system. The Lisbon European Council of 26 and 27 June 1992 already gave a first indication of this: 'The European Council considers that if the challenges of a EU composed of a large number of Member States are to be met successfully, parallel progress is needed as regards the internal development of the Union and in preparation for membership of other countries.'[14] One year later the internal institutional reform of the Union was set as the 'fourth Copenhagen criterion.'[15] The 1994 Essen European Council suggested that the necessary institutional reforms should take place 'before the start of the accession negotiations.'[16]

From then on, a clear parallel between the institutional reform and the enlargement process became (even more) apparent. The outcome of the first – and obviously failed – attempt to tackle the institutional challenges at the 1996-1997 Inter Governmental Conference (IGC) was clearly inspired by the widespread belief that enlargement would take place in stages. A protocol attached to the Amsterdam Treaty mentioned two phases for the institutional reform.[17] A first minor reform was foreseen 'at the date of entry into force of the first enlargement' whereas a more comprehensive review of the institutional provisions was deferred to a subsequent IGC to be held 'at least one year before the membership of the European Union exceeds twenty.' When the 1999 Cologne European Council decided to convene an IGC early 2000 in order to

---

[13] The Member States agreed that 'If Members of the Council representing a total of 23 to 25 votes indicate their intention to oppose the adoption by the Council of a Decision by qualified majority, the Council will do all in its power to reach, within a reasonable time and without prejudicing obligatory time limits laid down by the Treaties and by secondary law, such as in Articles 189 B and 189 C of the Treaty establishing the European Community, a satisfactory solution that could be adopted by at least 65 votes.' Council Decision of 29 March 1994 concerning the taking of Decision by qualified majority by the Council, *OJ* 1994 C 105/1; Council Decision of 1 January 1995 amending the Council Decision of 29 March 1994 concerning the taking of decisions by qualified majority by the Council, *OJ* 1995 C 1/1.

[14] Presidency Conclusions Lisbon European Council (26-27 June 1992), 4.

[15] Presidency Conclusions Copenhagen European Council (21-22 June 2003), 13.

[16] Presidency Conclusions Essen European Council of Essen (9-10 December 1994), Annex IV, Report from the Council to the Essen European Council on a strategy to prepare for accession of the associated CCE.

[17] Protocol on the institutions with prospect of enlargement of the European Union, *OJ* 1997 C 340/11.

settle the Amsterdam institutional left-overs,[18] a comprehensive institutional reform before the date of enlargement was again seen as essential.[19]

With the agreement on the Treaty of Nice, the candidate countries were given the assurance that the institutional 'housekeeping exercise' was complete and that, as from the date of entry into force of this Treaty, their accession would only depend on the evaluation of their economic and political achievements.[20] Both the Presidency Conclusions and the Declaration on the future of the Union (attached to the Nice Treaty) included this explicit message.[21] In practice, the Nice Treaty gave all the candidate countries, with the exception of Turkey – at that time still waiting for the opening of accession negotiations – a place in the various EU institutions.[22] Yet the institutional debate did not seem totally closed. In the same Declaration, the Heads of States or Government called for a deeper and wider debate on the future of the Union mentioning the delimitation of powers, the status of the Charter of Fundamental Rights, the simplification of the Treaties and the role of the national parliaments as examples of questions that had to be addressed.

The decision of the 2001 Laeken European Council to invite all candidate countries to take part in the Convention is a final example of the parallel between the enlargement process and the institutional debate.[23] The European Council had, as a matter of fact, agreed with the Commission that if the rate of progress of the negotiations and reforms in the candidate countries was maintained, the Czech Republic, Cyprus, Estonia, Hungary, Latvia, Lithuania, Malta, Poland, Slovakia, and Slovenia could join the Union in 2004. Bulgaria and Romania were given the perspective of opening negotiations on all chapters of the *acquis communautaire* in 2002. By involving these countries in fundamental discussions on the Union's future, the European Council confirmed their status as future Member States. At the same time, they were given partial responsibil-

[18] The Cologne European Council defined the Amsterdam left-overs as follows: size and composition of the Commission; weighting of the votes in the Council and possible extension of qualified majority voting in the Council.

[19] Presidency Conclusions of the June 1999 Cologne European Council.

[20] De Witte, op. cit. n. 4, at p. 217.

[21] Presidency Conclusions of the December 2000 Nice European Council; Declaration nr. 23 on the future of the Union, *OJ* 2001 C 80/85. According to this Declaration, '[...] *the conclusion of the Conference of Representatives of the Governments of the Member States opens the way for enlargement of the European Union and ..., with ratification of the Nice Treaty, the European Union will have completed the institutional changes necessary for the accession of new Member States*'.

[22] The idea that only a limited number of candidate countries would accede in a first wave, which was predominant at the time of the 1996 IGC, became obsolete as a result of the progress in the pre-accession process. The decision of the 1999 Helsinki European Council to start accession negotiations with 12 candidate countries increased the need for one comprehensive institutional reform.

[23] Presidency Conclusions of the December 2001 Laeken European Council (14-15 December 2001).

ity for the eventual outcome of the debate.[24] Then again, the very decision to organise this debate was most likely influenced by the notion that the accession of an unprecedented number of countries – at a time when the legitimacy of the EU institutions was still in question – became irreversible.[25]

3 Outcome of the institutional reform process

The current institutional situation is the result of a gradual reform process, starting with the so-called Amsterdam left-overs.[26] From a legal point of view, the actual composition of the EU institutions is governed by the Nice Treaty and the Treaty of Accession whereas the Constitutional Treaty defines the future institutional arrangements. Before discussing the outcome of the reform process with regard to the institutional triangle (European Parliament, Commission and Council), it is relevant to refer briefly to the composition of the European Court of Justice (ECJ). The rule that every Member State has one judge in the ECJ (and at least one in the Court of First Instance) was never really questioned. As a result, ten extra judges joined the Court on 1 May 2004.[27] In order to keep the judicial system workable, the Nice Treaty introduced some major changes such as the creation of specialised judicial panels, broadening the competences of the Court of First Instance and the creation of the Grand Chamber,[28] all more or less confirmed by the Convention and the IGC.[29]

3.1 The European Parliament

With regard to the composition of the European Parliament, it was obvious that the ceiling of 700 members as set out by the Amsterdam Treaty could not be maintained if the formula used to determine the number of parliamentarians per Member State was applied in respect of the new Member States. The number would have grown from 626 to 874 in total for a EU of 27

[24] Although Turkey was not given a place in the Nice Treaty, it was invited to participate in the Convention. This can be explained as a motivating signal for this country to continue its progress towards complying with the criteria.

[25] De Witte, op. cit. n. 4, at p. 209.

[26] See *supra* n. 18.

[27] The new judges took the oath on the formal sitting of 11 May. See Press Release N 41/04, 18 May 2004.

[28] For a critical comment, see P. Eeckhout, 'The European Courts after Nice', in M. Andenas and J. Usher, *The Treaty of Nice and Beyond. Enlargement and Constitutional Reform*, (Oxford, Hart Publishing 2003) pp. 313-333.

[29] Remarkably, the Constitutional Treaty changed the names of the Court of Justice and the Court of First Instance into 'the Court of Justice of the European Union' and 'the General Court' respectively. See Articles I-29 and III-353 to III-381 Constitutional Treaty.

Member States.[30] Consensus could not be reached on proposals to organise the allocation of seats keeping the maximum number of 700.[31] Instead, the 2000 IGC introduced a new ceiling of 732 (Art. 189 EC) and agreed on a new composition for the Parliament (Art. 190 EC; Art. 2 of the Protocol on the enlargement of the European Union and Declaration 20 on the enlargement of the European Union attached to the Nice Treaty) starting from the 2004-2009 term.[32] The arrangement involved reductions in the number of seats for all 15 Member States (total reduction from 626 to 535) except for Germany and Luxembourg.[33] The additional 197 seats (732-535) were divided among the twelve candidate countries with which negotiations had started. Remarkably, the Czech Republic and Hungary received only 20 seats whereas countries with a similar population size (Belgium, Greece and Portugal) received 22 seats. This anomaly arose from concessions made to Belgium in return for its 'defeat' with regard to the division of votes within the Council (cf. *infra*) and resulted in – with support from the European Parliament – [34] adjustments in the Treaty of Accession. As it became clear that in a first instance only ten new countries would join the Union, the 50 seats originally foreseen for Bulgaria (17) and Romania (33) were distributed among the twenty-five Member States of the enlarged Union, giving the Czech Republic and Hungary two 'extra' seats in order to restore the balance (Art. 11 Act of Accession).[35] It seems that the same balance could not be reached for the transitional period running from 1 May until the beginning of the 2004-2009 term. For this short period, the fifteen old Member States retained their number of seats whereas for the ten new Member States, the Nice formula was immediately applicable. This arrangement had two consequences. First, the Parliament counted from 1 May (until the start of the 2004-2009 term) 786 members.[36]

---

[30] D. Galloway, *The Treaty of Nice and Beyond, Realities and Illusions of Power in the EU,* (Sheffield, Sheffield Academic Press 2001) p. 117.

[31] Ibid., pp. 117-119.

[32] Belgium 22; Bulgaria 17; Czech Republic 20; Denmark 13; Germany 99; Estonia 6; Greece 22; Spain 50; France 72; Ireland 12; Italy 72; Cyprus 6; Latvia 8; Lithuania 12; Luxembourg 6; Hungary 20; Malta 5; Netherlands 25; Austria 17; Poland 50; Portugal 22; Romania 33; Slovenia 7; Slovakia 13; Finland 13; Sweden 18; United Kingdom 72. The figures for the 12 new Member States in the Declaration only reflected the common position to be adopted by the 15 Member States during the accession negotiations.

[33] Luxembourg kept its 6 seats. De facto, the Nice arrangements introduced a new minimum threshold granting only 5 seats to Malta.

[34] European Parliament resolution on the Treaty of Nice and the future of the European Union, A5-168/2001, 31 May 2001, p. 16.

[35] Belgium 24; Czech Republic 24; Denmark 14; Germany 99; Estonia 6; Greece 24; Spain 54; France 78; Ireland 13; Italy 78; Cyprus 6; Latvia 9; Lithuania 13; Luxembourg 6; Hungary 24; Malta 5; Netherlands 27; Austria 18; Poland 54; Portugal 24; Slovenia 7; Slovakia 14; Finland 14; Sweden 19; United Kingdom 78.

[36] For an overview, see wwwdb.europarl.eu.int/ep5/owa/p_meps2.repartition?ipid=0&ilg=EN&iorig=home&imsg=.

Second, an imbalance between the ten new and the old fifteen Member States appeared. Here again, we can refer to the Czech Republic and Hungary. Both countries had only 24 seats whereas Belgium, Greece and Portugal kept their 25 seats till the end of the transitional period. Other examples can be found by comparing Poland with Spain, Lithuania with Ireland, or Slovakia with Finland.[37]

The Convention suggested three changes to the system.[38] First, it proposed a new ceiling of 736 seats, increasing the number laid down in the Nice Treaty by four, in order to accommodate the additional four seats granted to the Czech Republic and Hungary in the Treaty of Accession. Second, the Convention proposed to replace the detailed listing in the Treaties of the number of seats for each Member State by an allocation rule according to which the representation of citizens should be degressively proportional, with a minimum threshold of four seats per Member State.[39] This decreased threshold – in comparison to the current situation[40] – entailed a third change, often criticised by the smallest Member States who argued that a sufficient number of seats is necessary to ensure the representation of the different political views in their Member State at the European level. Both the Italian and the Irish Presidency seemed sensitive to their demands, indicating that 'a limited or a modest increase' could be possible.[41] In the Constitutional Treaty, the minimum threshold has been raised to 6 seats per Member State. Furthermore, the Constitutional Treaty also introduced a maximum of 96 seats per Member State whereas the total number of parliamentarians has been fixed at 750. In practice, this implies that Germany will lose at least 3 seats and that Malta will win one extra seat (Art. I-20 Consti-

---

[37] Poland and Spain had 54 seats since the beginning of the new term. During the transitional period Spain had 64 seats while Poland only received 54. Lithuania and Ireland have 13 seats since the beginning of the new term. During the transitional period Ireland had 15 seats and Lithuania only 13. Slovakia and Finland have 14 seats since the beginning of the new term. During the transitional period Finland had 16 seats while Slovakia only received 14. For this transitional period the representatives in the European Parliament of the peoples of the new Member States were appointed by their own national parliaments (Art. 25 Act of Accession).

[38] Art. 19 Draft Treaty establishing a Constitution for Europe, adopted by consensus by the European Convention on 13 June and 10 July 2003, submitted to the president of the European Council in Rome, 18 July 2003, *OJ* 2003 C 169/1, hereafter Draft Constitution.

[39] Before the next elections in 2009, the European Council should adopt by unanimity, on the basis of a proposal from the Parliament, and with its consent, a decision establishing the composition of the Parliament.

[40] See n. 35.

[41] CIG 70/04, Presidency note, *Report on the Intergovernmental Conference*, Brussels, 24 Mach 2004, p. 4; CIG 60/03 ADD 2, *Intergovernmental Conference Addendum 2 to the Presidency note*, 11 December 2003, p. 4. At the end of May, it became clear that there was a general consensus on this issue, see 'Movement on voting issue in Constitution', www.euobserver.com, visited on 25 May 2004.

tutional Treaty). With the envisaged accession of Turkey, a further reallocation of seats seems to be unavoidable.[42]

3.2 The European Commission

With regard to the European Commission it was obvious that an extrapolation of the rule that the larger Member States had two Commissioners and the smaller States only one, would significantly increase the number of members of this institution. The Commission would grow from 20 to 33 in a Union of twenty-seven Member States. Already at the time of the 1996 IGC, it became clear that the big Member States were willing to give up their right to nominate a second Commissioner in return for a 'reweighting' of the votes in the Council.[43] The 2000 IGC went one step further but a comprehensive solution could not be reached. Article 4 of the Protocol on the enlargement of the European Union foresaw two phases for the reform. The new Commission that was foreseen to take up its duties on 1 November 2004 (the original date of 1 January 2005 was changed by Article 45 Act of Accession) includes one national of each Member State.[44] By maintaining one Commissioner per Member State, the request from a majority of the candidate countries to retain the principle of equality between States for the composition of the Commission was – at least for the first Commission term after their accession – taken into account.[45] Following the accession of the twenty seventh Member State, the principle of one national per Member State will be replaced by a rotation system. The decision on the concrete number and the practical implementation of this rotation system was left open. The Council will have to decide unanimously on the final arrangements, based on the principles laid down in the Nice Protocol. According to the latter, Member States should be treated on a strictly equal footing as regards determination of the sequence of, and the time spent by, their nationals as members of the Commission. Each successive College should be composed so as to reflect satisfactorily the demographic and geographical range of all the Member States of the Union.

---

42 According to the Commission 'in particular the medium and large countries will have to give up seats to accommodate Turkey's accession.' Commission Staff Working Document, *Issues arising from Turkey's Membership Perspective*, SEC (2004) 1202, Brussels, 6 October 2004, p. 45.

43 Article 1 Protocol on the institutions with prospect of enlargement of the European Union, *OJ* 1997 C 340/11.

44 Due to the postponement of the Parliamentary vote on the Council's nomination for a new European Commission, the Union found itself in a new political and legal situation. As a result, the new Commission could not start on 1 November 2004. For the time being, the Prodi Commission agreed to stay in office. At the time of writing it was not yet clear when the new Commission would start its activities.

45 C. Frank, and D. Pysna-Nigge, 'Full players or observers? Positions of acceding countries from Central Europe on the European Convention', *Annual report for the project 'CEEC-DEBATE'*, Université catholique de Louvain (August 2003) p. 25.

For the time period between 1 May and 31 October 2004, Article 45 Act of Accession stipulated that any acceding State was entitled to nominate one Commissioner. As a consequence, the Commission counted 30 members during the transitional period. Similarly to the transitional arrangement for the European Parliament, it seems that during this short period the ten new Member States were not treated on the same basis as the fifteen old Member States. Both their responsibility and their number illustrate this disparity. For instance, Poland, a big Member State, could nominate only one Commissioner, whereas the other big Member States kept their second Commissioner. Concerning their responsibility, it should be mentioned that, although a press release from the Commission stated that the ten new Commissioners would be 'full members of the College and will play a full and active role in the decision-making process'[46], they did not have a specific portfolio.

After tough discussions, both inside and outside the Convention meetings, the final Convention proposal seemed to be a compromise between two contradicting views: maintaining the principle of one Commissioner per Member State as an expression of the equality of States, or reducing the number of Commissioners in order to create a 'small' and well functioning College. According to Article 25 of the Draft Constitution the College would be restricted to 15 'full' members from 1 November 2009. In practice only the Commission President, the Union Minister of Foreign Affairs[47] and 13 Commissioners would have the right to vote. Member States not 'represented' by a Commissioner, would have the right to nominate 'a Commissioner without voting rights'. In order to preserve the equality between Member States, Article 25 Draft Constitution also stipulates that there should be an equal rotation between the two groups of Commissioners. Again, the means of implementation in practice is left open. It is the European Council that, on the basis of the same principles as stipulated in the Nice Protocol, will have to take the final decision.

The Convention proposal provoked a lot of questions and criticism from various, predominantly small, Member States.[48] Eventually, the Irish Presidency managed to come up with a compromise, which basically postpones the reduction of the size of the Commission. According to Article I-26 of the Constitutional Treaty, 'the first Commission appointed under the provisions of the Constitution shall consist of one national of each Member State.' The following

---

[46] IP/04/233, *Commission finalises preparations for arrival of new Commissioners on 1st May*, Brussels, 18 February 2004.

[47] This newly created function combines the post of the High Representative for the Common Foreign and Security Policy and the Commissioner responsible for External Relations; Cf. *infra*.

[48] See e.g., 'Reforming the Institutions: Principles and Premises', Brussels, 28 March 2003, CONV 646/03.

Commission will comprise two thirds of the number of Member States.[49] In a Union of 27 Member States, this would correspond to a Commission of 18 Commissioners. Such a smaller Commission could be appointed – at the earliest – in 2014. Significantly, however, the Constitutional Treaty leaves a stick behind the door: the European Council, acting unanimously, can decide to alter the proposed number of Commissioners. Furthermore, a declaration to Article I-26 accommodates the fears of those Member States without a national 'representative' within the Commission. The interests of these countries should be addressed 'by appropriate organisational arrangements' and the Commission is under an obligation to 'share information and consult with all Member States.'[50]

3.3 The Council

The composition and functioning of the Council also provoked extensive debate. Essentially, three core issues can be distinguished: the extension of QMV, the reweighting of votes and the Presidency.

3.3.1 The extension of QMV

Concerning the extension of QMV, it suffices to say that every Treaty revision constituted a step forward. The Nice Treaty already represented a credible progress.[51] The Convention went one step further and proposed to abandon the unanimity requirement in 32 cases. Still, 55 topics, including taxation and Common Foreign and Security Policy, continue to require a unanimous decision in the Council.[52] During the IGC talks, some Member States (especially the UK) even suggested the introduction of an 'emergency brake system', providing Member States with the possibility to refer an issue back to the European Council, in an attempt to wipe out the Convention's progress.[53] Other Member

---

49 The members of the Commission will be selected among the nationals of the Member States on the basis of a system of equal rotation to be established by a European Council Decision adopted unanimously by the European Council, taking account the equality of Member States as well as the demographic and geopolitical diversity of the Union.

50 Declaration on Article I-26 Constitution, CIG 87/04 ADD 2.

51 F. Laursen, 'Nice and Post-Nice: Explaining Current and Predicting Future Developments in the EU', Background paper for lecture on *'Current Issues in European Integration: Widening, the Treaty of Nice and the Post-Nice Agenda'* at the Graduate Institute of European Studies, (Tamkang University, Taipei, Taiwan March 2002) p. 5; K. Bradley, 'Institutional Design in the Treaty of Nice', *CMLRev.* 2001 pp. 1112-1113; Galloway, op. cit. n. 30, at pp. 94-114.

52 B.M.P Smulders, 'Kritische kanttekeningen bij de gevolgen van het 'ontwerp-verdrag tot vaststelling van een grondwet voor Europa' voor het institutionele evenwicht', *NTER*, (September 2003) pp. 248-249.

53 In IGC documents from the Italian Presidency examples can be found with regard to judicial cooperation in criminal affairs and social security. CIG 60/03 ADD 1, *Intergovernmental Conference Addendum1 to the Presidency proposal*, 9 December 2003, pp. 26 and 39. See also 'MEPs condemn backward steps in Constitution text', www.euobserver.com, visited on 25 May 2004.

States, however, supported a further extension of the QMV. In the Constitutional Treaty, QMV is generally extended in line with the proposals submitted by the European Convention. Opposition from various Member States, however, has ensured that a unanimity requirement is retained in a number of sensitive areas such as taxation, CFSP, aspects of social policy and the adoption of the multi-annual financial framework. Significantly, it is possible in some cases to move to QMV on the basis of a unanimous decision of the European Council and with the consent of the European Parliament. Such a decision may only be taken in the absence of opposition from the national parliaments and within six months of notification of the European Council's proposal. *A priori*, decisions with military implications or in the area of defence are excluded. These provisions, included in Article IV-444 of the Constitutional Treaty, clearly complicate this possibility when compared with the Draft Constitution.[54] It only included a requirement of prior notification to the national parliaments without providing for the possibility of objection and without mentioning a role for the European Parliament. Finally, the proposed 'emergency break system' has been included in Articles III-136(2) and III-270(3).

3.3.2 The reweighting of votes

The weighting of the votes in the Council proved to be the Achilles' heel of the institutional debate of the last years, and even the entire reform process. The rigid negotiating positions of some countries during the 2003-2004 IGC can partly be explained by the voting rules laid down in the Nice Treaty. The reason why the topic appeared as one of the priorities on the Nice agenda was twofold. First, as already mentioned, at the time of the 1996 IGC a re-weighting of the votes was 'promised' to the big Member States to balance the 'loss' of their second Commissioner. Second, the prospect of accession of a large number of small and medium-sized Member States raised concerns about the legitimacy of decision-making. Extending the existing system would accentuate the disparity between more populous States, already 'under-represented' in terms of voting strength and less populous States, already 'over-represented' in terms of their population size.[55] In addition, a qualified majority vote would represent less than 50 per cent of the population, whereas in the Union of fifteen Member States, a qualified majority vote represented in practice at least 58 per cent of the population.

One of the main discussion points on the redistribution of votes was whether the traditional grouping of Member States in clusters on the basis of their population and economic strength could be maintained or had to be replaced by a distribution system based purely on the demographic size of the countries. In

---

[54] See Article I-24 of the Draft Constitution.

[55] Galloway, op. cit. n. 30, at p. 67.

the end, no clear criterion was applied and the outcome was basically the result of a horse-trading exercise. Due to France's reluctance to give up its parity with Germany, the cluster of big Member States (Germany, France, UK and Italy) was preserved. However, the traditional parity between Belgium and The Netherlands was broken. In practice, Belgium was compensated in two ways. First, it was treated 'favourably' with regard to the division of seats in the European Parliament (see *supra*). Second, Brussels would become the permanent venue for the European Council meetings.[56]

Apart from Malta, categorised as a micro-state, the candidate countries were all clustered with the existing fifteen Member States, more or less on the basis of their population size. Latvian dissatisfaction with the outcome of the Nice redistribution of votes illustrates some anomalies in the arrangement.[57] According to the Nice settlement, Latvia has been granted 4 votes in the Council, Lithuania 7 and Estonia 4. In terms of population, Latvia has 2.3 million inhabitants, Lithuania 3.4 million and Estonia 1.3 million.[58] In other words, Lithuania has approximately one million inhabitants more than Latvia, which is almost equal to the population difference between Latvia and Estonia. Nevertheless, Latvia received as many votes as its smaller Baltic neighbour whereas Lithuania has been attributed a significantly higher number of votes. Moreover, Latvia has been granted the same number of votes as the tiny states of Cyprus (730.400 inhabitants) and Luxembourg (451.600 inhabitants).[59] The gap – in terms of population – between Latvia and the latter countries is bigger than the gap between Latvia and Lithuania. From this perspective, the attribution of only 4 votes to Latvia was perceived as inadequate. This issue can be linked with the attribution of votes to Lithuania and Ireland. In the first IGC proposals, Lithuania was granted only 4 votes whereas Ireland – with an almost identical number of inhabitants – received 7 votes. Only at the end of the deliberations were the two countries put at the same level (both 7 votes).[60]

---

56 Declaration on the venue for European Councils, *OJ* 2001 C 80/85.

57 The Latvian dissatisfaction is reflected in a declaration to the Treaty of Accession: 'Bearing in mind the need to ensure an adequate, comparable and equal representation of the Member States in the Council according to the number of their population, the Republic of Latvia declares that it reserves the rights to discuss the issue of the weighting of votes in the Council during the next Intergovernmental Conference.'

58 Population data provided by Eurostat, see Annex IIa of Council Decision amending the Council's Rules of Procedure, 12712/04, Brussels, 8 October 2004.

59 It has to be mentioned that Slovenia, with a population of approximately 2 million inhabitants, has also been granted 4 votes in the Council.

60 According to Peter Poole, 'during one all-night negotiation session, Lithuanian leaders managed to contact the German Chancellor's foreign policy advisor by phone, and he made sure they got the same number of votes as Ireland.' P. A. Poole, *The EU's Eastern Enlargement*, (Westport, Praeger 2003) p. 125.

Table 1: The weighting of votes according to Declaration 20 'on the enlargement of the European Union', attached to the Treaty of Nice:

Member States	*Population (x 1000)*	*Votes in Council*
Germany	82.531,70	29
France	61.684,70	29
UK	59.651,50	29
Italy	57.888,20	29
Spain	42.345,30	27
Poland	38.190,60	27
Romania	21.772,80	14
Netherlands	16.258,00	13
Greece	11.041,10	12
Portugal	10.474,70	12
Belgium	10.396,40	12
Czech Republic	10.211,50	12
Hungary	10.116,70	12
Sweden	8.975,70	10
Austria	8.114,00	10
Bulgaria	7.845,80	10
Denmark	5.397,60	7
Slovakia	5.380,10	7
Finland	5.219,70	7
Ireland	4.027,50	7
Lithuania	3.445,90	7
Latvia	2.319,20	4
Slovenia	1.996,40	4
Estonia	1.350,60	4
Cyprus	730,40	4
Luxembourg	451,60	4
Malta	399,90	3
Total	*488.217,60*	*345*

Apart from the fact that the Nice arrangement strongly increased the voting shares of the big Members States (with Spain and Poland gaining twice as much voting power than the other four big Member States), and therefore fulfilled one of the starting points of the debate, it is generally dispraised for its complexity and negative influence on the Union's ability to act. Under the Nice QMV system,[61] as adapted by the Act of Accession,[62] an act can only be adopted if the following three criteria are met:

- 232 votes out of 321 (72.27 per cent);[63]
- majority of the Members States (or two-thirds in case the act was not proposed by the Commission);
- 62 per cent of the total population of the Union (in case a Member State requests this verification).[64]

According to Baldwin and Widgren, this system entails the risk of a decision-making paralysis. They argue that the Nice settlement fails 'on efficiency grounds since it implies a level of efficiency that is far, far below that of the EU 15.'[65]

---

61 See Article 3 Protocol on the enlargement of the European Union; Declaration nr. 20 on the enlargement of the European Union; Declaration nr. 21 on the qualified majority threshold and the number of votes for a blocking minority in an enlarged Union. For the actual figures applicable from 1 November 2004 for the 25 Member States, see article 12 Act of Accession: Belgium 12; Czech Republic 12; Denmark 7; Germany 29; Estonia 4; Greece 12; Spain 27; France 29; Ireland 7; Italy 29; Cyprus 4; Latvia 4; Lithuania 7; Luxembourg 4; Hungary 12; Malta 3; Netherlands 13; Austria 10; Poland 27; Portugal 12; Slovenia 4; Slovakia 7; Finland 7; Sweden 10; United Kingdom 29.

62 For the transitional period between 1 May and end October 2004, Article 26 of the Accession Act applied. It seems that the candidate countries were, without many deliberations, included in the existing six clusters. Belgium 5; Czech Republic 5; Denmark 3; Germany 10; Estonia 3; Greece 5; Spain 8; France 10; Ireland 3; Italy 10; Cyprus 2; Latvia 3; Lithuania 3; Luxembourg 2; Hungary 5; Malta 2; Netherlands 5; Austria 4; Poland 8; Portugal 5; Slovenia 3; Slovakia 3; Finland 3; Sweden 4; United Kingdom 10.

63 Article 12 Act of Accession. This threshold (72.27 per cent) is lower than the one stipulated in the Nice Protocol (74,78 per cent).

64 According to the Council's new Rules of Procedure (see n. 58) this 62 per cent corresponds to 284.331 million people. This figure is based on data supplied by Eurostat following the definition of population provided by the Recommendations for the 2000 Censuses of Population and Housing in the ECE region (available at: www.unece.org/stats/documents/statistical_standards_&_studies/49.e.pdf). Remarkably, during the discussions on the adoption of the Decision amending the Council's Rules of Procedure, Italy insisted on having a debate on the criteria for the definition of the concept of 'European Population' to be applied once the Constitution enters into force. Italy argues that the population figure should be based on nationality rather than on the number of inhabitants. Therefore, the minutes of the Council meeting provide that the current system 'should not be considered as a precedent for the definition or interpretation of the notion of 'population' serving to determine the qualified majority in the context of the Treaty establishing a Constitution for Europe.'

65 R. Baldwin and M. Widgren, *A study of the Constitutional Treaty's voting reform dilemma*, November 2003, p. 4.

The Convention had proposed a much simpler, more transparent and more flexible system, which would have been introduced from 1 November 2009. According to Article 24 of the Draft Constitution, a qualified majority would be achieved when a decision is approved by the majority of Member States representing at least three-fifths (60 per cent) of the population of the Union.[66] In practice these voting rules would increase the relative voting power of the largest Member States, at the expense of Spain and Poland and most small Member States (although the very tiny States would gain some power).[67] In addition, the EU's ability to act would also be improved, as it would become much easier to reach a qualified majority. This innovative proposal also takes into account the dual nature of the European Union as a Union of States and Peoples. By replacing the weighting of votes through this double majority requirement, the Convention proposed to set out clear rules applicable in all circumstances, making tough negotiations in case of further enlargements redundant. In spite of these practical advantages, the Heads of States or Government could not agree on this proposal. Spain and Poland were particularly resistant as they were not willing to give up their extraordinary gains, which contributed to the failure of the 2003 IGC.

The establishment of a new Spanish government after the March 2003 terrorist attacks, combined with internal developments in Poland created a new atmosphere for discussion on this very sensitive issue. The Irish Presidency maintained the principle of double majority as the basis for negotiation. In the end, agreement was reached on a 65 per cent threshold in terms of population together with 55 per cent of the number of Member States.[68] In addition, a blocking minority cannot be possible without the participation of at least four Member States. This provision has been introduced to rule out the fear that the big three (France, Germany and the UK) might easily be able to block any decisions they do not like. In practice, this arrangement implies that in a Union of twenty-five Member States, a blocking minority may be formed by three big Member States and one more country (Article I-25 Constitutional Treaty). The ten new Member States cannot block a QMV decision whereas the eleven smallest Member States may do so. As an additional safeguard, the Member States

---

[66] In case the Council does not act on the initiative of the Commission or the Union Minister of Foreign Affairs, a qualified majority requires approval by two-thirds of the Member States representing three-fifths of the EU population.

[67] On the other hand, the facilitated decision-making procedure could cause more conflicts among Member States because the incentive for finding compromises will be reduced. Furthermore, the institutional balance will significantly shift from the Council to the Commission. Bobay, op. cit. n. 7, at p. 11.

[68] This arrangement reconciles the principles of equality between citizens and equality between Member States. This dual legitimacy of the Union can also be found in Article I-46(2) Constitutional Treaty. On the one hand, the citizens are directly represented in the European Parliament. On the other hand, Member States are represented in the (European) Council.

have also agreed on a draft Council Decision concerning the implementation of Article I-25. This Decision, to be adopted on the day the Constitutional Treaty enters into force, basically includes an Ioannina-like compromise to be applied until at least 2014.[69]

3.3.3 The Presidency

Finally, it was deemed necessary to revise the Presidency of the (European) Council in order to guarantee the efficient and coherent functioning of the Union. Maintaining the existing six months Presidency, which would imply that a Member State may only hold the Presidency each twelve and a half years, has important practical disadvantages. For instance, maintaining meetings with representatives from twenty-five Member States might be too time-consuming and demanding for one national government. Consequently, the Convention proposed a permanent President of the European Council and attributed the Presidency of the Foreign Affairs Council to the Union Minister of Foreign Affairs, whereas the Presidency of the Council in other formations would be reserved to Member States' representatives 'on the basis of equal rotation for periods of at least a year' (Arts. 21 and 23 Draft Constitution). The discussion on this issue continued during the IGC. Eventually, the Member States agreed on an institutional solution that is as close as possible to the current situation. Apart from the Foreign Affairs Council, which will be chaired by the Union Minister of Foreign Affairs (Art. I-24 Constitutional Treaty), the Presidency of the Council will be held by pre-established groups of three Member States for a period of 18 months. These so-called 'team-presidencies' shall be made up on a basis of equal rotation among the Member States, taking into account the diversity and geopolitical balance within the Union. The provision that 'each member of the group shall in turn chair for a six-month period all configurations of the Council' reveals the status quo in comparison to the current system of six-months rotating presidencies.[70] The only innova-

---

69 Declaration on Article I-25 Constitutional Treaty, CIG 87/04 ADD 2. The Declaration stipulates that: 'If members of the Council, representing: (a) at least three quarters of the population, or (b) at least three quarters of the number of Member States necessary to constitute a blocking minority resulting from the application of Article I-25(1), first subparagraph, or Article I-25(2), indicate their opposition to the Council adopting an act by a qualified majority, the Council shall discuss the issue. The Council shall, in the course of these discussions, do all in its power to reach, within a reasonable time and without prejudicing obligatory time limits laid down by Union law, a satisfactory solution to address concerns raised [...].To this end, the President of the Council, with the assistance of the Commission and in compliance with the Rules of Procedure of the Council, shall undertake any initiative necessary to facilitate a wider basis of agreement in the Council. The members of the Council shall lend him or her their assistance.'

70 Declaration on Article I-24(7) Constitutional Treaty concerning the European Council decision on the exercise of the Presidency of the Council, CIG 87/04 ADD 2.

tion is, therefore, that three Member States will be jointly responsible for the practical organisation of the Council meetings. With regard to the European Council, which is explicitly mentioned as a Union institution in Article I-19 of the Constitutional Treaty, a permanent president has been envisaged (Art. I-22 of the Constitutional Treaty). Together with the other institutional changes, this new post raises important questions concerning the principle of balance in the future European Union.

4 Balance in the future European Union

The Constitutional Treaty reflects the outcome of a difficult balancing act between divergent actors with divergent interests. According to the former Estonian Minister of Foreign Affairs, Tomas Hendrik Ilves, three interrelated dichotomies can be distinguished: '1) New vs. Old members; 2) Small vs. Large members; 3) Democratic Legitimacy vs. Effective Decision-making.'[71] These dichotomies are not new and all derive from the question of balance between Member States, on the one hand, and between institutions on the other.

4.1 Balance between Member States

In the original EEC a clear balance between three big and three small Member States could be identified. The system of weighted votes in the Council, the independence of the supranational institutions and the system of rotating presidencies, guaranteed a fair balance between the bigger and smaller Member States.[72] The continuous deepening and widening of the European integration process gradually altered the original equilibrium. The fifth enlargement wave, with the accession of predominantly small and medium-sized countries, further raised the debate on balance in the European Union.

The tensions between the bigger and smaller Member States became obvious during the Convention deliberations. Proposals from the biggest Member States with regard to the abolition of the rotating presidency in the Council and the establishment of a permanent European Council President provoked fierce opposition from the smaller Member States.[73] The Benelux countries, for instance, which have always considered their regional co-operation as a neces-

[71] *Constructing a New Europe*, Lecture by T.H. Ilves, Minister of Foreign Affairs Estonia at Humboldt University, Berlin, 5 February 2001.

[72] Magnette and Niclolaïdis, op. cit. n. 8, at pp. 5-7.

[73] The proposition to appoint a permanent President of the European Council was formulated in the so-called ABC-proposal (Aznar, Blair, Chirac). Later on, a French-German paper confirmed the big countries' preference for a permanent Presidency.

sary counterbalance to the weight of the big Member States,[74] reacted with the adoption of a Joint Memorandum.[75] In this document, the Benelux governments expressed their preference for strong common institutions and an extension of the Community method. They rejected the idea of creating new institutions, such as a Congress of the peoples of Europe, as well as the proposal for a long-term European Council President appointed outside the circle of its members. The Benelux countries repeated these statements in their joint reaction to the Franco-German proposals on the future institutional architecture of the Union,[76] in the form of a Benelux Memorandum on the reform of the Council[77] and in a separate contribution on 'the Union's institutions' within the Convention.[78]

Clearly, the Benelux countries saw themselves as the spokesmen of the small Member States. In this regard, the Benelux Three took the initiative to bring 18 small countries together with the aim of creating a united front ahead of a meeting with Convention President Giscard D'Estaing.[79] It would, however, be an oversimplification to reduce the institutional debate to a clash between big and small Member States. Sweden and Denmark, for instance, refused to support the Benelux initiative and defended the big Member States' plea for a permanent president of the European Council.[80] The joint French-Dutch contribution to the Convention,[81] entitled 'strengthening the Commission's role', also illustrates that the dividing line between small and big Member States is not straightforward. Finally, and somewhat ironically, it has to be mentioned that the Benelux States – as the traditional defenders of the small States – did not take part in a small countries' meeting ahead of the 2003 IGC, mainly because of the

---

74 B. Kerremans, 'België, de Benelux en de IGC. Van maximalisme naar pragmatisme?'[Belgium, the Benelux and the IGC: From maximum to pragmatism?], 50 *Internationale Spectator* 6 (1996), p. 312.

75 Memorandum of the Benelux: a balanced institutional framework for an enlarged, more effective and more transparent Union, CONV 457/02, Brussels, 11 December 2002, available at www.european-convention.eu.int.

76 Prise de position du Benelux suite à la contribution franco-allemande à la Convention européenne sur l'architecture institutionnelle de l'Union, available at www.gouvernement.lu/salle_presse/actualite/2003/01/20benelux/.

77 Benelux Memorandum on the reform of the Council, the Hague, 4 June 2002, available at europa.eu.int/futurum /documents/other/oth040602_en.htm.

78 Contribution by the Benelux countries on 'The Union's Institutions', CONV 732/03, Brussels, 8 May 2003.

79 18 small countries unite in Athens on EU future, 16 April 2003, available at www.euobserver.com.

80 Ibid.

81 Franco-Netherlands contribution from Mr. Gijs de Vries and Mr. Dominque de Villepin, 'Strengthening the Commission's role', CONV 664/03, Brussels, 2 April 2003.

predominant intergovernmental position of many participants.[82] Hence, they did not join a coalition of small States that basically subscribed to the principle of one Commissioner per Member State, promoted the preservation of the rotating Council Presidency and opposed the creation of new institutions that could upset the existing balances.[83]

Be that as it may, the outcome of the deliberations clearly reflects a compromise between the priorities of the smaller and bigger Member States. The preoccupation with the requirement of balance is, for instance, reflected in the principles for the future rotation of Commissioners. According to Article I-26 of the Constitutional Treaty, Member States shall be treated on a strictly equal footing and 'each successive Commission shall be so composed as to reflect satisfactorily the demographic and geographical range of all the Member States'.[84] Another example can be found in the Declaration on Articles I-22, I-27 and I-28, which proclaims that in the choice of the President of the European Council, the President of the Commission and the Union Minister of Foreign Affairs 'due account is to be taken of the need to respect the geographical and demographic diversity of the Union and its Member States.'[85] The latter provisions are clearly introduced to reassure the small Member States, which feared that these important positions might automatically be reserved for nationals of the biggest Member States. On the other hand, the small Member States accepted the idea of a European Council President whereas the system of rotating (team) presidencies was maintained. The requirement that these teams 'shall be made up on a basis of equal rotation among Member States, taking into account their diversity and geographical balance within the Union'[86] clearly illustrates the objective to find an appropriate mix of Member States with divergent interests. This does not only imply a balance between small and big Member States but also a balance between Northern and Southern countries and countries defending a more intergovernmental or supranational vision of the future of the Union.

---

[82] X, Small countries meet in Prague ahead of IGC, *EUObserver*, 1 September 2003, available at www.euobserver.com.

[83] Contribution submitted by Mr. M. Attalidis, Mr. P. Balazs, Mr. H. Christophersen, Mr. H. Farnleitner, Mr. L. Hjelm-Wallen, Ms. S. Kalniete, Mr. J. Kohout, Mr. I. Korcok, Ms. M. Kuneva, Mr. E. Lopes, Mr. R. Martikonis, Mr. L. Meri, Mr. D. Roche, Mr. D. Rupel, Mr. P. Serracino-Inglott, Mr. T. Tiikiakainen, members of the Convention, on 'Reforming the Institutions: Principles and Premises', CONV 646/03, Brussels, 28 March 2003. Notwithstanding the observation that the Representatives of the Benelux countries did not sign this document, the text stipulated that 'it should be read in conjunction with a number of papers previously submitted, in particular that by the Benelux countries.'

[84] Emphasis added.

[85] Declaration on Articles I-22, I-27 and I-28 Constitutional Treaty. Emphasis added.

[86] See n.70. Emphasis added.

Consequently, the formation of coalitions between countries with similar interests will become increasingly important because, as a result of enlargement, the relative power of each individual Member State has decreased. The Convention already provided an interesting test-case for future coalition building. Apart from the traditional Benelux and Franco-German co-operation, coalitions between big and small or new and old Member States may be identified. In this context, it seems that the importance of regional sub-groups will grow in an enlarged EU. It has even been argued that an extended form of regional co-operation could be reflected at the institutional level. Hanna Ojanen, for instance, suggested that the Nordic countries could better share one Commissioner with important assignments rather than having three Commissioners with limited influence in an oversized Commission.[87] Whereas this innovative proposal provides an interesting line of thought and a potential solution to current institutional problems, it seems unthinkable that Member States would agree to such a far-reaching change. The Benelux countries, for instance, always avoided behaving too openly as one political bloc in order to avoid being treated as one country.[88] This observation does not exclude the perceived benefits of pragmatic co-operation between Member States with similar interests.

4.2 The institutional balance

Apart from the envisaged balance between Member States, the European Union is characterised by a balance between the institutions. The preservation of this institutional balance was one of the issues raised in the Laeken Declaration[89] and formed a central theme of many contributions to the Convention.[90] Despite the widespread use of this 'buzz-word',[91] the institutional

---

87 'Nordic Cooperation in an enlarged EU', 28 August 2001, www.euobserver.com.

88 Moreover, the strategic adoption of common Benelux positions does not necessarily imply that the three countries have an identical view on all issues at stake. For instance, the Netherlands – as a net-contributor to the EU budget – generally adopted a more cautious attitude on proposals for the extension of the EU's competences. See e.g. D.J. Eppink, 'Benelux moet hoeder zijn van belangen kleine EU-landen' [Benelux has to safeguard the interests of smaller EU states], *NRC Handelsblad*, 25 July 2004; A. Pijpers and S. Vanhoonacker, 'The Position of the Benelux Countries', in A. Pijpers and G. Edwards, eds., *The Politics of European Treaty Reform. The 1996 Intergovernmental Conference and Beyond*, (London, Pinter 1997) pp. 127-129.

89 With regard to the democratic legitimacy and transparency of the institutions, the Laeken Declaration *inter alia* contained the following question: 'How, finally, should the balance and reciprocal control between the institutions be ensured?'.

90 For instance, the European Commission's contribution mentioned the need that 'the Union's modus operandi be simplified and its institutions reformed, but without changing the current institutional balance.' Communication from the Commission on the institutional architecture, CONV 448/02. See also the Benelux Memorandum, op. cit. n. 75.

91 L.W. Gormley, 'The Institutional Balance in the European Union', in P. Xuereb, ed., *The Value(s) of a Constitution for Europe* (Malta, EDRC 2004), p. 102.

balance seems to be an extremely diffuse concept.[92] It is therefore of no surprise that States stressing the need for the preservation of this balance came up with entirely contrasting proposals.[93] This ambiguity can be linked with the dual interpretation of the concept. On the one hand, institutional balance is a legal principle referring to the obligation that the institutions must act within the limits of their competences, as reflected in Article 7(1) EC. On the other hand, the term 'institutional balance' is also a political concept relating to the way the relationship between the institutions is organised.[94]

The legal definition of the institutional balance can be seen as the Union's alternative to the Montesquieu model of a clear separation of powers between a legislative, executive and judicial branch.[95] This principle has been included in the Treaties from the very beginning and is supervised by the Court of Justice. Already in the *Meroni* judgment of 1958, the ECJ emphasised that the balance of powers characterising the institutional structure of the Community constitutes a 'fundamental guarantee granted by the Treaty.'[96] The Court further expressed its vision on the institutional balance in cases relating to the comitology principle[97] and with regard to the prerogatives of the European Parliament.[98] Finally, direct and indirect references to the institutional balance form an essential element of most inter-institutional cases. For instance, in the *European Parliament* v. *Council* judgment of 1990 the Court clearly explained the meaning of 'institutional balance' as a principle of law:

---

[92] J. Rood, 'The Community Method and the Institutional Balance after the European Convention, in A. Michalski, ed., *The Political Dynamics of Institutional Reform* (The Hague, Clingendael 2004), p. 77.

[93] For instance, both the ABC proposal and the Benelux Memorandum claimed to proceed from the principle of institutional balance notwithstanding their entirely opposite views with regard to the establishment of a permanent European Council President.

[94] J.P. Jacqué, 'The Principle of Institutional Balance' 41 *CMLRev.* (2004) p. 383.

[95] On the distinction between the legislative and executive powers within the European Union, see: K. Lenaerts and M. Desomer, 'La recherche d'un equilibre pour l'Union. Répartition des compétences et équilibre institutionnel dans le projet de Constitution', in O. De Schutter and P. Nihoul, eds., 'Une constitution pour l'Europe: réflexions sur les tranformations du droit de l'Union européenne, (Bruxelles, Larcier 2004) pp. 53-80.

[96] ECJ, Case 9/56 *Meroni* v. *High Authority* [1957-1958] *ECR* 133 at 152.

[97] ECJ, Case 25/70 *Einfuhr- und Vorratsstelle für Getreide und Futtermittel* v. *Köster* [1970] *ECR* 1161 at 1172; ECJ, Case 30/70 *Scheer* v. *Einfuhr- und Vorratsstelle für Getreide und Futtermittel* [1970] *ECR* 1197 at 1208-1209.

[98] For instance, in the *Isoglucose* case the Court declared the consultation of the European Parliament in the legislative process of the Communities as 'an essential factor in the institutional balance intended by the Treaty.' ECJ, Case 138/79 *SA Roquette Frères* v. *Council* [1980] *ECR* 333 at 3360; ECJ, Case 139/79 *Maizena GmbH* v. *Council* [1980] *ECR* 3393 at 3424.

'The Treaties set up a system for distributing powers among the different Community institutions, assigning to each institution its own role in the institutional structure of the Community and the accomplishment of the tasks entrusted to the Community.

Observance of the institutional balance means that each of the institutions must exercise its powers with due regard for the powers of the other institutions.'[99]

The Constitutional Treaty confirms this principle in Article I-19(2). Whereas from a strict legal point of view, the institutional balance is thus maintained, the more important question of relations between the institutions is also more controversial. It first has to be mentioned that the institutional balance, understood as a reflection of the division of powers within the institutional triangle constituted by the Commission, the Council and the European Parliament, has always been a rather dynamic concept.[100] Of particular importance are the progressively increased powers attributed to the European Parliament. Originally entrusted with a rather limited advisory role, the Parliament has developed into the Union's co-legislative body, on a par with the Council. It has also achieved a role in the appointment of the Commission, is responsible for the non-mandatory expenditure and, since the Treaty of Nice, is a privileged party in actions for annulment of legislation on the basis of Article 230 EC. The Constitutional Treaty further confirms and strengthens the increasing powers of the European Parliament.[101] First, Article I-20(1) explicitly endows the Parliament with the right to 'elect' the President of the Commission.[102] Second, the application of the co-decision procedure, enshrined in the Constitutional Treaty as the 'ordinary legislative procedure' (Art. I-34 and III-396), is further extended. Finally, the Parliament's budgetary powers are enhanced since the budgetary procedure will reflect the ordinary legislative procedure (Art. III-404). Moreover, the old distinction between mandatory and non-mandatory expenditure has been eliminated, which means that the Parliament's influence now extends to the entire budget.

Whereas the powers of the European Parliament have progressively increased throughout the European integration process, the Commission appears to be on the losing side.[103] The Commission's formal competences and its primary role of policy initiator have not changed but the establishment of the

---

99 ECJ, Case C-70/88 *Parliament* v. *Council* [1990] *ECR* I-2041 para. 21-22 at I-2072-2073.

100 Rood, op. cit. n. 92, at p. 77.

101 See: M. Delgado-Iribarren, 'The New Legislative and Budgetary Competences of the European Parliament in the European Constitution', available at www.realinstitutoelcano.org/analisis/569/569.pdf.

102 In practice, the role of the Parliament in the nomination procedure will not change fundamentally. Already under the current provisions, the Parliament has to 'approve' the nomination of the Commission President (Art. 214(2) EC).

103 Jacqué, op. cit. n. 94, at pp. 389-390.

European Council and the increased legislative powers of the European Parliament have acted as a check upon the political weight of this institution.[104] The Parliament and the European Council have a 'right of quasi initiative', i.e. they can request the Commission to submit a proposal.[105] In combination with the more frequent use of conciliation in the context of the co-decision procedure, where the Council and the Parliament play the most dominant role, the impact of the Commission in the decision-making process has decreased.[106] Notwithstanding the observation that the Commission has required major functions in other fields, for instance in the pre-accession process,[107] the Constitutional Treaty seems to put the position of the Commission further under pressure. For instance, the establishment of a European Council President and a Union Minister of Foreign Affairs (UMFA) might challenge the role of the Commission President. It is hard to see how these three functions can be separated. The position of the 'double-hatted' UMFA clearly complicates the institutional power balance. On the one hand, the UMFA is responsible for the Union's CFSP/EDSP, a task which shall be carried out as mandated by the Council. On the other hand, the UMFA shall be one of the Vice-Presidents of the Commission. In exercising his responsibilities within the Commission, he shall be bound by the Commission procedures to the extent that this is consistent with his tasks within the Foreign Affairs Council, which he will chair. Moreover, the Foreign Minister will be appointed by the European Council, which also has a right to end his term of office (Art. I-28). Hence, the UMFA draws his legitimacy from this institution and not primarily from the Commission. There is, in other words, a danger of 'intergovernmental contamination' of the Union's policy.[108] At the least, it is questionable whether this new arrangement will strengthen the Commission's role. The institutional changes envisaged in the Constitutional Treaty therefore tend to reinforce the existing tendencies. On the one hand, the role of the European Parliament and the (European) Council will be strengthened, whereas the position of the Commission will largely depend on the political charisma and vision of the Commission's president.

---

[104] This has been clearly illustrated by demission of the Santer Commission and the problems with regard to the establishment of the Barroso Commission.

[105] Gormley, op. cit. n. 91, at p. 110.

[106] Rood, op. cit. n. 92, at pp. 77-78.

[107] A. Ott, 'The European Union, its Constitution and Institutional Future', in N. Neuwahl, ed., *European Union Enlargement. Law and Socio-Economic Changes* (Montréal, Thémis 2004), p. 243.

[108] Rood, op. cit. n. 92, at p. 83.

5 Conclusion

The parallel processes of EU enlargement and institutional reform have determined the EU agenda for more than a decade. The joint accession of ten predominantly small Member States required a revision of the traditional balance between the equality of states and the equality of citizens. Three successive Intergovernmental Conferences dealt with this challenge. The Nice Treaty and the Treaty of Accession mathematically incorporated the new Member States in the EU institutions. This exercise led to a very complex and non-transparent system. In particular, the reweighting of votes in the Council forms a very complicated compromise between divergent interests. For the acceding countries, it was specifically important to have as many votes assigned as those Member States having comparable populations. The EU Fifteen were mainly concerned that the Amsterdam formula would compensate the bigger Member States for the loss of their second Commissioner. Moreover, each Member State wanted to preserve its relative voting power as much as possible. Eventually, the outcome proved to be inconsistent. Whereas countries with a comparable population received an equal number of votes (Poland versus Spain and Lithuania versus Ireland), the relative gap between different clusters of states is hard to explain from a demographic point of view. A comparison between the Baltic States illustrates this anomaly. Furthermore, the Nice allocation of seats in the European Parliament created certain incomprehensible differences between Member States with a comparable population size (Czech Republic and Hungary versus Belgium, Greece and Portugal). The Act of Accession rectified the latter inconsistency but could not avoid different treatment during the transitional period.

In spite of its complexity, the Nice settlement paved the way for the accession of ten new Member States. However, the question remained whether this enlargement would not jeopardise 'the momentum of European integration.' Particularly those Member States defending a communitarian view on the integration process, most notably the Benelux countries, urged for a more profound revision of the institutional framework.[109] The European Convention and later the Intergovernmental Conference prepared the adoption of a 'Treaty establishing a Constitution for Europe.' The debates in the Convention and the IGC proved that, notwithstanding the fact that it would be a simplification to reduce the institutional discussions to a row between small and big Member States, it is possible to identify certain coalitions of countries defending similar positions on institutional issues. As was the case with previous Treaty amendments, the

[109] A June 2001 Benelux Memorandum 'on the Future of Europe' called for a comprehensive debate on the future of the EU and suggested the Convention method leading to a draft Treaty establishing a Constitution for Europe. Benelux Memorandum on the Future of Europe, available at www.europa-web.de/europa/03euinf/10counc/future.htm.

Constitutional Treaty reflects a compromise between these interests. A clear example is, for instance, the future establishment of a permanent European Council President, primarily supported by the bigger Member States, and the retention of a kind of rotating Presidency system in the Council, a major interest for a majority of small Member States. The continuous postponement of decisions on sensitive issues, such as the reduction of the number of Commissioners, is another characteristic of the institutional reform process.

With regard to the controversial concept of 'institutional balance' it seems clear that the role of the European Parliament and the (European) Council will be strengthened whereas the Union Minister of Foreign Affairs creates a rather hybrid position which breaks the separation of powers between the Council and the Commission. It is obvious that this new structure raises many questions and it remains to be seen in practice whether it will bring more democracy, transparency and efficiency in the European Union, the points of departure of the institutional reform process.[110] Moreover, the prospective accession of Turkey will give new impetus to the question of balance within the EU.

110 See: The Future of the European Union - Laeken Declaration, available at europa.eu.int/futurum/documents/offtext/doc151201_en.htm.

CHAPTER 4

The National Parliaments in an Enlarged Europe and the Constitutional Treaty

Philipp Kiiver

1 Introduction

Accession to the European Union entails far-reaching consequences for the internal constitutional orders of the new Member States. Their national parliaments, having ratified the Accession Treaty where and in as far as they were competent to do so, have transferred key legislative competences to international and supranational institutions, in particular to the Council of Ministers. Having done so, the parliaments now face the new challenge to established practices of government-parliament relations: national ministers will be able to negotiate European legislation in Brussels, which will be directly binding upon the domestic legislators. Still, as national ministers remain answerable to their respective national parliaments at home, under domestic standards of parliamentary democracy, their conduct of policies in the Council may be subject to domestic parliamentary scrutiny. The degree and mechanisms of such *European scrutiny*, however, depend on the will and capacities of the national parliaments themselves. The parliamentary institutions and procedures in the fifteen old Member States (hereinafter 'the Fifteen') for instance, which have faced the same challenge for some years already, vary significantly from one Member State to another.

The present paper first outlines the challenges that lie ahead for the new Member States' parliaments. A brief overview then points out the variations in parliamentary practice within the Fifteen, and provides a reference framework for what to expect of the new Member States. Finally, the discussion shall be placed in the wider context of the role of national parliaments in the European architecture. Since the Council of Ministers is usually seen to derive its democratic legitimacy from the fact that all the individual Ministers are accountable to their national parliaments at home, the domestic scrutiny mechanisms in the ten new Member States may hold broader implications. A scenario of weak national parliaments outnumbering the stronger ones in an enlarged EU shall, therefore, be discussed in the context of the democratic deficit of the EU. An outlook at the possible consequences of and for the Treaty establishing a Constitution for Europe shall then conclude the discussion.

2 The parliaments of the new Member States and the European challenge

Throughout the 1990s, the national parliaments within the EU have been increasingly attracting attention in the debate on the future of Europe. Conventionally, the national parliaments are seen as the losers of European integration, having underestimated the European dimension[1] and having

---

1 See A. Duff, 'Building a Parliamentary Europe', 29 *Government and Opposition* (1994) pp. 147-165, at p. 164.

allowed the governments to escape effective democratic accountability.[2] Since the Council as such is indeed not accountable to the European parliament, the only formal accountability link there remains the individual ministers' reliance on parliamentary confidence at home. Most national parliaments are, however, widely perceived to be rather modest and ineffective in exercising scrutiny over their ministers concerning European policy.[3] This is what lies at the very heart of the perceived democratic deficit, or parliamentary gap, of the European Union.[4]

The basis for any national parliamentary involvement in the decision-making at the EU level so far, is essentially the link of ministerial accountability towards parliament. As in a parliamentary system, the cabinet relies on parliamentary confidence or tolerance to stay in office, parliament is able to supervise the executive, to demand the disclosure of information, to question and press ministers and, ultimately, to threaten them with a motion of no-confidence, interpellations or comparable measures, depending on the applicable constitutional rules. During the pre-accession period, the national parliaments of the new Member States, on the one hand, had the main task of supervising the negotiation process by scrutinising their governments' performance. On the other hand, they had the legislative task of implementing, where competent, the *acquis communautaire* into national law. Finally, they ratified the Accession Treaty, whether or not combined with a referendum. Post-accession scrutiny of the governments' EU policy will now bring about a new challenge, a preview of which could have already been experienced during the pre-accession negotiation stage. The following overview points out some of the main aspects of the challenge to national parliaments.[5]

1. Formal input of national parliaments is, at least so far, not provided for in the EU decision-making process. Ratification of legislative acts is not necessary.

---

[2] See J. Lodge, 'The European Parliament', in E. Smith, ed., *National Parliaments as Cornerstones of European Integration* (London/The Hague/Boston, Kluwer Law International) p. 188; see Swedish Riksdag, *National Parliaments and the European Union* (Discussion Document for the COSAC Meeting in Stockholm, May 2001) p. 11.

[3] See K. Neunreither, 'The Democratic Deficit of the European Union: Towards Closer Cooperation between the European Parliament and the National Parliaments', 29 *Government and Opposition* (1994) pp. 299-314; Ph. Norton, ed., 'National Parliaments and the European Union', 1 *The Journal of Legislative Studies* (1995) special issue no. 3; E. Smith, ed., *National Parliaments as Cornerstones of European Integration* (London/The Hague/Boston, Kluwer Law International 1996; T. Raunio, 'Always One Step Behind? National Legislatures and the European Union'', 34 *Government and Opposition* (1999) pp. 180-202; D. Dimitrakopoulos, 'Incrementalism and Path Dependence: European Integration and Institutional Change in National Parliaments', 39 *Journal of Common Market Studies* (2001) pp. 405-422.

[4] See J. Lodge, 'Democratic Legitimacy and European Union', 6 *Public Policy and Administration* (1991) pp. 21-29 at p. 23.

[5] Cf. Norton, op. cit. n. 3.

Meanwhile, the task of implementing Directives into domestic law, assigned to 'the national authorities' which anyway may or may not be the parliaments,[6] mostly leaves little discretion. Failure to timely and properly implement Directives constitutes a violation of Community Law.

2. The technical complexity of EU legislation requires great specialisation, expertise and resources which are usually available only to the executive. This means that parliaments will lag further behind, in terms of information, the apparatus of civil servants in the ministries, as well as in COREPER.[7] Even when the government or the Commission provides relevant documents, sorting them according to importance alone is time-consuming, not to mention the scrutiny of their substance.

3. The transnational character of EU decision-making adds to the information lag in that the interests of other Member States, sometimes expressed only informally, have to be taken into account. Co-decision by the Council with the European Parliament further means that a legislative draft and a common position can change in a series of readings, so that keeping track of it becomes even more difficult to outsiders.

4. Supranational decision-making under qualified-majority voting (QMV) in the Council means that no matter how strict parliamentary supervision of a minister might be, the latter can still be outvoted. The Council's meeting behind closed doors has further led to impediments to parliamentary scrutiny of ministers' conduct in the past.

Again, parliamentary practice in the new Member States might not even change fundamentally after accession, but continue along the patterns of the monitoring of the pre-accession negotiation phase. Nevertheless, any adaptation to this negotiation process itself constitutes a form of parliamentary response to the European challenge, as it presupposes the realisation that EU membership is no longer a matter of classical foreign policy. In order to respond to the outlined European challenge, the national parliaments of the Fifteen have gradually adapted their approach to EU policy, and so have, as said above, the parliaments of the new Member States. An overview over the differences in approach is provided in the following paragraphs.

6 Art. 249 EC; Art. I-33 of the Constitutional Treaty.

7 See V. Miller and R. Ware, 'Keeping National Parliaments Informed: The Problem of European Legislation', 2 *The Journal of Legislative Studies* (1996) pp. 184-197; Raunio op. cit. n. 3.

3 Existing variations in European scrutiny

The national parliaments of the Fifteen have gradually responded to the European challenge by adapting their institutions and procedures for parliamentary scrutiny. Especially, they have strengthened their scrutiny mechanisms in the period following the adoption of the Single European Act and the Maastricht Treaty.[8] Indeed, a relative increase in scrutiny powers of the EU national parliaments over the EU can be observed in the course of European integration. In absolute terms, however, the efforts are still widely considered to be insufficient and calls for yet greater efforts do not subside. Thus, several contributions to the European Convention emphasised the demand for stronger mechanisms and greater involvement of national parliaments in EU policy, primarily by holding their own governments to account.[9]

3.1 The Fifteen

When comparing the parliamentary mechanisms for exercising European scrutiny as they exist in the Fifteen's national parliaments today, it becomes evident first of all, that great differences exist in terms of procedural and institutional set-ups. While all parliaments have established European Affairs Committees, or assigned a pre-existing committee such a function, the role, competence and composition of these committees differ greatly. In some national parliaments they are central and powerful bodies, while in others they are mere advisory EU expert groups. These differences are closely related to whether European affairs are treated centrally as being 'European' in nature, or whether their treatment is decentralised among the sectoral committees, such as on trade or agriculture, according to subject-matter. Further differences exist as regards the committees' size, their frequency of meetings and their productivity, their constitutional status and the personality of their members, as well as the procedures under which they operate.[10] Parliaments thus have different posi-

---

8 See Norton, op. cit. n. 3.; D. Judge, 'The Failure of National Parliaments?', 18 *West European Politics* (1995) pp. 79-100.

9 See e.g. V. Andriukaitis and D. Kutraite-Giedraitiene, *Strengthening the role of national parliaments* (CONV 220/02); F. Basile, *The Role of National Parliaments* (CONV 239/02); D. Hübner, *The role of national Parliaments* (CONV 390/02); K. Kiljunen, et al., *Contribution from members of the Convention representing the Finnish Parliament on the role of National Parliaments in the European Union structure* (CONV 82/02); P. Kreitzberg and T. Kelam, *Role of National Parliaments* (CONV 95/02).

10 The bulk of information for this overview is derived from the edited volumes by V. Herman and R. van Schendelen, eds., *The European Parliament and the National Parliaments* (Farnborough, Saxon House 1979), Norton, op. cit. n. 3, F. Laursen and S. Pappas, eds., *The Changing Role of Parliaments in the European Union* (Maastricht, European Institute of Public Administration 1995), E. Smith, op. cit. n. 3, Finnish Eduskunta, *National Parliaments and the EU - Stock-Taking for the Post-Amsterdam Era,*

tions and powers in supervising their respective governments' EU policy. Where parliamentary opinions are not legally binding, their impact, if an opinion is expressed at all, is of varying political weight to the respective government.

The most straightforward, although not entirely unproblematic, way to roughly categorise Member States parliaments in terms of relative strength is to assess the impact they can have on their governments' policy-formulation. In the context of European decision-making this would relate to the parliamentary contribution to the national standpoint in the Council. A frequently employed categorisation therefore is essentially based on a distinction between:

1. strong 'policy-making' parliaments which can reject government policies and substitute them with their own,
2. moderate 'policy-influencing' parliaments which are able to reject or amend government policies but not substitute them, and
3. weak parliaments with 'little or no policy effect'.[11]

Other authors also use a categorisation of strong, moderate and weak parliaments, with different determining factors, such as, *inter alia,* the binding effect of parliamentary opinions,[12] the involvement of sectoral standing committees in the scrutiny process as adding to expertise[13] or the timing and management of scrutiny.[14]

Eventually the Danish parliament, where ministers of typically a minority Cabinet are briefed by the parliament's European Affairs Committee and receive negotiating mandates for upcoming Council meetings, emerges as being undisputedly strong. The parliaments of Finland and Sweden and the Austrian *Nationalrat,* which have adopted a Danish-style briefing routine, are considered strong or moderate. The strength of the Finnish model mainly derives from its optimised input from sectoral standing committees in the scrutiny work, while the process remains largely centralised in Denmark, Sweden and Austria. Finn-

October 1999 COSAC seminar paper (Eduskunnan Kanslian Julkaisu 1/2000) and A. Maurer and W. Wessels, eds., *National Parliaments on their Ways to Europe: Losers or Latecomers?* (Baden-Baden, Nomos 2001), from fact-sheet reports by European Parliament, *Bodies within national parliaments specialising in European Community affairs* (Luxembourg, Office for Official Publications of the European Communities 1990), European Parliament, *Bodies within national parliaments specialising in European Community affairs* (Luxembourg, EP 1992) and Travers, et al., *European Affairs Committees - The Influence of National Parliaments on European Policies: An Overview* (Brussels, European Centre for Parliamentary Research and Documentation 2003), as well as from country-specific sources.

11 See Norton, op. cit. n. 3, at p. 2, Maurer and Wessels, op. cit. n. 10.

12 See T. Bergman, 'National parliaments and EU Affairs Committees: notes on empirical variation and competing explanations', 4 *Journal of European Public Policy* (1997) pp. 373-387.

13 See T. Raunio and M. Wiberg, 'Does Support Lead to Ignorance? National Parliaments and the Legitimacy of EU Governance', 35 *Acta Politica* (2000) pp. 146-168.

14 See Maurer and Wessels, op. cit. n. 10.

ish and Swedish negotiating mandates are politically binding, so that ministers may deviate from the given line in the Council but have to explain their actions afterwards, although such deviations practically never occur. Danish mandates are politically binding as well but so authoritative in practice that they constitute a quasi-legally binding instruction. The Austrian *Nationalrat* has the option to impose opinions that are legally binding or, otherwise, to adopt politically binding resolutions.[15] The German *Bundesrat* also appears to be moderate or strong, especially in EU matters where *Länder* interests are affected. The Dutch parliament, whose assent is required for measures under the Third EU Pillar, is qualified as moderate in that area, while being weaker in other areas of EU policy. The UK Commons and the German *Bundestag* are moderate, the French parliament moderate or weak, and the rest of the national parliaments of the old Member States – Belgium, Luxembourg, Ireland, Portugal, Spain, Italy and Greece – turn out to be weak. Weakness in the present context is mainly indicated by a passive or reactive attitude as regards the government's policy formulation, a low level of expertise among MPs in EU matters and little interest in scrutinising this policy area. Scrutiny is then mainly carried out *ex post*, for instance by questioning ministers during the implementation stage of legislation or by considering annual government reports, which is just about the minimum form of parliamentary involvement.

3.2 Newcomers' adaptations

The form and degree of European scrutiny in a national parliament is primarily a matter of domestic history, political culture, attitudes of political parties and institutional balance of power.[16] It is tempting to picture an ideal prototype model of parliamentary scrutiny. However, it should be noted that national parliaments are a highly heterogeneous group, if one may speak of a group at all. Each national parliament represents the political preferences of its own electorate in terms of composition and the placement of political parties into either government or opposition. A parliament also reflects wider constitutional preferences, which relate, *inter alia*, to the competences a parliament has. Thus, for each parliament one has to ask which powers it shares with a president in a semi-presidential system, which powers it shares with the government, with an upper chamber, with sub-national entities such as autonomous provinces

[15] See W. Urbantschitsch, *National Parliaments in the European Union - The Austrian Experience* (Graz, Forschungsinstitut für Europarecht 1998).

[16] See Norton, op. cit. n. 3, R. Pahre, 'Endogenous Domestic Institutions in Two-Level Games and Parliamentary Oversight of the European Union', 41 *Journal of Conflict Resolution* (1997) pp. 147-174, Bergman, op. cit. n. 12, M. Agostini, 'The Role of National Parliaments in the Future EU', 36 *The International Spectator* (2001) pp. 29-41, A. Maurer, *National Parliaments in the European Architecture: Elements for Establishing a Best Practice Mechanism* (CONV WG IV working document no. 8).

or federal states, or with the electorate itself in those cases where referenda are possible.

A particularly telling example of how practice may diverge while formal rules are inspired by one and the same model, can be found in the accession countries of 1995.[17] Sweden, Finland and Austria joined the European Union in the post-Maastricht period, at a time when the debate about the role of national parliaments in addressing the EU democratic deficit was of increased controversy. The three countries could observe and learn from the experience of older Member States and could adapt beforehand to issues such as the co-decision procedure, QMV, the internal market, Monetary Union, the Schengen *acquis*, the Second and Third Pillars, and broadened EU competences under the First Pillar. All three countries of the 1995 enlargement observed that the Danish parliament had the tightest grip at supervising the government in EU policy. Inspired by this model, the parliaments of Sweden, Finland and Austria set up a mechanism of centralised briefing and debriefing of Brussels-bound ministers. Yet while the parliaments of Austria and Sweden kept the sifting of EU documents centralised in their respective European Affairs Committees as well, the Finnish parliament adopted a model of decentralised sifting in the sectoral standing committees according to subject-matter, followed by a centralised briefing of ministers in the Grand Committee. Then, as mentioned earlier, in Finland and Sweden, parliamentary opinions are only politically binding. The Austrian model, which does feature legally binding opinions, is applied moderately in practice.[18] Mandates are worded in a broad manner so as to leave the minister sufficient manoeuvring space for compromise-finding in the Council. The restrictive Danish mandating model has, thus, not been reproduced in practice, not even in Austria where formal rules are even more far-reaching than the Danish model, which is not even codified but essentially based on a committee report of 1973.[19] Again, the Danish uniqueness lies in the tradition of having minority cabinets, as well as persisting Euro-scepticism, the peculiar behaviour

---

17 Cf. H. Hegeland and Chr. Neuhold, *Parliamentary participation in EU affairs in Austria, Finland and Sweden: Newcomers with different approaches* (European Integration online paper 6/10).

18 See Urbantschitsch, op. cit. n. 15, B. Blümel and Chr. Neuhold, Blümel, 'The Parliament of Austria: A Large Potential with Little Implications', in A. Maurer and W. Wessels, op. cit. n. 10.

19 Folketing Market Relations Committee Report of 29 March 1973; parliamentary participation in EEC affairs in general was based on Article 6(2) of the Danish Accession Act of 1972. Due to the variations in the implementation of formal rules, it has been suggested to depart from categorisations of national Parliaments along strong-moderate-weak scales, and instead to apply method-based categorisations as regards the treatment of EU matters. This would allow to take into account that a broadly worded mandate might be no more binding upon a Government than a concerted parliamentary effort in an informal policy-influencing practice, see A. Fraga, 'Wanting more power... a struggle for what?', in Finnish Eduskunta, op. cit. n. 10, and her contribution to Maurer and Wessels, op. cit. n. 10.

of opposition parties,[20] and a Nordic culture of transparent governance.[21] In such a combination the Danish tradition is not likely to be equalled anywhere else in the European Union.

Just like Finland, Austria and Sweden, the new Member States may now profit from the experience of the older Member States. Later accession alone however, does not guarantee strong European scrutiny in the national parliaments by itself. Denmark and the UK entered the EEC with a relatively strong parliamentary culture in 1973, while Ireland did not, and does not, feature a strong parliament, and nor do Greece, Portugal and Spain, although these countries acceded to the EEC even later. Variations as well as similarities in approach among the accession countries of 2004 are in fact observable already now. To point out some examples, the Estonian parliament has amended its Rules of Procedure to set up an overview system inspired by the Finnish model. Its European Affairs Committee consists of at least one member of each of the other standing committees, to ensure specialist input via overlapping committee membership. The European Affairs Committee also receives opinions from the sectoral standing committees, and deliberates with the competent minister on Fridays. The Committee is entitled to issue a politically binding negotiating mandate.[22] Experience during the first weeks of Estonia's EU membership in terms of timely provision of information from the government has been positive.[23] Parliament has already even turned down a negotiating position proposed by the government, and the minister stuck to the parliamentary opinion in the Council. The parliament of Slovenia has also modelled its scrutiny system after the Finnish example[24] and so did the Hungarian National Assembly.[25] The Latvian parliament is meanwhile influenced more by the Danish system.[26] The practice is quite strong as far as the authority of the European Affairs Committee is concerned, yet just as in the Danish parliament and other parliaments also for that matter, the sectoral standing committees hardly pay any attention to EU affairs, so that the scrutiny remains highly centralised in the European Affairs Committee.[27] To import additional EU-related expertise, the parliament

---

[20] See Pahre, op. cit. n. 16.

[21] See Bergman, op. cit. n. 12.

[22] Art. 152.1-152.5 Estonian Riigikogu Rules of Procedure.

[23] Telephone interview with a staff member of the Riigikogu European Affairs Committee on 8 June 2004.

[24] See P. Vehar, 'The National assembly of the Republic of Slovenia and EU Affairs After Accession, 2 *Forum Parlament* (2004) pp. 16-20.

[25] See Office of the Hungarian National Assembly, 'How Does the Hungarian Parliament Deal with EU Affairs?', 2 *Forum Parlament* (2004) pp. 6-11.

[26] Art. 185.3 and 185.4 Latvian Saeima Rules of Procedure.

[27] Telephone interview with a staff member of the Saeima European Affairs Committee on 8 June 2004. See generally on the disadvantages of centralisation of European scrutiny, S. Ramstedt, 'Comments on the report by Mr Tapio Raunio - Parliamentary Scrutiny of EU Decision-Making: Comparing National Systems', in Finnish Eduskunta, op. cit. n. 10.

of Malta envisages informal participation of Maltese MEPs in the European Affairs Committee's scrutiny procedure.[28] Malta thus follows the examples set earlier by the German *Bundestag*, as well as the parliaments of Belgium, Ireland and Greece. In these parliaments, however, the MEPs rarely attend meetings in practice, so it remains to be seen whether the Maltese MEPs have time or interest to join deliberations in the Maltese parliament. Turning to the legal basis for scrutiny, the Czech Republic has amended its Constitution to enshrine parliamentary participation in the country's EU policy, envisaging rights of information and expression of parliamentary opinions.[29] So have Slovenia[30] and Hungary.[31] Again compared to older Member States, it should, however, be noted that a constitutional basis alone neither ensures nor indicates stronger scrutiny. Several of the old Member States, ranging between strong, moderate and weak scrutiny in practice, have such provisions concerning parliamentary involvement in EU matters in their respective Constitutions, including Finland and Germany, but also Portugal and Belgium.

It is too early to evaluate the practice in the new Member States, apart from the past experience gained during the accession negotiation process. Even for the Fifteen, a categorisation of national parliaments into groups of stronger and weaker players is less straightforward than it may seem. Using conventional means, the parliaments of Estonia, Latvia, Slovenia or Hungary might indeed have the potential to maintain a relatively strong scrutiny system. Nevertheless, one might consider that most of the new Member States have stable majority governments and a dominant executive, that most of them are neither Eurosceptic nor particularly 'Nordic', and that practically all of them saw an interruption of their parliamentary culture during decades of authoritarian rule. Even though all of the new Member States can enjoy the advantages of late accession and the experience of implementing the *acquis*, other factors may still outweigh these advantages in the longer term, such as the small size and resources of a parliament or permissive pro-European consensus. Nevertheless, what is possible already now is to estimate the impact of the national parliaments in the new Member States on the democratic legitimacy of EU decision-making as a whole. For instance a scenario of *all* the parliaments of the new Member States being weak or moderate in their European scrutiny, or a more likely scenario of a mix across the strength range, can be reviewed in the context of parliamentarism, accountability and legitimacy in the European constitutional architecture.

---

[28] Art. 120F Maltese House of Representatives Standing Orders.

[29] Art. 10b Czech Constitution.

[30] Art. 3a (4) Slovenian Constitution.

[31] Art. 35/A Hungarian Constitution; see generally on the constitutional adaptations to EU membership in the new Member States: A. Albi, 'EU Amendments of the Central and Eastern European Candidate Countries', in J. Ziller, ed., *The Europeanisation of Constitutional Law in the Light of the Constitution for Europe* (Paris, L'Harmattan 2003).

4 National parliaments in the European architecture

What will be the impact of the accession of new Member States, some of which may turn out to have modest European scrutiny in their parliaments, on the democratic legitimacy of the European Union as a whole? Recalling that the Council of Ministers is conventionally seen to be deriving its legitimacy from the accountability of its individual members at home, what will be the consequences of weak or moderate national parliaments outnumbering their stronger counterparts in an enlarged European Union? Conversely, what will be the effects of an opposite scenario featuring strong newcomers? To address these questions, the role of national parliaments in the EU, as well as within their own Member States, will need closer examination.

As mentioned at the outset, the reason why national parliaments attract attention in the first place is that they are perceived as contributing to democratic legitimacy in EU decision-making and bringing Europe 'closer to its citizens'. This argument is based on the assumption that national parliaments are familiar and important focal points for debate in their national publics and trigger greater voter mobilisation than the European Parliament does. Such reasoning can, however, be deceptive, in that it implies that national parliaments are a homogenous collective of institutions which share the same status and function in their respective countries, the same role as a 'victim' of European integration, and that they share a common interest in confronting their governments and in together holding the Council to account. Accordingly, the Council would command a sort of aggregate legitimacy, being the sum of its component members, and more national parliaments with stronger European scrutiny would add up to more democratic legitimacy for the Council as a whole. Following that line of reasoning, an influx of modest parliaments might have a strategically detrimental impact. Critically reviewing these notions would now allow to draw a more realistic picture , as set out in the following paragraphs.

Firstly, as regards the balance of power in a parliamentary democracy, it should be noted that simplified government-versus-parliament juxtapositions usually do not reflect reality, nor even the theoretical model of the relevant Constitution.[32] A parliament is elected to support a functioning government for the period of its term, after which the electorate can decide again on the distribution of seats. The supervising and deliberative functions of a parliament in fact mainly derive from the activity of opposition parties, which challenge the government in the hope of gaining a parliamentary majority in the future.[33] Parliaments are, thus, not unitary bodies but assemblies of political parties

[32] See Maurer and Wessels, op. cit. n. 10, at p. 451; Pahre, op. cit. n. 16; Ph. Norton, ed., *Parliaments and Governments in Western Europe* (London, Frank Cass 1998).

[33] See R. Holzhacker, 'National Parliamentary Scrutiny over EU Issues', 3 *European Union Politics* (2002) pp. 459-479.

either in government or in opposition, while parliamentary majorities are typically supportive of, or controlled by, the executive.

Secondly, national parliaments are not a collective but, as said, individual focal points for their own national publics. Rooted in their own systems' history, political culture and constitutional setting, their heterogeneity is considerable. Different electoral systems, for instance, lead to different modes of electoral representation and of government formation. The number of political parties represented in a parliament varies from effective bipartisanism to heavy fragmentation. Some Member States tend to have single-party majority cabinets (e.g. Greece, UK), some tend to have two-party coalitions (e.g. Germany, Austria), others have three (e.g. the Netherlands) or more political parties (e.g. Belgium, Italy), while in some Member States (most notably Denmark) even minority cabinets are not uncommon. Party discipline and mutual compatibility of coalition partners differs. In terms of political culture, even the capacity of parliaments to act as fora for public debate differs from one Member State to another. While in some Member States, televised parliamentary debates, written parliamentary questions and ministers' replies attract broad public attention, in others the arguments are more often exchanged outside the plenary in committees or even outside parliament itself in the media.

Thirdly, a national parliament's preferences are coined in the domestic setting, as political parties' agendas are heavily dominated by domestic policy issues. Domestic government-opposition cleavages, however, do not necessarily apply to the Council arena, as transnational alliances may be formed beyond party lines, and domestic cleavages as regards European policy may run through political parties internally. To assume that national parliaments can collectively maintain a form of European parliamentarism would mean to ignore the reason why a given national parliament is composed the way it is. Apart from that, it would ignore the fact that national parliaments can scrutinise government policy from a national point of view only, since a parliament has an electoral mandate to represent its own nation, and its own nation only. Transnational decision-making, however, addresses cross-border problems involving the interests of several Member States.

Fourthly and finally, it should be noted that each parliament is oriented towards its own electorate and that the national publics, in turn, focus on their own parliament. National parliaments thus represent particularised interests of politically and culturally isolated entities. Because of that isolation, which is rooted in the exclusiveness of the electorate and its linguistic delimitations, greater parliamentary scrutiny over EU policy in one Member State will not increase the legitimacy of EU decision-making in the eyes of the public of another Member State. To illustrate that, the French will not feel any closer to the EU knowing that the Danish parliament conducts an effective European scrutiny, and they will not feel any worse about it believing that the Greek parliament is rather toothless. Therefore, for the public of any given Member State, effective scrutiny in eight of the Member States parliaments will be no better than effective scrutiny in six and no worse than effective scrutiny in ten of the national parliaments. An influx of weak parliaments into the EU following the enlargement, should that be the case, might thus have a statistical impact in comparative studies along the strong-moderate-weak scale, but in the general public of the individual Member States it will go unnoticed.

The above four points are to show that discussions on the role of national parliaments in an enlarged EU should not be flawed by misconceptions about the parliaments' role and nature. For instance, assuming an aggregate democratic legitimacy of the Council deriving from a collective of national parliaments would mean that each set of national parliamentary scrutiny procedures with respect to a government's EU policy constitutes one-twenty-fifth of European parliamentarism. However, in the light of the above considerations, neither the presence of a collective interest, nor the capacity of cross-border spillover effects, in terms of EU legitimacy perception, can be assumed. As to the converse scenario of more parliaments adopting hand-tying scrutiny practices in EU affairs, instead of remaining restrained, it would hamper the efficiency of Council decision-making,[34] without adding to increased collective legitimacy either. Now the Treaty establishing a Constitution for Europe, on the one hand, addresses national parliaments in their individual capacity of holding their governments to account. On the other hand, however, it still seeks to promote the misleading idea of a quasi-collective of solidarity among national parliaments. Both dimensions shall be elaborated in the following paragraphs.

5 The Constitutional Treaty and beyond

In as far as national parliaments are concerned, the Constitutional Treaty continues the development of greater awareness of the issue the run-up to the Maastricht IGC, when the national parliaments' contributions to the Union became a subject of intergovernmental discussions. Maastricht Declaration 13 aimed in two directions. Firstly, co-operation and exchange of information between the national parliaments and the European Parliament should be enhanced. Secondly, national parliaments should receive EU legislative proposals 'in good time' as a prerequisite to effective scrutiny. The Amsterdam Treaty sought to further formalise the role of national parliaments, building on the two-pronged approach of the Maastricht Declaration, and aiming at inter-parliamentary co-operation, as well as improved information flows. It also reserved a six-week time window in the EU legislative process for national parliamentary influence *ex ante*, and invited collective inter-parliamentary contributions to be

---

[34] See Urbantschitsch, op. cit. n. 15, F. Hayes-Renshaw and H. Wallace, *The Council of Ministers* (London, Macmillan), p. 291.

adopted. The Nice IGC, in its Declaration 23, Article 5(4), as well as the Laeken Declaration, reiterated the need to further address the role of the national parliaments in the Union's architecture.

The Constitutional Treaty now formally recognises the national parliaments as links in the chain of representative democracy, leading from the citizens via the parliaments and the governments up to the Council.[35] The Constitutional Treaty also strengthens national parliaments' access to EU documentation, which is now sent to them directly from the Commission instead of being forwarded to them by the governments.[36] Thus, parliaments, provided they can handle the flood of paper[37] and provided they are still interested in exercising their powers of scrutiny, can dispose of more timely information. The most prominent feature of the Treaty as regards the national parliaments in terms of institutional and procedural innovation, however is the inclusion of an entirely new device for national parliamentary involvement in EU politics: the 'early warning system' for the principle of subsidiarity, providing national parliaments with a collective and direct legislative intervention device. Each national parliament receives two votes, one per chamber in the case of bicameral parliaments, and if parliaments or chambers, which, taken together constitute one-third of the votes[38] submit 'reasoned opinions' stating that a Commission proposal violates the subsidiarity principle, (meaning that the addressed policy area should not be dealt with on EU level) the Commission is to reconsider, although not necessarily to amend or withdraw, the proposal.[39]

A preliminary assessment of the early warning system, which will be new to both new Member States the Fifteen alike, reveals that it is an inherently weak mechanism.[40] The 'reasoned opinions' are not of a binding nature and if a national parliament wanted to send a letter to the Commission, it could do so all along.[41] The six week period, during which parliaments may issue reasoned opinions, affirms the delay that has already been introduced by the Amsterdam Protocol. Furthermore, the parliaments are not awarded separate standing before the ECJ as privileged applicants for annulment actions on the ground of subsidiarity. Such standing would probably not have provided any added value

---

35 Art. I-46(2) of the Constitutional Treaty.

36 The Protocol of the Constitutional Treaty on the Role of the national Parliaments in the European Union.

37 See S. Weatherill, 'Competence', in B. de Witte, ed., *Ten Reflections on the Constitutional Treaty of Europe* (Florence, European University Institute 2003), at p. 911.

38 The threshold is one-fourth on the area of freedom, security and justice.

39 Arts. I-11(3) of the Constitutional Treaty and Art. 3 of the Protocol to the Constitutional Treaty on the role of the national Parliaments in the European Union, Art. 6 and 7 Protocol to the Constitutional Treaty on the Application of the Principles of Subsidiarity and Proportionality.

40 See also the contribution by F. Amtenbrink in Chapter 2.

41 Thanks to Hans Hegeland for this remark.

anyway, since the ECJ does not treat subsidiarity as a legally enforceable principle .[42] To do so would even have caused distortions in national constitutional arrangements, for instance in those cases where parliaments do not have legal personality to bring independent court actions.[43]

Yet in the light of the earlier considerations above, concerning the conventional misconceptions about the role of national parliaments, the system appears to be flawed for even more fundamental reasons. Firstly, government-parliament relations are rarely adversarial. Whenever a parliament as an institution is called upon to become active, the institution's position will be determined by the parliamentary majority, which usually coincides with the political colour of the government in office. Thus, even if a national parliament, that is, the majority therein, issues a reasoned opinion, it can mean two things. Either the parliamentary majority wishes to damage and embarrass its own government, when the latter has already agreed with the policy measure being taken at the EU level, or – more likely – the parliamentary majority does what the government asks it to do after having failed to obstruct the measure in Brussels itself. A special situation might emerge in cases of bicameral parliaments, when the majority in the upper chamber is of an opposing political colour with respect to the government and its majority in the lower chamber. In either scenario, since national parliaments form no collective positioned against the EU institutions or their governments, reasoned opinions, if adopted at all, will be a matter of domestic power struggles or evidence of loyalty to the government but not an expression of collective involvement of national parliaments in EU affairs. This is also an inherent constraint upon inter-parliamentary co-operation for the sake of direct, collective contributions by national parliaments. While benchmarking and non-binding best practice comparisons are reasonably successful, for instance in the framework of COSAC, a half-yearly inter-parliamentary conference, apart from the fact that different parliaments have different ideas about the desirable role for COSAC itself, a meaningful and substantive collective parliamentary stance would effectively bypass the own governments. It is, consequently, unlikely to emerge.

6 Conclusion

It is difficult to estimate the strength of the national parliaments of the new Member States as regards scrutiny of their governments' EU policy. In fact, finding appropriate criteria and empirical evidence for generalisations is not easy even for the old Member States. European scrutiny is, after

[42] See A. Estella, *The EU Principle of Subsidiarity and its Critique* (Oxford, Oxford University Press, 2002).

[43] See M. Claes, *The National Courts' Mandate in the European Constitution*, (Oxford, Hart Publishing 2005, forthcoming), theme 3, chapter 6.3.

all, still a feature of domestic constitutional and cultural particularities in each Member State. Indeed, every national parliament is as unique as the people it represents. Meanwhile, a greater number of weak, moderate or strong national parliaments within the EU after enlargement will have little effect on the democratic legitimacy of the EU institutions, in particular the Council. As has been pointed out, national parliaments are neither homogenous nor a collective, and it would be deceptive to equate European scrutiny in a national parliament as being one-twenty-fifth of a larger legitimacy scheme. The share of strong, moderate or weak scrutinisers among the twenty-five national parliaments will be irrelevant to any single national public and its perception of the legitimacy of Council decision-making. If there is demand for more national parliamentary input, then this is either based on highly abstract notions, tending to ignore or even welcoming the detrimental effects on Council efficiency, or, from the individual national perspective, it represents a call for greater transparency of government policies in the own Member State alone. Accordingly, demands for sharper parliamentarism need to be considered separately, in each Member State, so that a nuanced view can be ensured. Arguments from an all-European perspective, however, tend to rely on crude generalisations. For example, the Constitutional Treaty seeks to assist national parliaments in their scrutiny efforts by providing them with a direct access to more documentation. The constitutional implications of the fact that the Commission sends documents to the national parliaments directly, however, remain largely blacked out. The term 'national parliaments', for instance, seems to include the German *Bundesrat*, which is a law-maker but not a parliament, the federal parliament of Belgium, which is a Parliament but not always a law-maker,[44] the French National Assembly, which does not control the President, the Dutch Senate which does not elect the government, and the UK House of Lords which is not even elected itself. The crude nature of the European standard employed is intimately connected to the wider misconceptions about a collective role for 'the' national parliaments.

---

44 Cf. the very telling Declaration No. 49 annexed to the Constitutional Treaty, in which the Belgian Government wishes 'to make clear' that the assemblies of the Belgian Regions and Communities belong to the national parliamentary system as component parts thereof, or as Chambers of the national Parliament. The Subsidiarity Protocol's early warning system however merely allocates two votes to each national Parliament, to be shared out in cases of bicameralism (Art. 7), and leaves possible consultation of regional parliaments with legislative powers to the national Parliaments themselves (Art. 6). Practice will show which assemblies will effectively cast the votes under the system, and how the arising problem will be solved that in Belgium there are two Chambers of the federal Parliament, three Regions and three Communities. The Declaration is even more important in the context of the Constitutional Treaty passerelle clause, Article IV-444, the application of which can be vetoed by any one national parliament. Sub-national parliaments are not explicitly addressed to wield such a power, yet the Belgian Declaration seems to aim at creating such an effect.

Again, European scrutiny will remain a feature of essentially domestic politics and government-parliament relations. The early warning system on the subsidiarity principle will not alter the domestic character of scrutiny and debate of EU matters in the national parliaments. For the future development of the European constitutional architecture, this should be reason again to review critically the possible sources of democratic legitimacy of EU decision-making. Solving European democratic deficits by parliamentarising the national level, for instance, seems questionable in this light. For the new Member States themselves, these considerations imply that European scrutiny will naturally develop as a new feature of parliamentary practice. It will have to be separately examined against the background of the particularities of each political system, history and culture. Both aspects may form the starting point for further research. Empirical and comparative studies of European scrutiny in the parliaments of the new Member States are still scarce. Generally speaking, somewhat more critical reflections about the currently fashionable notion of strengthening a collective role for the national parliaments in the EU are very much in order.

PART 2 – DIFFERENTIATION IN EU AND POLICY

CHAPTER 5

The 'Principle' of Differentiation in an Enlarged European Union

Unity in Diversity?

Andrea Ott

1 Between Differentiation and Disintegration – Flexibility in EU law and policy

The European Union is built on a set of fundamental principles that have been developed through the evolution of European Community and Union law, the practice of the institutions and the case law of the European Court of Justice. Some of these principles have found their way into the existing EC/EU Treaties, some others have sought to find their way into the Union via the Treaty establishing a Constitution for Europe (hereinafter Constitutional Treaty).[1] Such fundamental principles are the principle of supremacy and direct effect, the principle of supranationality[2], the principle of non-discrimination and co-operation or sincere co-operation among Member States (Art.10 EC).[3] With new forms of co-operation and policies in an ever growing European Union however, new forms or set of principles come to forefront, among them the concept or 'principle' of flexibility or differentiation can be distinguished to characterise law and policy making in the enlarged European Union.

From the outset, it is disputable whether flexibility can be considered a principle at all.[4] Neither is it clearly defined nor does it entail a clearly defined concept compared with the rule of law or the principle of supremacy. Differentiation or flexibility is viewed by many as a means to enable some Member States to further integrate without exercising their veto to prevent other Member States from integrating or, in contrast, enabling Member States to preserve their identities on a national, regional and local level.[5] Others see an element of disintegration in it, a European Union of different legal regimes and different speeds in opposition to supranationality, embodying the Member States' acceptance of Community interests, the establishment of an effective Community

1 See Art.I-2: 'The Union is founded on the values of respect for human dignity, freedom, democracy, equality, the rule of law and respect for human rights, including the rights of persons belonging to minorities. These values are common to the Member States in a society in which pluralism, non-discrimination, tolerance, justice, solidarity and equality between women and men prevail.'

2 On supranationality as a form of a genuine principle: H. P. Ipsen, 'Über Supranationalität', pp. 97, in H. P. Ipsen, ed., *Verfassungsperspektiven der europäischen Integration* (Baden-Baden, Nomos, 1984); see generally: A. von Bogdandy, Doctrine of Principles, *Jean Monnet Working Paper* No.9/03.

3 For details: A.Ott, 'Fundamental and Basic Principles', pp. 13, in A. Ott and K. Inglis, eds., *Handbook on European Enlargement* (The Hague, TMC Asser Press, 2002).

4 A general definition of principles is not given in the Treaties, in the literature principles are defined in opposition to rules as in difference to rules do not set legal consequences but state reasons which give particular arguments. See R. Dworkin, *Taking Rights seriously*, (Cambridge, Harvard University Press, 1977), pp. 24-31.

5 J.Shaw, 'European Union Legal Studies in Crisis? Towards a New Dynamic', *Oxford Journal of Legal Studies* 1996, pp. 231-253 at p. 232.

power, the autonomy and efficiency of Community law[6], uniformly applied by the European Court of Justice. In consequence this policy form enables certain Member States to integrate more closely without others as the EU enlarges and becomes more diverse politically and economically.[7] Two different forms of flexibility are classified in this contribution, reflecting practice and the structure of the Treaties/Constitutional Treaty. One is the form of differentiation achieved by an accession treaty. The other forms are reflected by the EU constitutional or institutional system.

With an enlarged European Union the concept and understanding of differentiation needs to be revisited. How much diversity in the European Union can be justified to keep the momentum of integration and supranationality? This contribution argues that despite all trends to the 'Europe of bits and pieces'[8] or 'disintegration', certain common fundamental principles underpin the constitutional legal order of the European Union. These need to be better defined and reaffirmed with an enlargement and constitutionalisation process that is characterised by opposing forces of a piecemeal approach to the application of European Union law in new and old Member States and an exercise of consolidation and simplification by a novel Constitutional Treaty.

2 Differentiation after accession in the Constitutional Treaty

2.1 Enhanced co-operation or constitutional differentiation

The topic of constitutional differentiation was brought to the fore with the perspective of an enlarged and more diverse European Union to secure the widening without loosing the momentum of further integration or deepening. The original six Member States expressed in the 1996 IGC, when preparing to enlargement – the need for a constitutionally legitimised version in the form of a general enabling clause.[9] This was long discussed but also

---

6 Ipsen, op. cit., or see Pierre Pescatore's definition of recognition by a group of states of certain common interests and values and the creation of effective Community power and the autonomy of this power, P. Pescatore, *The Law of Integration* (Leiden, Sijthoff, 1974) at p. 26.

7 D.Dinan, ed., *Encyclopaedia of the European Union* (London, Palgrave Macmillan, 2000), at p. 236.

8 D. Curtin, The Constitutional Structure of the European Union: A Europe of Bits and Pieces *CML Rev.* 1993, pp. 17-70 and see the substantial literature which has been written about the forms of differentiation/flexibility in the EU: F. Tuytschaever, *Differentiation in European Union Law,* (Oxford, Hart Publishing, 1999); G. de Búrca and J. Scott, *Constitutional Change in the EU,* (Oxford, Hart Publishing, 2000); B. Witte, D.Hanf and E.Vos, *The Many Faces of Differentiation in EU Law,* (Antwerpen, Intersentia, 2001); J.A. Usher, 'Variable geometry or concentric circles: Patterns for the EU', *ICLQ* 46(1997) pp. 243, C.-D. Ehlermann, Engere Zusammenarbeit nach dem Amsterdamer Vertrag: Ein neues Vertragsprinzip, *EuR* 1997, pp. 362 at pp. 366-367.

9 B. P. G. Smith, *Constitution building in the European Union*, p. 110 (The Hague, Kluwer, 2002).

avoided enabling some Member States to further integrate. Subsequent changes were made to the structures of the European Community to make it a European Union with different policies such as the Common Foreign and Security Policy, the establishment of the Economic and Monetary Union diversified policies and pillars of the legal order.[10] The European Community/Union widened with Spain and Portugal in 1986 and Austria, Finland and Sweden in 1995 and undertook its fifth enlargement with eight Central and Eastern European countries, Malta and Cyprus on 1 May 2004.

Consequently, the Amsterdam Treaty introduced in 1997, through Articles 40 to 45 EU;

- a constitutionally legitimised version of closer co-operation;
- an enabling clause in its third pillar and;
- Article 11 EC on closer co-operation into the Community pillar.

Simply by reference to the wording, the complexity of a justified use of closer co-operation became obvious. The provisions were a strange mix of procedural and material norms of overlapping scope.[11] In addition, no practical use was made of these instruments. A majority of Member States had to participate and a dubious 'Luxembourg compromise' sort of veto was introduced that could block its application when an opposing, non-participating member invoked important and stated reasons of national policy.[12]

With the enactment of the Treaty of Nice on 1 February 2003, 'closer co-operation' has been renamed as 'enhanced co-operation' and extended to foreign policy (excluding matters having military or defence implications).[13] Furthermore, without major resistance from the smaller Member States and with the emergence of interesting new alliances among Member States, some changes to the flexibility clause in the Treaties could be introduced. These changes improved the application of the provisions. With the amendment of Article 40

---

10 On this, see S. Douglas-Scott, *Constitutional Law of the European Union*, (London, Longman, 2002), at p. 31.

11 The original idea of a general clause on flexibility paved the way for specific provisions in the different pillars, even though Articles 43 and 44 EU needed to be read in conjunction with Article 11 EC for measures in the first pillar.

12 Tuytschaever, op. cit., n. 8 at p. 55. It is also illustrative that the first draft articles set up by the Irish Presidency during the IGC 1996 on flexibility included a modest list of closer integration: education, vocational training, youth, culture, public health, tourism, energy, civil protection, trans-European networks, industry, research and technology, development co-operation and the fight against social exclusion. Most of these areas already give examples of successful closer co-operation schemes among Member States, and it would not be wise to include these areas under the much stricter and intransparent institutional and procedural requirements of the general enabling clause.

13 See in preparation the proposals by Germany and Italy, CONFER 4783/00, Belgium, CONFER 4765/00, and Spain, CONFER 4760/00. General reservations were expressed by the UK, Sweden and Denmark.

EU, enhanced co-operation is given a clearer definition and the 'Luxembourg compromise' restriction has been eliminated in the first pillar as well as in the third pillar. The minimum number of participating Member States has also been lowered to eight, the majority of the former Union of Fifteen before the fifth enlargement. Secondly, the individual criteria mentioned in Article 11 EC have been integrated into the general provision of Article 43 EU to avoid the repetition of criteria in different pillars. In this respect Article 43(a)EU has been amended to reinforce the process of integration. Thus, areas of enhanced co-operation cannot fall within the exclusive competence of the Community (criterion (d)). In general, the procedural requirements have been made more transparent, separating them from the substantive requirements for cooperation in Article 40a EU. The position of the Commission has also been slightly improved in the third pillar (Article 40(a), paragraph 1), Member States must address requests for enhanced cooperation to the Commission, which in turn will submit a proposal to the Council.[14] Whether the position of the Parliament has been strengthened is debatable. The Parliament already had a right of consultation. However, now it clearly spells out that the European Parliament has to be consulted (Art. 40(a), (2)).[15] In respect of the first pillar, it does strengthen the position of the European Parliament. In principle the Council may act on a majority of votes when assessing a proposal from the Commission after consultation with the European Parliament. However, when enhanced co-operation is used in an area covered by the co-decision procedure, the assent of the European Parliament is now required. But legal review of enhanced co-operation remains a problem. Article 40 EU (Amsterdam version) stated, in paragraph 4, that Article 35 in respect of judicial protection applies, however limited, to paragraphs Article 40(1) to (3). This appears to clearly restrict legal review to formal and procedural requirements for initiating closer or enhanced co-operation.

Further changes were foreseen in the Constitutional Treaty.[16] With its main task of simplification of the existing Treaty provisions, this Constitutional Treaty includes a general flexibility clause in Articles I-44 and Articles III-416 to III-436. This does not go much beyond what already has been achieved by the tidying-up exercise of Nice but extends its use. It includes a separate form of permanent structured co-operation for mutual defense[17] and enhanced co-operation

---

[14] If the Commission does not act, Member States may submit an initiative to the Council nevertheless.

[15] As far as an area is covered by enhanced cooperation for which the procedure of Art. 251 EC applies, the assent of the EP is necessary.

[16] Art. IV-447 (2) Constitutional Treaty.

[17] Art. I-41 (6) in connection with Art. III-312 Constitutional Treaty: 'Those Member States whose military capabilities fulfil higher criteria and which have made more binding commitments to one another in this area with a view to the most demanding missions shall establish permanent structured cooperation within the Union framework. Such cooperation shall be governed by Article III-312. It shall not affect the provisions of Article III-309'.

in judicial co-operation in criminal matters (Art. III-270(4)). It strengthens the role of the Commission in CFSP and the European Parliament in general. The constitutional provision of Article I-44 refers in its paragraph 1 to the substantial and procedural requirements of Article III-416 to III-423, paragraph (2) Constitutional Treaty sets the number of Member States required for enhanced co-operation at one-third of the current Member States. This would raise the current threshold of participation of eight Member States to nine countries in a Union of twenty-five, and to at least ten Member States in a Union of thirty.[18]

2.2 What happens to the general enabling clause after accession?

Enlargement to the East and the South with ten new Member States led to a more diverse group of countries in the European Union.[19] Further accessions are planned with Romania and Bulgaria in 2007, with Croatia and Turkey in the waiting line.[20] Whether a larger and more heterogeneous Union leads to a more frequent use of constitutional flexibility is doubtful.[21] This has several explanations. One is that even though the enabling clause has been improved to make constitutional flexibility more feasible in the future, its application still lacks clarity and depends more on political than legal interpretation. Secondly, the Treaty reforms of Amsterdam, Nice and the Constitution show the limits of any simplification in this area. The fundamental principles of non-discrimination, fair competition, internal market or economic, social and territorial cohesion shall not be put at stake (Art. III-416). Successful forms of flexibility such as in EMU, the Social Protocol and Schengen, would not have met the requirements of the current general enabling clause.

In EU practice, concrete examples have been discussed in relation to the EURO-group, the statute on European company law and the European Arrest Warrant. It has been advocated to institutionalise the EURO-group by using closer or enhanced co-operation,[22] which resulted in the Commission's propos-

---

[18] See further: M. Dougan, 'A Tidying-up exercise that needs some tidying up of its own', *The Federal Trust*, August 2003, p. 12.

[19] A. Hatje, Art. 44 EUV para.28, in J. Schwarze, ed, EU-Kommentar (Baden-Baden, Nomos 2000).

[20] 'Romania finishes EU Talks', *EUobserver* www.euobserver.com visited on 9 December 2004. On Croatia and the postponement of negotiations talks due to the lack of co-operation of the Croatian government with the UN international tribunal: EU talks with Croatia postponed, *EUobserver* www.euobserver.com visited on 6 March 2005.

[21] B. de Witte is sceptical, 'The Impact of Enlargement on the Constitution of the European Union', pp. 209, in M. Cremona, ed., *The enlargement of the European Union*, Oxford University Press, 2003) see also W. Wessels, 'Die Vertragsreformen von Nizza. Zur zukünftigen Handlungsfähigkeit einer 27er Union', *Integration* 1/2001 at pp. 8-25.

als in 2001 to formally strengthen the EURO group.[23] The Commission's proposal was far from clear as to whether it considered the general enabling clause a legal basis for enhanced co-operation or an implementing measure according to Article 99(5) EC.[24] Both legal bases encountered legal difficulties in relation to enhanced co-operation. Firstly, enhanced co-operation should not concern an area falling into the exclusive competence of the Community and, secondly, it would contradict the situation leading to the EMU with the UK clearly opposing an institutionalisation of the EURO group.[25] Aside from legal questions connected with enhanced co-operation, Member States prefer to achieve common agreements in sensitive areas of national sovereignty before resorting to the last resort of excluding other Member States by enhanced co-operation. This is apparent in the discussions about enhanced co-operation in the cases of the European Company Statute and the European Arrest Warrant. Spain was the only country to object to a European Company Statute despite the Council Legal Service argument that co-operation would meet all the procedural and substantive requirements of the Treaty provisions.[26] As for the European Arrest Warrant, the European Parliament asked the Council to resort to enhanced co-operation in 2001 before Italy dropped its opposition and enabled all the Member States to adopt this measure.[27]

Thus, enhanced co-operation is used more as a political instrument or bargaining tool to 'convince' resistant Member States and achieve a consensus. In practice the last resort of enhanced co-operation or of co-operation among some Member States on the basis of international law is not used. Seen from the perspective of the new Member States, their scepticism and ambivalence stands out and might be considered another stumbling block to its use in practice.[28] It is generally seen by all new Member States, maybe with the exception of Poland as a bigger new Member State, as demoting them to second class Member

---

[22] J.-V. Louis, 'Differentiation and the EMU', p. 62, in de Witte, Hanf and Vos, eds., op. cit. n.8 ; I. Pernice and F. Hoffmeister, 'The Division of Economic Policy Powers', pp. 376, in: A. von Bogdandy, P. Mavroidis and Y. Mény, eds., *European Integration and International Coordination* (The Hague, Kluwer Law International, 2002).

[23] COM(2001) 82 final, 7, paras.19-21.

[24] On this Pernice and Hoffmeister, op. cit. n.8 at pp. 378.

[25] See Pernice and Hoffmeister, op. cit. n.8 at p. 379 and Louis calling it necessary adaptation of the concrete clauses or Treaty revision, op. cit. n.8, at p. 62.

[26] See J.M. de Areilza, 'The Reform of Enhanced Co-operation Rules: Towards less flexibility?', in de Witte, Hanf and Vos, op. cit. n.8 at p. 33.

[27] J. Wouters and F. Naert, 'The European Union and 'September 11', *Working Paper No.4- -* January 2003, p. 1 Institute for International Law, K.U. Leuven, law.kuleuven.be/iir/eng/wp/WP40ed2e.pdf visited on 25 June 2005.

[28] R. Trzaskowski, 'National Report Poland', p. 77, in *Positions of 10 Central and Eastern European Countries on EU Institutional Reform*, Université Catholique de Louvain, (June 2003).

States, belonging not to the avantgarde circle but to the outer circle.[29] In general, new Member States see the general obligation of solidarity and coherence as being strained[30] or they are worried whether the principle of solidarity will be applied in an enlarged Union.[31].

As described above, the Constitutional Treaty includes further changes and amendments to the existing general enabling clause. While certain forms of flexibility are kept, the Constitutional Treaty tries to achieve more coherence and consistency by merging the Community pillar with the two intergovernmental pillars and creating a single legal personality for the European Union. But a major change in the time-consuming ratification process, which would have been consistent with international law,[32] could not be achieved.[33] External coherence might not necessarily result in internal coherence as differences will continue to prevail between the pillars in their respective structure, decision-making and instruments. And the door would open, after the ratification of the Constitutional Treaty by all twenty-five Member States, to voluntary withdrawal from the European Union. This is a new and ultimate form of flexibility; to leave the European Union and establish another framework for relations between former Members and current Members.[34] This presupposes that this Constitutional Treaty will be ratified by all EU Member States. In France, the United

---

29 R. Trzaskowski, 'From candidate to member state: Poland and the future of the EU', *Institute for Security Studies, Occasional Papers* no.37 September 2002, p. 19; P. Krotohvil, 'National Report Czech Republic', p. 34, *Positions of 10 Central and Eastern European Countries on EU Institutional Reform*, op. cit.; M. Apostol, 'National Report Romania', p. 90, in *Positions of 10 Central and Eastern European Countries on EU Institutional Reform*, op. cit. The Polish government saw the changes introduced by the Nice Treaty in a positive light because its openness would be secured and foresaw its active participation in an avantgarde group or centre of gravity, see R.Trzaskowski, 'From candidate to member state: Poland and the future of the EU', *Institute for Security Studies Occasional Papers*, p. 21.

30 So the Prime Minister of Romania Adrian Nastase, in a speech of 6 June 2002 at the European Policy Center, Brussels, Romania in the European Union and the Future of Europe, www.theepc.be; without taking a position, see the speech by the Slovenian representative D. Rupel, 'The Future of Europe – Debate', 3 July 2001, p. 9.

31 R. Martikonis, 'The case of Lithuania', p. 31, B. Hajos et al., 'The future of the European integration process: Ideas and concepts of candidate countries', *Discussion Paper C 107*, 2002 Centre for European Integration Studies, www.zei.de, p. 5. These concerns had already been raised by the Greek government against the Nice changes. P. Xuereb, The Future of Europe: Solidarity and Constitutionalism. Towards a Solidarity Model, *ELRev.* 2002, pp. 643.

32 See further on this: B. de Witte, 'Entry into Force and Revision', in: B. de Witte, ed., *Ten Reflections on the Constitutional Treaty for Europe,* Robert Schuman Centre for Advanced Studies (2003), www.iue.it .

33 Article IV-6 paragraph 4 foresees, once the Constitutional Treaty is constitutionally accepted by all Member States and that when the constitutional amendments have been ratified by four-fifth, the matter is referred to the European Council. This might be a possibility to put these individual country under political pressure.

34 Art. I-60 Constitutional Treaty .

Kingdom, Ireland, Luxembourg, Denmark, Spain, Portugal, Poland and the Netherlands referendums were scheduled and complicate the adoption of the new Constitutional Treaty. After the referendums in France and the Netherlands have failed in May and June 2005 and while ten Member States have already ratified the Constitutional Treaty, the European Council in June 2005 decided to put the ratification process for one year on hold.[35] These difficulties and disagreements might result in new forms of differentiated co-operation among willing Member States[36] outside the existing Treaties or the new Constitutional Treaty.[37]

3 Differentiation in Accession Treaties

Predetermined flexibility results from the accession treaties agreed between current and future members. Special regimes were negotiated in past enlargement processes with Denmark, the UK and Ireland in 1973, Greece in 1981, Spain and Portugal in 1986 and Sweden, Finland and Austria in 1995[38] and the fifth enlargement of 2004. Usually the differentiations are only temporary, especially when involving the core part of the Community *acquis*, but may also be of more permanent nature when involving marginal matters. Such differentiation or derogations among Member States can be generally divided into:

a) temporary derogations;
b) temporary provisions;
c) safeguard clauses and
d) transitional regimes.

They fall into two groups: one group of exemptions is motivated by technical, financial or practical reasons; the other is imposed for political reasons. Derogations form part of the modalities of accession and hold implications for primary and secondary law.[39]

---

35 Referenda on EU Constitution – let the people vote?, www.euractiv.com visited on 28 June 2005.

36 See for the different scenarios: L. Rossi, 'What if the Constitutional Treaty is not ratified?' www.euractiv.com visited on 6 July 2004.

37 The majority in the literature argues that despite a general enabling clause in the Treaties, co-operation among Member States under international law remain possible, see for instance: B. de Witte, Chameleonic Member States, pp. 238, in de Witte, Hanf and Vos, eds., op. cit n.8.; A. Hatje, in Schwarze, ed., op. cit. n.19.

38 The previous enlargement processes with Denmark, the UK and Ireland in 1973, Greece in 1981, Spain and Portugal in 1986 and Sweden, Finland and Austria in 1995; Czech Republic, Estonia, Cyprus, Latvia, Lithuania, Hungary, Malta, Poland, Slovenia and Slovakia, *OJ* 2003 L 236.

39 See examples in A.Lopian, *Übergangsregime für Mitgliedstaaten der Europäischen Gemeinschaften*, (Baden-Baden, Nomos, 1994).

General derogations, especially for the complex Common Agricultural Policy[40] and state aid have been applied from the first enlargement and will also be extended in the current accession treaty. Similarly, specific safeguard clauses to suspend rights and obligations under certain circumstances of economic difficulties have employed in previous enlargements in 1972, 1979 and 1985.[41] These safeguard clauses have been further refined in this accession treaty in extending pre-accession conditionality to the post-accession phase as Kirstyn Inglis describes in her contribution. A transitional period for the non-application of certain parts of the *acquis* was applied for the first time in respect of the southern enlargements for political reasons. Greek, Spanish and Portuguese workers only gained full access to the EC market after a transitional period of seven years,[42] which was later reduced to six years for Spanish and Portuguese workers.[43]

Due to the numbers of countries acceding at the same time and the efforts taken to prepare countries of former communist regimes to have working economic and political systems in line with western democracies and economies, substantial efforts of adjustments after accession must still be taken, which are highlighted by new forms of transitional regimes and safeguard clauses. The Accession Treaties of the current enlargement process include concrete conditions or modalities of admission to the European Union and are complemented by the Act of Accession. The Act of Accession divides into five parts with part one consisting of principles, part two including adjustments to the Treaties, part three permanent provisions, part four involving temporary provisions and part five containing the provisions relating to the implementation of the Act of Accession. The conditions are further specified in 18 Annexes, 10 Protocols, a substantial number of declarations by Member States and including joint declarations and declarations of the European Commission. From these provisions it becomes clear that the European Union ensures a strict post-accession monitoring system that creates a complicated web of differentiation between current and new Member States and new forms of potential application of specific institutional enabling clauses to deviate from the *acquis*.

3.1 Temporary derogations from the *acquis communautaire:* Schengen and EMU

The Schengen agreement has been considered a showcase for successful differentiation in the aim of furthering integration among Member States. It started off as an international agreement among Germany, France and the Benelux countries in 1985 (Schengen I) to gradually abolish checks

40 See on this Sandra Marco Colino, The impact of agriculture on the success of enlargement.

41 These safeguard clauses were modelled after the former Art. 226 EC.

42 Article 56 of the Act of Accession of Spain.

43 *OJ* 1991, L 206/1.

on persons at common borders. A Schengen Implementing Convention was unveiled in 1990 (Schengen II).[44] Most Member States signed both but the UK resisted any commitment to lift internal border controls and Ireland followed due to its Common Travel Area established with the UK. Similarly, Denmark did not participate because of the Nordic Travel Area. Later, in 1996, Denmark acceded to Schengen but objected to the introduction of Justice and Home Affairs into the institutional and legal framework of the Treaties.[45] With the Treaty of Maastricht, a third pillar for intergovernmental co-operation in Justice and Home Affairs was established but without practical consequences for closer co-operation as Article K.7 EU legitimised the existing forms of intergovernmental co-operation.[46] Following the changes introduced by the Amsterdam Treaty, the Schengen members decided to incorporate the Schengen *acquis* into the EU legal system. The protocol that integrates the Schengen *acquis* clarifies the different special status of Denmark, Ireland and the UK. Article 1 of the Protocol, integrating the Schengen *acquis* into the framework of the European Union specifies this as closer co-operation. Article 3 described the special status of Denmark as having rights and obligations in regard to the Schengen *acquis*. Denmark is bound by the Schengen *acquis* but the integration has no Community legal force and the further implementation of the Schengen *acquis* is built on international law. This has to be seen in contrast to Article 4, which applies to Ireland and the UK and enables them to opt in to some or all provisions of the Schengen *acquis* as happened in practice.[47] Furthermore, Article 6 stipulates that the Republic of Iceland and the Kingdom of Norway shall be associated with the implementation of the Schengen *acquis* and its further development on the basis of the Agreement signed in Luxembourg on 19 December 1996.[48] There-

---

44 E.Denza, *The Intergovernmental Pillars of the European Union* (Oxford, Oxford University Press, 2002), pp. 66.

45 See on this and especially the, in the Danish view, problematic so-called passarelle clause in Art.K.9 of the EU Treaty, K.U. Kjaer, 'How many borders in the EU?', pp. 169 (at p. 177) in: K.Groenendijk, E.Guild and P. Minderhoud, eds., *In Search of Europe's borders* (The Hague, Kluwer Law International, 2003).

46 G. Papagianni, 'Flexibility in Justice and Home Affairs an Old Phenomenon taking new forms', p. 104, in de Witte et al., op. cit.n.8.

47 Council decision of 29 May 2000 concerning the request of the UK of Great Britain and Northern Ireland to take part in some of the provisions of the Schengen *acquis*, *OJ* 2000 L 131/43; Council Decision of 28 February 2002 concerning Ireland's request to take part in some of the provisions of the Schengen *acquis*, *OJ* 2002 L 64/20.

48 Den Boer and Kerchove have identified five different configurations of countries: a. The EU members which committed themselves to create an area of freedom, security and justice minus UK, Ireland and Denmark, b. 13 EU Member States that have signed the Schengen Agreement, c the same 13 Member States plus the two associated members Iceland and Norway who together with the UK and Ireland form the so-called Mixed Committee, d. the 13 Schengen EU Member States together with the partial participants (UK and Ireland) who have requested an opt-in in respect to certain elements of the Schengen

fore, the current complex situation differentiates between the Schengen members excluding Ireland and the UK who can opt in under European law, while Denmark, Norway, Iceland, Switzerland and Liechtenstein are Schengen states but apply the Schengen system and build on the Schengen *acquis* according to international law.[49]

Under these circumstances, it was the intention of the Union not to have another special regime applying to the new Member States. They are obliged to integrate the Schengen *acquis* from the date of accession. The Act of Accession in its Article 3 stipulates that the new Member States are bound but only part of this *acquis* will apply immediately. However, it divides into directly binding Schengen *acquis* and other provisions of the Schengen *acquis* that only apply in a new Member State depending on a Council decision verifying whether the necessary conditions for the application of all parts of the *acquis* concerned have been met in that new Member State.[50] Due to the opt-in of Ireland and the United Kingdom to certain parts of the Schengen *acquis*, they will participate in the decision only as far as it relates to acts in which they participate. To aid the new Member States to fully comply with the *acquis* in this area, extra funding is secured by the European Union. Article 34 sets up a fund for transitional issues such as JHA matters and by Article 35 Act of Accession a 'Schengen facility' is established which provides funding of external border controls with an amount of € 300 million per year. In consequence, with accession the different forms of application in the European Union prevail and differences between the full application under EU law (twelve Member States), the optional opt-in (UK and Ireland) for certain matters, application under international law (Denmark,

---

acquis and e. the acceding countries which have to implement the Schengen *acquis*, on whom, however, according to Art.3 of the Act of Accession only parts of the *acquis* will immediately apply after accession. See M. den Boer and G. de Kerchove, 'Schengen *Acquis* and Enlargement', pp. 315 in, V. Kronenberger, *The European Union and the International Legal Order: Discord or Harmony?*, (The Hague, TMC Asser Press, 2001).

49 On Norway, Iceland and Switzerland: Agreement concluded by the Council of the European Union and the Republic of Iceland and the Kingdom of Norway concerning the latters' association with the implementation, application and development of the Schengen *acquis* - Final Act, *OJ* 1999 L 176/35 and Council Decision of 25 October 2004 on the signing, on behalf of the European Community, and on the provisional application of certain provisions of the Agreement between the European Union, the European Community and the Swiss Confederation, concerning the Swiss Confederation's association with the implementation, application and development of the Schengen *acquis*, *OJ* 2004 L 370/78.

50 According to Annex I, directly applicable *acquis* parts include external border controls, illegal immigration, criminal law cooperation, aspects of police cooperation, drugs, firearms and data protection, while the abolition of internal borders, visa policy, freedom to travel, the core of police cooperation and SIS only apply when the Council takes a positive decision. See further S. Peers, The EU Accession Treaty, Statewatch analysis of the EU Accession Treaty.

Norway, Liechtenstein, Iceland and Switzerland) and the partial non-application under EU law and the accession treaty for the new Member States can be made in such a way that these countries fully implement the Schengen *acquis* but cannot fully participate in the Schengen system and lift internal borders.[51] The consequences of this partial application of the Schengen regime for the new Member States is further discussed by Przemyslaw Zysk in his contribution on '*European counter-Terrorism and enlargement*'.

Another example for a co-operation established originally outside the EEC Treaty and which is further discussed in the contribution by Beata Dziechciarz is the co-operation and co-ordination of economic policies. Initially the plan to establish an Economic Monetary Union failed in the Nineteen-seventies.[52] it was taken up again with the Maastricht Treaty to complete the Economic and Monetary Union in which eleven Member States participated in since 1 January 1999, with the late comer, Greece, on 1 January 2001, and with a special and specific status of United Kingdom and Denmark of non-participation in the third stage.[53] While Denmark has been excluded since 1992,[54] the UK has the option to opt-out of stage three of EMU in the absence of a positive decision of the government and Parliament.[55] In Sweden, since 1999 the government has lacked the necessary support to advocate the participation in EMU and Sweden is not willing to participate in the Exchange Rate Mechanism.[56] The new Member States have accepted, under the Copenhagen criteria, the obligation to join once they fulfil the necessary preconditions. Until then they are Member States with derogations according to Article 122 EC in conjunction with Article 4 Act of Accession.

3.2 Temporary derogations from the internal market *acquis:* the example of the movement of workers

An extensive differentiation in legal regimes applying to workers results from the derogations found in the Accession Treaty for workers between the fifteen receiving Member States ('the Fifteen') and the eight new

---

[51] This depends on a fully functioning Schengen Information System which enables authorities to consult personal data.

[52] F. Amtenbrink, 'Economic and Monetary Policy (in the framework of the EMU)', in Ott and Inglis, op. cit. n.3.

[53] The Danish population decided against introduction of the Euro by referendum in September 2000.

[54] These special conditions are laid in Protocol 12 on certain provisions relating to Denmark.

[55] Protocol No.11 on certain provisions relating to the UK and Northern Ireland. In October 1997 the UK informed the Council that it did not intend to move to the third stage. See K.P. E. Lasok , *Law & Institutions of the European Union* 7th edn. (London, Butterworths, 2001), p. 585.

[56] This was confirmed by the negative outcome of a referendum in September 2003, 'Bigger than expected Swedish 'no' throws doubts on future of the euro', www.euractiv.com visited on 15 September 2003.

CEEC Member States, excluding Cyprus and Malta.[57] The applicable temporary provisions are listed in the respective annexes and are applied individually to the new Member States. Article 24 stipulates the temporary provisions in connection with individual country annexes V to XIV.[58]

Article 24 Act of Accession in connection with, for instance, the Poland Annex XII of the Act of Accession stipulates that in the field of free movement of persons: 'Article 39 EC and the first paragraph of Article 49 EC shall only fully apply in relation to the freedom of movement of workers and the freedom to provide services involving temporary movement as defined in Article 1 of Directive 96/71/EC (therefore posted workers do not fall under the scope of the transitional arrangements)'.[59] Instead, the Fifteen Member States apply national measures or those resulting from bilateral agreements, regulating the access to their labour markets for a two year period. Furthermore, Polish nationals legally working in a present Member State at the date of accession and admitted to the labour market of that Member State for an uninterrupted period of 12 months or longer will enjoy access to the labour market of that Member State.[60] The family members of a worker only have access to the labour market as far as the worker is legally admitted to the labour market for a period of at least 12 months or when the workers arrives after accession, only after eighteen months of residence. Austria and Germany have secured specific flanking measures to address serious disturbances in certain specified sectors such as construction, industrial cleaning and interior decorators of their labour markets.

The Council will review the situation on the basis of a report submitted by the European Commission on the functioning of the transitional provisions, and then the present Member States must notify the Commission as to whether they intend to continue applying national measures or measures resulting from bilateral agreements or whether they apply the Community *acquis*.

---

57 Malta and Cyprus due to their size and economic situation were excluded from these transitional derogations.

58 Article 40 of the Act of Accession clarifies for the application of the transitional periods set in Annexes V to XIV that the new Member States' national rules imposed during the transitional period shall not lead to border controls between Member States and therefore hamper the proper functioning of the internal market. See the identical wording in Article 153 Act of Accession for Austria, Finland and Sweden: *OJ* 1994 C 241/9-404. Inglis calls this specified transitional arrangements for the new Member States which provide for technical adaptations to various laws, see K. Inglis, The Accession Treaties and transitional arrangements: A twilight zone for the new Member States in C.Hillion, ed., *EU Enlargement: A Legal Approach*, (Oxford, Hart Publishing 2004).

59 This is reflecting the previous case law on the Accession Treaty with Portugal and Spain: ECJ Case C-113/89 *Rush Portuguesa Ldt.* v. *Office national d'immigration* [1990] *ECR* I-1417.

60 This is again which has been clarified by the Court in the previous enlargement, even though now a one year minimum legal employment has to be proofed. ECJ, *Mário Lopes da Veiga* v. *Staatssecretaris van Justitie* [1989] *ECR* 2989.

A further extension is given to the Member States according to paragraph 5 in the form of a special safeguard clause: in the case of serious disturbances of their labour market or of a threat thereof, and after notifying the Commission, it can continue to apply these measures until the end of the seven year period following the date of accession. In a most extreme situation, the *acquis* in this field would not apply until 2011. A two year period applies automatically with these national measures (para.2) and three more years (until 2009) will be added to this provided the (Fifteen) Member States notify the Commission that they will continue applying national measures (para.5), upon proof of serious disturbances on the labour market or the threat thereof the Commission may grant another two-year-extension until 2011.[61]

While at the moment of signing the Accession Treaty in April 2003 some of the Member States promised to grant CEEC nationals full access to their labour markets from accession, one year later, twelve of the Fifteen, except Ireland, Sweden and the United Kingdom, have announced that they extend national measures or impose restrictions beyond the date of accession.[62] The nature of the national measures varies from country to country, from access to the labour market (Sweden,[63] Ireland and the UK)[64], to transitional measures of different nature and length in the other 12 Member States.[65] In a Joint Declaration by all the Member States annexed to the Accession Treaty, the Fifteen stress the strong elements of differentiation and flexibility in this particular arrangement.[66] These elements, however, also result in complexity and legal uncertainties.[67]

---

[61] List referred to in Article 24: Czech Republic, Freedom of Movement of Persons Points 3 and 5.

[62] See Workers from the new EU face benefit ban, 18.2.2004; Czech leaders criticise Dutch for closing off labour market, www.euobserver.com visited on 17 February 2004. See also Summary of Transitional Arrangements by County, 29 April 2004, *European Citizen Action Service – Press Release Annex.*

[63] The Swedish parliament turned down at the last moment restrictive measures which were announced previously by the government, 'Sweden opens its doors to new EU workers', www.euobserver.com visited on 28 April 2004.

[64] See 'Row in Ireland over immediate freedom of movement', www.euobserver.com visited on 4 July 2002; 'UK will not close its borders', www.euobserver.com visited on 9 February 2004.

[65] See on a summary of transitional arrangements by country, 29.4.2004, European Citizens Action Service – Press Release Annex.

[66] So for instance for Poland: 'The EU stresses the strong elements of differentiation and flexibility in the arrangement for the free movement of workers. Member States shall endeavour to grant increased labour market access to Polish nationals under national law, with a view to speeding up the approximation to the *acquis*. As a consequence, the employment opportunities in the EU for Polish nationals should improve substantially upon Poland's accession. Moreover, the EU Member States will make best use of the proposed arrangement to move as quickly as possible to the full application of the *acquis* in the area of free movement of workers.'

[67] On this: K. Inglis, 'Treading the tightrope between flexibility and legal certainty: The temporary derogations from the *acquis* on the freedom of movement of workers and safeguard measures under the Accession Treaty', *Conference Paper* 2004.

The current restrictions have to be seen in the light of the provisions spelt out in the Accession Treaty such as a standstill clause and Community preference principle and in light of the limits set by European law in the form of a general non-discrimination for EU citizens. Five problem areas arise. One legal problem concerns the interpretation of market access in relation to the non-discrimination principle of EU citizens. Secondly, the status of family dependants in light of the standstill clause and Community preference and in comparison with the rights deriving from the Europe Agreements is problematic. Third, the rights of EU citizens in comparison with rights of citizens from the EEA countries and Switzerland need to be analysed. Fourth, the special situation of Cyprus and its citizens under the accession treaty deserves attention which will be addressed by Nikolaos Skoutaris in his contribution 'Differentiation in European Union citizenship law – the Cyprus problem' in this volume.

National measures restrict the access to the labour market of the Fifteen which results in the restriction of the comprehensive rights of job-seekers under Article 39 EC to seek work, change their job and reside in another Member State. Despite these restrictions, the new Member States citizens are full EU citizens with all the rights of Articles 12 and 18 EC and are not restricted by the transitional arrangements found in the Accession Treaty and its annexes. The ECJ has given these rights a broad interpretation within its jurisdiction, a right to non-discrimination and residence are included and can only be restricted by legitimate, proportional and non-discriminatory measures.[68]

In practice, this could lead to difficult borderline cases. The British government decided to open its job market and therefore not to impose national measures. However, it obliges workers from the eight CEEC Member States to register with the Home Office and restricts their social benefits. Only those registered and working in the UK for at least 12 months are entitled to job-related benefits.[69] Due to the Common Travel Area, Ireland decided also to amend its social welfare legislation at the beginning of 2004 and requires that individuals have to be habitually resident for two years before being entitled to social benefits.[70] These changes are disputable in two respects; the standstill clause and the non-discrimination right of EU citizens. The standstill clause, contained in paragraph 14 of the individual CEEC country annexes to the Accession Treaty guarantees that national measures applied by the Fifteen shall not be more restrictive than those prevailing on the date of signature of the Treaty of

---

[68] See further: ECJ, Case C-184/99 *Grzelcyk* [2001] *ECR* I-6193; ECJ, Case C-413/99 *Baumbast* [2002] *ECR* I-7091; M.Dougan, 'A Spectre is Haunting Europe.... Free Movement of Persons and the Eastern Enlargement', in Hillion, ed., op. cit. n.58, pp. 114.

[69] The Social Security (Habitual Residence) Amendment Regulation 2004, Note from the Social Advisory Committee, www.ssac.org.uk visited on 23 March 2004.

[70] Social Welfare (Miscellaneous Provisions) Act 2004.

Accession in April 2003. In addition, Member States are allowed to deviate from Article 39 EC in regard to access to the labour market and from Articles 1 to 6 Regulation 1618/68 (excluding the remainder of the Articles, including Art. 7 of this Regulation which regulates the non-discrimination of workers in regard to social benefits). According to Article 12 EC, citizens of CEEC Member States have a right to non-discrimination, and Article 7 of the Regulation 1618/68 emphasises this for workers and work-related benefits. These rights of EU citizens are also not restricted by the Accession Treaty. Member States can require from EU citizens, independent of their worker' status that they have sufficient financial resources but that they are not allowed to discriminate directly or indirectly between EU citizens as concerns their social and tax benefits relating to their employment.

These derogations are all the more dubious when compared to the legal status of third-country nationals. For instance, it is not clear which consequences the standstill clause in combination with Community preference (para.14 of the country annexes) has with regard to family members of the worker from the new CEEC Member States. By comparison the regime that applied under the Europe Agreements, a stricter exception is included in the second paragraph of the CEEC country annexes to the Accession Treaty, so that CEEC nationals legally working in an existing Member State have access to the labour market of that Member State provided this individual was admitted to the labour market on the date of accession for an uninterrupted period of twelve months and was legally working there. Their family dependants have, according to paragraph 8, different rights depending on whether they were already residing with the worker in Fifteen Member States concerned on the date of accession. However, when they entered this Member State after accession, they only have access to the labour market once they have been resident for eighteen months. Under the Europe Agreements, the relevant provisions on movement of workers and freedom of establishment have been interpreted in the case law of the ECJ in such a way as to include a directly effective right, giving a corollary right of entry and residency once the individual has become legally established or resident in one of the Member States.[71]

According to Article 37 of the Europe Agreement Poland, family members have access to the labour market when they are legally resident. This differentiation might run counter to paragraph 14 of the country annexes to the Accession Treaty, which includes the mentioned standstill clause and a Community preference. It guarantees no worse conditions after accession and CEEC workers from the new Member States get preference over third-country nationals. However, it is not obvious how the Accession Treaty relates to the previously

---

[71] See for establishment: ECJ, Case C-63/99 *Gloszczuk* [2001] *ECR* I-6369; ECJ, Case C-235/99 *Kondova* [2001] *ECR* I-6427, on workers: ECJ, Case C-162/00 *Pokrzeptowicz-Meyer* [2002] *ECR* I-1049; ECJ, Case *Deutscher Handballbund* v. *Kolpak* [2003] *ECR* I-4135.

applicable Europe Agreements. Moreover, two Europe Agreements remain in force – those with the candidate countries Bulgaria and Romania. The standstill clause applies to national measures but it remains disputable as to how it relates to the status achieved under Community law which includes association agreements concluded by the European Union and its Member States. A direct reference to the Europe Agreement is missing which might restrict the application of the standstill clause only to national measures and therefore the previous association status is irrelevant for judging the previous legal condition of family members.[72] Despite this and in an overall judgment, it can be considered problematic when the CEEC workers receive a better treatment than nationals from Bulgaria and Romania but their family members are treated worse after accession.

Another discriminatory differentiation can be seen when comparing the legal status of workers from the EEA and Switzerland with the CEEC citizens. Icelandic, Liechtenstein, Norwegian and Swiss citizens, while not being EU citizens but EEA and EFTA nationals, will enjoy better labour market access for the upcoming years and consequently, better treatment than EU citizens from new Member States including Bulgaria and Romania when they join (which is envisaged for 2007). The EEA Agreement extends the four freedoms to EEA citizens. With enlargement, this agreement has been extended with the EEA Enlargement Agreement. However, in favour of the EEA countries, the transitional arrangement and safeguard measures will also apply. According to Article 3 of the EEA Enlargement Agreement, the Act of Accession is incorporated into the EEA Agreement.[73] As concerns the Swiss-EU relations and due to the non-participation of Switzerland in the EEA, bilateral relations between the EU and Switzerland have, since 1999, been based on seven sectoral agreements. One of the Swiss Sectoral Agreements which came into force in 2002 concerns the free movement of persons of Swiss and EU citizens.[74] Unlike the EEA Agreement, the *acquis* is not automatically extended but the Swiss labour market will open gradually over twelve years, after seven years of which the Swiss will hold a referendum to ask their population whether to continue with this sectoral agreement for an indefinite time period. From its entry into force, EU citizens lawfully resident in Switzerland have a right to nondiscriminatory treatment (Article 2 of the sectoral agreement), after two years the priority given to Swiss nationals

72 See for the argument that these principles apply to the Europe Agreement: P. Tschäpe, Die *Übergangsbestimmungen zur Arbeitnehmerfreizügigkeit und zum Grundstücksverkehr im Rahmen der Osterweiterung* (Baden-Baden, Nomos, 2004); doubting: K.Inglis, Treading the tightrope between flexibility and legal certainty. The temporary derogations from the *acquis* on the free movement of workers and safeguard measures under the Accession Treaty, *Conference paper* 2004.

73 See the agreement on http://secretariat.efta.int.

74 See S. Breitenmoser, 'Sectoral Agreements between the EC and Switzerland: Content and Context', *CMLRev* 2003, p. 1137.

will be abolished and after five years the quota for Community workers shall be abolished. Thus, it will take 12 years to accomplish complete free movement.[75]

In the first half of 2004, the EU negotiated with Switzerland to extend this agreement to the incoming Member States. While the EU insisted at the beginning of the negotiations on the same treatment of current and incoming EU citizens by the Swiss government, Switzerland used to its favour the fact that the Fifteen proposed to maintain national measures, as it could mean that Switzerland would have opened its labour market earlier than the Fifteen. Switzerland and the EU have agreed that Switzerland may keep a seven year transitional year period until 30 April 2011, together with a quota system, and they are able to differentiate between Fifteen Member States citizens who will get full access to the Swiss labour market by 2007, while EU citizens from the CEECs will be restricted until 2011.[76] Independently of this obvious discrimination between EU citizens externally,[77] legal uncertainties arise from the question of whether this agreement and arrangement will provisionally apply as of 1 May 2004 or only from the moment it takes effect following the anticipated Swiss referendum.[78]

4 Differentiation in a common constitutional system

The accession treaties, with their derogations from the *acquis* for political, economic and legal reasons, introduce new forms of differentiation between current and incoming Member States and this differentiating regime is also extended to countries closely associated to the EU such as Switzerland and the EEA. They create two different groups of Member States for parts of the internal market *acquis* at least for two years after accession, and for other forms of predetermined flexibility in forms of opt-outs on parts of the Schengen and *acquis* and the participation of the EMU for an indefinite time. In addition, the Amsterdam and Nice Treaties, introduced a new form of institutional enabling clause to differentiate among Member States (so-called enhanced co-operation, Art. 11 EC Treaty with Arts. 40 to 45 EU). A European Union of 25 or 30 members is more diverse due to sheer numbers and dynamics initiated by Commu-

75 In case of serious economic of social difficulties, a Joint Committee shall examine appropriate measures to remedy the situation, see Art.14 para.2 Swiss Sectoral Agreement.

76 In addition, a general safeguard clause until 2014 is applicable. Further: Neuerungen beim freien Personenverkehr Schweiz – EU ab 1.Juni 2004, Medienmitteilung Staatssekretariat für Wirtschaft.

77 It is highly doubtful whether this form of 'external' discrimination is at all relevant for EC law. See further: A.Ott, 'Grundfreiheiten', in F.Merli and S.Huster, eds., *Systematische Erläuterung zum Vertrag über den Beitritt der MOE-Staaten, Zyperns und Maltas zur Europäischen Union*, (Berliner Wissenschafts-verlag, 2005).

78 This is expected in mid-2005.

nity and Union policy with the Treaty changes of Maastricht, Amsterdam and Nice. Consecutively, acknowledging more diversity among Member States, the current Members and the Commission have emphasized a minimum standard of consistent and efficient application of the *acquis communautaire* on which the special legal order, the constitutional legal order of the European Union, is built.

Therefore the Member States make use of flexible tools such as transitional arrangements, safeguard clauses and predetermined flexibility which find their limits, in the case of the Accession Treaty, in general principles of EU citizenship and non-discrimination together with the standstill clause included in the annexes of the Accession Treaty. In addition, the case law on EU citizenship has progressed[79] and new changes are expected with a new Directive on Free Movement[80] and perhaps also with the Constitutional Treaty with a binding human rights charter. This flexibility results in legal complexity and uncertainties in interpretation which threaten the uniform application of EU law by the courts and test the limits for such developments in the EU legal order.

The scope and definition of a minimum standard, consisting of the constitutional and fundamental principles of EC and EU law, vary but include at least the elements of democracy, the rule of law, the principle of supremacy, direct effect of EC law, the protection of human rights and sincere co-operation among Member States. These principles also include obligations towards the EU citizen such as democracy, the protection of human rights and non-discrimination. Among Member States and governing their relations, the principles of coherence and unity of EU law,[81] the rule of law and democracy,[82] equality and solidarity[83] among Member States need to be mentioned. Leading commentators are divided as to whether these fundamental principles restrict changes introduced by an accession treaty. Neither Treaty nor the ECJ clarify what legal status fundamental constitutional principles acquire in the constitutional legal order of the EU.[84] Some commentators believe these fundamental constitutional principles influence the interpretation of primary law but yet more hold the view

---

79 On the case law: ECJ, Case C-184/99 *Grzelczyk* [2001] *ECR* I-6193: ECJ, Case C-413/99 *Baumbast and R* [2002] *ECR* I-7091.

80 Directive 2004/38/EC *OJ* 2004 L 229/35 to come into force on 1 May 2006.

81 A.Hatje, 'Europäische Rechtseinheit durch einheitliche Rechtsdurchsetzung', pp. 7 and U.Becker, 'Differenzierungen der Rechtseinheit durch „abgestufte Integration', pp. 29, both in: J.Schwarze and P-C. Müller-Graff, eds., Europäische Rechtseinheit durch einheitliche Rechtsdurchsetzung, *EuR* Beiheft 1/1998.

82 See for instance: ECJ, Case 294/83 *Les Verts* [1986] *ECR* 1339.

83 On the principle of equality: J. Wouters, 'Constitutional Limits of Differentiation: the Principle of Equality', pp. 301, in de Witte, Hanf and Vos, op. cit. n.8.

84 See: A.Ott, 'Fundamental and Basic Principles of the EC and the EU', p. 15 in Ott and Inglis, op. cit ..3.

that certain supra-constitutional principles exist that cannot be altered by an accession treaty.[85]

This latter view is supported by several arguments.[86] First it becomes obvious from the Treaty provisions that the differentiation between Treaty amendment according to Article 48 EU and accession according to Article 49 EU has to be made, changes to the Treaties which go beyond mere adjustments need to follow the amendment procedure.[87] This is underlined by the case law of the ECJ on accession treaties.[88] And the idea of minimum principles which remain out of reach of change within a constitutional system such as the European Union, are reflected in national constitutions, like the German one and the Maastricht decision by the German *Bundesverfassungsgericht*.[89]

According to the eternity clause of the German constitution, the German constitution can only be amended under certain circumstances but with the exclusion of the basic principles laid down in Articles 1 and 20 of the German Constitution; the dignity of man, basic human rights and Germany as a social, federal and democratic state bound by the rule of law.[90] In this Maastricht deci-

---

85 On supraconstitutional principles: F. Snyder, *General Course on Constitutional Law of the European Union*, Academy of European Law, ed. Volume VI, Book I, 1998, pp. 76; J.L. Cruz Vilaca and N.Picarra, Y a-t-il des limites matérielles a la révision des traits instituant les CE?, *CDE* 1993, p. 29; J.Wouters, Constitutional Limits of Differentiation: the Principle of Equality, p. 326, in de Witte, Hanf and Vos, op. cit. n.8.

86 In the literature also the EEA Opinion is seen as an indication for this view: ECJ, *EEA* Opinion 1/91, [1991] *ECR* 6084.

87 See also U. Becker, 'EU enlargement and limits of amendments of the EC Treaty', Jean Monnet Working Paper 15/2001, p. 9; *P. Tschäpe*, op. cit. n. 72, 106, 129, G. Nicolaysen, *Europarecht I* (Nomos, Baden-Baden,2nd edn., 2002); contra: B. de Witte, 'Rules of Change in International Law: How special is the European Community?', *NYIL* 1994, p. 321; B. de Witte, The Semi/Permanent Treaty Revision Process, p. 51, in P. Beaumont, C. Lyons and N. Walker, eds., *Convergence and Divergence in European Public Law* (Oxford, Hart Publishing, 2002); M. Pechstein and C. Koenig, *Die Europäische Union*, (Tübingen, Mohr, 2nd. edn, 1998), pp. 251-252.

88 See: ECJ, Case 185/73 *Hauptzollamt Bielefeld* v. *OHG König* [1974] *ECR*, 607: 'No Provision in the Treaty of Accession or in the Act accompanying can be construed as validating measures, whatever their form, which are incompatible with the Treaties establishing the Communities.'

89 Maastricht judgment: BVerfGE 89, 155, *CMLRev.*1994, p. 57.

90 Article 79 (Amendment of the Basic Law; amended March 27, 1954). (1) The Basic law can be amended only by a law which expressly amends or supplements the text thereof. With respect to international treaties the subject of which is a peace settlement, the preparation of a peace settlement or the abolition of an occupation regime, or which are designed to serve the defense of the Federal Republic, it shall be sufficient, for the purpose of a clarifying interpretation to the effect that the provisions of the Basic Law are not contrary to the conclusion and entry into force of such treaties, to effect a supplementation of the Basic Law confined to this clarifying interpretation.

sion, the German judges emphasized, on the one hand, the role of the Member States as master of the Treaties but also that minimum standards of democracy and human rights standards from the perspective of the German Constitutional Court are inviolable.[91] Such a view has to be treated with caution not only at the German level but also at the European level with its own constitutional legal order. More difficult than establishing the existence of supraconstitutional principles exist is to define their precise content to establish infringements. Apart from the rule of law, all of these principles are closely connected with the principle of sincere co-operation enshrined in Article 10 EC and are closely linked.

4.1 EU fundamental principles in relations among Member States

The obligation of coherence among Member States is explicitly mentioned in Article 1 EU. Coherence or consistency, as a guiding criteria for the Union's measures, is mentioned in detail in Article 3 EU and Article 11 paragraph 2 for the CFSP.[92] Some authors have stressed a principle of unity of law (Rechtseinheit) which can be defined by the unified or consistent application of European Union law.[93] This is a general principle that is not explicitly defined or named in the Treaties but shines out through Article 2 EU ('maintaining in full the *acquis communautaire*') and is primarily an overarching principle of the judicial system of the EU. Even though Article 220 EC mentions only the interpretation and application of the Treaty, the uniform application of EU law becomes evident from the interpretation of the European Union as a special legal order and from the function of the supervision through the preliminary ruling system (Art. 234 EC). However, referring to the substantial list of various forms of differentiation applied among Member States and listed above, substantial limits apply to the unity or uniform application of EU law, sanctioned by primary law and the Accession Treaties.

The principle of solidarity derives from the Treaty's wording; the Union's 'task shall be to organised, in a manner demonstrating consistency and solidarity, relations between the Member States and between their peoples' (according

(2) Such a law requires the affirmative vote of two thirds of the members of the Bundestag and two-thirds of the votes of the Bundesrat. (3) An amendment of this Basic Law affecting the division of the Federation into Länder, the participation in principle of the Länder in legislation, or the basic principles laid down in Articles 1 and 20, is inadmissible.

91 The judgment resulted in constitutional changes with the changed Article 23 which renders Article 79 II and III applicable on the delegation of sovereign powers on the European Union.

92 Other authors seem to use instead the term unity of law: U. Becker 2001, op. cit. n.87.

93 On this especially: T.Oppermann, Die Dritte Gewalt in der Europäischen Union, *Deutsche Verwaltungsblatt* 1994, p. 901; and further: A.Hatje, 'Europäische Rechtseinheit durch einheitliche Rechtsdurchsetzung', op. cit. n.81, at pp. 7; U.Becker, op. cit. n.81.

to Art.1 subparagraph 3 EU)[94] and also finds its basis as an obligation among Member States (Art.10 EC).[95] Article 10 spells out the principle of co-operation that applies between the Community's institutions, between the Community and the Member States and between the Member States and the Community (sincere co-operation). The court spelled out in its case law that Article 10 EC imposes mutual duties of genuine co-operation and assistance.[96] Furthermore, this principle finds its special expression in the inclusion of cohesion in the Articles 158 to 162 EC and is generally reflected in Article 2 EC.[97] Even though there are clear manifestations of this obligation, a clear definition as to what it entails and how far it reaches is more difficult to extract and has not as yet been specified by the Treaties or the Court.[98]

Solidarity can be separated into solidarity among Member States and Member States towards their citizens and vice versa. However, in certain policy areas such a distinction cannot be made. Such distinction cannot be drawn in the policy goals of consumer, environment, health and social policies.[99] Specific references to solidarity can also be found in the provisions on structural funding and economic and social cohesion of Articles 158 to 162 EC, where the reduction of disparities in economic and social development is the policy aim.[100] There have been few judgments of relevance to interpreting solidarity in recent years. In comparison to subsidiarity, Community solidarity has kept a low profile.[101] However, both concepts have in common the fact that their definition remains difficult but also that they restrict one another.[102] In the 1970s the ECJ stated that, in permitting Member States to profit from the advantages of the Community, the Treaty also imposes on them the obligation to respect its rules. For a

94 C.Calliess, Art.1, C. Calliess and M. Ruffert, eds., *EU-Vertrag* (Neuwied, Luchterhand 1999), para.48, C. Stumpf, Art. 1 EUV, para.46, Schwarze, ed., op. cit. n. 19.

95 This has been confirmed by the jurisdiction of the court as early as 1973: ECJ, Case 49/72 *Commission* v. *Italy* [1973] *ECR* 101; ECJ Joined cases 6 and 11/69 *Commission* v. *France* [1969] *ECR* 523.

96 ECJ, Case 44/84 *Hurd* v. *Jones* [1986] *ECR* 29, especially in regard to solidarity: ECJ, Joined cases C-63/90 and C-67/90 *Portugal and Spain* v. Council [1992] *ECR* I-5073.

97 See further. C. Calliess, Art.1 EU-Vertrag, paras 44 to 49, C. Calliess and M. Ruffert, eds., *Kommentar zum EU-Vertrag und EG-Vertrag* (Neuwied, Luchterhand, 1999).

98 Stumpf, Artikel 1 EUV, para.47, in Schwarze, op. cit.n.19.

99 Stumpf, Artikel 1 EUV, in Schwarze, op. cit. n.19.

100 This includes the fair financial transfer among Member States: see For the European Union, Peace, Freedom and Solidarity, Communication of the Commission on the institutional Architecture, COM (2002) 728 final, p. 14.

101 See: E. A. Marias, 'Solidarity as an Objective of the European Union and the European Community', *LIEI* (1994/2), pp. 85 (at p. 85) and especially it becomes manifest when looking at the British EU law literature and the lack of consideration of solidarity.

102 Calliess, Art.1 EUV para.49, in Calliess and Ruffert, op. cit n.97; C.Calliess, *Subsidiaritätsprinzip und Solidaritätsprinzip in der Europäischen Union* (Baden-Baden, Nomos, 1996).

state unilaterally to break or to profit from, according to its own conception of national interest, the equilibrium between advantages and obligations flowing from its adherence to the Community would bring into question the equality of Member States.[103]

The judges clarified that a failure in the duty of solidarity accepted by Member States strikes at the fundamental basis of the Community legal order. The diversity of 'solidarities' also becomes clear when analysing the Constitutional Treaty. Article I-2 of the Constitutional Treaty clarifies that the Member States' values include a society of pluralism and, *inter alia*, solidarity. In Article I-5 of the Constitutional Treaty (the current Art. 10 EC) solidarity is mentioned as a principle of loyal co-operation. The novelty of a solidarity clause in Article I-42 of the Constitutional Treaty applies if a Member State has fallen victim to a terrorist attack or a natural or man-made disaster. This gives the impression that essential aspects of solidarity found in the current EU and EC Treaty would be even less prominent and clearly drafted under the new Constitutional Treaty. Even though solidarity as a concept remains fuzzy at its edges, it underpins the constitutional structure of the European Union which is not built on power politics but on equal treatment of Member States ensuring the support for a weaker Member State by regional policies and structural funding, and the achievement of common policies and goals in spite of the size and strength of the respective Member State. Therefore, it is clear that the principle of solidarity is closely connected with the equality of Member States, and finds its main manifestation in Article 10 EC.

The principle of equal treatment or non-discrimination is mainly used in the relationship between the individual and the EU but is as a separate notion relevant in the relations among Member States. Again, the legal point of reference is the principle of sincere co-operation stipulated in Article 10 EC. However, one has to keep in mind that this principle has a clearer image. A general principle of equality of states and therefore Member States, derives already from international law.[104] This equality of sovereign states is one of the major principles of international law and is reflected in the way the accession negotiations were conducted. The Member States were parties to the accession negotiations, deciding by unanimity in the bilateral intergovernmental 'Conference for accession to the European Union' between the Fifteen and the candidate countries individually and the Accession Treaty has been signed by each Member State and each acceding country.[105] The ECJ has interpreted this principle in connec-

[103] ECJ Case 39-72 *Commission* v. *Italy* [1973] *ECR* 101; ECJ, Case 128/78 *Commission* v. *UK and Northern Ireland*, [1979] *ECR* 419 (para.12).

[104] See for instance, J. Wouters, Constitutional Limits of Differentiation. The Principle of Equality, pp. 301, at p. 319, in de Witte et al. op. cit. n.8 He refers to Article 2 (1) of the Charter of the United Nations and the Helsinki Final Act.

[105] L. Maurer, Negotiations in progress, pp. 125, in Ott and Inglis, op. cit. n.3.

tion with the above mentioned solidarity principle when Member States were not completely implementing Community law or only implementing them in respect of the parts of the *acquis* which was advantageous for them.[106]

4.2 EU principles limiting differentiation?

All of these principles are found in the EC and EU Treaties and most of them have been interpreted by the ECJ. While their importance in an enlarged and more diverse Union grows, their limits or definitions stay diffuse and debatable. The Constitutional Treaty is a missed opportunity to clarify the fundamental principles within the Union. It uses terms such as 'values' in Article I-2 consisting of such political and legal principles of democracy, solidarity and the rule of law, while fundamental principles are listed in Article I-11 with the principles of conferral, proportionality and subsidiarity. This last provision leaves the previous content of Article 5 EC untouched and achieves no restructuring to clarify fundamental principles applying among the Member States.

How far these principles can limit differentiation in primary law is closely connected with the question of how much differentiation can be undertaken and its consequences – are open to legal review by the courts. Pre-empted differentiation agreed by the Member States and manifested in protocols attached to EU and EC Treaties and in primary law, cannot automatically be reviewed by the ECJ. In contrast, they form the basis for review. Accession treaties and acts of accession are characterised by their double legal nature: firstly, they are considered international agreements among the Member States and the incoming state[107] and secondly, they also form EU primary law because they modify primary law.[108] With these legal measures a line has to be drawn between the legal nature of the instrument in which the differentiated regime is manifested and the legal instruments installed in the EC Treaty to monitor infringements of secondary law or primary law.[109] Any request to declare the Accession Treaty null and void is inadmissible, regardless of whether it is introduced by an individual or by a privileged claimant under Article 230 EC.[110]

However, provisions of an accession treaty can give rise to preliminary rulings under Article 234 EC.[111] These conditions have to be seen in context of the procedural law of the Community, according to Article 234 EC, subject-matter is, *inter alia*, the interpretation of the Treaty including an accession

---

[106] ECJ, Case 39/72 *Commission* v. *Italy* [1973] *ECR* 101; ECJ, Case 128/78 *Commission* v. *UK* [1979] *ECR* 419.

[107] See the wording of Article 49 EU.

[108] See the case law: ECJ, Case 185/73 *Hauptzollamt Bielefeld* v. *OHG König* [1974] *ECR* 607; ECJ, Joined Cases 194/85 and 241/85 *Commission* v. *Greece*, [1988] *ECR* 1037.

[109] Hoffmeister, 'Changing requirements for membership', in Ott and Inglis, op. cit n.3, at. p. 102.

[110] ECJ, Joined Cases 194/85 and 241/85 *Commission* v. *Greece* [1988] *ECR* 1037.

[111] ECJ, Case C-355/97 *Landesgrundverkehrsreferent der Tiroler Landesregierung* [1999] *ECR* I-4977.

treaty[112] and the annulment procedure of Article 230 EC reviews the legality of acts[113] on the grounds of an infringement this Treaty, including the accession treaties.[114] Under certain circumstances the legal review may be opened; if the act of accession has been infringed or secondary law has been modified with respect to the act of accession. This limited review has also been extended to the concrete application of safeguard clauses in the accession treaty.[115] In line with the ECJ's general reluctance to scrutinise measures concerning common policies and external relations,[116] the judgments have given the Commission a broad scope of application.

5 Conclusion: How much unity in diversity?

What conclusions can be drawn for the application of differentiated integration after enlargement when comparing its different forms? On a political level, the discussion about a Constitution for Europe and the institutional proposals introduced during the Convention on the Future of Europe manoeuvre between more federal and more intergovernmental structures. Could this process lead the Union into a federation of European states which decides to give Europe a constitutional basis if Member States agree to further transfer competences? Or is the other option the creation of a customs union *de luxe* of some 25 or 30 Member States in which broader policies can only be achieved by the enhanced co-operation of a few of them? The Constitutional Treaty clarifies the current status quo with some new elements already discussed in previous intergovernmental conferences, such as the merging of the pillars and granting the European Union one single legal personality. Thus, both elements, confederate in some, intergovernmental in others, still coexist and therefore actions of simplification and giving the European Union clearer constitutional structures might entail two opposing elements: a more homogeneous yet a more flexible structure. A more homogeneous structure might

[112] Not that clear in K. Lenaerts and D.Arts, *Procedural Law of the European Union* (London, Sweet and Maxwell, 1999) p. 116 but see B.Wegener, Art.234 para.5 in Calliess and Ruffert, op. cit. n.97.

[113] This excludes primary law but includes all measures which intend to have legal effect.

[114] Lenaerts and Arts, op. cit. n.112, at p. 197.

[115] ECJ, Case SA *Piraiki-Patrakai and others* v. *Commission* [1985] *ECR* 207, in another case the Court characterised the conditions as precise in substance and procedure: ECJ, Case 258/81 *Metallurgiki Halyps* v. *Commission*, [1982] *ECR* 4261.

[116] See for instance, A. Ott, 'Der EuGH und das WTO-Recht: Die Entdeckung der politischen Gegenseitigkeit – altes Phänomen oder neuer Ansatz?', *EuR* 3/2003, pp. 504; contra and expecting a strict scrutiny by the ECJ: See F. Bignami, 'The Challenge of Co-operative Regulatory Relations' in G.A. Berman and K. Pistor, *Law and Governance in an Enlarged European Union* (Oxford and Portland, Hart Publishing, 2004), pp. 97-140.

result from the abolition of a complicated system of differentiations,[117] entailing opt-outs and opt-ins and different scopes of application of the EU *acquis*. On the other hand, this rigidity could only work with a strong flexibility clause in order to cope with all eventualities, which might not fit into a constitutional 'strait-jacket'.[118] In addition, the option to leave the European Union/European Communities has been disputed but with a larger Union the Constitutional Treaty opened the door for voluntary withdrawal (Art. I-60).

Also relevant is whether enlargement will lead to greater flexibility through the use of the general enabling clause. This can be disputed for legal and political reasons outlined above.[119] The substantial differentiation established between the receiving and the new Member States by the current Accession Treaties already creates complex legal regimes for the upcoming years. The acceding Member States have temporary derogations without concrete time limits from the application of various parts of the Schengen *acquis* and from the EMU *acquis*. In addition, potential derogations apply in core areas relating to Internal Market *acquis* with the abstract possibility to extend it with broad variations of safeguard clauses.[120] Consequently, these differentiations among the incoming and current Member States lead to the question of whether this is still consistent with fundamental principles governing EU law and, therefore, whether it will limit the possibility to differentiate among Member States. Such limits can be seen in the obligations of consistency and unity of law, the principle of solidarity, equality among states and the principle of democracy and the rule of law. All of these principles are linked and underpin the constitutional structure of the European Union and the relations between Member States and towards Community institutions, which is reflected in Article 10 EC and in Article 1 EU.[121]

While uncertainties prevail as to their precise content and judiciability, their importance in an enlarging Union is growing. Additionally, the role of the Commission in the process following accession has been strengthened and new forms of safeguard measures have been introduced which extend conditionality to the first years after accession.[122] The future assessment of these measures

[117] At least this 'illusion' is given when reading the Constitutional Treaty.

[118] In this regard see the opening clause for voluntary retreat from the European Union and closer cooperation in defence matters.

[119] However, judicial and administrative flexibility which leads to negative side effects could be seen in the new Member States even though these countries engaged in substantial pre-accession preparations involving constitutional matters and training of judges in EU law.

[120] However, the application of such derogations and transitional regimes has to be proportional and not of a permanent basis.

[121] See solidarity and equality reflected in Art. I-2 and Art. I-5 of the Constitutional Treaty. A so-called solidarity clause in Art. I-42 points at solidarity in cases of terrorist attack and disasters.

[122] See in this regard Art. 37 and especially Art. 38 Act of Accession which entails a post-accession conditionality instrument: 'If a new Member State has failed to implement commitments undertaken in the

depends on the role of the European Commission in the coming months and the next three years after accession. In addition, the role of the Court of Justice will require extension and the judges will need to assess more closely the concrete application of the modalities of accession set in the act of accession, particularly to counterbalance the administrative powers of the Commission and the flexible and untransparent national measures taken in the area of movement of workers. This differentiation in EU law and policy, necessary due to political and economic differences between new and old Member States as much as a lack of trust among Member States, provokes the question of how the gap between desired minimal unity and unavoidable diversity might be bridged or, in other words, how much diversity is desirable in unity. Hence, the constitutional framework for changes in the current structure and the constitutional limits of changes and the clearer definition of the common fundamental constitutional principles, grow in importance. Fundamental principles, even though ill-defined, such as solidarity and equality among Member States and non-discrimination among EU citizens deserve special attention and need to be further refined in a constitutional context to meet the challenges of the current accession process and future enlargements.

context of the accession negotiations, causing a serious breach of the functioning of the internal market, including any commitments in all sectoral policies which concern economic activities with cross-border effect, or an imminent risk of such breach the Commission may, until the end of a period of up to three years after the date of entry into force of this Act, upon motivated request of a Member State or on its own initiative, take appropriate measures'.

CHAPTER 6

Impact of European Union Enlargement on EMU

Monetary Split-up into 'Ins' and 'Outs' as a Temporary or Permanent Phenomenon?

Beata Dziechciarz

1 Introductory remark

On 1 May 2004, the day when the fifth Accession Treaty of 16 April 2003[1] entered into force, the EU increased from 15 to 25 Member States. This enlargement was the first to occur after the start of the Economic and Monetary Union (EMU) on 1 January 1999. The 10 Newcomers from Central and Eastern Europe and from the Mediterranean joined the EU at the time when EMU was celebrating its 5 years of existence. Remarkably, not all 'old' Member States, namely Sweden, Denmark and the United Kingdom did not introduce the single currency at that time. And none of the new Member States adopted the Euro upon their accession of 1 May 2004. Instead, under the Accession Treaty, they became Member States with a derogation in the meaning of Article 122 EC.

2 Differentiation in the monetary integration

It must be noted in the first place that the division of the Community into those Member States that introduced the Euro and those that did not, is not a phenomenon resulting merely from the Accession Treaty of 2003. EMU is perhaps the most important EU policy field where the concept of differentiated integration was put in practice. Broadly speaking, differentiation means that not all Member States are involved in the same way in integration within the Community.[2] The differentiation within EMU was visible already in the beginnings of monetary integration.[3] But it was the Maastricht Treaty that formally introduced it. The Maastricht Treaty pre-programmed differentiated monetary integration in that it required Member States to fulfil specific conditions in order that they be able to introduce the single currency.[4] Since it was already apparent at the time of the IGC in Maastricht that not all Member States would fulfil these conditions at the same time,[5] it was necessary to draft a special set of

---

1 *OJ* 2003 L 236/23. Hereafter, the Accession Treaty.

2 See, e.g., for the origins, definition and concepts of differentiated integration, E. Grabitz, ed., *Abgestufte Integration. Eine Alternative zum herkömmlichen Integrationskonzept* (Kehl am Rhein, Engel 1984); C.D. Ehlermann, 'Increased Differentiation or Stronger Uniformity', in J.A. Winter, et al., eds., *Reforming the Treaty on European Union: The Legal Debate* (The Hague, Kluwer 1996) p. 27.

3 For example, in the framework of the European Monetary System. See, e.g., V. Grieser, *Flexible Integration in der Europäischen Union: neue Dynamik oder Gefährdung der Rechtseinheit* (Berlin, Duncker und Humblot 2003) pp. 200 et seq.

4 See, e.g., for flexible integration in the field of EMU, U. Häde, 'Währungsintegration mit abgestufter Geschwindigkeit', in A. Weber, ed., *Währung und Wirtschaft: Das Geld im Recht* (Baden-Baden, Nomos 1997) p. 141; P. Vigneron and M.R. Molica, 'La Différenciation dans L'Union Economique et Monétaire. Dispositions juridiques et processus décisionnel', *Euredia* (2000) p. 197.

5 Cf., H. Tietmeyer, *Die Europäische Wirtschafts- und Währungsunion* (Stuttgart, G. Fischer 1992) p. 37.

provisions that would take into account the situation of those Member States not capable of fulfilling the criteria at the time of the convergence assessment.[6]

A second category of differentiation in the field of EMU includes special arrangements negotiated by Denmark and the United Kingdom in Maastricht.[7] These two Member States were given the right unilaterally to decide whether to join the Euro area. They made use of their so called 'opt-outs'.[8] Therefore, their special status results from the respective protocols annexed to the EC Treaty.[9] The Protocols form primary law.[10]

As a consequence of the differentiated monetary integration, from the beginning of the final stage of EMU (1 January 1999), the status of the Member States with regard to EMU can be threefold:[11]

- Member States that introduced the Euro (they form the so called Euro area[12]) of which there are currently 12;
- Member States with a derogation, currently being Sweden and the ten new Member States;
- and Member States having a special status namely, Denmark and the United Kingdom.

Differentiated monetary integration has also terminological consequences. In primary law, only the terms 'Member States with a derogation' (e.g., Art. 122(1) EC) and 'Member States without a derogation' (e.g., Art. 122(4) EC), are used. In secondary Community law, differentiation between 'participating' and

---

6 See J.-V. Louis, in *Commentaire Mégret. Le droit de la CEE*, Vol. 6, 2nd edn. (Bruxelles, Éd. de l'Univ. de Bruxelles 1995) pp. 147 et seq.

7 See, for the dichotomy of the special arrangements within the EMU, J. A. Usher, 'Variable Geometry or Concentric circles: Patterns for the European Union', *ICLQ* (1997) p. 243 at p. 255.

8 See the 5th and 6th recitals of the preamble of the Council Decision 98/317/EC of 3 May 1998 in accordance with Article 109j (4) of the Treaty, *OJ* 1998 L 139/30.

9 These are respectively: Protocol No. 26 on Certain Provisions relating to Denmark (hereafter, the Danish Protocol) and Protocol No. 25 on Certain Provisions relating to the United Kingdom of Great Britain and Northern Ireland (hereafter, the UK Protocol).

10 According to Art. 311 EC, the protocols annexed to the EC Treaty form an integral part thereof.

11 See, e.g., R. Stadler, *Der rechtliche Handlungsspielraum des ESZB*, (Baden-Baden, Nomos 1996) p. 79 ('dreifach abgestufte Währungsintegration'); Ch. Zilioli and M. Selmayr, *The Law of the ECB*, (Oxford, Hart 2001) p. 134.

12 According to the definition of the European Monetary Institute (Annual Report 1997, p. 116), 'Euro area' means 'area covering those Member States which have adopted the Euro as the single currency in accordance with the Treaty.' Note that it is not (yet) a legal term. This will change when the Treaty establishing a Constitution for Europe (hereafter, Constitutional Treaty) will enter into force (see, e.g., Art. III-197(2)(a) Constitutional Treaty).

'non-participating' Member States also arises.[13] The latter term includes 'those Member States which have not adopted the single currency'[14] and thus covers both Member States with a derogation and Member States with a special status. Colloquial equivalents for 'participating Member States' and 'non-participating Member States' are the 'Ins' and the 'Outs', respectively.

3 The new Member States and EMU

3.1 Under the Accession Treaty

The Act of Accession forms an 'integral part' of the Accession Treaty and stipulates the conditions of admission and the adjustments to the Treaties on which the Union is founded and which such admission entails.[15] With regard to EMU, Article 4 of the Act of Accession reads as follows: 'Each of the new Member States shall participate in Economic and Monetary Union from the date of accession as a Member State with a derogation within the meaning of Article 122 of the EC Treaty.' It follows that the new Member States now have the same status with respect to EMU as Member States that did not comply with the necessary conditions for the adoption of the single currency at the time of the first assessment of convergence (according to Article 121(4) EC) in 1998 and in the consecutive convergence assessments (according to Article 122(2) in conjunction with Article 121(1) EC).[16] Those Member States were to have a derogation according to Article 122(1)(2) EC. Hence, the Accession Treaty implicitly assumes that the new Member States have not yet fulfilled the 'necessary conditions' in the meaning of Article 122(2) EC. Although it could have been recognised that some of the acceding countries were not too far off from compliance with the convergence criteria before their EU accession,[17] it must be borne in mind that there was no mechanism available for formally evaluating

---

[13] See, e.g., Council Regulation 1103/97 of 17 June 1997 on certain provisions relating to the introduction of the Euro, OJ 1997 L 162/1; Council Regulation 1467/97 of 7 July 1997 on speeding up and clarifying the implementation of the excessive deficit procedure, *OJ* 1997 L 209/6.

[14] See e.g. Art. 1 (2) of the Council Regulation 1467/97, *OJ* 1997 L 209/6.

[15] Art. 1 (2) Accession Treaty. Note that accession treaties form primary law (see, e.g., ECJ, Joined Cases C-63/90 and C-67/90 *Portugal and Spain* v. *Council* [1992] *ECR* I-5073, para. 49).

[16] In 1998, these Member States were Greece and Sweden (see 2nd and 4th recital of the Council Decision 98/317/EC, *OJ* 1998 L 139/30). On 1 January 2001, Greece joined the Euro area (Council Decision 2000/427 of 19 June 2000 in accordance with Article 122 (2) of the EC Treaty on the adoption by Greece of the single currency on 1 January 2001, *OJ* 2000 L 167/19).

[17] See, e.g., R. Beck, 'EMU enlargement: no big bang', *Deutsche Bank Research EU Monitor No. 12* (Frankfurt am Main, April 2, 2004) p. 9 at pp. 9-11.

their convergence under the EC Treaty. Article 122(2) EC is applicable exclusively to EU Member States.[18] Accordingly, neither the Commission nor the ECB are obliged to prepare the so called Convergence Reports as regards candidate countries.[19] The procedures foreseen for the introduction of the Euro in the EC Treaty (Article 122(2) in conjunction with Article 121(1)) thus preclude entry to the EU and the Euro area at one and the same time. It follows that these are legal grounds, and not only the economic ones[20] that preclude the contemporaneous entry to the EU and the Euro area.[21] In consequence, each new Member State becomes a 'Member State with a derogation' upon EU accession unless some special arrangements with respect to EMU is specifically stipulated within their accession treaty.[22] The latter not being the case in the fifth Accession Treaty, the consequence of the Article 4 Act of Accession is that the relevant provisions of the EC Treaty on the derogation status apply to the new Member States.

3.2 Under Article 122 EC

The central provision on the legal situation of the Member States with a derogation is Article 122(3) EC. It entails the exclusion of these Member States from certain rights and obligations in the field of EMU. As far as the 'economic' part of EMU (Art. 98 et seq. EC) is concerned, Article 122(3) EC only excludes the application of Article 104(9) and (11) EC, which means that sanctions resulting from a contravention of budgetary discipline cannot be applied with regard to those Member States with a derogation. By contrast, a derogation has far more reaching consequences for the monetary policy. Accord-

---

[18] In the same sense Commission (DG for Economic and Financial Affairs), *Enlargement argumentaire*, Enlargement Paper No. 5 (Brussels, September 2001) p. 28.

[19] See also Commission, *Composite Paper. Reports on Progress Towards Accession by Each of the Candidate Countries* (Brussels, 4 November 1998) p. 11.

[20] Nonetheless, it is the main reason in the case of 2004 enlargement. See A. Nowak-Far, 'Unia Gospodarcza i Walutowa' [Economic and Monetary Union], in Z. Brodecki et al., eds., *Finanse. Acquis communautaire* [Finance. *Acquis communautaire*] (Warszawa, LexisNexis 2004) p. 159 at p. 161.

[21] See also Commission, *Towards the Enlarged Union. Strategy Paper and Report of the European Commission on the Progress Towards Accession by Each of the Candidate Countries*, COM (2002) 700, 9 October 2002 at p. 27.

[22] Cf., Commission, DG for Economic and Financial Affairs, 'Accession to the EU and implication for EMU', in Commission, DG for Economic and Financial Affairs, *Seminar on Currency Board in the context of EU accession. Summary of proceedings and papers*, Enlargement Paper No. 1 (Brussels, May 2000) p. 33 at p. 36 ('To define from the outset the EMU status of a new Member State, without having to create a new category, the status of a new Member State should be determined in the Accession Treaty, which should grant the derogation for the adoption of the euro'). See also U. Häde, in Ch. Calliess and M. Ruffert, eds., *Kommentar zum EUV und EGV*, 2nd edn. (Neuwied, Luchterhand 2002), Art. 122 EC, para. 36.

ing to Article 122(3) EC, the following provisions do not apply to Member States with a derogation:

- Article 105(1), (2), (3) and (5) EC (objectives and basic tasks of the ESCB);
- Article 106 EC (issue of banknotes and coins);
- Article 110 EC (legal acts of the ECB);
- Article 111 EC (exchange rate policy in respect of third currencies);
- Article 112(2)(b) EC (appointment of members of the Executive Board of the ECB).

Further exceptions concerning the rights and obligations in the framework of the ESCB are regulated in chapter IX of the Statute of the ESCB and the ECB.[23]

Against this background, one can conclude that the Member States with a derogation – by contrast with the participating Member States – do not transfer their monetary sovereignty to the Community.[24] Consequently, they retain their national currencies.[25] Article 43.2 ESCB Statute explicitly states therefore that the national banks of those Member States with a derogation 'retain their powers in the field of monetary policy according to their national law'. Here, a certain parallel with the legal situation of the Member States in the second stage of EMU (1 January 1994 to 1 January 1999)[26] can be drawn.[27] According to Article 121(4) EC in conjunction with the Protocol No. 24 on the transition to the third stage of EMU, the Community as a whole moved to the third – and final – stage of EMU on 1 January 1999.[28] Therefore, also those Member States with a derogation participate in the third stage of EMU.[29] Consequently, all provisions that are applicable in the third stage of EMU and are not excluded by Article 122(3) EC (or chapter IX of the ESCB Statute) apply to them.[30] Looked at from the other way round, the provisions which ceased to apply in the third stage of EMU are applicable to Member States with a derogation only if the EC Treaty

---

23 Protocol No. 18 annexed to the EC Treaty. Hereafter, the ESCB Statute.

24 Article 122(3) in conjunction with Article 105 (2) 1st indent EC.

25 Article 122(3) in conjunction with Article 106 EC.

26 Art. 116(1) in conjunction with Art. 121 (4) EC.

27 See also P. Vigneron and M. Molica, op. cit. n. 4 at p. 200.

28 Emphasis added. See U. Wölker, 'The Continuity of Contracts in the Transition to the Third Stage of Economic and Monetary Union', *CMLRev.* (1996) p. 117 at p. 1128; R. Torrent, 'Whom is the European Central Bank of?: Reaction to Zilioli and Selmayr', *CMLRev.* (1999), p. 1229 at p. 1232.

29 See G. Nicolaysen, 'Der rechtliche Status Griechenlands als Mitgliedstaat mit einer Ausnahmeregelung', in M. Papaschinopoulou, ed., *Griechenland auf dem Weg zur EWWU* (Baden-Baden, Nomos 1999) p. 39 at p. 40; U. Wölker, in GTE, eds., *Kommentar zum Vertrag über die Europäische Union und zur Gründung der Europäischen Gemeinschaft*, 6th edn. (Baden-Baden, Nomos 2003), Art. 122 EC, para. 1. Contra, e.g., W. Schill, in C.O. Lenz, ed., *Kommentar zum EG-Vertrag* (Cologne, Bundesanzeiger 1994), Art. 109k EC, para. 2.

30 See Ch. Zilioli and M. Selmayr, op. cit. n. 11 at p. 136.

explicitly states so. Article 122(6) EC confirms this.[31] According to this provision, Article 119 on mutual assistance in case of difficulties as regards the balance of payments of a Member State and Article 120 EC, on protective measures in case of sudden crisis in the balance of payments of a Member State continue to apply to Member States with a derogation – despite the fact that both regulations ceased to apply[32] from the beginning of the third stage of the EMU.

As a counterpart to the retention of monetary sovereignty, Article 122(5) EC stipulates the suspension of voting rights of the Member States with a derogation in the Council when taking decisions referred to in the provisions that do not apply to these States. In such cases, they are excluded from voting but not from participating in meetings and deliberations.[33]

3.3 Opt-outs for new Member States?

As already noted,[34] in Maastricht Denmark and the United Kingdom were given a special right not to introduce the single currency. Their legal situation – unlike that of a Member State with a derogation - is regulated in the Protocols annexed to the EC Treaty. The history of the negotiations in Maastricht and, consequently, the recitals of the preamble to the respective Protocols show that the special status of these two Member States is based on political grounds.[35] Therefore, the procedure leading to abrogation of the Opt-out can only be initiated at the request of the Member State in question.[36] Nonetheless, the status of Denmark and of the United Kingdom is not identical. Briefly speaking, under the Danish Protocol, Denmark has an 'exemption'.[37] Its effect is that all provisions of the EC Treaty and the ESCB Statute referring to a derogation are applicable to this Member State.[38] The analysis of the UK Protocol leads to quite the contrary conclusion that the United Kingdom was granted more exceptions than Denmark and, consequently, than those Member States with a derogation.[39] In contrast with the Danish Protocol, the UK Protocol does not refer generally to the relevant EC Treaty provisions concerning a derogation but individually

---

31 See also Art. 124(2) EC.

32 See Arts. 119(4) and 120(4) EC.

33 R. Bandilla, in E. Grabitz and M. Hilf, eds., *Kommentar zur EU* (München, Beck October 1997), Art. 109k EC, para. 18.

34 See *supra* 2.

35 See, for details, E. Flores, in: GTE, eds., *Kommentar zum EU-/ EG-Vertrag*, 5th edn. (Baden-Baden, Nomos 1999), following Art. 109m, Protocols No. 11 und No. 12, paras. 2 et seq.

36 See point 4 of the Danish Protocol and point 10a of the UK Protocol.

37 Point 2 of the Danish Protocol.

38 *Idem.*

39 Just compare Art. 122(3) EC with point 5 of the UK Protocol and Art. 43.1 ESCB Statute with point 8 of the UK Protocol.

regulates the situation of the United Kingdom. The most spectacular exception negotiated by the United Kingdom is that this country is not bound by the objective of establishing monetary union since Article 4(2) EC does not apply to the United Kingdom by virtue of point 5 of the UK Protocol.

Against this background, one can consider whether an accession country might claim an opt-out from EMU following the example set by Denmark or the United Kingdom. The Danish and the UK Protocols form primary law.[40] However, compared to the regime applicable to a derogation, each of these protocols explicitly refers to a country mentioned by name.[41] Accordingly, point 5 Danish Protocol and point 10(2) UK Protocol state that the provisions cease to apply in the event of abrogation of the special status. It follows that these two Protocols cannot be applied by analogy.[42] Furthermore, the Treaty does not contain any general clause allowing the Member States to unilaterally decide whether to join the Euro area or not. The reality is quite the opposite; such a clause – although generally taken into consideration – was finally laid to rest in Maastricht.[43] As a result, under the EC Treaty (and disregarding the country-specific arrangements), a Member State *either* introduces the Euro (if it fulfils the necessary conditions) *or* has a derogation (in the case where it does not fulfil the necessary conditions).[44] Therefore, any new opt-out would have to be regulated in primary law[45] and consequently would require amendment of the EC Treaty.[46]

Finally, the inclusion of an opt-out for a new Member State in the relevant accession treaty can be considered. The fundamental objective of an act of accession is "the integration of the new Member States into the community".[47] Thereby, the acceding countries are expected to take on the whole *acquis communautaire*. In the joint cases C-63/90 and C-67/90 *Portugal and Spain* v. *Council*, the ECJ held that 'the accession of new Member States to the Community

40 See *supra* 2.

41 See A. Nowak-Far, *Unia Gospodarcza i Walutowa w Europie* [Economic and Monetary Union in Europe] (Warszawa, C.H. Beck 2001) p. 328f.; P. Vigneron and M. Molica, op. cit. n. 4 at p. 228.

42 See P. Vigneron and M. Molica, op. cit. n. 4 at p. 228; Ch. Zilioli and M. Selmayr, op. cit. n. 11 at p. 143.

43 See, e.g., R. Smits, *The European Central Bank. Institutional aspects* (The Hague, Kluwer 1997) p. 133.

44 Cf., Art. 122(2)(2) EC. See also Commission, DG for Economic and Financial Affairs, May 2000, op. cit. 22 at p. 36.

45 Cf., R. Bandilla, in: E. Grabitz and M. Hilf, eds., *Kommentar zur EU* (Munich, Beck January 2000) Art. 4 EC, para. 3.

46 In this context, see the proposal of Sideek Mohamed to amend the Treaty according to Art. 48 EU in order to codify the lacking political will of Sweden to introduce the Euro (S. Mohamed, 'Sweden from the Euroland. Is the purported exclusion of Sweden from the Euroland justified?', in *EBLR* (2000) p. 363 at p. 371).

47 ECJ, Case 231/78 *Commission of the European Communities* v. *United Kingdom of Great Britain and Northern Ireland* [1979] *ECR* 1447, paras. 10 et seq.

is carried out by means of acts which have the status of primary law and can change pre-existing situations in any area of Community law whatsoever, the maintenance in force of existing Community rules being the course generally followed'.[48] At the same time, it should be borne in mind that, as a rule, an act of accession is the outcome of complicated political compromises intended to facilitate the integration of the new Member State.[49]

Turning to the fifth enlargement, the fifth Accession Treaty (as well as former accession treaties) does not include any exceptions in the area of EMU. They have not even been taken into consideration.[50] Moreover, they have not even been requested by the applicant countries during the accession negotiations.[51] Quite the opposite, the acceding Member States accepted unreservedly the aim of EMU.[52] Remarkably, the adherence to the aims of economic and monetary union was required by the accession criteria as formulated by the European Council in Copenhagen in June 1993 (i.e. in the first stage of EMU).[53] This criterion can be regarded as a political signal from the side of the Community that no opt-out or any variation on the same theme from the EMU would be taken into consideration in the future enlargement processes.[54] In consequence, the Member States that joined the EU after 1993 have actually been obligated to take on more than those Member States participating in the IGC in Maastricht[55] although one could have expected that similar solutions to those negotiated by Denmark and the United Kingdom would have been offered to the new Member States.[56] Fortunately, and corresponding to the lack of political will on the part

---

48 ECJ, Case C-63/90 and C-67/90 *Portugal and Spain* v. *Council*. [1992] *ECR* I-5073, para. 49.

49 Cf., ECJ, Joined Cases 31 and 35/86 *LAISA* v. *Council of the European Communities* [1988] *ECR* 2285, para. 15 ('the provisions of the act of accession affirm the results of the accession negotiations which constitute a totality intended to resolve difficulties which accession entails either for the community or for the applicant state'). See also M. Pechstein and P. Kubicki, 'The Legal Framework of Accession to the European Union', in W. Czaplinski, ed., *Poland's Way to the European Union. Legal aspects* (Warszawa, Scholar 2002) p. 231 at pp. 243 et seq.

50 See, e.g., ECB, 'The Eurosystem and the EU enlargement process', *Monthly Report* (Frankfurt am Main, February 2000) p. 39 at p. 46.

51 See, e.g., Poland's negotiation position in the area of EMU: 'Poland will not request derogations or transition periods concerning the *acquis* in the area of Economic and Monetary Union.' (available at www.negocjacje.gov.pl/neg/stne/pdf/stne11en.pdf).

52 See Commission (DG for Economic and Financial Affairs), May 2000, op. cit. n. 22 at p. 40.

53 Conclusions of the European Council in Copenhagen, 21-22 June 1993, *Bull. EC* 6-1993 (point 1.13).

54 See also M. Cremona, 'Accession to the European Union: Membership Conditionality and Accession Criteria', in W. Czaplinski, ed., op. cit. n. 49 at pp. 263 et seq.

55 See T. Bruha and O. Vogt, 'Rechtliche Grundfragen der EU-Erweiterung', *Verfassung und Recht in Übersee* (1997) p. 477 at p. 489; K. Inglis, 'The Europe Agreements Compared in the Light of their Pre-accession Reorientation', in *CMLRev.* (2000) p. 1173 at p. 1179.

56 See T. Oppermann, *Europarecht*, 2nd edn. (Munich, C.H. Beck 1999) para. 1846.

of the EU, there was no factual need on the side of the candidates to consider granting special rights concerning participation in the EMU.[57]

4 Termination of the derogation or the special status

The termination of a derogation status is regulated by Article 122(2) in conjunction with Article 121(1) EC. These provisions regulate the procedure and criteria for the abrogation of a derogation. Accordingly, at least once every two years, or at the request of a Member State with a derogation, the Commission and the ECB report[58] to the Council on the progress made by the countries concerned on their path to convergence. In the case of Denmark and the United Kingdom, this procedure can only be initiated at the request of the respective country.[59]

The decision on an abrogation of the derogation or the special status is taken by the Ecofin-Council,[60] acting by a qualified majority on a proposal from the Commission, after consulting the European Parliament and after discussion in the Council meeting in the composition of the Heads of State or Government. The Constitutional Treaty introduces an additional step in this procedure. According to Article III-198(2)(2), the Council will in future act on a basis of a recommendation of a majority of the participating Member States comprising at least 65% of the population of those Member States.

The criteria forming the basis for the Convergence Reports and for the Council decision are set out in Article 121(1) EC and defined in a protocol annexed to the EC Treaty[61]. They comprise the compatibility between each Member State's national legislation and Articles 108 and 109 EC and the ESCB Statute (i.e., the so-called legal convergence[62]) and four economic criteria, the fulfilment of which shows whether the country concerned has achieved a high degree of sustainable convergence. For the Member State concerned, it means that:

1. the inflation rate in the year before the examination may not be more than 1½ percentage points above the average rate of the three best-performing

[57] See also Ch. Zilioli and M. Selmayr, op. cit. n. 11 at p. 143.

[58] These are the so called 'Convergence Reports'. See, e.g., the title of the EMI Report of 1998 (available at: www.ecb.int/pub/pdf/othemi/englishen.pdf).

[59] See point 4 of the Danish Protocol and point 10a of the UK Protocol.

[60] According to Declaration No. 3 on Part Three, Titles III and VII of the Treaty establishing the European Community, under the provisions concerned the Council meets in the composition of Economic and Finance Ministers .

[61] Protocol No. 21 on the convergence criteria referred to in Art. 121 EC. Hereafter, Convergence Criteria Protocol.

[62] See EMI, Convergence Report (Frankfurt am Main, 1998) p. 288.

Member States;[63]

2. long-term interest rates may not exceed the level in these three countries by more than 2 percentage points;[64]
3. the government's financial position must be sustainable, i.e. at the time of its examination, the country may not be the subject of a Council decision under Article 104(6) EC that an excessive deficit exists;[65]
4. for at least two years, the currency of the Member State must have participated in ERM and remained within the normal fluctuation margins without devaluing at the initiative of the Member State.[66]

Furthermore, some additional real economic aspects (such as the results of the integration of markets, the situation and development of the balances of payments on current account and the development of unit labour costs and other price indices) have to be taken into consideration.[67]

After the Council takes a decision to abrogate a derogation or special status, the conversion rate at which the Euro will be substituted for the currency of the Member State concerned, is adopted according to the procedure laid down in Article 123(5) EC. On the day when the decision on the conversion rate comes into force, the Member State concerned joins the Euro area.

The procedure leading to the termination of a derogation status was first put into practice with regard to Greece and Sweden in 2000. Greece then introduced the Euro on 1 January 2001.[68] According to the 2 years intervals (Article 122(2) EC), the first convergence assessment concerning the new Member States took place in October 2004. The Convergence Reports prepared by the Commission and the ECB concluded that none of them (Sweden included) fulfilled all the necessary conditions for adopting the Euro and, therefore also, that there should be no change in their status as 'Member States with a derogation'.[69] It was striking that, while some of the countries examined fulfilled 3 criteria of a total of 4 economic convergence criteria (in particular, Sweden and Lithuania), none of the countries examined complied fully with the legal requirement of convergence.[70]

---

63 Art. 121(1) 1st indent EC in conjunction with Art. 1 Convergence Criteria Protocol.

64 Art. 121(1) 2nd indent EC in conjunction with Art. 2 Convergence Criteria Protocol.

65 Art. 121(1) 3rd indent EC in conjunction with Art. 3 Convergence Criteria Protocol.

66 Art. 121(1) 4th indent EC in conjunction with Art. 4 Convergence Criteria Protocol.

67 Art. 121(1) last sentence EC.

68 See Council Decision 2000/427 *supra* n. 16.

69 Convergence Reports 2004 are available at: europa.eu.int/comm/economy_finance/publications/european_economy/convergencereports2004_en.htm and www.ecb.int/pub/pdf/conrep/cr2004en.pdf .

70 *Idem.*

5 Consequences for the Community

5.1 Visibility of the monetary division of the Community

The last stage of EMU started on 1 January 1999 with the majority of Member States introducing the Euro. Those Member States that did not qualify for the introduction of the single currency have had a derogation under Article 122 EC. Two Member States decided not to introduce the single currency and made use of their Opt-outs. With regard to the numbers of 'Ins' and 'Outs', there were eleven participating and four non-participating Member States in 1999. Since January 2001, after the derogation of Greece was abrogated, there were twelve participating and three non-participating Member States. After the 2004 enlargement, the ratio has changed radically. Since May 2004, the Euro has been legal currency in twelve Member States and thirteen Member States remain outside the Euro area.

Fig. Monetary division of the Community in 2004

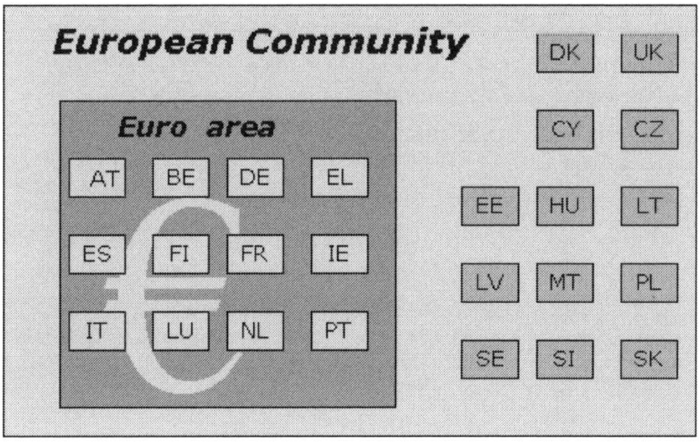

5.2 Durability of the monetary division of the Community

The analysis of the procedure leading to abrogation of a derogation or special status leads inevitably to some conclusions on the projected durability of the monetary division of the Community.

First, the regularity of the procedure leading to abrogation of a derogation – as provided for in Article 122(2) EC where, remarkably, the conjunction 'or' and not 'and' is used – indicates that the derogation was meant to be temporary.[71]

---

[71] See R. Bandilla, in: E. Grabitz and M. Hilf, eds., op. cit. 33, Art. 109k EC, para. 5; J.A. Usher, *The Law of Money and Financial Services in the EC*, 2nd edn. (Oxford, Oxford University Press 2000) p. 200; Ch. Zilioli and M. Selmayr, op. cit. n. 11 at p. 136.

The wording and headings of Treaty provisions concerning a derogation reflect this.[72] The situation of Denmark or the United Kingdom is different since the procedure according to Article 122(2) EC can be initiated only at the request of the relevant Member State.[73] It follows that their special status can be – at least theoretically – even permanent. However, both the Danish and the UK Protocols indicate that the abrogation of the special status will be irreversible: once the special status is abrogated, the Protocols will cease to apply.[74]

Second, the introduction of the Euro depends on the fulfilment of necessary criteria in the meaning of Article 122(2) EC. This applies both to the Member States with a derogation and those Member States with an opt-out.[75] The only difference is that Denmark or the United Kingdom are free to decide if legal consequence can be drawn from the fact that it fulfils convergence criteria. As already noted, no other Member State has been given an opt-out.[76] The Treaties emphasise repeatedly that one of the aims of the EU is 'to establish an economic and monetary union including a single currency' (seventh recital of the preamble of the EU Treaty, Art.2, first indent EU, Art. 2 EC and Art. 4(2) EC).[77] None of these provisions is excluded from application in Article 122(3) EC. It can be argued, therefore, that the Member States with a derogation are obliged to introduce the Euro as soon as they fulfil the necessary conditions.[78] Hence, in accordance with the loyalty clause of Article 10 EC, they must strive for 'a high degree of sustainable convergence' (as formulated in Article 121(1) EC) and to take all appropriate measures in order to be able to adopt the Euro within the acceptable[79] time.[80]

---

[72] Cf., e.g., Art. 123(3) EC ('If and as long as there are Member States with a derogation'). Cf. also the headings of Chapter 4 of the Title VII of the EC Treaty and chapter IX of the ESCB Statute ('Transitional provisions').

[73] See point 4 of the Danish Protocol and point 10a of the UK Protocol.

[74] Cf. point 5 of the Danish Protocol and point 10 *in fine* of the UK Protocol.

[75] Cf., point 4 of the Danish Protocol in conjunction with Art. 122(2) EC; point 10 lit. a of the UK Protocol in conjunction with Art. 122(2) EC.

[76] See *supra* 3.3.

[77] S. U. Häde, in Ch. Calliess and M. Ruffert, eds., op. cit. n. 22, Art. 4 EC, para. 12.

[78] That is why the term 'pre-ins' seems to be more appropriate than 'outs' to describe Member States with a derogation.

[79] In this context, Protocol No. 24 on the transition of the Community into the third stage of EMU can be recalled. It expresses the will of the Community to 'enter swiftly' into the last stage of EMU.

[80] See Paul J.G. Kapteyn, P. Ver Loren van Themaat and Laurence W. Gormley (eds.), *Introduction to the Law of the European Communities. From Maastricht to Amsterdam*, 3rd ed. (London, Kluwer 1998), p. 994; Ch. Zilioli and Martin Selmayr, op. cit. n. 11 at p. 137.

With regard to the new Member States, it can be assumed that once they have ratified the Accession Treaty, which does not include an opt-out clause, they have undertaken to participate fully in EMU.[81] Naturally, it cannot be predicted exactly when the new Member States will achieve the necessary state of convergence. Taking into consideration the fact that the majority of newcomers are economically weaker than any of the 'old' Member States,[82] it can be expected that the convergence process will last for a considerable period of time[83] even though some of the newcomers are not far from fulfilling the nominal economic convergence criteria.[84] This means that the current monetary 'split-up' of the Community will be prolonged accordingly. The different state of convergence in the new Member States indicates at least that the process of enlarging the Euro area will be staggered over time.

As a last remark, it must be remembered that, due to the fact that every new Member State becomes a Member State with a derogation upon accession,[85] the monetary division of the Community will then be prolonged accordingly, or – alternatively – it would be revived if all Member States are participating Member States at that time of enlargement.

5.3 Co-ordination mechanisms foreseen in the EC Treaty

5.3.1 Enhanced need for co-ordination

As a consequence of a derogation, new Member States participate in the EMU in its final stage but do not introduce the Euro.[86] As already noted,[87] Member States with a derogation and with an opt-out are excluded from most rights and obligations in the field of monetary union. Nonetheless, since the derogation status is meant as a temporary one, the EC Treaty provides for the restricted participation of Member States with a derogation as well as of the opt-out Member States in EMU.

---

81 See R. Cortés Herrera, 'Suecia y la UEM: ¿Hecha la Ley, hecha la trampa?', *Revista de derecho comunitario europeo* (2002) p. 209 at p. 214.

82 See also ECB, 'The EU economy following the accession of the new Member States', *Monthly Bulletin* (Frankfurt am Main, May 2004) pp. 49 et seq.

83 See also R. Smits, op. cit. n. 43 at p. 514; E. Vranes, 'The 'Internal' External Relations of EMU – on the Legal Framework of the Relationship of 'In' and 'Out' States', *Columbia Journal of European Law* (2000) p. 361 at p. 382.

84 For example, in 2004 Lithuania failed to fulfil only one of the 4 economic convergence criteria, viz. the criterion on exchange rate stability which follows mainly from the fact that its currency has not participated in ERM II for the required period.

85 Unless it negotiates some special arrangement. See *supra* 3.1.

86 Cf. the wording of Art. 4 of the Act of Accession. See also Ch. Zilioli/ M. Selmayr, op. cit. n. 11 at p. 144.

87 See *supra* 3.2.

The division into participating and non-participating Member States increases the need for co-operation and co-ordination between the Euro area as a whole and the non-participating Member States.[88] Indeed, the increased number of non-participating states requires suitable co-ordination mechanisms. Inevitably, the increased number of non-participating states makes co-ordination more difficult.[89] Also, it increases the tendency of the participating Member States to form informal bodies in order to co-ordinate their views.[90] An example is the existence of the so called 'Euro Group', an informal body created at the Luxembourg Summit in 1997.[91] The need for an enhanced dialogue between the participating Member States within the Euro area is explicitly recognised in the Constitutional Treaty. First, it regulates the arrangements for meetings of the Euro Group,[92] albeit without giving any decision-making competences to this body. Second, the Constitutional Treaty introduces the possibility of closer co-ordination between those 'Member States whose currency is the Euro' in the field of economic policy.[93]

5.3.2 Co-ordination in the field of economic policy

Non-participating Member States are fully involved in the procedures of economic policy co-ordination and budgetary surveillance under the EC Treaty (Art. 99 and 104 EC, respectively) and the Stability and Growth Pact.[94] However, the sanctions foreseen in Article 104(9) and (11) EC and in Regulation 1467/97[95] cannot be applied with respect to these Member States.[96] Moreover,

---

88 Cf. Paul J.G. Kapteyn and Pieter Ver Loren van Themaat/ Laurence W. Gormley, op. cit. 79 at p. 996. See also H.J. Hahn and U. Häde, 'Europa im Wartestand', in O. Due, ed., *Festschrift für Ulrich Everling* (Baden-Baden, Nomos 1995) p. 381 at p. 391.

89 See R. Smits, op. cit. n. 43 at p. 504 et seq.

90 See R. Smits, op. cit. n. 43 at p. 507.

91 See Resolution of the European Council of 13 December 1997 on economic policy co-ordination in stage 3 of EMU and on Treaty Articles 109 and 109b of the EC Treaty, *OJ* 1998 C 35/1 (section I, point 6). See, for the Euro Group, J.-V. Louis: *The Euro Group and Economic Policy Co-ordination*, EuroSpectator Report (April 2001), available at: www.iue.it .

92 Article III-195 Constitutional Treaty and Protocol on the Euro Group.

93 Articles III-194 et seq. Constitutional Treaty.

94 The Stability and Growth Pact is based on a Resolution of the European Council on the Stability and Growth Pact (Amsterdam, 17 June 1997, *OJ* 1997 C 236/1), and two regulations: the Council Regulation 1466/97/EC of 7 July 1997 on the strengthening of the surveillance of budgetary positions and the surveillance and coordination of economic policies (*OJ* 1997 L 209 / 1), and the Council Regulation 1467/97/EC of 7 July 1997 on speeding up and clarifying the implementation of the excessive deficit procedure (*OJ* 1997 L 209/ 6).

95 *OJ* 1997 L 209/ 6.

96 Art. 122(3) in conjunction with Art. 104(9) and (11) EC; point 5 of the UK Protocol in conjunction with Art. 104(9) and (11) EC.

the United Kingdom enjoys a special exception since Article 104(1) EC stipulating that the Member States have to avoid excessive government deficits does not apply to this Member State.[97]

In the framework of economic policy co-ordination, the non-participating Member States are obliged to submit convergence programmes (Art. 7 et seq. of Regulation 1466/97) whereas, since 1999, the participating Member States annually submit their stability programmes (Art. 3 et seq. of the Regulation 1466/97). The new Member States had to submit their first convergence programmes by 15 May 2004.[98]

Furthermore, the escape clauses of Article 119 and Article 120 EC continue to apply to Member States with a derogation as well as to Denmark[99] and the United Kingdom[100] in the final stage of EMU.

5.3.3 Co-ordination in the field of monetary policy

Compared to the participating Member States transferring their monetary competences to the Community level,[101] the non-participating Member States define and conduct their monetary policies according to national law.[102] The single monetary policy – as envisaged in Article 4(2) EC – has been defined and implemented by the European System of Central Banks (ESCB) since 1 January 1999.[103]

According to Article 107(1) EC, the ESCB is composed of the European Central Bank (ECB) being at the top of the System[104] and the national central banks. Remarkably, the national central banks of the non-participating Member States are also part of the ESCB since neither Article 122(3) EC nor point 5 of the UK Protocol exclude the application of Article 107(1) EC. Therefore, not only the ECB and the central banks of the participating Member States but also the central banks from outside the Euro area – with the noteworthy exception of the Bank of England[105] – were granted independence under Article 108 EC (Art. 7 ESCB Statute).[106]

---

97 Point 5 of the UK Protocol. For the United Kingdom, Article 116(4) EC remains in force, which means that this Member State has (only) to 'endeavour' to avoid excessive deficits (point 6 of the UK Protocol).

98 See, for details, at http://ue.eu.int/showPage.asp?id=699&lang=en&mode=g .

99 Point 2 of the Denmark Protocol.

100 Point 6 of the UK Protocol.

101 See, e.g., U. Häde, in Ch. Calliess and M. Ruffert, eds., op. cit. n. 22, Art. 105 EC, para. 7; A. Hatje, in: J. Schwarze, ed., *EU-Kommentar* (Baden-Baden Nomos 2000), Art. 4 EC, para. 11.

102 See *supra* 3.2.

103 See Art. 8 EC and Art. 105(2) first indent EC; Art. 1.1 and 3.1, first indent ESCB Statute.

104 Cf. Art. 107(3) EC, according to which the ESCB is governed by the decision-making bodies of the ECB. See also J.-V. Louis, in *Commentaire Mégret*. op. cit. n. 6 at p. 69.

105 See Point 5 of the UK Protocol.

106 Art. 122 (3) does not exclude the application of Art. 108 EC.

However, whereas all national central banks together with the ECB form the ESCB, only the central banks from the Euro area are 'integral parts' of the ESCB and, thus, are subject to the guidelines and instructions of the ECB as provided for by Article 14.3 ESCB Statute. Therefore, in the words of the ECB, 'two realities' coexist within the ESCB.[107] First, there is the ESCB comprising the ECB and all national central banks. Second, there is a subsystem comprising only the ECB and the national central banks of those Member States that have adopted the Euro. Only in the latter form does the system carry out the basic tasks of the ESCB including definition and implementation of the monetary policy of the Euro area, conduct of foreign-exchange operations, holding and management of the official foreign reserves of the Member States and promoting the smooth operation of payment systems.[108] This subsystem became known as a 'Eurosystem'.[109]

In the context of the existence of the Eurosystem, it is actually striking that the national central banks of non-participating Member States do not form any separate subsystem within the ESCB. The option to let the EMI continue in parallel with the ESCB in the last stage of the EMU was taken into consideration during the IGC in Maastricht but finally rejected.[110] Under the EC Treaty, the co-ordination of the monetary policy of the Euro area and the non-participating Member States takes place within the ESCB.

The national central banks from outside the Eurosystem are not subject to guidelines and instructions from the ECB.[111] Their rights and obligations within the framework of the ESCB are restricted to activities which do not directly concern the monetary policy of the Community. For example, the national central banks of the non-participating Member States are involved in the collection of statistical information under Article 5 ESCB Statute.[112] Furthermore, the national central banks from outside the Eurosystem do not participate in the decision-making process within the Governing Council and the Executive Board of the ECB.[113] Instead, the governors of these central banks have a seat and vote in the third decision-making body of the ECB, being the General Council, which is the third decision-making body of the ECB according to Art. 123(3) EC.[114]

---

[107] See Opinion of the European Central Bank of 19 September 2003 at the request of the Council of the European Union on the draft Treaty establishing a Constitution for Europe, *OJ* 2003 C 229/7, para. 14.

[108] Article 105 (2) EC.

[109] *See ECB, 'The Eurosystem and the European System of Central Banks (ESCB)', Monthly Report (Frankfurt am Main, January 1999) p. 7.* It has to be noted that the 'Eurosystem' is not a legal term. It will change when the Constitutional Treaty comes into force (Art. I-30(1)).

[110] See J.-V. Louis, 'Differentiation and the EMU', in B. de Witte et al., eds., *The Many Faces of Differentiation in EU Law* (Antwerp, Intersentia 2001) p. 43 at pp. 47 et seq.

[111] Art. 43(1) in conjunction with Art. 14.3 ESCB Statute.

[112] Neither Art. 43 ESCB Statute nor point 8 of the UK Protocol exclude the application of Art. 5 ESCB Statute.

[113] Art. 43(1) in conjunction with Art. 10.1 and 11.1 ESCB Statute.

[114] See Art. 123(3) EC and Art. 45.1 ESCB Statute.

According to Article 45.2 ESCB Statute, the General Council is composed of the President and Vice President of the ECB and the Governors of all (twenty-five Member States') national central banks. Thus, the General Council provides for an institutional link between the Eurosystem and the other national central banks. The responsibilities of the General Council include, on the one hand, tasks which refer only to the non-participating Member States, in particular the tasks of the European Monetary Institute (EMI), which, because of the derogation or the opt-out, still have to be performed in the third stage of EMU.[115] It includes the monetary policy co-ordination between the Euro area and the non-participating Member States.[116] On the other hand, the General Council has to 'contribute' to the tasks which concern all Member States and do not refer to the single monetary policy (such as, for example, the collection of the statistical data under Article 5 ESCB Statute).[117] As a transitional body, the General Council will exist as long as there are Member States with a derogation or as long as the United Kingdom does not introduce the euro.[118]

5.3.4 Co-ordination in the field of exchange-rate policy

Because of a derogation or special status, Article 111 EC, concerning the formulation of the exchange-rate policy of the Euro area, does not apply to the non-participating Member States.[119] In the area of exchange-rate policy, they retain their competences according to national law. However, under Article 124 EC, each of the non-participating Member States[120] has to treat its exchange-rate policy as 'a matter of common interest' and to consider the interests of the other non-participating Member States as well as the interests of the Euro area.[121] In this context, Article 124 EC requires these Member States to take account of the experience acquired in co-operation within the framework of the European Monetary System (EMS).[122]

The EC Treaty does not regulate the exchange-rate relationship between the Euro area and the non-participating Member States. The existing Exchange Rate Mechanism II – like its predecessor, the ERM of the EMS – does not have a

[115] See Art. 47.1, first indent in conjunction with Art. 44 ESCB Statute; point 9 lit. a and b of the UK Protocol.

[116] Cf., Art. 117(2), second indent EC.

[117] Cf. Art. 47.1, second indent and Art. 47.2 ESCB Statute.

[118] Art. 123(3) EC in conjunction with point 9 of the UK Protocol.

[119] Art. 122(3) EC and point 5 of the UK Protocol in conjunction with Art. 111 EC.

[120] According to point 6 of the UK Protocol, Art. 124 EC applies to the UK as if it had a derogation.

[121] See, for details, R. Smits, in GTE, eds., *Kommentar zum EWG-Vertrag*, 4th edn. (Baden-Baden, Nomos 1991) Art. 107 EEC, paras. 7 et seq.

[122] Art. 124(2) in conjunction with 124(1) EC and, with regard to the United Kingdom, point 6 of the UK Protocol.

Treaty background. Its political basis[123] is the Resolution of the European Council on the establishment of an exchange-rate mechanism in the third stage of the economic and monetary union (Amsterdam, 16 June 1997).[124] The operating procedures of the ERM II are determined by the Agreement of 1 September 1998 between the European Central Bank and the national central banks of the Member States outside the Euro area.[125]

According to point 1.6 of the – politically binding – ERM II Resolution, participation in the ERM II is 'voluntary' for the non-participating Member States.[126] With regard to those Member States with a derogation, the Resolution additionally expresses the expectation that these Member States join the mechanism either at the time of its foundation or at a later date.[127] However, it must be borne in mind that formal participation in the ERM II is necessary for the fulfilment of the exchange rate convergence criterion as defined in Article 121(1), third indent, EC and Article 3 of the Convergence Protocol.[128] Since the Member States with a derogation are obliged to strive for the fulfilment of the convergence criteria, including the ERM II criterion,[129] it can be argued that under the EC Treaty they are obliged to join the ERM II.[130] Otherwise, a factual opt-out from the EMU would be possible.[131] And such a possibility – as already argued[132] – cannot be regarded as compatible with the EC Treaty since only Denmark and the United Kingdom were given opt-outs.

---

[123] See B. Martenczuk, 'Der Europäische Rat und die Wirtschafts- und Währungsunion', *EuR* (1998) p. 151 at p. 156.

[124] *OJ* 1997 C 236/5. Hereafter, the ERM II Resolution.

[125] *OJ* 1998 C 345/6. Hereafter, the ERM II Agreement.

[126] The ERM II Agreement repeats this statement in its 4th recital.

[127] Cf., Point 1.6 of the ERM II Resolution and the fourth recital of the ERM II Agreement.

[128] However, it remains a controversial point. See, for the necessity of formal participation in the ERM II, R. Smits, op. cit. n. 43 at p. 126; U. Häde, in Ch. Calliess and M. Ruffert, eds., op. cit. n. 22, Art. 121 EC, paras. 17 et seq.; M. Selmayr, *Das Recht der Wirtschafts- und Währungsunion* (Baden-Banden, Nomos 2002) pp. 367 et seq. Contra S. Mohamed, op. cit. n. 46 at p. 365; R. Cortés Herrera, op. cit. n. 80 at pp. 218 et seq.

[129] See *supra* 5.2. See also – with regard to Sweden – ECB, Convergence Report (Frankfurt am Main, 2000) p. 5; ECB, Convergence Report (Frankfurt am Main, 2002) p. 3; ECB, *Convergence Report* (Frankfurt am Main, 2004) p. 80.

[130] See R. Smits, op. cit. n. 43 at pp. 465 et seq.; M. Selmayr, op. cit. n. 129 at p. 390; E. Vranes, op. cit. n. 82 at p. 380 et seq.; J.-V. Louis, 'The EMU: Law and Institutions', *CMLRev.* (2004) p. 575 at p. 604. Contra J.A. Usher, op. cit. n. 70 at p. 186.

[131] See U. Häde, in: Ch. Calliess and M. Ruffert, eds., op. cit. n. 22, Art. 121 EC, para. 21. An example is the non-participation of Sweden, although this Member State has not been given an opt-out.

[132] See *supra* 3.3.

One should remember that participation in the ERM II requires a certain degree of stability of the exchange-rates.[133] Consequently, a Member State with a derogation is obliged to join ERM II if and as soon as it is economically 'fit' to participate in the Mechanism.[134]

6 Monetary integration strategies of the new Member States

All national central banks of the new Member States signed the ERM II Agreement upon accession and, thus, recognised its necessity and its procedures.[135] This does not mean participation in the ERM II. After a decision is made at national level, the national currency of the concerned non-participating Member State can only join the ERM II once an agreement on the central parity and fluctuation band is achieved at Community level.[136] Until then, the obligations of the national central banks from outside the Euro area are limited to a co-operation with the ECB and the national central banks participating in the ERM II in concertation and the other exchanges of information necessary for the proper functioning of the ERM II.[137]

Since the timing of the entry into the ERM II depends on the economic situation of the Member State concerned,[138] it should be considered in a broader context of the overall macroeconomic situation of this country.[139] Therefore, the EU generally advises against a premature entry into the ERM II.[140] Interestingly, the Economic and Social Committee recommends a contemporaneous entry into the EU and into the ERM II in order to 'avoid prolonging the EMU acces-

---

[133] Cf. Point 1.1 and 1.3 of the ERM II Resolution. See also ECB, Policy position of the Governing Council of the ECB on exchange rate issues relating to the Acceding Countries of 18 December 2003 (available at: www.ecb.int), pp. 3 et seq.

[134] See, e.g., E. Vranes, op. cit. n. 82 at p. 381.

[135] Agreement of 29 April 2004 between the European Central Bank and the national central banks of the Member States outside the Euro area on 1 May 2004 amending the Agreement of 1 September 1998 laying down the operating procedures for ERM II, *OJ* 2004 C 135/3.

[136] The procedure is regulated in point 2.3 of the ERM II Resolution and in Art. 1 of the ERM II Agreement.

[137] Art. 19 of the ERM II Agreement.

[138] See *supra* 5.3.3.2.

[139] See, in particular, Commission, Comprehensive monitoring report on the state of preparedness for EU membership (Brussels, November 2003) p. 22; ECB, Policy position of the Governing Council..., op. cit. n. 130 at p. 5. See also, for the economic point of view, B. Égert et al., 'Challenges for EU Acceding Countries' Exchange Rate Strategies after EU Accession and Asymmetric Application of the Exchange Rate Criterion', in Oesterreichische Nationalbank, ed., *Focus on Transition* (No. 2, 2003) p. 152 at pp. 162 et seq.

[140] Commission, Comprehensive monitoring report on the state of preparedness for EU membership (Brussels, November 2003) p. 22; ECB, Policy position of the Governing Council..., op. cit. n. 130 at p. 5.

sion process excessively' and, in particular, to remove the 'risk of one or other of these countries opting out of EMU'.[141]

Generally speaking, most of the new Member States have opted for an early entry into the ERM II and for a participation limited to 2 years (as required in Article 121(1), third indent, EC).[142] However, the national strategies vary from one country to the other, as shown in the table *infra*.[143] It indicates that there is probably no universal path to the EMU (in terms of one solution for the exchange-rate regime and the timing of entry to the ERM II). The specific solutions will depend rather on the economic and political situation of the countries concerned.

After Greece joined the Euro area in 2001, only Denmark has participated in the ERM II. In June 2004, three new Member States joined the Mechanism. At the request of Estonia, Lithuania and Slovenia and in accordance with the procedure set out in the ERM II Resolution,[144] it was decided on 27 June 2004 to include the Estonian *kroon*, Lithuanian *litas* and Slovenian *tolar* in the ERM II.[145]

---

[141] Opinion of the Economic and Social Committee on 'The impact of enlargement on EMU' of 19 September 2002, *OJ* 2003 C 61/55, (points 1.4 and 3.2.7.3).

[142] Such attitude is mainly based on a conviction that the ERM II participation is a formal requirement for the adoption of the euro ('waiting room'). See Backé et al., *The Acceding Countries' Strategies towards ERM II and the Adoption of the Euro: An Analytical Review*, ECB Occasional Paper No. 10 (February 2004), p. 6 (available at www.ecb.int/pub/scientific/wps/date/html/index.en.html).

[143] See also P. Backé et al., op. cit. n. 142, at pp. 6 et seq.

[144] Point 2.3.

[145] See, for details ECB press releases of 27 and 28 June 2004 (available at www.ecb.int/press/pr/activities/intco/html/index.en.html).

[146] Following Commission (DG Economy and Finance), 2003 pre-accession economic programmes of acceding and other candidate countries: overview and assessment, Enlargement Paper No. 20 (Brussels, November 2003) p. 13 (table 6).

Table Monetary integration strategies of the new Member States according to their Convergence Programmes 2004[146]

Country	*ERM II entry target date*	*Entry to the ERM II*	*Euro introduction target date*
Cyprus	'early participation'	-	'by 2007'
Czech Republic	'only after conditions have been established for successful fulfilment of convergence criteria'	-	'around 2009/2010'
Estonia	'immediately after EU accession'	28.06.2004	'as soon as possible'[147]
Hungary	not specified[148]	-	not specified[149]
Latvia	'at the beginning of 2005'	-	'1 January 2008'
Lithuania	not specified[150]	28.06.2004	not specified[151]
Malta	not specified[152]	-	'as rapidly as economic convergence permits'[153]
Poland	not specified	-	not specified[154]
Slovak Republic	'2005 or one year thereafter'	-	'2008 or 2009 at the latest'
Slovenia	'by the end of 2004 at the latest'	28.06.2004	'at the beginning of 2007'

7 Conclusions

Under the EC Treaty, all Member States participate in the EMU. However, the participation of Member States with a derogation as well as of Denmark and the United Kingdom, is limited since they do not introduce the Euro. Due to the differentiation within the monetary integration, there are Member States which introduced the Euro, Member States with a derogation

[147] See also the Position of the Bank of Estonia on Participating in EMU (available at www.bankofestonia.info/pub/en/majandus/euroopaliit/) where the date 2006 is specified.

[148] But see the Hungarian Pre-Accession Economic Programme (PEP) 2003 ('as soon as possible').

[149] But see the Hungarian PEP 2003 ('2008').

[150] But see press release of the Lithuanian Central Bank on the information concerning ERM II and the adoption of the euro of 9 June 2004, available at www.lb.lt/news/pg.dll?f=1&did=773&lng=EN ('at the earliest possible date').

[151] But see press release of the Lithuanian Central Bank on the information concerning ERM II and the adoption of the euro of 9 June 2004, available at www.lb.lt/news/pg.dll?f=1&did=773&lng=EN ('late 2006 or early 2007').

[152] But see the Maltese PEP 2003 ('as soon as possible').

[153] But see the Maltese PEP 2003 ('2007/2008').

[154] But see the Polish PEP 2003 ('2008/2009').

and Member States with a special status. Since the legal situation of Denmark differs from that of the United Kingdom, four different legal regimes can actually be observed within EMU.[155] Such a complex structure is not easy to understand, even for experts in monetary matters.[156]

The last enlargement did not create any new legal regime within the EMU. Under the Accession Treaty, the new Member States became Member States with a derogation. Nonetheless, the last enlargement intensified the monetary division of the Community. Due to the fact that there are currently more non-participating (13) than participating Member States (12), the 'singleness' of the monetary policy and of the currency of the Community as envisaged by Article 4(2) EC Treaty seems today to be diluted to a considerable extent.[157] Furthermore, the increased number of non-participating Member States poses challenges to the co-ordination between the Euro area and the 'Outs'. On the other hand, one cannot forget that it is exactly the differentiation between 'Ins' and Member States with a derogation as pre-programmed in the Maastricht Treaty (disregarding the special arrangements) that allows a parallel pursuit of two seemingly incompatible concepts, that of deepening (in the sense of the creation of the EMU) and that of widening within the EU (in the sense of the inclusion of new and economically weaker Member States).[158]

The analysis of the consequences of the monetary division of the enlarged Community leads to the following conclusions. The 'Outs' stay outside the Euro area either on economic grounds (Member States with a derogation) or on political grounds (Member States with a special status). Accordingly, the possible duration of the monetary division of the Community depends on economic and political factors. With regard to the first ones, it can be concluded that plausible and efficient co-ordination between the Euro area and the 'Outs' is vital, both to ensuring the smooth functioning of the whole EMU enterprise, and to help the 'pre-Ins' in their efforts to adopt the Euro. Time will show how efficient the co-ordination mechanisms foreseen in the EC Treaty are. However, in this context, the role of these mechanisms for the successful integration of Greece must be recognised.

Finally, with regard to the fact that certain Member States lack the political will to introduce the Euro (regrettably, also certain Member States with a derogation[159]), it must be borne in mind that no Member State can be forced to intro-

---

155 See U. Wölker, in GTE, eds., op. cit. n. 29, Art. 122 EC, para. 2.

156 In the same sense S. Weinbörner, *Die Stellung der EZB und der nationalen Zentralbanken in der Wirtschafts- und Währungsunion nach dem Vertrag von Maastricht* (Frankfurt am Main, Lang 1998) p. 411; V. Grieser, op. cit. n. 3 at pp. 216 and 221.

157 Cf., R. Smits, op. cit. n. 43 at pp. 514 et seq.

158 Cf., H. Tietmeyer, op. cit. n. 5 at p. 37.

159 See, for the case of Sweden, a Member State which unilaterally reserved the right to decide when to adopt the Euro, U. Bernitz, 'Sweden and the European Union: On Sweden's Implementation and Application of European Law', *CMLRev.* (2001) p. 903 at pp. 931 et seq.

duce the Euro against its will.[160] Therefore, in the end it is the political readiness of the Member States concerned (including the support of their citizens)[161] that will make it possible for the Community to coincide with the Euro area in the foreseeable future.[162]

---

[160] See U. Wölker, *Der Eintritt in die dritte Stufe der Wirtschafts- und Währungsunion* (Bonn, Europa Union Verlag 1999) p. 33; U. Häde, in Ch. Calliess and M. Ruffert, op. cit. n. 22, Art. 121 EC, para. 48. Cf. also, J.-V- Louis, op. cit. n. 131 at pp. 603 et seq.

[161] Note that in the 'euro' referendum in September 2000, Denmark decided to stay outside the Euro area. Also the Swedish referendum on introduction of the Euro ended with a 'no' vote (56,2%) in September 2003. However, from the point of view of the Community law, only Denmark has the right to opt-out on the ground that its Constitution implies a referendum on the introduction of the Euro (see 2nd recital of the preamble of the Danish Protocol).

[162] Cf., U. Häde, in Ch. Calliess and M. Ruffert, eds., op. cit. n. 22, Art. 121 EC, para. 21, who recalls the judgment of the German Federal Constitutional Court of 12 October 1993 (*Maastricht judgment*), BVerfGE 89, 155, 201 ('Die (...) Wirtschafts- und Währungsunion lässt sich (...) nur bei der stetigen ernsthaften Vollzugsbereitschaft aller Mitgliedstaaten verwirklichen.').

CHAPTER 7

Differentiation in European Union Citizenship Law

The Cyprus Problem

Nikolaos Skoutaris

My father says: 'Love your country'
But my own country is divided into two.
I do not know which part I should love more.[1]

1 Introduction

On 1 May 2004, one of the most ambitious projects of the European Union was realised; its fifth enlargement. Now, with the accession of the Ten new Member States, the European Union almost reaches its geographical limits, becomes a union of 450,000,000 people and has 20 different official languages. The citizens of Lithuania, Estonia, Latvia, Hungary, Poland, the Slovak Republic, the Czech Republic, Slovenia, Malta and the Republic of Cyprus have become European Union citizens in accordance with Article 17 of the EC Treaty. But, in contrast with the rest of the new Member States, Cyprus does not exercise effective control over all the areas envisaged by its own Constitution. Thus, the reality created by the 1974 Turkish invasion of the [occupied] areas in which the Government of the Republic of Cyprus does not exercise effective control (beyond the Green Line – see further)[2], poses many legal questions. Lead among them is the status of the inhabitants of the [occupied] areas in which the Government of the Republic of Cyprus does not exercise effective control with regard to EU citizenship.

The present paper addresses this issue by briefly reviewing the concept of EU citizenship, referring to the historical background of this legal Gordian knot, analysing thoroughly the relevant provisions of the Constitution of Cyprus and the citizenship laws of that State, describing the *sui generis* case of the settlers, questioning whether the new 'Green Line' Regulation creates a de facto citizenship status for the inhabitants of the [occupied] areas in which the Government of the Republic of Cyprus does not exercise effective control and discussing possible implications of *Loizidou* v. *Turkey*[3] cases of the European Court of Human Rights.

---

1 Poem from the Turkish Cypriot poet Nese Yasin.

2 Finding a workable description for the purposes of the present paper for those areas was one of the most important issues. The term 'Occupied Territories in Cyprus' was the first choice. But, the fact that the EU has never spoken of occupied territories, preferring rather to refer to them as 'those areas in which the Government of the Republic of Cyprus does not exercise effective control' (Council Regulation 8208/04 (hereinafter referred to as 'the Green-Line Regulation')), was convincing enough about the inaccuracy of the formerly mentioned term. After rejecting inadequate terms (e.g. Northern Cyprus) and discussing with the Cypriot judge of the ECJ Mr. Arestis as to what would be the most accurate term, it was decided that the 'politically gentle' term used by the EU with the addition of the word 'occupied' in brackets, was the most accurate term to describe the legal and political status quo of those areas.

3 European Court of Human Rights *Loizidou* v. *Turkey* judgment of 23 March 1995 (*preliminary objections*), Series A no. 310; *Loizidou* v. *Turkey* judgment of 18 December 1996 (*Merits*), Reports of Judgments and Decisions 1996-VI, no.26.

2 The concept of EU citizenship

Before we analyse the issue of the status of the inhabitants of the [occupied] areas in which the Government of the Republic of Cyprus does not exercise effective control with regard to the citizenship of EU, the relevant concept must be outlined. The symbolism of the move at Maastricht on 7 February 1992, from European Economic Community to European Community, and from Community to Union, was evident also in a number of specific EC Treaty provisions, such as the introduction for the first time of a systematic concept of citizenship of the Union through Articles 8 to 8e EC Treaty. Although, previously, there had been no formal concept of Union/Community citizenship, most of the rights and characteristics attached to the concept of citizenship were partially outlined with the scope of the Rome Treaties and the Single European Act, such as the rights of freedom of movement and residence. The Treaty on European Union (hereinafter 'TEU') took the initiative in the form of a statement that all nationals of the Member States were citizens of the EU, which was accompanied by a short list of rights attached to this status, such as the right to free movement and residence (subject to limitations)4; electoral rights as far as concerns the European Parliament and municipal elections[5]; diplomatic and consular protection[6]; access to the ombudsman[7]; the right to petition the European Parliament[8]. The wording of the Articles relating to citizenship was not substantially altered by the Amsterdam Treaty (now Arts. 17-22 EC) but Article 18 EC, relating to the right of citizens to move and reside within the EU, has been amended under the Treaty of Nice.[9]

Much of the academic commentary at the time of the TEU was critical of the inadequacy of the citizenship provisions and tended also to highlight their seemingly mere symbolic nature. It has been suggested by B. Wilkinson[10], for example, that the European Citizen could protest, using the words of Mark

4 Article 18 (ex 8a) EC.

5 Article 19 (ex 8b) EC.

6 Article 20 (ex 8c) EC.

7 Article 21 (ex 8d) EC.

8 Article 22 (ex 8e) EC.

9 Art. 18(1) remains unaltered, but Art. 18(2) has been changed, and Art. 18(3) has been added.
2. If action by the Community should prove necessary to attain this objective and this Treaty has not provided the necessary powers, the Council may adopt provisions with a view to facilitating the exercise of the rights referred to in paragraph 1. The Council shall act in accordance with the procedure referred to in Article 251.
3. Paragraph 2 shall not apply to provisions on passports, identity cards, residence permits or any other such document or to provisions on social security or social protection.

10 B. Wilkinson, 'Towards European Citizenship? Nationality, discrimination, and free movement of workers in the European Union', 1 *EPL* (1995) p. 417, at p. 437.

Twain, that 'rumours of his or her birth have been greatly exaggerated' and D'Oliveira suggests[11] that '[c]itizenship is, in other words, nearly exclusively a symbolic plaything without substantive content'. Moreover, although citizenship in general is regarded as an ideal to be aspired to, expressing a deep commitment to public, communal life, which describes the citizen's legal-political status and her/his relations with the polity, the TEU endorsed the Spanish proposal, which had differentiated the definition of the concept of citizenship (which was regarded per se as the basis of the democratic legitimacy) from the status *civitatis*, which can be defined as a set of rights, freedoms and obligations of citizens of the European Union.[12] Hence, the notion of European demos was not defined accurately by adopting a fully fledged citizenship, which would have led – as Weiler points out[13] – to the democratic legitimisation of the European Union and fundamentally changed the very telos of European integration from its unique concept of Community to a more banal notion of nation-building.

However, despite the fact that, when introducing citizenship at the Maastricht IGC, the Member States had intended this very instrumental, limited concept of citizenship as clearly depicted by the set of rights attached to the right of citizenship, it is the recent jurisprudence of the European Court of Justice (hereinafter 'ECJ'), and especially the cases of *Martinez Sala*[14] and *Grzelczyk*,[15] that might suggest – as Helen Toner points out[16] – that nationals of the Member States can say, to use Advocate General Jacobs' adaptation of the famous words of Cicero and St Paul that *'civis europaeus sum'*. But still, those decisions do not significantly alter the legal status quo for access to EU citizenship[17] via the nationality of a Member State. So, the main question is, for the purposes of this paper, whether according to Article 17(1) '[e]very person holding the nationality of a Member State shall be a citizen of the Union' who, among the inhabitants of the [occupied] areas in which the Government of the Republic of Cyprus does not exercise effective control, are entitled to the nationality of this Member State.

---

11 H. Jessurun D' Oliveira, 'European Citizenship – Pie in the Sky', in Rosas and Antola, eds., *A Citizen's Europe: in search of a new order* (London, Sage Publications, 1995) p. 82.

12 C. Colsa, 'The Concept of Citizenship in the Treaty on European Union' 29 *CMLR* p. 1137, at p. 1160.

13 J.H.H. Weiler, 'To be a European Citizen: Eros and Civilisation' in J.H.H. Weiler, *The Constitution of Europe*,(Cambridge University Press, 1999), p. 324 at p. 337.

14 ECJ, Case C-85/96, *Maria Martinez Sala* v. *Freistaat Bayern* [1998] *ECR* I-2691.

15 ECJ, Case C-184/99, *Rudy Grzelczyk* v. *Centre Public d'Aide Sociale d'Ottignes-Louvain-la-Neuve (CPAS)* [2001] *ECR* I-6193.

16 H. Toner, 'Judicial Interpretation of European Union Citizenship – Transformation or Consolidation' 7 *MJ* (2000) p. 158 at p. 159.

17 For proposals for amendments of the law concerning the access to EU citizenship read in general the Opinion of the European Economic and Social Committee on 'Access to European Union Citizenship' (2003/C 208/19).

3 Historical background[18]

Before we analyse the provisions in the Constitution of the Republic of Cyprus (hereinafter 'the Constitution') and the relevant citizenship laws thoroughly, it is necessary to briefly describe the historical background of this legal problem. The Republic of Cyprus gained its sovereign independence from the United Kingdom by virtue of a constitution and three treaties,[19] namely the Treaty of Guarantee, the Treaty of Alliance, and the Treaty of Establishment, all of which came into operation the same day – 16 August 1960. The Cyprus agreements,[20] forged in Zurich and London in 1959, have been successfully characterised as the political compromise between the United Kingdom, Greece and Turkey, since on the one hand, the struggle against the British colonial powers for Enosis[21] and, on the other hand, the first shy suggestions for taksim[22] were expressed during the 1950's.

The Constitution was drawn up explicitly in terms of the two communities and was referred to subsequently by the Turkish Cypriots as 'a functional federation', though that expression does not actually appear. The country was defined as 'an independent and sovereign Republic with a presidential regime, the President being Greek and the Vice-President[23] being Turkish elected by the Greek and the Turkish communities of Cyprus respectively'.[24] The legislative system[25] was unicameral. The House of Representatives comprised 35 Representatives belonging to the Greek community and 15 belonging to the Turkish one. Outside the House of Representatives two communal chambers[26], were to be elected – one Greek and one other Turkish – which were given separate functions that were not entrusted to the House. The judicial system was headed both by the Supreme Constitutional Court[27] and by the High Court of Justice[28], each consisting of Greek and Turkish Cypriot judges, each with a neutral president (and, therefore, neither Cypriot, Greek, Turkish nor British). Finally, the Constitution recognised the bicommunal nature of Cyprus in its arrangements for administration.

---

[18] See in general *The Cyprus Conflict*; available at www.cyprus-conflict.net/narrative-main.htm.

[19] See in general www.kypros.org/Constitution/English/.

[20] For an analysis of the Cyprus Agreements see in general the Intelligence Report No.8047, U.S. Department of State, Bureau of Intelligence and Research, 'Analysis of the Cyprus Agreement'.

[21] Enosis means union in Greek; it depicted the devotion of the Greek Cypriots to union with Greece.

[22] Taksim means partition in Turkish; it denoted the intention of the Turkish Cypriots for self-governance.

[23] See in general Part 3 (Articles 36 - 60) of the Constitution of the Republic of Cyprus.

[24] Article 1 of the Constitution of the Republic of Cyprus.

[25] See in general Part 4 (Articles 61 - 85) of the Constitution of the Republic of Cyprus.

[26] See in general Part 5 (Articles 86 - 111) of the Constitution of the Republic of Cyprus.

[27] See in general Part 9 (Articles 133 - 151) of the Constitution of the Republic of Cyprus.

[28] See in general Part 10 (Articles 152 - 164) of the Constitution of the Republic of Cyprus.

The viability of this very elaborate and rigid Constitution was brought into question from the very first years of its life. The first President of Cyprus, Archbishop Makarios, proposed thirteen amendments[29] to the Vice-president Dr. Kucuk, which would 'remove obstacles to the smooth functioning and development of the state'. The atmosphere after the presentation of the thirteen proposals was very tense, with the Turkish Cypriots interpreting the move as a preparation to slide into Enosis. This tension[30] was the main cause that led to the first, low-scale, intercommunal armed conflict. It started on 21 December 1963 and led to the establishment of the 'Green Line', a neutral zone between the Greek and the Turkish quarters in the capital city, Nicosia. From that moment on and until 1974, the two Communities together with the three guarantor states and the United Nations were negotiating in order to find a viable solution for Cyprus while disorder and anarchy prevailed on the island – mainly because of the large number of weapons in the hands of para-military groups.

In 1974, following a coup against Archbishop Makarios; the President of Cyprus, organised by the military regime in Greece, Turkish forces invaded the island. The Security Council, in Resolution 353 (1974),[31] called upon all states to respect the sovereignty and territorial integrity of Cyprus and demanded an immediate end to foreign military intervention in the island that was contrary to such respect. On 13 February 1975 the Turkish Federated State of Cyprus was proclaimed in the area occupied by Turkish forces. A resolution adopted at the same meeting of the so-called Council of Ministers and Legislative Assembly of the Autonomous Turkish Cypriot Administration at which the proclamation was made, emphasised their determination 'to oppose resolutely all attempts against the independence of Cyprus and its partition or union with any other state' and resolved to establish a separate administration until such time as the 1960 Cyprus Constitution was amended to provide for a federal republic.[32]

On 15 November 1983, the Turkish Cypriots proclaimed their independence as the so-called 'Turkish Republic of Northern Cyprus'. This was declared illegal by the Security Council in Resolution 541 (1983)[33] and called for its withdrawal. All States were requested to refuse to recognise the 'purported state' or assist it in any way. This was reiterated in Security Council Resolution 550 (1984)[34]. The Council of Ministers of the Council of Europe decided that it continued to regard the government of the Republic of Cyprus as the sole legitimate government of Cyprus and called for respect for the independence and territorial integrity for Cyprus.[35]

---

[29] See in general *The 13 Points* November 1963; available at www.cyprus-conflict.net/13_points.htm.

[30] See supra n. 18.

[31] United Nations Security Council Resolution 353 (1974).

[32] Resolution No. 2 in Supplement IV, Official Gazette of the so-called Turkish Federated State of Cyprus.

[33] United Nations Security Council Resolution 541 (1983).

[34] United Nations Security Council Resolution 550 (1984).

[35] Resolution 83 (13) adopted on 24 November 1983.

On 4 July 1990, the Republic of Cyprus had applied for membership of the European Community. In its historic report, 'Agenda 2000'[36] containing its final recommendations on Accession negotiations, the European Commission noted, inter alia, that: 'The Union is determined to play a positive role in bringing about a just and lasting settlement in accordance with the relevant United Nations Resolutions'. On the other hand, the Helsinki European Council[37] in December 1999, clarified that the non-solution of the Cyprus problem could not hinder the island's efforts to join the EU.[38] On 16 April 2003 the President of the Republic of Cyprus, Mr. Tassos Papadopoulos signed the Treaty of Accession of the Republic of Cyprus to the European Union in Athens. The Protocol on Cyprus[39], attached to the Treaty of Accession 2003, provides for 'the suspension of the application of the acquis in those areas of the Republic of Cyprus in which the government of the Republic of Cyprus does not exercise effective control'. It adds that in the event of a settlement of the Cyprus problem, 'the Council, acting unanimously on the basis of a proposal from the Commission, shall decide on the adaptations to the terms concerning the accession of Cyprus to the European Union with regard to the Turkish Cypriot community'. Thus, the Republic of Cyprus as it was envisaged in the Cyprus Agreements of 1960 is a Member State of the EU but the application of the *acquis communautaire* is suspended for those areas in which the Republic does not exercise effective control. This status quo is analogous to that applied in Germany before its unification. It is obvious from the aforementioned that for EU purposes, the executive of the Republic of Cyprus is the only legitimate government of Cyprus and as such it is the laws of this government that regulate the status of Cypriot nationals for EU citizenship purposes.

---

[36] European Commission, *Agenda 2000 For a Stronger and Wider Union, COM (1997) 2000, 15 July 1997*. available at europa.eu.int/comm/agenda2000/index_en.htm.

[37] December 1999 Helsinki European Council Presidency Conclusions); available at europa.eu.int/council/off/conclu/dec99/dec99_en.htm.

[38] That position of the EU has been criticised especially in the light of the fact that the Greek Cypriots did not vote in favour of the settlement of the Cyprus problem as it was envisaged according to the Annan plan. The main argument against that position can be summarised as follows: if the solution of the Cyprus problem was a condition for the accession of the Republic of Cyprus to the EU, this would have either led to the settlement of the problem or the Cyprus problem would not have taken on an EU dimension. But that EU position is in full accordance with the prudent view that the Republic of Cyprus cannot be condemned because of a problem that has been created by an invasion from another State.

[39] The Treaty of Accession 2003 signed in Athens on 16 April 2003, *OJ* 2003 L 236/23 see Protocol 10 on Cyprus.

4 The Constitution and the Citizenship laws of the Republic of Cyprus

Article 14 of the Constitution of the Republic of Cyprus provides that '[n]o citizen shall be banished or excluded from the Republic under any circumstances'. Article 198[40] of the Constitution provides that 'any matter relating to citizenship shall be governed by the provisions of Annex D to the Treaty of Establishment' until such time as a law of citizenship is made incorporating such provisions. The Republic of Cyprus Citizenship Law of 1967,[41] which has been amended in 1972[42] and 1983,[43] makes provision for the acquisition and renunciation and deprivation of citizenship. According to section 3 of the aforementioned law: '[c]itizens of the Republic shall be the persons who, on the date of entry into force of the Law, have either acquired or are entitled to acquire citizenship of the Republic under the provisions of Annex D or who acquire thereafter such citizenship under the provisions of this Law'.

According to section 2 of Annex D[44] of the Treaty of Establishment, any person who became a British subject under the provisions of the Cyprus (Annexation) orders in Council, 1914 to 1943, or descended in the male line from such a person, or was born in the Island of Cyprus on or after 5 November 1914, and was ordinarily resident on the island of Cyprus at any time in the period of 5 years immediately before the date of said Treaty shall, on the date of the same Treaty become a citizen of the Republic of Cyprus. Moreover, section 4 provides the possibility for such persons, who, although they fall under the *ratione personae* of section 2 because they fall under one of the qualifications listed in paragraph 2 of section 3, do not automatically become citizens of the Republic of Cyprus, to apply to the appropriate authority in order for the Cypriot citizenship to be granted to them. Furthermore, section 5 makes provision for those who were granted a certificate of naturalisation by the Governor of

---

40 Article 198(1) reads as follows:

1. The following provisions shall have effect until a law of citizenship is made incorporating such provisions –

a) any matter relating to citizenship shall be governed by the provisions of Annex D to the Treaty of Establishment;

b) any person born in Cyprus, on or after the date of the coming into operation of this Constitution, shall become on the date of his birth a citizen of the Republic if on that date of his birth a citizen of the Republic or would but for his death have become such a citizen under the provisions of Annex D to the Treaty of Establishment.

41 The Republic of Cyprus Citizenship Law 1967.

42 The Republic of Cyprus Citizenship (Amendment) Law 1972.

43 The Republic of Cyprus Citizenship (Amendment) Law 1983.

44 Annex D of the Treaty of Establishment; available at www.kypros.org/Constitution/English/annex_d.html.

Cyprus, those who were registered as a citizen of the United Kingdom and Colonies by the Governor of Cyprus and for those descended in the male line from persons in the aforementioned categories, so that they may apply to the appropriate authority to be granted the citizenship of the Republic. Finally, section 6 provides for the right to citizenship of the spouses[45] of the persons who are entitled to citizenship of the Republic of Cyprus.

According to The Republic of Cyprus Citizenship Law of 1967[46] a person acquires citizenship by birth, by registration or by naturalisation. Section 4 of this law provides that a person acquires citizenship of the Republic of Cyprus by birth if any of his/her parents was a citizen at the time of their birth. Moreover, in accordance with paragraph 2 of section 5, a person becomes a citizen of Cyprus if s/he is married to a citizen of the Republic and the two have lived together for at least two years. Furthermore, if a citizen of the United Kingdom or of a Commonwealth country is of Cypriot origin, is ordinarily resident in Cyprus or is in the public service of the Republic and has been resident in Cyprus throughout the period of one year, is of good character and intends to continue reside in the Republic or to continue in the public service of the Republic, that person shall be entitled to apply to the Minister to be registered as a citizen of the Republic.

On the other hand, a citizen may renounce citizenship[47] by making a formal declaration which must be registered; the registration may be withheld if the reason for the renunciation is to avoid military service and so also to evade criminal prosecution. In addition, a citizen may be deprived[48] of citizenship by a decision of the Council of Ministers in cases where citizenship was first acquired by registration or by naturalisation. Section 8 of the Law states that the Council of Ministers may deprive a citizen of citizenship if:

1. it was obtained by fraud, false representation or by the concealment of any material fact;
2. a naturalised person shows himself or herself to be disloyal or disaffected towards the Republic;
3. the naturalised person had dealings with the enemy in time of war;
4. a naturalised person was sentenced to a term of imprisonment of not less than 12 months within 5 years from the date of his/her naturalisation;
5. a naturalised person has been resident in a foreign country for a period of 7 years during which time that person has not, at any time, been in the service of the Republic or of an international organisation of which the Republic was a member, and nor has that person been registered annually

---

[45] Although the wording of the provision mentions only women in the light of the evolution of the western societies in matters of gender equality we can read the word woman as spouse.

[46] Supra n. 41.

[47] Section 7 of The Republic of Cyprus Citizenship Law of 1967.

[48] Section 8 of The Republic of Cyprus Citizenship Law of 1967.

in the prescribed manner at a consulate of the Republic expressing the intention to retain citizenship of the Republic.

Thus, as far as concerns the situation of the inhabitants of the [occupied] areas in which the Government of the Republic of Cyprus does not exercise effective control, the Republic of Cyprus[49] continues to recognise citizenship and the right to citizenship, in accordance with the aforementioned legal status quo, of all Turkish Cypriots and Cyprus Republic passports issued to any persons who can provide proper documentation. Hence, they possess an EU citizenship in 'hibernation', which can be activated if they provide proper documentation to the relevant authority of the only recognised government in the island. The citizens of the Democratic Republic of Germany faced an analogous situation before the fall of the Berlin wall and they were considered to fall under the *ratione personae* of the EEC Treaty.

5 A special case: the settlers

This section of the chapter deals with the special category of inhabitants of the [occupied] areas in which the Government of the Republic of Cyprus does not exercise effective control, created in the aftermath of the 1974 invasion as a result of the policy of the so-called Turkish Republic of Northern Cyprus and the Occupation Forces, otherwise known as 'the settlers'.

In the part of Cyprus occupied by the Turkish army since 1974, Turkey has implemented a policy of systematic colonisation in order to change the demographic character of the island.[50] According to reports confirmed in both the Turkish and Turkish Cypriot press, those settlers come from the Turkish mainland and are of Turkish citizenship. Today in the occupied part of Cyprus, according to the Republic of Cyprus authorities[51] there are about 115,000 settlers. On the other hand, Turkish Cypriot sources refer to a number less than 90,000. There is, of course, also, the presence of 35,000 Turkish occupation troops.[52] Turkey's policy of colonisation is contrary to the 1960 Treaty of Establishment[53] of the Republic of Cyprus. Annex D to the Treaty, as formerly mentioned, governs Cypriot citizenship and makes it impossible and unlawful for either Community to upset the demographic balance by bringing in large numbers of ethnic Turks or Greeks and, further, contends that they were of Greek Cypriot

49 See in general U.S. Office of Personnel Management Investigation Service, *Citizenship of the world*, March 2001, page 62; available at labs.ucop. edu/internet/security/forms/citizenship. pdf

50 See in general the Cyprus question in www.mfa.gov.cy.

51 *Ibid.*

52 *Ibid.*

53 Supra n. 19.

or Turkish Cypriot descent and entitled to come to Cyprus as a result thereof. Section 4(7) imposes quotas regarding the grant of citizenship to persons who had emigrated to Greece, Turkey or the British Commonwealth before 1955 having been resident in Cyprus or descended from Ottoman subjects resident in Cyprus in 1914. The Republic of Cyprus does not consider those alien persons, who have settled illegally and without permission in the areas under control of the Turkish forces, as legitimate claimants to Cypriot citizenship[54] and thus they do not have access to EU citizenship via the citizenship laws of the Republic of Cyprus.

But if the United Cyprus Republic, as envisaged in the Annan plan[55], was established by the two referenda that had taken place in Cyprus on 24 April 2004, the situation concerning the settlers and EU citizenship would have been quite different. It is quite important to examine the provisions of the Annan Plan referring to Cypriot citizenship and especially to the settlers because not only do the provisions of the Constitution attached to that unification plan differentiate from the policy adopted by the Republic of Cyprus but there is also a possibility that a new referendum will take place for the establishment of the United Cyprus Republic, in accordance with a slightly amended Annan plan. According to Article 12 of the Constitution of the United Cyprus Republic[56], there is one single Cypriot citizenship. Moreover, '[a]ll persons holding Cypriot citizenship shall also enjoy internal constituent state citizenship status as provided for by Constitutional law. Such status is complementary to and does not replace Cypriot citizenship'.[57] Provisions, which state that the internal constituent state citizenship status shall be regulated by the Constitutional Law on Internal Constituent State Citizenship Status and Constituent State Residency Rights[58], are included in the Constitutions of both the constituent Cypriot States.[59] But, it is the Federal Law to Provide for the Citizenship of the United Cyprus Republic and For Matters Connected Therewith or Incidental Thereto[60] that regulates Cypriot citizenship and, thus also, the EU citizenship

---

54 Supra n. 49.

55 The UN plan for Cyprus; available at www.cyprus-un-plan.org/.

56 The Constitution of the United Cyprus Republic; available at www.cyprus-un-plan.org/AnnexI/AnnexI.pdf.

57 *Ibid.* at Art. 12(2).

58 Constitutional Law on Internal Constituent State Citizenship Status and Constituent State Residency Rights; available at www.cyprus-un-plan.org/AnnexII/AnIIAt3_Constitutional_Law_on_Internal_Constituent_State_Cit.pdf.

59 Art. 8 of the Constitution of the Greek Cypriot State; available at www.cyprus-un-plan.org/AnnexI/CONSTITUTION_OF_THE_GREEK_CYPRIOT_STATE.pdf; and 73 of the Constitution of the Turkish Cypriot; available at www.cyprus-un-plan.org/AnnexI/CONSTITUTION_OF_THE_TURKISH_CYPRIOT_STATE.pdf .

60 Federal Law to Provide for the Citizenship of the United Cyprus Republic and For Matters Connected Therewith or Incidental Thereto; available at www.cyprus-un-plan.org/AnnexIII/AnIIIAt4_Federal_Law_on_Citizenship. pdf.

for nationals of this state. According to section 3(1) of the Federal Law to Provide for the Citizenship of the United Cyprus Republic and For Matters Connected Therewith or Incidental Thereto, any person who held Cypriot citizenship on 31 December 1963[61], the descendants of those persons and the spouses of such persons shall be considered citizens of the United Cyprus Republic upon the relevant date. In addition to the above, persons whose names[62] are on a list handed over to the UN Secretary-General by each side shall be considered citizens of the Republic. These two lists may number no more than 45,000 persons, inclusive of their spouses and children. Applicants should be included on the list according to the following criteria and in the following order of priority:

1. persons who enjoyed permanent residence on Cyprus for at least 7 years before reaching the age of 18 and for at least 1 year during the 5 years immediately preceding the relevant date, and;
2. other persons who have enjoyed permanent residence on Cyprus for more than 7 consecutive years based on the length of their stay.

This provision clearly offers 45,000 settlers the possibility of becoming EU citizens. And, although the figure in a possible future unification of the island may be altered, it is inevitable that similar provisions will give a significant number of settlers the opportunity to obtain access to EU citizenship, which, until now under the formerly mentioned legal status quo of the Republic of Cyprus, has been impossible.

6 De facto citizenship?

This part of the paper addresses the issue of whether the new 'Green Line' regulation adopted after the rejection from the Greek Cypriots of the Annan plan in the referendum of 24 April 2004, provides for the inhabitants of the [occupied] areas in which the Government of the Republic of Cyprus does not exercise effective control, such rights that they may be deemed *de facto* EU citizens. The Council[63] adopted Regulation 866/2004 on a regime under Article 2 of Protocol 10[64] on Cyprus of the Act of Accession on 29 April 2004 (hereinafter 'the Regulation'). The Regulation defines the terms under which the provisions of EU law will apply to the line between the areas in which the

---

[61] This date is connected with the incidents that led to the establishment of the 'Green Line' during December 1963. See in general section 3. Historical Background below.

[62] Section 3(2); supra n. 58.

[63] EU Council press release 8572/04 *Cyprus / accession – Council adopts Regulation on the "green line"*; available at ue.eu.int/ueDocs/cms_Data/docs/pressData/en/misc/80092.pdf.

[64] Supra n. 39.

Government of the Republic of Cyprus exercises effective control and the areas in which it does not ('Green Line'). Since this line does not constitute an external border of the EU, special rules concerning the crossing of goods, services and persons need to be established. The Regulation is intended to facilitate trade and other links between the areas in which the Government of the Republic of Cyprus exercises effective control and the areas in which it does not, all the while ensuring that appropriate standards are maintained. Regarding persons, the Green Line Regulation indicates in particular that, while taking into account the legitimate concerns of the Government of the Republic of Cyprus, it is necessary to enable EU citizens to exercise their right of free movement within the EU and set the minimum rules for carrying out checks on persons at the Green Line.[65] Although, in the light of the recent developments, according to which there is an opening of the 'Green Line Border'[66], and of the fact that the Republic of Cyprus is more than willing to grant the status of Cypriot citizen to those entitled to it according to the Constitution and the laws of the State, it seems that the free movement of EU citizens is far less hindered at present than it used to be. So, this Regulation still neither solves the 'state of siege' for the Karpas Greek Cypriot and Maronites, who are entitled to the EU citizenship status, nor does it protect the Turkish Cypriots who want to become citizens of the Republic of Cyprus but are concerned with the consequences of such decision because of the oppressive regime in the North. Furthermore, although the Regulation contains provisions about the right of free movement that the EU citizens should enjoy, there is no mention of the other rights attached to the status of EU citizenship. Hence, it seems misleading to speak about *de facto* citizenship. The inhabitants of the [occupied] areas in which the Government of the Republic of Cyprus does not exercise effective control in Cyprus, therefore, possess an EU citizenship status in 'hibernation'.

7 Possible implications of *Loizidou* v. *Turkey*[67] cases

In the *Loizidou* v. *Turkey* cases[68], the European Court of Human Rights, was conscious of the need to avoid a regrettable vacuum in the system of human rights protection. Although both Cyprus and Turkey are Contracting Parties of the European Convention of Human Rights, the inhabitants of the [occupied] areas in which the Government of the Republic of Cyprus does not exercise effective control may not fall under the *ratione loci* and nor may the inhabitants fall under the *ratione personae* of the Convention because those areas

---

65 Supra n.2, Art. 2.

66 Supra n. 18.

67 Supra n. 3.

68 Op. cit. n.3.

are not *de facto* under the effective control of the Republic of Cyprus. Turkey also argues that it does not exercise effective control over those areas that are the independent 'pseudo-state' Turkish Republic of Northern Cyprus, which has been recognised only by the Turkish Republic.[69] Hence, in order to respect its obligation to protect the European public order for the protection of individual human rights, the European Court of Human Rights held that the Turkish forces do indeed have effective control over Northern Cyprus and, thus, the Turkish Republic is responsible for protecting the human rights in those areas. It follows, therefore, that the inhabitants of the [occupied] areas where the Government of the Republic of Cyprus does not exercise effective control, according to the ratio decidendi of this case, can secure their rights that derive from the European Convention of Human Rights through the Turkish judicial system since, on the one hand, the Turkish Republic is a Contracting Party to the Convention and, on the other hand, Turkey has effective control over those areas.

But what would be the result if the European Court of Justice were to adopt an analogous ratio decidendi and agreed with the Strasbourg Court that Turkey has effective control of those areas?

To trace the formerly mentioned legal reasoning to the Community law environment, the same vacuum arises in the protection of the EC freedoms of the inhabitants of the [occupied] areas in which the Government of the Republic of Cyprus does not exercise effective control in Cyprus. That is because on the one hand, the citizens of the Republic of Cyprus are EU citizens and on the other hand, the Turkish citizens enjoy the rights provided by the Association Agreement with Turkey, the so-called Ankara Agreement,[70] and at some future moment they may even enjoy full EU citizenship rights. Undoubtedly, there is a substantial difference between the rights conferred on the citizens of the Cyprus Republic and to those of the Turkish Republic. But there is still a lacuna concerning the Community rights of the inhabitants of the [occupied] areas in which the Government of the Republic of Cyprus does not exercise effective control. Those citizens enjoy neither the rights that the former enjoy as EU citizens nor the rights that the latter enjoy under the so-called Ankara Agreement. Thus, in the highly improbable situation that the European Court of Justice would endorse an analogous ratio decidendi, the inhabitants of the [occupied] areas in which the Government of the Republic of Cyprus does not exercise effective control should;

a. either be conferred the rights enjoyed by the citizens of Turkey because of the Association Agreement since they are under the effective control of the same government as the Turkish citizens, or;

---

69 See in general section 3. Historical Background below.

70 Association Agreement with Turkey *JO* 1964 217 (French language version), *OJ* 1973 C 113/2 (English language version).

b. Turkey should be found liable for restricting access to the EU citizenship status and the rights attached thereof to persons entitled to them.

On the other hand, if the Court endorses such a rationale, thus taking the lead of the Strasbourg Court that Turkey has the effective control of those areas, the Union would automatically stop referring to those areas merely as areas over which the Republic of Cyprus does not have effective control, a *sui generis* 'no man's land'. It would, for the first time, recognise those areas as EU areas over which a non-EU state has effective control which hinders the rights of EU citizens. It remains improbable that the ECJ would endorse such a rationale. Whether the regime in the [occupied] areas where the Government of the Republic of Cyprus does not exercise effective control could or would be challenged in front of the ECJ is a most topical question, especially in the context of Turkey's pre-accession efforts to join the Union.

8 Conclusion

It is obvious from the aforementioned analysis of the status of the inhabitants of the [occupied] areas where the Government of the Republic of Cyprus does not exercise effective control with regard to EU Citizenship, is rather complex. The 1974 invasion created an anomaly concerning the status of such persons. And, although the Constitution and the Citizenship laws of the universally recognised Republic of Cyprus offer something of a solution, the reality created by the Occupation sets the limits to it. As far as it concerns the status of those persons, legal certainty will be established only when the island is unified again under the aegis of a new sovereign and independent state. The European Union should be determined to play 'a positive role in bringing about a just and lasting settlement in accordance with the relevant United Nations Resolutions'[71] since the very *telos* of the Union is to secure the values of peace, democracy and prosperity for its citizens.

71 Supra n. 36.

CHAPTER 8

The Impact of Agriculture on the Success of Enlargement

Sandra Marco Colino[1]

1 Introduction

The recent Central and Eastern enlargement of the EU has been top of the political agenda since 1993, when the historic decision of widening the EU territory towards the East was taken in the European Council of Copenhagen. Negotiations leading to this 'venture into the unknown'[2] began in March 1998 and proved to be very challenging for the EU and candidates alike, at times appearing to put at risk the entire process of integration. This paper assesses the monumental effect of enlargement towards Central and Eastern Europe on the CAP with the intention of predicting how the reform of the policy has been and will continue to be affected by the presence of the new members. The latest impulse for reform of this common policy is aimed at fostering an entirely new perspective on agriculture in Europe and also the global context. The challenge is to construct alternative tools of integration to enable the successful convergence of nations with major economic differences.

The first widening of the EU territory since the ratification of the Nice Treaty aggravated a number of sensitive issues in EU integration. In particular, the complexity of the enlargement process unavoidably led to a climate of tension in the intergovernmental give-and-take that is the decision-making process of the Union. Moreover in addition to the Ten new members, that joined the EU on 1 May 2004,[3] and Romania and Bulgaria are set to join in 2007 and Turkey is on the brink of opening accession negotiations.[4] The Thirteen new Members bring 100 million new consumers with an average purchasing power of less than a third of that of the Fifteen to the Union's market. From the point of view of agriculture, enlarging the EU implies expanding by 50 percent the total area of farming and a doubling of the agricultural labour force. These challenges naturally prompted much political debate within the Union at a time of deep concern over budgetary reform and the need for a new agricultural policy at EU level.

Difficulties aside, enlargement is said to be the perfect occasion for achieving 'higher goals of European unity.'[5] In opting to extend the benefits of membership to the CEEC, political rhetoric and abstract theorising have played

---

1 This paper would never have materialised but for the unconditional help and invaluable advice of Mr. Martin J. Doris.

2 Expression used in the *Editorial comments*, 35 *CMLRev.* (1998).

3 These countries are: the Czech Republic, Cyprus, Estonia, Hungary, Latvia, Lithuania, Malta, Slovakia and Slovenia.

4 In principle, the accession of Romania and Bulgaria is expected to take place in 2007. The case for Turkey is less certain. On this topic, see yaleglobal.yale.edu/display.article?id=3475, www.qantara.de/webcom/show_article.php/_c-301/_nr-42/_p-1/i.html or www.eubusiness.com/afp/041006125211.gdjpr1xj.

5 D. Baker, 'Agriculture in the EU's Eastern Enlargement', (Copenhagen, Fødevareøkonomisk Institut 2002), p. 144.

an important role. It is often claimed that enlargement poses a unique opportunity for Europe to unite by peaceful means.[6] Others argue that the economic arguments in favour of an amplified Union are stronger still: it has been estimated that the stability and prosperity of the single market will be widened, bringing a boost in economic activity throughout the whole of the EU. Regardless of whether it is security or prosperity – or indeed both – that has motivated the decision to enlarge, this paper focuses on whether or not the accession of these countries will be economically sustainable. This paper analyses the cost of the enlargement by examining the most expensive common policy, the Common Agricultural Policy (CAP).

The first part of the paper provides a brief analysis of the relevant aspects of the enlargement process. The CAP and the reforms of agricultural policy introduced in preparation for enlargement are assessed in the second part. The third part highlights a number of political problems that may arise between the Member States and within the domestic politics of the new members.

2 The enlargement process in context: The Copenhagen criteria and the CAP

In order to provide workable suggestions on how the CAP has been affected by the accession of the new members on 1 May 2004, it is necessary to explore the background to the most recent enlargement. Even before agreeing to the inclusion of the Central and Eastern European countries (CEEC) within the EU, the Union had been implementing a strategy of support towards this area of Europe. After the fall of the Berlin Wall in November 1989, the PHARE Programme was immediately established,[7] providing not only emergency aid but also economic support for modernisation and restructuring. Shortly afterwards, in December 1991, the Europe Agreements were concluded after almost a year of negotiations with four countries: Poland, Hungary, the Czech Republic and Slovakia.[8] These agreements provide the legal basis for bilateral relations and agricultural trade between the mentioned nations and the Community and aimed to promote co-operation in order to modernise, restructure and privatise agriculture. Throughout the 1990s, similar agreements were signed with the remainder of the CEEC candidates for accession. The most controversial part of the Europe Agreements proved to be the trade-related protocols, which not only aimed at reducing tariffs and regulating export subsidies

---

6 See, *inter alia*, europa.eu.int/pol/enlarg/overview_en.htm, and A. Downer, 'EU Enlargement: Meeting the Challenges of Global Security and Trade Environment', speech, *National Europe Centre Conference on EU Enlargement*, (Canberra 2003).

7 See *infra* 3.2.

8 The Europe Agreements are also referred to as the Association Agreements.

but also sought the bilateral asymmetrical liberalisation of market access. Whilst initially they applied solely to industrial products, soon agricultural products and processed foods were also affected. In principle, they feature mutual Tariff Rate Quota market access, on a two-stage schedule for liberalisation actions for each associated country and the EU.[9] In practice, numerous amendments to these protocols were made with all applicant countries. These adjustments imply substantial differences between the then candidates for accession in the amount, scheduling and emphasis of trade access under these Agreements.

In 1993, the crucial leap towards integrating the CEEC into the Union was taken in the Copenhagen summit, when the European Council agreed to accept as EU members nations which until now had been only associated countries. It was then that the conditions for entry, the so-called Copenhagen criteria, were decided. The first of these required that candidates have a stable democratic political system. A functioning market economy with the potential to compete inside the single market was a second requirement. Finally, the capacity to fulfil the responsibilities of membership by implementing the *acquis communautaire* was also requested. As regards this third condition, it is precisely the agricultural elements of the *acquis* which have proved to be the most demanding. However, it was not only the candidates for membership that had to undergo action. The fifteen old Member states (hereinafter 'the Fifteen') also needed to make changes. One of the conditions it had to comply with in order to smooth the path for enlargement was to bring forward new orientations for the CAP. The reform of the CAP was, even then, considered one of the priorities to be tackled for making the Enlargement a success. Already before 1993, the CEEC had been proceeding with programmes of economic transition and integration into the world economy. They had been assisted by aid from the EU and other countries as well as by private investments. Also during this period the EU has been building its internal market and defining the role of that market in the context of agriculture. Simultaneously, the World Trade Organisation (WTO) expanded its membership and its scope of operations into agricultural trade and domestic support.[10]

The effects on agricultural policy are more than substantial. The new Members are transition economies and as such they have populations that are less wealthy and more rural than those of the veteran Fifteen. The agricultural sectors of the CEEC set out as technologically limited and dominated by peasant-style production system. Over the last ten years, immense improvements have been made in the countries' production and marketing systems, land use patterns, pricing mechanisms, ownership and systems of governance. The complexity of bringing so many diverse transition economies simultaneously

---

9 For more details on these Agreements, see Baker, *supra* n. 5.

10 See also A. Mayhew, 'The Financial and Budgetary Impact of Enlargement and Accession', in C. Hillion, ed., *EU Enlargement: A Legal Approach*, (Oxford, Hart Publishing 2004) pp. 143-167.

into a single market and policy regime is an unprecedented challenge for the EU and its institutions. One of the priorities to be addressed in the Union is how to reduce the huge budgetary impact of the CAP that so much worries the so-called net contributors like the UK or Germany. However, enlargement implies the disbursement of even larger funds for the Fifteen. How can these two contradictory tendencies be reconciled in a satisfactory way for everyone? Complex political discussions will have to take place so that such opposing goals can somehow come together in a way that grants coherence and political strength.

3 A common policy no longer 'in common'? The CAP before and after enlargement

The CAP affects the daily lives of the entire European population. Apart from the direct consequences on those who are dedicated to agricultural activity, every individual as a consumer and often also as taxpayers are concerned. It is estimated that the CAP costs the citizens of the EU more than €100 billion a year.[11] High cost proves to be a constant source of political friction and, thus, particular attention is paid to how the CAP is financed and how the new enlarged Union will increase the bill.

3.1 The evolution of the CAP from its origins

The CAP is a key element in a wider process of integration, a process in which political union is being preceded by and achieved through economic unification. Integration is being promoted via the harmonisation of divergent national economic strategies and the eventual creation of new common policies. Of all such EU agendas, the CAP presents itself as the most significant ongoing project. Since its conception in 1958 at the Stresa Conference,[12] the third oldest common policy[13] has played a crucial role in the development of the EU, being dubbed 'an icon of European integration.'[14] Indeed, traditionally the idea of the European Community was primarily associated with the establishment of uniform rules for agriculture. Since it began functioning in 1962, it has become a crucial pillar of European integration.

---

11 OECD, *Monitoring Agricultural Support*, Paris, as cited in J. Rollo, 'Agriculture, the Structural Funds and the Budget after Enlargement', 68 *Sussex European Institute* (2003) p. 4.

12 In this Conference, the then six members of the European Economic Community established the creation of Common Market Organisations.

13 It was created after the customs union and competition policy.

14 J. Rollo, op. cit. n. 11, at p. 4.

The motivation that led to the creation of the CAP are varied. First and foremost is the fact that increasingly urban modern societies remain dependent upon the supply of agricultural products whilst those dedicated to the essential task of providing such commodities must be encouraged to continue to undertake this form of labour. Equally important are the risks inherent to agricultural activity, such as harsh weather conditions capable of destroying a season's harvest. Thus the CAP sought to buffer the farming community from losses suffered as a result. Also farmers typically reside in underprivileged areas, which implies a disincentive to farmers from continuing to provide such an indispensable activity.[15] From the point of view of consumers, and market stability the main concern is the need to guarantee the supply of goods at affordable prices. Besides these general characteristics, agricultural trade in Europe is of particular importance, as the EU is the world's leading importer and second largest exporter of agricultural produce. Each enlargement has steadily increased the Union's self-sufficiency (See Chart 1 below). In turn the result has been a reduction in the Union's dependency on agricultural imports and this has been further guarded against by means of a markedly protectionist policy against such imports.

Chart 1. Self-supply of the European Union 'Agriculture, the Structural Funds and the Budget after Enlargement', 68 Sussex European Institute (2003) p. 4.

Source: European Commission DG I Foreign Relations and DG VI Agriculture, and EUROSTAT.

[15] See B. Hervieu and C. Beranger, 'New Regulation of Agriculture and Rural Development in Europe Particularly in France through Multifunctional Character of Agriculture and Land', in *International Conference on European Rural Policy at the Crossroads*, (Arkleton Centre for Rural Development and Research, University of Aberdeen 2002).

The primary legal bases for the CAP are contained in Articles 32 to 38 EC (ex Arts 34-47 ECT) which set out the uniform criteria applicable. EU policies on agriculture and rural development are implemented by the Directorate-General for Agriculture of the European Commission.[16] However, the modifications need to be considered in the wider context of the WTO. The obligations the EU in the context of the General Agreement on Trade and Tariffs (GATT) also exert a substantial influence on the shape of the CAP. Negotiations under the Uruguay Round established ceilings for the total amount of agricultural export subsidies.[17] Within the Europe of Twenty-five these limits had to become duties. The EU will continue to aim for a broad based agreement, as it will leave all WTO partners more room for manoeuvre in the context of a global package. Given the general consensus within the WTO that trade liberalisation is economically beneficial, the CAP is striving towards liberalisation.[18]

The main social, economic and political objectives of the CAP are established in Article 33 EC (ex Art. 35 ECT).[19] These objectives have been deliberately framed in a broad, open-ended manner in order that they can be more easily adapted as the process of integration evolves. An abundant case law from the European Court of Justice has evolved in this field, particularly as concerns the free movement of goods. The instruments adopted to put the CAP into practice vary from a wide range of activities and the Common Organisations of the Market (CMO) are the most important. They are the group of rules which organise the market of each product or group of similar products, rules that are to be applied by the institutions of the Union as well as by the national authorities of each Member State.

Financing the CAP remains the most delicate issue. The burden falls on the Member States, who must contribute to the Community Budget in proportion to each country's individual economic capacity. Created in 1962, it is the European Agricultural Guidance and Guarantee Fund (hereinafter 'the EAGGF') that is in charge of determining the distribution of funds. As its name suggests, the EAGGF comprises two parts: the Guidance Section, which takes care of the structural policy and deals with the development of less favoured regions and rural areas, and the Guarantee Section, where trade policy is examined and financed (See Table 1 which provides a clarifying example of how these funds are allocated by showing the distribution of the 1999 budget.) A total of EUR

---

16 See also www.europarl.eu.int/comm/dg06.

17 J. M. Sumpsi and L. V. Barceló Vila, *La Ronda Uruguay y el Sector Agroalimentario Español* (Madrid, Ministerio de Agricultura, Pesca y Alimentación 1996).

18 See also Mayhew, *supra* n. 10, pp. 145-147.

19 The objectives are: to increase the productivity of the agriculture; to ensure a fair standard of living for the agricultural community; to guarantee the stabilisation of markets; to ensure a supply of food at reasonable prices for consumers.

40,440 million was allocated to the EAGGF Guarantee Section, broken down as follows (in million Euro):

Table 1. Financing the common agricultural policy: the EAGGF

Crop products	26,982
Livestock products	9,666
Other measures (excluding clearance of accounting)	1,500
Accompanying measures	2,597
(i) Guarantee section total	40,745

Source: General Report 1999-Chapter IV: The Community economic and social area. Section 19: Agricultural policy (35/38).

The reality of enlargement further exacerbates the financing problems of the agricultural policy. Without the new members, the CAP already comprised the largest share of the EU budget, at no less than 0.6 per cent of GNP. If the policy was already too costly in a Union of Fifteen, the entry of new Member States (hereinafter 'Ten'), with their outstandingly large and inefficient agricultural sectors and with limited capacity to contribute towards the Budget, seems implausible. The estimated additional costs needed to administrate the agricultural sector in an enlarged Union fluctuate between EUR 5,000 and EUR 50,000 million.

It was long evident that adaptations to the policy were urgently required. Building a new policy in which less money is spent on each commodity whilst keeping the traditional CAP guidelines, is designed to make it possible to invest in the newcomers. A slight increase of expenditure for the Fifteen is also necessary.[20] The policy is therefore changing in order to adapt to the recent needs of Europe, cutting expenses where possible so as to be able to invest in new, emerging realities. These adaptations are analysed in the following pages.

3.2 Pre-accession aid provided to the new members for agricultural issues

The pre-accession preparations of the Ten demanded enormous efforts on their part in order to adapt and build their legal, political and economic frameworks in order to prepare for their inclusion in the CAP as Member States. The EU had already provided economic help to the CEEC from

20 For instance, the Budget rose from ECU 41 billion in the year 2000 to 42 billion the following year. See OFCE, *Observations et diagnostics économiques*, No. 66 (Paris, 1998), p. 37-60.

the outset[21] but this aid was granted for economic and social transition and not, initially, with future membership in mind. The reasoning behind pre-accession funding was twofold. From the perspective of the CEEC, had they not received such assistance, the supposed benefits of accession may have been undermined, resulting in a negative attitude towards membership in the Fifteen and the Ten. For the Fifteen, it was considered more advantageous to begin providing financial benefits incrementally in order to commence the process of raising CEEC standards to those of the EU.

Specific Community programmes aimed to better organise the distribution of financial aid and identify the activities eligible for financing. In the period of the present financial framework 2000-2006, a total of EUR 22 billion was assigned to the eight CEEC through: PHARE, ISPA and SAPARD.

Table 2. Indicative Budget Allocations for All Three Pre-Accession Instruments from the Year 2000.

€ million p.a. (1997 prices)	
SAPARD	500
ISPA	1000
Phare	1500
Total	3000

Source: www.europa.eu.int/comm/dg06/publi/fact/sapard/index_en.htm

Technical support was provided through the Poland-Hungary Assistance for Reconstruction of the Economy (PHARE), which has been concerned with the development of new institutions and investment for the adoption of the *acquis* in these countries. The Instrument for Structural Policies for Pre-Accession (ISPA) was used for regional policy. It provides financial assistance for development of infrastructure for the environment and transport, focusing on cohesion and social development. The primary pre-accession instrument was the Special Accession Programme for Agriculture and Rural Development (SAPARD), set up to provide financial and institutional assistance to agriculture and for rural development through the establishment of framework aid and to implement the *acquis communautaire* concerning the CAP. In particular, it set out the criteria for the allocation of agriculture and rural development assistance in the pre-accession phase. The measures to be taken in order to achieve these goals are also outlined in the programme, and include investment in agricultural holdings, the improvement of product marketing, protection of the environment, the re-parcelling of land, the improvement of vocational training and, more

[21] See *supra* n. 2.

generally, the diversifying of economic activities in order to create alternative incomes.

The SAPARD beneficiaries were required to draft a plan of action for the promotion of agriculture and rural development. This action plan required the new members to specify the final targets for economic assistance,[22] and the measures to be taken. The Commission thereafter distributed the funds available according to four basic criteria: Agricultural population, agricultural area, GDP per capita, and specific situation of the area.

Both SAPARD and ISPA were in operation from 2000 until the date of accession. However, SAPARD, ISPA and PHARE were not the only ways of providing subsidies for agriculture. Pre-accession assistance took many forms, including technical assistance where transfers are less direct and more long-term than, for example, the supply of equipment. There were other projects which emerged from different initiatives. For instance, the Commission and the COPA/COCEGA and CEJA (representative organisations of farmers at EU level) launched a 15 month project in order to assist the national agricultural organisations in the ten CEEC applicant countries to build know-how and to enforce the body of EU legislation in the agriculture and food sectors. This aid materialised in the form of long-term experts, trainee placements and high level seminars and workshops. The sum of money invested was EUR 2.5 million.[23] This is one of the numerous examples of activities carried out which reflect the effort made by both the EU and the new members into the enlargement project.

'The integrated and sustainable countryside based on the participation of every man and woman'[24] was highlighted as a key priority at a conference in Cork in 1996, where representatives of the then candidates for accession were in attendance. This event, defined by the Irish State Minister for rural development Mr. Jimmy Deenihan, as the most important conference on this subject ever in Europe, led to the Cork Declaration.[25] It insisted on the importance of placing agriculture at the heart of rural development. In addition, the Joint Venture Programme (JOP) was set up in order to promote productive investments, notably the creation of joint ventures, involving one enterprise from the Fifteen and one from the CEEC. It provided integration and financial aid to those wishing to create, develop or restructure a joint venture. All productive sectors may benefit except for the financial service sector. Other secondary events for integration

---

22 The so-called 'final beneficiaries' are, as described in the SAPARD, the 'public or private enterprises responsible for performing the operations', as well as the 'institutions entrusted by the national authorities to grant public aids.'

23 IP/99/700, Brussels, 27 September 1999. See www.europa.eu.int/rapid/start/cgi/guesten.ksh?p_action.gettxt=gt&.

24 Commissioner Franz Fischler, *A Living Countryside*, www.rural-europe.aeidl.be/rural-en/biblio/cork/art02.htm.

25 See europa.eu.int/comm/archives/ leader2/dossier_p/en/dossier/cork.pdf.

take place simultaneously, such as the Die East-West Festival, which was hosted annually in the little German town of the same name. Each year, a different CEEC country was the focus of the festivities and the event is becoming increasingly popular, establishing a network of activities with these States. One of the priorities is the exchange of know-how, technologies and complementary products in different areas, including those related to the CAP. It is therefore an impulse towards the desired closer co-operation with the new and the future members.

3.3 Adaptations in agriculture since the Agenda 2000

3.3.1 Motivation behind the changes

Officially, the new reforms of the agricultural policy are said to have emerged independently of enlargement. Indeed, this is to some extent true when it is considered that Agenda 2000 was not the first attempt to renew the CAP. Reforms date as far back as 1969, when the second Mansholt Plan attempted to address the first problems of agricultural surpluses and the high expenditure that resulted from the immense growth experienced by EU agriculture since the CAP's inception. The Fifteen had already sought to respond to the new challenges of agriculture. The CAP was already proving too costly to implement in practice and resulting in a highly inefficient allocation of resources. Moreover, in the context of globalisation and the evolution of the Union, an ever growing necessity to protect the environment, health and social standards as well as cultural diversity, the priorities and concerns governing sustainable agriculture had to be reassessed. The concept of multifunctionality in agriculture emerged. While seeking its share in the expansion of world trade for agricultural products, the EU also sought to ensure that progress in trade would not damage the legitimate concerns of the public related to food safety and quality, maintaining the territorial balance and preserving the landscape and the environment. In this sense, the CAP needed to be modified even in the former smaller Union of fifteen Member States in order to create a policy in accordance with these priorities.[26] One of the aims of the Agenda 2000 was to ensure that farming throughout the Union be 'sustainable and competitive, capable of maintaining the landscape, preserving nature, contributing to vitality of the countryside and responding to the concerns and demands of customers in terms of food quality and safety, environmental protection and animal welfare.' The reform evidently concerns all stakeholders, from consumers to farmers.

---

[26] For a detailed study of multifunctionalism in agriculture, see B. Hervieu and C. Beranger, *supra* n. 15.

Apart from the above motivations for the new changes, it is clear that the main purpose in mind when reforming the CAP has been the accession of the CEEC, including Bulgaria and Romania. The CAP clearly held crucial implications for the enlargement process. The final conditions offered to the new Members in the agricultural sector. As such, enlargement provided a most opportune moment for such a complete review of the CAP.[27] Indeed, a detailed examination of previous major reforms reveals that a heightened concern for rural development coincided with former enlargements. Socio-structural policies were introduced in 1971 just prior to the accession of the United Kingdom, Ireland and Denmark in 1973. Even more important were the reforms that occurred in 1985, a year before Spain and Portugal entered the Community, when the *Green Paper on Perspectives for the Common Agricultural Policy* was published and the structural funds were modernised. Again, in 1994, new GATT agreements bringing the CAP somewhat closer to the WTO standards were signed in Marrakesh and in less than a year, the fourth enlargement took place when Finland, Sweden and Austria became members.

Thus, the proposals made by the Commission in 1997 in the *Agenda 2000* can be considered far more than a mere declaration of intent to practice sustainable agriculture: it was the first attempt to deal with the enormous challenge of wider integration involved in enlargement. It intended to show how the CAP needed adapting if enlargement were to be carried out in an affordable way in the context of the 2000-2006 Financial Framework.

3.3.2 The difficulty in reaching a consensus on the reforms

In 1999, the Commission presented its proposals before the European Council in Berlin. A reform of the agricultural policy was suggested as one of the key considerations when fixing the 2000-2006 budgetary strategy.[28] The Commission's proposals were substantially altered when they were presented before the European Council in Berlin 1999 as a consequence of the opposition of France – a net contributor – was worried about limiting the increase of the Budget. Jacques Chirac used his power to block and reduce the price cuts put forward. Despite this opposition, the Commission fought and managed to obtain a Mid-Term Review (MTR), scheduled for 2003, completing it in June of that year. Despite the partial rejection of the Commission's propos-

[27] See European Commission, 'Study on Alternative Strategies for the Development of Relations in the Field of Agriculture between the EU and the Associated Countries with a View to Future Accession', Agricultural Strategy Paper, Brussels (1995).

[28] The 2000-2006 Financial Framework has been criticised for being limited to 'reshuffling' the quotas assigned to each category of products. For a critical view, see A. Massot Martí, 'El Acuerdo Agrícola de Berlín sobre la Agenda 2000: ¿Los Estados contra la Unión Europea?', 22 *Cuadernos Europeos de Deusto*, (Bilbao, 2002), p. 174.

als, *Agenda 2000* had its impact on the fifth enlargement, as producer support was restructured to a certain extent and certain production quotas were continued.[29] In Berlin, the number of candidates for accession was also increased from six to ten, and the date of the fifth accession was delayed from 2002 to mid 2004. These two factors required a further consideration of the budgetary framework by the Fifteen, which took place at the Brussels European Council in October 2002, where the heads of government agreed on the shape of the budgetary offer to be made to the future new Member States in Copenhagen the following December.

The *raison d'être* for the objections made by France to the Commission's proposals hinged on the fact that: the strategy was based on further support price cuts for all products except sugar, and a 'decoupling' of direct payments to farmers, which would also be received in the form of a single payment each year.[30] Normally, these payments would be linked to the production of predetermined products. That link was to disappear under the Commission's plan and, thus, producers would be free to dedicate their efforts to the products of their choice. The downside was that there is no longer any incentive to produce particular products. To receive these decoupled payments, producers would have to pursue environmental standards, food safety standards and animal health standards above the minimum required by EU law. The MTR also promoted 'modulating' direct payments, implying a transfer of a proportion of the direct payments to environmental and regional development programmes. These changes favoured most new members but had a negative impact on the leading contributors to the CAP.

The two measures proposed – the reduction of price support and decoupling – were an attempt to assimilate the CAP to a social income based policy. Using Rollo's terminology, borrowed from the American debate on social welfare, the intention was to go from 'workfare' towards 'welfare' – much to the dislike of farmers, who would be received by the public as social security recipients rather than as a crucial part of the economy. The 'Club Med',[31] which includes Spain, Italy, France, Greece and Ireland – even if the latter is not a Mediterranean country geographically speaking – was reluctant to adopt these changes. France and Germany agreed, prior to the official negotiations, that the agricultural budget should be frozen until 2013 and imposed this in the Brussels European Council of October 2002. They also managed to achieve that the degree of price cuts and the proportion of production covered by decoupling should be less than that proposed by the Commission.

---

[29] On the Agenda 2000, see also europa.eu.int/comm/agenda2000/index_en.htm and europa.eu.int/scadplus/leg/en/s60000.htm.

[30] The first € 5,000 of any payment would be given in total. Above 5,000 it was proposed they be subject to reductions of one percent in 2006, rising to six percent per annum by year 2011.

[31] Expression used by Rollo, *supra* n. 11, p. 12.

The type of enlargement put forward in the Berlin Council implied a dual phase project according to which all ten CEEC would have joined the EU by 2007. New financial guidelines were established in January 2002, retargeted at a 2004 enlargement involving ten countries including the eight CEEC. The 2002 Communication maintains the Berlin financial guidelines and takes into account issues arising from the accession negotiations, particularly direct payments. A gradual increase in direct payments to the future new Member States following their accession was part of this proposal.

The Brussels summit of October 2002 maintained the Agenda 2000 budget and the 2004 schedule for the fifth enlargement. Simultaneously, EU members agreed to maintain direct payment expenditures at 2007 levels thereafter. These proposals for the adjustments of the CAP and the CAP budget have yet to be transformed into formal policy.

3.3.3 State of the art: what has been achieved so far?

It was not until October 2002 that, after almost a decade of hectic preparation, the schedule for the eastern enlargement became clear. Undoubtedly, one of the major setbacks for the delay has been reaching a consensus on the conditions under which the new Member States will adopt the CAP. The difficulties were not only posed by the acceding countries but also by how complicated it proved to adopt a common position among the Fifteen in advance of their accession.

The current status, just months after the Ten became members of the EU, is complex. The acceding countries had been trying very hard and their meeting of the vague criteria established in Copenhagen was satisfactory. The new Members had already adopted most of the *acquis*.[32] The majority were also making good – but slow – progress, in the process of creating the management and information systems necessary for the operation of CAP instruments, and control systems for payment. Border controls are also being set up. For these purposes, they are being granted additional EU funding. The implementation of the PECA Protocols to the Europe Agreements was also in practice, and it was proving most difficult regarding standard product descriptions and the adoption of Farm Accounting Data Network (FADN). The 2002 report rarely mentions the PECA Protocol, but urges the early and rapid introduction of FADN, particularly in Slovakia.

The obligations that the newly acceded countries have had to fulfil to receive the necessary funding and enter the EU were established annually in the Regular Reports and the annual Accession Partnerships. One important reform that the new Members had to carry out was to create their own Common Organisations of the Market (COMs).[33] Harmonised quality descriptions, storage and

[32] Estonia, Slovenia, Lithuania and Slovakia have already adopted all the *acquis communautaire*.

[33] This need to create CMO is referred to as 'urgent' in the Regular Reports. See Baker, *supra* n.5, p. 14.

warehouse functions as well as market intelligence systems were some of the main priorities in these reports. Many CEECs introduced policy regimes similar to the CAP. Buying agencies for several crops and animal products were created. The 2002 Report called for the establishment of Integrated Administration and Control Systems (IACS) for the disbursement of funds under the CAP. The duties of the IACS include the 'nomination and accreditation of paying agencies, training and institutional development, establishment of registries for land parcels and livestock and operational information systems.'[34] For each CEEC, a similar set of requirements surrounded accreditation of a SAPARD administrative agency and procedures. All new members had achieved this upon accession and some of them as early as 2002.

One challenge that the CEEC were confronted with upon accession was the switch from SAPARD to post-accession aid. Under the SAPARD Regulation,[35] upon accession the beneficiaries stopped being entitled to SAPARD support. A detailed and extensive draft of the *Guidelines for the Switch from SAPARD to Post-accession Rural Development Instruments* appeared late in 2003,[36] with specific instructions on how to make this transition 'seamless'.[37] This Draft points out the duties of the national administrations in order to be entitled to receive post-accession funds, which will now come from the EAGGF. The new members implemented these changes in due time.[38] For this and the other adaptations, transitional arrangements for state aids have been agreed within the Accession Treaty. Harmonisation of safety standards and transitional agreements for upgrading food processing establishments are also dealt with.[39]

Despite the enormous sacrifices made prior to accession, the benefits of membership were drastically reduced after the controversial Berlin summit. The outcome of the Council after the opposition of France and Germany was disappointing for the Ten, and did not improve after the MTR. While decoupling was introduced, it was done in a differential, much less ambitious way than the original proposals, and proposed price cuts or production quota increases were significantly reduced in sugar, arable and dairy products. Mediterranean agri-

---

34 D. Baker, *supra* n.5, p. 13.

35 Council Regulation 1268/1999, *OJ* 1999 L 161/87.

36 *Draft Guidelines for the Switch from SAPARD to Post-accession Rural Development Instruments*, 17 December 2003.

37 Draft Guidelines, p. 3.

38 See also Network of Independent Agricultural Experts in the CEE Candidate Countries, 'Social Security Systems and Demographic Developments in Agriculture in the CEE Candidate Countries', *Institut für Agrarentwicklung in Mittel- und Osteuropa* (2003), for DG Agriculture, European Commission.

39 Each CEEC has undertaken to survey all food processing establishments for veterinary and food safety and determine the potential for each to satisfy the EC directives before accession. For those that are suitable for upgrading, an action plan was to have been established by each CEEC. While all of Estonia's establishments are already surveyed, urgent action needed for Slovakia, Poland, Latvia and Lithuania.

culture has not been modified. The degree of potential decoupling was reduced from 100 to 75 for arable subsidies and to between 75 and zero percent for beef and sheep subsidies. It is a voluntary measure that can be introduced any time between 2005 and 2007. The result could be a Union in which some Member states have reached complete decoupling in the eligible products by 2005 and other countries with no signs of decoupling or with only partial decoupling until 2007. But the worst news for the Ten, especially the CEECs, is that despite their efforts during the negotiations to implement the acquis so that their farmers could be eligible for direct payments in full immediately upon accession, only 25 percent of direct payments have been granted. Thereafter, the percentage will increase steadily every year until 2013, when the new Members will finally receive the payments in full.[40] In November 2002, the EU suggested that these direct payments be topped up by each State to a level equal to 40 percent of the levels enjoyed by existing EU farmers from national funds or EAGGF rural development funds.[41]

The new Member States, contrary to their high expectations about accession, are being given a differentiated and worse treatment compared to the Fifteen. Farmers in the new Member States are dissatisfied and taxpayers from the Fifteen are reluctant to pay more for receiving less. Furthermore, the differentiated decoupling, along with the different treatment of the Ten for the receipt of direct payments, is endangering the 'common' character of the Common Agricultural Policy. Moreover, this approach can be expected to set a precedent for future divergences within the CAP in future enlargements. It would be politically difficult in the Fifteen, to support both complete decoupling for domestic farmers and also impose contributions to production subsidies to competitors who would then undercut domestic producers in the market.

On the one hand, the agricultural situation of the Ten and the help they have needed implies an enormous expenditure for the Fifteen, both before and after enlargement. On the other hand, despite the enormous efforts of the Ten to comply with the Copenhagen criteria, they will experience a differentiated worse treatment on agriculture and structural funds until 2013. In short, the current situation favours no Member State entirely, thus creating a different climate of political discomfort in the CAP of the enlarged Union of twenty-five.

---

40 See Commission Regulation 1972/2003, *OJ* 2003 L 293, and Commission Regulation 60/2004, *OJ* 2004 L9. These Regulations are now on appeal before the CFI following a complaint from Poland. See *infra* Section 3.3.

41 In the case of Slovenia, two options were suggested for direct payments. In both cases, the original 25 percent limit remains in place, but the first option means that top-up levels may reach 30 percent subject to earlier restrictions on their use of rural development funds. The second option is that like schemes for direct payments may be topped up by 10 percent.

4 Consequential political frictions

The political consequences for future discussions concerning agricultural issues in our enlarged Union are particularly worrying. As Mayhew has pointed out, 'at the end of every European Union accession negotiation, there is a fight about finance.'[42] In this sense, the 2004 enlargement is no exception. It has been established that at the very origin of the controversy around the CAP is the high cost of the necessary agricultural adaptations, both for the Fifteen and for the new Member States. Some advocated that enlargement could only be successful if the interests of the Fifteen were fully respected. Heinemann, for instance, claimed that since the Fifteen could veto the entry of the newcomers, the priority of the negotiations for enlargement should be the protection of their wishes.[43] This was a realist's approach to the utopia that called for supranational, common objectives to guide joint actions and policies. Decision-making happens inside the Council and therefore it is subject to the intergovernmental give and take. It is naïve to believe that national Governments, would ignore the wishes of the population that elected them faced with the pressures of re-election. The defence of national interests is not necessarily entirely negative. It is beneficial for the future strength of the Union to address local needs giving a sense of satisfaction among the population and making the benefits of integrating palpable for all. However, it is self-evident that claims that the interests of the Fifteen are the deciding factor are short-sighted. The position of the newcomers must be safeguarded within the Union in the interests of integration at EU level especially to counteract a growing Euroscepticism in these new members, which may prove damaging longer-term now that these countries are inside the Union and enjoy the right to vote. Self-interest that manifests itself in extremes of differentiation may lead to serious confrontations and blockages in progress or advances made to date.

Three potential types of political frictions resulting from agricultural issues on enlargement can be identified: Those between the Fifteen, those that impact upon former members and newcomers, and those that affect the national domestic politics of the CEEC, Malta and Cyprus. Each of these categories is commented upon below.

4.1 Confrontations within Fifteen

Tensions among the Fifteen may well emerge concerning changes in the distribution of structural funds. The Club Med Member States have traditionally been recipients of these funds and wants to remain so. Up until now, the Fifteen beneficiaries were able to control expenditure in the

---

[42] See Mayhew, *supra* n. 10, p. 143.

[43] See F. Heinemann, *The Political Economy of EU Enlargement and the Treaty of Nice*, (Mannheim, Zentrum für Europäische Wirtschaftsforschung 2001).

approved budgets. However, upon accession the Ten have acquired the right to vote too. Previously, it was the Mediterranean countries that possessed larger agricultural sectors and were less well off. Moreover, the economic loss that the enlargement implies for these countries has been enhanced by the fact that these nations have fewer cultural and commercial links with the Ten. This is due to historical and geographical reasons and it is logical considering that they tend to produce similar products and thus the need for trade between them has been limited. Therefore the benefits of having the CEECs and Malta and Cyprus within the single market are not so important to the Club Med countries as the loss they will suffer through the diminution of their entitlement to EU funds.

4.2 Conflicts between the new and old

While the general opinion in most CEEC favoured entry into the EU,[44] the media in the Fifteen was generally rather sceptical about the benefits of an enlarged Community. Even so, it is possible to find voices supporting these advantages and trying to convince the public opinion of the positive aspects of enlargement.[45]

Prior to enlargement, the most fervent discussions between the candidates and the Fifteen concerned the quotas to be allocated to each CEEC for each commodity and direct payments. As regards the allocation of quotas, the controversy revolved around the fact that, up until accession farmers in the CEEC were able to produce as much as their capacity allowed them. Now they face production quotas limiting the quantity they may produce. The offers made by the EU fell substantially short of the amounts originally proposed by the candidates. The amount of quota allocated to each new Member State is crucial, as it determines the number of farmers and establishments that may benefit from CAP instruments. The root of the disagreement is the EU's decision to choose late 1992 as a reference period, which failed to acknowledge the CEEC decline in both production and consumption since 1990. The new members wanted to use 1987-89 as a baseline, just like the rest of the EU Members States and, in particular, those that joined the EU in 1995.[46] The EU hides behind the fact that the performance during the years 1987-89 was the consequence of central planning and failed to reflect production capacity in a market context.

44 See A. Szczerbiak, *'Public Opinion and Eastern Enlargement. Explaining Declining Support for EU Membership in Poland'*, 34 *Sussex European Institute* (2000).

45 As an example, the Swedish newspaper *Dagens Industri* published an article in 2000 explaining how the GDP of some of the forthcoming members was rising, meaning less costs than expected for the Union. *Dagens Industri*, Stockholm, 26.05.2000, p. 16.

46 Austria, Finland and Sweden were the Member Status who joined the EC in 1995. See Baker, *supra* n. 5, p. 17.

The problem of the ten-year timeframe for full direct payments to farmers from the new members is even more complex. The Commission argues that direct payments compensate for price reductions, which have not been suffered by farmers in the new Member States. Also, it claims that direct payments would slow down the necessary restructuring of farms as they are said still to lack the necessary administrative capacity to accommodate direct payments. Nevertheless, differential rates run counter to the CAP principles established in Article 33 EC, in particular equality of support and treatment. With the delay in the full direct payments, there will be an unfair transitional period of almost ten years when farmers in Spain, for instance, will receive much more than those in Poland, even if they are carrying out the same activity and both nations have exactly the same amount of voting power in the decision-making process for legislative and policy development purposes. Besides, the Austrian, Finnish and Swedish farmers received the payments in full even if they acceded after 1992, when the programme for direct payments began functioning. This asymmetric treatment can be harmful to the process of farm restructuring. The political consequences can be disastrous.

There are other issues that have accentuated the tensions between former and new Members. One of these has to do with the competitiveness of CEEC products. Reduced production (including labour) costs in Central and Eastern Europe have proven a threat to farmers in the Fifteen. Fear persists that cheap CEEC products will flood the EU markets to the detriment of competing products from other former EU members. However, such enhanced competition cannot be considered a negative aspect of enlargement in a Union that claims to have the protection of competition and the free movement of goods as major objectives. If products enter the market at lower prices, competing producers will have an incentive to look for more efficient means of production to reduce costs and meet their competitive demands. The entry of the products from the Ten poses a common risk inherent to competition. That risk is typical and an ideal motivation for innovation and progress. Even so, numerous studies support the idea that the threat posed by the newcomers is not so great because of quality differentials existing between the agricultural products from the CEEC and those available in the EU.[47] When it comes to food products, the preferences of buyers are not always influenced by price as they are inexpensive goods and consumers are normally prepared to pay more for quality. The trade tendencies during the accession period largely favoured the EU. Also, for the time being, it does not (yet) seem to be profitable for farmers of the new Member States to expand into new markets.

Finally, one particular source of concern for the Ten is worthy of special mention: that of the ownership of farmland. The CEEC are worried that foreign-

---

47 Duponcel, Swinnen, and Berschmidt and Hartman have elaborated studies for beef, fruit, vegetables and processed foods. See Baker, *supra* n. 5, pp. 21-22.

ers with large spending power will be willing to invest in the relatively inexpensive farmland of the CEEC. The preoccupation of farmers from the Ten as well as Bulgaria and Romania has to do with the fact that these nations had, until recently, a very different concept of private property. Transitional measures have been adopted, accompanied by restrictions on foreign ownership of temporary residences.[48]

4.3 Importance of agriculture in the internal politics of the candidates (now Member States)

So, the conditions for accession were disappointing from the perspective of farmers from the new Member States. The rules of the game were agreed upon before the new Member States had any voting power and, consequently, they have been totally dependent on what the Fifteen decided. Such harsh treatment may well be one of the main causes of the decline in support for EU membership in Poland – one of the most fervent supporters of enlargement – and this is reflected in recent studies.[49]

It is often believed that the weight of enlarging the EU falls entirely on the shoulders of the EU. However, farmers and rural populations of the new Member States have been heavily affected by the economic transition. Membership of the EU was seen as a unique opportunity to renovate this sector of the economy, and therefore enlargement had been eagerly awaited in these countries with large agricultural populations, many on small holdings, and have poor rural infrastructures. *Agenda 2000* included promising proposals and the support for accession was granted. However, the Copenhagen summit left the new Member States with no more than 25 per cent of direct payments upon accession in 2004. The budgetary pressures for new members are outstanding. The suggestion that each State could top up direct payments from their own budget poses difficult financial problems at a time when these countries are struggling to invest in the necessary administrative reforms to adopt the *aquis communautaire.* Under these pressures, they will encounter difficulties in meeting the excessive deficit procedures of the EU, further complicating their passage into the EMU. This, at the end of the day, endangers the entire economic integration project.

The cuts in economic support towards the rural areas of the CEEC are further enhanced by the difficulties these countries will face in order to fully profit from the EU funding as a consequence of the deficiencies of their admin-

---

48 See *Treaty of Accession of the Czech Republic, Estonia, Cyprus, Latvia, Lithuania, Hungary, Malta, Poland, Slovenia and Slovakia*, signed in Athens, 16 April 2003, OJ 2003 L 236/23. See also K. Inglis, 'The Union's Fifth Accession Treaty: New Means to Make Enlargement Possible', 41 *CMLRev.* (2004), pp. 937-973. See Press Release, supra n. 45.

49 See, *inter alia*, A. Szczerbiak, *supra* n. 44, p. 5.

istrative capacity and the hard task of meeting the cross compliance standards necessary to qualify for direct payments. As a consequence, farmers are now aware that the benefits of enlarging will not have a noticeable impact for quite some time, and they are threatening to maintain tariffs and border protection unless they are granted better conditions. The Polish Minister of Agriculture, Jaroslaw Kalinowski, has stated that unless the EU improves its offer, trade barriers against farm products from other Member states will be maintained.[50]

From the perspective of the population of the CEEC, accession criteria imply sacrifices for farmers in the new Member States, and yet the benefits of the CAP will not be fully extended to these Members for at least ten years. This less than privileged situation is beginning to have its impact in the domestic politics of the new Members. In Poland, for instance, the agricultural sector exerts important political influence. The farmers' ability to exert political influence cannot be ignored. The radicalised agricultural lobby had its impact on the 2001 elections, with the victory of two eurosceptic parties, one of which is agriculturally based.[51]

The discomforting situation has even led Poland to appeal against certain provisions of the Regulations on excessive stocks and on the extension of the phasing-in mechanism to direct payments. The Council of Ministers recently decided to lodge a complaint to the CFI.[52] In particular, the government of Poland claimed that analogous criteria to those of the 1995 enlargement should be applied as regards the selection of agricultural products subject to charges on excessive stocks. They also estimate that the Regulations substantially amend the terms of accession set out in the Treaty of Accession as regards Poland.[53] Among other claims, the Commission is alleged to have violated the principle of free movement of goods and the principle of non-discrimination due to nationality for providing a differentiated treatment for Poland than for the Fifteen. The case is still pending, though it serves to dramatically highlight those key political tensions that are developing over the issue of agriculture, and the case for reform.[54]

Bearing in mind these problems, it can be expected that agricultural issues will be the Achilles heel of an enlarged Union. In this context, deciding the next financial framework promises to be a true war of irreconcilable interests where anything can be expected, except for consensus.

---

50 Press Release *Information on an appeal lodged by Poland against EU Regulations on excessive stocks and new direct payments*, Urzad Komitetu Integracji Europejskiej (2004) which can be found on www2.ukie.gov.pl/WWW/en.nsf/0/EBFB099CB0520054C1256ECB002E62A0?Open.

51 See R. Epstein, 'International Institutions and the Depoliticization of Economic Policy in Postcommunist Poland: Central Banking and Agriculture Compared', 4 *ECPR Workshop on Enlargement and European Governance* (2000).

52 See also Press Release, *supra* n. 45.

53 See Treaty of Accession, *supra* n. 48.

54 See Press Release, supra n. 45.

5 Conclusions

In the process of integration of the CEEC countries, the CAP remains a key issue given the importance of agriculture in the ten new Member States. The agricultural terms and conditions for enlargement have been drawn overwhelmingly in favour of the Fifteen as a result of the fact that these countries had the power to negotiate and vote. This is defendable in the sense that these countries can veto the accession of newcomers if their interests are harmed. If the expenditure gets too high, the situation might become unbearable for the net contributors. However, great damage is caused to the opinion of the CEECs' population about entering the EU, which, as this paper shows, may well have a very negative impact on the process of integration as a whole. The solutions adopted in Berlin and after the MTR can only be regarded as transitional measures to respond to a critical situation. To have a group of countries relegated to a second-class status, unable to fully benefit from membership is an undesirable and unprecedented solution and should be avoided in the future.

Whilst the current situation remains problematic, it is clear that the likelihood of pleasing all actors, new or well established, is slim. Experts had long been claiming that enlargement was unaffordable unless the new Members were treated in a less beneficial way.[55] Former and new Members need to be aware of these economic obstacles and must be prepared to make sacrifices if they believe in the benefits of an enlarged Union in terms of economic prosperity and peace in Europe. It is still too early to evaluate the true extent to which the political tensions originated by agricultural issues will evolve. The true challenges of enlargement can be determined only once these countries are given the chance to express their opinions through votes. In any case, as usual, 'widening' the Union bears the danger of slowing down the process of integration, thus making it difficult to 'deepen' the existing links between Member States.[56] Enlargement is a demanding task and it is up to all the countries involved to evoke the principle of solidarity established in the Treaties. After all, budgetary increases are a small price to pay for the incalculable advantages of peace and prosperity in a larger Union. One can only hope that concrete results of these noble pursuits become palpable in the short term so that the political tensions can be overcome.

---

55 R. Baldwin, *Towards an Integrated Europe*, CEPR, London, cited by Rollo, *supra* n.11, p. 3.

56 Having these countries as members will affect the decision-making process, and if they come together when it comes to voting they may actually block or slow down the adoption of certain decisions.

CHAPTER 9

European Counter-terrorism in the Context of Enlargement: Challenges Ahead

Przemysław Zysk

1 Counter-terrorism in the pre-enlargement era

Terrorism has long been viewed in Europe as a purely domestic issue. When the Paris and Rome Treaties were signed, the idea of placing counter-terrorism or the wider area of justice and home affairs within the framework of the Communities was not even considered. The Member States preferred to counter acts of indigenous terrorism by pursuing their own national, rather than collective, policies. Each state fought terrorism alone, vigilantly guarding its sovereign powers against any intrusions. When counter-terrorism co-operation was undertaken, often after discovering links between terrorist groups residing in different Member States, it was essentially carried out through bilateral channels on a case-by-case basis.

The late Nineteen-sixties and early Nineteen-seventies altered the situation to a certain degree as a series of terrorist acts claimed attention across the world.[1] Acts of indigenous political violence that were fuelled by separatist ideas[2] or left-wing ideologies[3] swept across the larger part of the continent. These domestic incidents were accompanied, and increasingly often overshadowed, by a relatively new phenomenon on European soil: trans-national terrorism inspired by extremist Islamic conceptions. The most spectacular and attention-grabbing was perhaps the terror attack carried out during the Munich Olympic Games in 1972, when the Black September Organisation launched its attack against Israeli athletes.[4]

The need for more co-ordinated action was growing steadily. The escalation of trans-national terrorism and increasingly compelling pressures from within states were persuasive enough to force states to adopt a more co-ordinated approach in place of the widely prevailing national policies. However, as it was impossible to adopt effective measures against the spate of international terrorism at global level, a more regionally orientated approach in Western Europe seemed to be the only viable option.[5] Member States began to realise that they

1 P. Chalk, *West European Terrorism and Counter-Terrorism. The Evolving Dynamic* (London, Macmillan Press 1996) p. 173.

2 The most prominent examples are ETA (Euskadi ta Askatasuna – Basque Fatherland and Liberty) operating in Basque provinces of Spain, and IRA (Irish Republican Army) in the Northern Ireland. These two organisations have been, by far, the most deadly of all West European terrorist groups for several decades.

3 Among the most prominent organisations of this type, characterised by anti-US, anti-NATO and anti-capitalist stance, should be mentioned the Italian BR (*Brigade Rosse* – Red Brigades), the German RAF (*Rote Armee Fraktion* – Red Army Faction), the French AD (*Action Directe* – Action Direct), the Greek ELA (Revolutionary People's Struggle) and the Portuguese FP-25 (Popular Forces of 15 April).

4 Al-Fatah is one of the oldest Palestinian guerrilla groups and was founded in 1975 to establish an independent Palestinian state with means recognised as terrorist. S. Anderson & S. Sloan, *Historical Dictionary of Terrorism* (Metuchen, Scarecrow Press, 1995) pp. 60-62, at 109-113.

5 It did not concern the Eastern European Countries, the members of the Soviet bloc, as they were themselves sometimes perceived as state sponsors of terrorism or at least as passive supporters.

would do well to pool their resources, thus benefiting from shared experience. Accordingly, a number of informal meetings on counter-terrorism were held in the course of the early Nineteen-seventies. This occasional collaboration was soon transformed by the Rome Council of Ministers of December 1975 into a permanent special group on terrorism called the TREVI group.[6]

Thus the decision to set up the TREVI forum for co-operation had finally been taken. But the problem of how the co-operation should be placed in a complex legal space was not easy. Neither the EEC Treaty nor the ECSC and Euratom Treaties provided a legal basis that could accommodate new integrative needs and permit further integration in the counter-terrorism field. As the political atmosphere and the level of advancement of the European integration project precluded the broadening of the Communities' powers, the only way to accommodate further integrative impulses was to place counter-terrorism co-operation on a separate intergovernmental plane. The TREVI group was accordingly set up outside the formal legal framework of the existing Communities structures and, consequently, outside the mainstream of EC decision-making. Thus, a new stream of European integration in the so-called 'black market' of European integration appeared, parallel to the stream of the deep-rooted supranational Communities focused on economic development.

Although the TREVI co-operation functioned with varying intensity for almost twenty years, its palpable results were quite modest. Some observers, such as a Spanish police officer, went as far as to suggest that the TREVI group was essentially irrelevant to practical and operational levels of police co-operation, dismissing it as little more than an overindulgent form of ministerial rhetoric or 'TREVI speak'.[7] On the other hand, it should not be overlooked that not only did TREVI initiate counter-terrorism co-operation among European governments on a multi-lateral basis but it also fostered co-operation through bilateral links. This was believed to have contributed to some successes in the fight against terrorism, notably the thwarting of the IRA bomb plot in Gibraltar in March 1988 by common Anglo-Spanish efforts. Most likely, TREVI was neither as effective as government officials suggested, nor as futile as the Spanish police officer above said. The truth probably lies somewhere in between. It might sound surprising today but some of the core EU anti-terrorism measures date back no further than the TREVI era. To give an example, it was with the TREVI forum that began to draw up a list of terrorists and terrorist organisations, elaborated the overall analysis of the terrorist threat and disseminated good practices on counter-terrorism. Of equal importance was the promotion of personal contacts and close working relationships among government officials

---

6 The origin of the initiative is problematic. Some sources claim it was put forward by UK representatives whereas others favour Dutch delegates.

7 Chalk, op. cit n. 1, at p. 129. See also M. Anderson et al., *Policing the European Union* (Oxford, Clarendon Press 1995) p. 56.

that significantly contributed to the increase in mutual trust between participants and, thus, permitted a more efficient exchange of information on internal security threats, including the movement of suspects, airport security, technological advances and the like.[8]

The Maastricht Treaty changed the institutional framework substantially by way of introducing a single institutional framework, oft referred to as a temple-like edifice, within which numerous strands of co-operation were placed.[9] The integration of various counter-terrorism frameworks and circles of co-operation, previously scattered throughout the legal space into one firm structure, resulted in a more efficient, streamlined co-ordination of counter-terrorist efforts.[10]

The Maastricht Treaty expressly recognised terrorism to be of common interest to Member States and a serious form of international crime to be prevented and combated through police co-operation within the third pillar. As this was the only place where terrorism was mentioned *expressis verbis*, there was a risk that this would be the only or predominant framework for anti-terrorist actions. Unsurprisingly, these concerns proved grounded. Counter-terrorism remained limited to the police co-operation field while other potential fields of action became marginalized. The third pillar measures appeared to be at the vanguard of the fight against terrorism only rarely supported by common efforts in the field of foreign affairs.

Numerous institutional defects along with the lack of a commonly shared vision as to the role and goal of the EU in the justice and home affairs alike[11] together with concerns over sovereignty, were largely responsible for the limited involvement of the Member States in counter-terrorism within the EU in the Maastricht era. Both the heavily restricted powers entrusted to the EU by the Maastricht Treaty and the subsequent, rather meagre, anti-terrorism developments confirmed the distrust for and some opposition to a major role for the EU in this area. However, the growing uneasiness with growing security threats steadily superseded the reluctance to go down the path of closer co-operation.

As a consequence, the provisions on co-operation in the field of justice and home affairs that had framed the mainstream response to terrorism became the main focus of the 1996-7 IGC.[12] The Amsterdam Treaty introduced a number

---

8 The exchange of information was ameliorated by liaison offices in each country and by establishing a secure communication network. Liaison offices exchanged both administrative and sensitive information by telephone, facsimile or telex. In the event of terrorist crimes, Member States were required to inform the other Member States within 24 hours. Anderson et al., op. cit. n. 5, at p. 54.

9 The 'pillar' terminology was coined during the negotiations of the Maastricht Treaty.

10 It must, however, be noted that the Schengen *acquis* remained outside the Union framework.

11 A good account on the divergences can be found in M. den Boer and W. Wallace, 'Justice and Home Affairs', in H. Wallace and W. Wallace, eds., *Policy-making in the European Union* (Oxford, University Press 2000) pp. 499-500.

12 See also B. Tonra, 'From Maastricht to Amsterdam' in Tonra, ed., *Amsterdam. What Treaty Means* (Dublin, Institute of European Affairs 1997) pp. 13-19.

of important changes to the defective framework, one of which expanded the Union's counter-terrorism reach from police to judicial co-operation in criminal matters. This signalled a shift of focus from the down-to-earth co-operation in policing and information exchange to a more complex and challenging judicial co-operation. At the same time new fields of common action were identified.[13] Particular attention should be given to those grounds that allowed the facilitation of extradition and the establishment of minimum rules relating to constituent elements of criminal acts, as they were crucial for efficient counter-terrorism and were soon to advance to the forefront of the fight against terrorism.

However, despite the expansion of EU powers, the day-to-day co-operation in counter-terrorism was striking in that it recalled past decades as it still revolved around the dissemination of information and best practices as well as the occasional elaboration of instruments of less prominent legal value. The EU counter-terrorism by no means represented a coherent and legally binding set of co-ordinated measures adopted by common accord but, rather, a series of reactive and uncoordinated responses adopted within a small circle without a widely approved and long-term anti-terrorism programme. The declining terrorist activity throughout the EU from the second half of the Nineteen-nineties[14] led to a decrease in the political salience of terrorism and lessened the Member States' willingness to continue along the path of closer integration. The focus shifted from terrorism to crime in general, with special attention given to organised crime. As some sensitive anti-terrorism measures were included in specific action plans as a part of the fight against organised crime, while the remaining measures were left aside, two distinct anti-terrorism streams of decision-making came into existence. There are numerous differences between them stretching from the prominence of envisaged measures, the choice of legal instruments, the level of transparency and predictability, the degree of Commission and European Parliament involvement as well as the potential role of the European Court of Justice.

The outrageous terrorist attacks in the United States of America in September 2001 dramatically transformed the situation. Although these events took place far away, their magnitude as well as their dire consequences, reverberated loudly throughout Europe. A successful attack against a close European ally considered a world superpower highlighted the potential vulnerability of European states to Islamic terrorism. It was also realised that a swift and robust response to 11/09 aimed at quenching thriving security concerns could also be utilised for political purposes. Whatever the actual reason, many Member States adopted extensive legislative programmes directed at countering terrorism, increasingly accompanied by an outcry from human rights watchdogs and academic circles.

---

13 Art. 31 EU (ex. K 3).

14 'Patterns of Global Terrorism', *Europe Overview*, www.usis.usemb.se/terror/index.html.

The anti-terrorism policy also changed radically at EU level. Counter-terrorism preoccupations jumped to the top of the EU political agenda, weakening significantly, though rather temporarily, long-standing concerns over national sovereignty. This encouraged decision-makers, especially the Commission, to press ahead into hitherto uncharted waters. The events in the United States proved a much more effective catalyst for deeper co-operation in the Union than its multi-annual action plans on organised crime – under which counter-terrorism used to be placed – or the lofty slogans of Freedom, Security and Justice expressed in the Amsterdam Treaty. The swiftly convened Justice and Home Affairs Council and the Brussels European Council adopted an action plan which was dedicated to combating terrorism alone for the first time in the history of the European integration project.[15]

Soon afterwards the candidate countries expressed their solidarity with the United States and aligned themselves with the broad EU response to the events of 11/09.[16] Although this declaration did not have any prominent legal value, it did have an important political significance. Its adoption sent a signal to other states and their societies that the soon to be Member States shared the same values and principles as well as, broadly speaking, the general approach of the EU in its counter-terrorism efforts, as enshrined in the Action Plan. This was all the more important since the plan was adopted without their active participation, let alone the right to vote. The adoption of the declaration could boost mutual trust between the Member States and candidate countries. It was also likely to counter the sense of detachment felt by the latter due to their inability to affect the end product, with which they had to comply at any rate, and from a relatively low level of terrorist vulnerability. The adoption of the declaration also helped to highlight the importance of the field of Justice and Home Affairs, which has on occasion been disregarded in their preparations for EU membership.

The sense of commitment and urgency that prevailed after 11/09 soon dissipated among the Member States. Lofty political declarations made by various European bodies and politicians across Europe were soon forgotten and the far-reaching commitments made to deepen counter-terrorism co-operation remained largely on paper. As the sense of insecurity waned and concerns with national sovereignty re-emerged, the end result of a number of commitments disappointed initial expectations.

The Madrid atrocities of 11 March 2004 – Europe's worst terror attack since the 1988 Lockerbie bombing – were an acute reminder of terrorist threat. Those

[15] Conclusions and Plan of Action of the Extraordinary European Council Meeting on 21 September 2001, SN 140/01. This document was later updated by Laeken and Seville European Councils.

[16] Press Releases by the Belgian EU Presidency on the alignment of the candidate-countries with the conclusions of the European Council of 22 September 2001, www.europa.eu.int/news/110901/september.htm.

who claimed that Europe would not be a target of Islamic terrorism – due to the qualitatively different foreign policy compared to that of the United States and many examples of successful assimilation of Muslim minorities – were proved very wrong.

The Madrid attack renewed the political momentum dissipated over the last two and a half years and brought about a real sense of urgency. It accentuated the fact that European soil might equally be a logistical base for Islamic terrorists. Ernst Sentner, a widely respected international security expert, was to say that, "all the signs now point to Europe being the target. The Madrid atrocity could be just the first in a series of similarly spectacular strikes."[17] Unsurprisingly, in a Declaration on Combating Terrorism made by the European Council on 25 March 2004, the Heads of State and Government renewed their political commitments and agreed on an extensive legislative/operational programme that ensures that counter-terrorism will be high on the political agenda and guarantees that Justice and Home Affairs will remain one of the fastest-growing areas of European co-operation.[18]

The Madrid attack was significant for the countries preparing their accession to the Union. A series of Islamic terrorist attacks carried out around the world, the endorsement and/or active participation in the Iraq war and the vulnerability of Europe, removed the all-embracing feeling of security induced by the prospect of enlargement and NATO membership. They also gained a stronger position in the EU circuit. The accession negotiations were already closed and the enlargement day was imminent. The officials of the acceding countries could fully participate in the discussions over the response to 11/03, albeit without the right to vote, and were better versed in the procedures. This meant that they were now better equipped to affect its results and also take more responsibility therefore.

2 Expansion of the area of freedom, security and justice

The Amsterdam Treaty introduced in Article 29 (ex Art. K.1) EU a new, ambitious objective for the Union formulated as follows:

'[...] the Union's objective shall be to provide citizens with a high level of safety within an area of freedom, security and justice[...]'.

It was clear that the objective was supposed to play a major role given its position in the Treaty: it was not only laid down in Title VI EU as a sectoral goal but also in other far more prominent places. Its recognition in the preamble to the Treaty

---

17 'European cooperation vital in war on terror', *European Voice*, 18 March 2004, p. 16.

18 See the Presidency Conclusion of the Brussels European Council of 25/26 March 2004, point II.5.

in itself suggested its salience while its inclusion in the Article 2 EU (ex-Art. B) amongst other general and overarching objectives of the Union, such as the common market or the economic and monetary union, implied a broad and practical dimension of this new objective. Indeed, its introduction has proved not a legislative caprice but rather a prelude to, and a brief projection of, an intense and rapid legislative programme in the JHA area that we see today.

Combating terrorism has been closely associated with this objective. Although the formulation of Article 2 EU does not contain any mention of "terrorism" but only a general reference to 'crime',[19] Article 29 EU, contained in Title VI EU, sets out more precisely that 'a high level of safety within an area of freedom, security and justice' shall be achieved by preventing and combating crime, and then enumerates seven generic types of criminal offences, including that of terrorism.

However, for a long time it was not clear what this objective meant exactly. While for some observers it was, essentially, only a further and rather meaningless "advertising slogan" for a closer integration in JHA,[20] it captured the imagination of a number of European movers and shakers as well as EU officials.[21] Soon afterwards, the 1998 Vienna Action Plan cast some light on the concepts of Freedom, Security and Justice as understood by Commission and Council officials. But only the Conclusions of the 1999 Tampere European Council summit advanced detailed programmes to put these rather vague concepts into practice.

As far as an Area of Freedom is concerned, its expansion has involved three main aspects. The core aspect is the fundamental freedom of movement of people across internal borders. This cornerstone of European integration has, however, been seriously curtailed for the new Member States as they are set to remain outside the Schengen area for the next few years.[22] Although all entrants were required to transpose the bulk of Schengen *acquis* ahead of the enlargement day,[23] there is no specified date for their full inclusion in the Schengen area. A lengthy period of technical preparations, including the setting up of the second-generation Schengen Information System can be expected, to be followed by evaluation procedures and a unanimous decision of the Council before the Schengen area expands.[24] In the meantime, new EU citizens will

---

19 Art. 2 reads: 'The Union shall set itself the following objectives: (...) to maintain and develop the Union as an area of freedom, security and justice, in which the free movement of person is assured in conjunction with appropriate measures with respect to external border controls, asylum, immigration and the prevention and combating of crime'.

20 S. Peers, *EU Justice and Home Affairs Law* (Harlow, Pearson Education Limited 2000), p. 13.

21 Which could perhaps be viewed in some cases as a sign of institutional self-interest.

22 See K. Inglis, 'The Union's Fifth Accession Treaty: New Means to Make Enlargement Possible', 41 *CMLRev.* (2004) p. 949.

23 See Art. 3(1) Act of Accession and Annex I.

24 See Art. 3(3) Act of Accesion.

continue to look with envy at the Fifteens' citizens who are free from any border checks at internal frontiers while lawyers will be grappling with legal loopholes arising from partial application of the Schengen regime.[25] The second aspect mentioned by the Vienna Action Plan is the freedom to live in a law-abiding environment. This is, however, only a nicely worded declaration, tantamount to providing citizens with safety that is essentially covered by the notion of Security. Moreover, the responsibility for internal security lies in the hands of the Member States, with the Union's role restricted basically to facilitation of cross-border co-operation.[26] The third aspect of freedom comprises the 'full range of fundamental human rights, including specifically the protection against discrimination'. There is no denying that the *acquis* affords, in the main, a much higher level of protection against discrimination on the basis of Articles 12, 13 and 141 EC than the earlier legislation of the new Member States. However, the 'full range' of fundamental rights seems far from the reality given the case-by-case and rather fragmentary ECJ jurisprudence as well as the unclear legal status of its 'creative distillation'[27] contained in the Charter of Fundamental Rights.

Enlargement should also imply the extension of the Area of Security. The EU does not, however, intend to create a European security area in the sense of a common territory with uniform detection and investigation procedures but, rather, to provide an institutional framework to facilitate common actions and benefit from the synergy effect as a result. This is the role of a great many and diverse acts on mutual recognition, freezing of assets, extradition adopted within this framework as well as the two European agencies that strive to facilitate, albeit with limited success, cross-border co-operation. Clearly, security is the dimension that counter-terrorism has been most closely connected with. The overwhelming majority of measures adopted in the wake of 11/09 and 11/03 seek to strengthen safety across the continent against a backdrop of complaints about their disregard for fundamental freedoms. Although EU officials tend to refer to 'inconveniences' rather than to the curtailment of human rights,[28] the security rationale seems to have acquired a prominent role in political discourse after 11/09 and 11/03, clearly putting aside the dimension of human rights and fundamental freedoms. Doubts about a balance between efficiency and protection of fundamental freedoms[29] or whether sufficient thought is given to privacy

25 See also K. Inglis, 'The Union's Fifth Accession Treaty: New Means to Make Enlargement Possible', op. cit. n. 22, p. 950.

26 Art. 33 EU reads that "maintenance of law and order and the safeguarding of internal security" is a competence of Member States.

27 P. Craig and G. de Búrca, *EU Law: Text, Cases and Materials* (Oxford, Oxford University Press, 3rd edn. 2003) pp. 358-363.

28 'Security hasn't hurt liberty', *The International Herald Tribune* (electronic version),visited on 3 June 2004.

29 J. Apap and S. Carrera, *Judicial Cooperation in Criminal Matters*, CEPS Policy Brief No. 46, February 2004.

and data protection in the future SIS II (the new Schengen Information System) are good cases in point.[30]

The Area of Justice seeks to give all citizens a common feeling of justice throughout the Union by way of, *inter alia*, bringing to justice all those that threaten freedom and security of individuals and society. This is achieved by creating a common institutional framework within which efficient judicial co-operation can be co-ordinated and a certain degree of harmonisation performed. Within this important dimension of counter-terrorism the harmonisation of the definition of terrorism and rules on extradition was carried out as well as the co-ordination of cross-border investigations via Eurojust. Justice should not only, however, be felt as a result of the effective prosecution of criminals but also by guaranteeing the accused or suspect full enjoyment of his/her rights in criminal proceedings throughout the EU. This more 'positive' aspect of justice is still lacking. A Commission proposal on certain procedural rights in criminal proceedings is, however, a step in the right direction.[31]

Enlargement has many faces. One such face is the expansion of the Area of Freedom, Security and Justice further to the East and the South. A closer examination reveals, however, that the enlargement is set to extend Security and Justice to a significantly greater extent than Freedom. The extensive counter-terrorism programmes adopted after the events of 11/09 and 11/03 are likely to increase this imbalance.

3 Progressive enlargement

A practical dimension of the new Member States' alignment to the area of Freedom, Security and Justice is the possibility of enhancing trans-national co-operation through a common set of instruments. The enhancement of co-operation should not, however, be perceived as a one-day event where the toolkit is handed over to the newly admitted countries with the passage of 1 May 2004, since in reality there is no 'magic date' on which the security co-operation between new and old members is dramatically transformed. Rather, it has been a long and incremental process during which the toolkit was made gradually available over the passage of time and with steadily rising trust. Some counter-terrorism measures were already applied by the new members before accession, while others are still not fully in use. Two examples are particularly topical: the so-called 'blacklist' and the European Arrest Warrant.

---

30 Opinion of the Chairman of the Schengen Joint Supervisory Authority of 24 May 2004, SCHAC 2504/04.

31 Commission Proposal for a Council Framework Decision on certain procedural rights in criminal proceedings throughout the European Union, COM(2004) 328 final, 28 April 2004.

Following the terrorist attacks of 11/09, the EU criminalized the financing of terrorism[32] and established a common list of persons, groups and entities involved in terrorist acts whose assets are to be frozen across the Union.[33] These measures permitted national law enforcement authorities to extend the freezing of terrorist assets well beyond national boundaries while at the same time they ensured that national concerns are addressed via the unanimity voting requirement.[34]

The accession of ten new countries implies a considerable extension of the area where the duty to freeze such assets is applied. The existence of safe havens in Europe, where terrorist money could be safely transferred or property acquired, has thus been severely restricted through a certain degree of uniformity in practices. The concerns over a potential blockage of the freezing mechanism due to unanimity voting in a large twenty-five-member club seem exaggerated. If the procedure needs any change, it should be to exercise greater scrutiny over the choice of persons put on the 'blacklist' rather than any relaxation in procedural constraints. Human rights watchdogs, including Statewatch, have repeatedly warned that greater attention should be paid to the choice of persons so as to avoid erroneous decisions causing grave personal difficulties for those directly concerned and the consequent outcry among the general public at large.[35]

As a matter of fact, the list was applied by the candidate states before the date of enlargement on 1 May 2004. In 2002, the accession states declared that they shared the objectives of the measures underpinning the list and voluntarily took on the obligation to conform national policies accordingly.[36] Thus, they associated themselves with the EU list and promised to bring their policies into line

---

32 Council Common Position 2001/930/CFSP of 27 December 2001 on combating terrorism, *OJ* 2001 L 344/90.

33 Council Common Position 2001/931/CFSP of 27 December 2001 on the application of specific measures to combat terrorism, *OJ* 2001 L 344/93, and Council Regulation 2580/2001 of 27 December 2001 on specific restrictive measures directed against certain persons and entities with a view to combating terrorism, *OJ* 2001 L 344/83.

34 It is interesting to note that an informal list of people involved in the support for a terrorist cause was elaborated and disseminated in the TREVI era. To avoid abuse of diplomatic privileges, officials participating in TREVI meetings exchanged information about undesired people. Certainly, inclusion in the 'black list' was not associated with the freezing of assets but merely a potential refusal of the right of entry.

35 Statewatch is a leading human rights watchdog routinely examining EU law in the field of JHA. www.statewatch.com.

36 Declaration by the Presidency on behalf of the European Union, the Central and Eastern European countries associated with the European Union, the associated countries Cyprus, Malta and Turkey, and the EFTA countries, members of the European Economic Area, on the application of specific measures to combat terrorism of 23 December 2002, 15762/02, PESC/02/195.

with those of the old Member States long before their accession. The accession date brought about, however, two significant differences. First, the basically political declaration embodied in an instrument of a persuasive value, which was accompanied by a general duty of an acceding state to bring into line its legislation, has been replaced by a direct legal duty of implementation flowing from directly effective and applicable regulation. Second, the accession provided entrants with the leeway to shape the list on the same terms as applicable to the Fifteen receiving Member States. The entrants thus gained the opportunity of shape the EU list, that have long been desired by non-member states.[37]

A common list of terrorists was one of many items on the list of counter-terrorism instruments in place before the accession. Also co-operation through Europol and Eurojust was pursued before 1 May 2004, albeit to a limited extent. In contrast, some measures were not in use although it had been planned that they would be in place before the date of enlargement. The European Arrest Warrant, designed to replace extradition procedures, is the most conspicuous example. It was supposed to be implemented by the Fifteen by 1 January 2004 while the deadline for the Ten was set for the day of their accession. In practice, upon enlargement roughly half of the entrants[38] and three of the Fifteen Member States had failed to transpose the Framework Decision on the European Arrest Warrant into their national legislation.[39] Effectively, it was not fully ready before enlargement, as the Commission had hoped. Its openly divergent implementation in the Member States and the resurfacing political opposition to it, exemplified recently by the refusal of the President of the Czech Republic to approve the European Arrest Warrant because it touched national sovereignty too deeply, bring the promise of further complications before a single post-extradition regime across Europe may be established.[40] And this instrument is only one item on the long list of non-transposed measures in various areas under the now obsolete third pillar.[41] The problem has become particularly acute in recent years following the adoption of the Brussels Action Plan against terrorism and the ambitious Tampere programme that prompted intensive legislative activity, putting a strain on the implementation capabilities of the Member States.

---

37 Notably, Norway has routinely complained about the list of terrorists. They put into question the inclusion of several organisations recognised as terrorist by the EU.

38 Cyprus, Hungary, Lithuania, Poland and Slovenia.

39 Germany, Greece and Italy.

40 'Czech President vetoes bill on European Arrest Warrant', *Euobserver*, 24 August 2004.

41 See *infra* 5.4.

4 Selected challenges in context of enlargement

4.1 Complexity

EU counter-terrorism represents an area of particular intricacy. The Justice and Home Affairs area that has framed counter-terrorism co-operation at the EU level for the last three decades is difficult to grasp for external observers and national delegates alike. It has been subject to far-reaching treaty revisions that have transfigured the institutional setting and created two different regimes within the first and third pillars, under the Title IV EC and Title VI EU respectively. This fragmented legal foundation containing rules and procedures different from those applicable in the Communities core has been compounded by fluctuating institutional structure both inside and outside the treaty framework. The vibrant and unstable fabric of the JHA gave birth to the third-pillar-oriented Counter-Terrorism Co-ordinator, although he was formally appointed by the second-pillar Secretary-General/High Representative for the Common Foreign and Security Policy (CFSP). The establishment of other structures is a frequent topic at the Article 36 Committee, Coreper and JHA Council meetings. The Austrian idea of a separate FBI-style agency or the Counter-Terrorism Co-ordinator's proposals on the Council structures are good cases in point. But JHA extend much beyond the treaty frameworks. The informal form of enhanced co-operation by the so-called 'Big Five' and the Counter-Terrorism Group have been placed outside this framework.

Moreover, quite surprisingly for many bystanders, the Amsterdam Treaty incorporated the Schengen *acquis* into the Treaties and replaced its institutions with their communitarian counterparts.[42] This undoubtedly positive development gave rise to serious misgivings about the manner in which the bulky Schengen *acquis* was incorporated. Instead of incorporating the entire *acquis* into the 'third pillar' and, possibly, subsequent transposition of its revised version to the first pillar, 'Schengen was glued in un ungainly manner on to both the first and third pillars'.[43] Not only did this contribute to the already "unprecedented degree of complexity"[44] of the JHA area and its consequent opacity, standing in stark contrast with lofty and frequently voiced ideas of simplicity, comprehensibility and transparency for citizens but also preserving the compartmentalisation of the internal security perimeter, yet this time within the EU framework.

Institutional transformations aside, the field of counter-terrorism is now becoming challenging in itself. After decades of the JHA lead in counter-terror-

42 Den Boer and Wallace, op. cit. n. 11, at pp. 513-514.

43 See A. Duff, *The Treaty of Amsterdam. Text and Commentary* (London, Sweet & Maxwell 1997) p. 53.

44 J. Monar, 'Institutionalising Freedom, Security and Justice' in J. Peterson & M. Shackleton, eds., *The Institutions of the European Union* (Oxford, University Press 2002) p. 189.

ism a more comprehensive approach is being promoted. Among a variety of measures proposed by the Revised Action Plan adopted by the European Council on 25 March 2004, one will find novelties like the elaboration of a long-term strategy to address factors contributing to recruitment to terrorism or the investigation of links between extreme religious beliefs and support for terrorism. Seven identified objectives that are to be pursued by the Union in the fight against terrorism are formulated in a wide-ranging and cross-pillar fashion that struggles to ignore the pillar logics. Their implementation will, without the shadow of doubt, necessitate comprehensive efforts in many policy fields by dozens of workgroups, committees and other bodies placed within all three pillars and at different levels of EU governance. The increasingly wide policy coverage of EU responses adds to the already swollen problem of co-ordination which was recently underlined by the appointment of the Counter-Terrorism Co-ordinator. This comprehensiveness of the EU approach and the challenge of coordination mean that it will difficult for national authorities and delegates to keep track of developments and have a good overview of EU counter-terrorism.

Fourthly, the complexity is further boosted by the swift advancement of EU counter-terrorism in the wake of the events of 11/09 and, more recently, 11/03. First, the occurrences in New York imparted a strong impulse to the third pillar machinery and rapidly pushed the JHA co-operation beyond previously unknown limits; then the Madrid terrorist attacks renewed the slackened impetus guaranteeing the flourishing of legislative and extra-legislative activity in the EU counter-terrorism, now in a wider cross-pillar framework.

These factors resulted in an unprecedented degree of complexity in EU counter-terrorism, which will be something of a headache for national delegates from new Member States, especially those working in capital cities. In a large arena of actors dealing with terrorism who are subject to diverse procedures and practices and frequently working under pressure of events, it will take a good deal of time for the officials to find their way, let alone have a complete picture of EU counter-terrorism.

Moreover, enlargement will also make the task even more challenging for their fellow colleagues from the Fifteen Member States as it will heighten again the degree of complexity. Each new entrant brings with it a package of its own approaches, fears and security concerns. Although these seemed largely muted during the accession negotiation and in any event did not constitute a substantial hurdle to the candidate states' ultimate goal of full membership, unequal and asymmetrical bargaining relationships in the enlargement negotiations does not guarantee that muted fears and objections will not manifest themselves at a later stage.[45] These might embrace a wide range of issues including the fear

[45] N. Walker 'The Problem of Trust in an Enlarged Area of Freedom Security and Justice: A Conceptual Analysis', in M. Anderson and J. Apap, eds., *Police and Justice Co-operation and the New European Borders* (The Hague, Kluwer International 2002) p. 27.

for the perceived Russian expansionism, regional border co-operation with non-member states after the accession or reluctance towards transferring power over vital policy areas to Brussels.[46] Still more importantly, these potential tensions will have to be tackled pursuant to the unworkable unanimity requirement that seems to be increasingly at odds with efficient and effective governance in the Union framework.[47]

4.2 Legal and structural diversity

This decade will be remembered as one of unprecedented intensification in justice and home affairs co-operation, measured by the growth of the body of legislation or the number of texts produced to meet the needs of various working parties in this area. Counter-terrorism is not an exception to this rule but rather an exemplary case. The swift progress has not, however, gone as far as to touch upon the internal institutional structures of the Member States. This field has been widely viewed as a 'sacred cow', which must remain untouched by the EU *acquis* as it is arguably too close to the heart of national sovereignty. Indeed, internal structures reflect deep-rooted national traditions and experiences gained over many years. Unsurprisingly, the EU Treaty does not grant powers to legislate in this area and, additionally, explicitly guarantees that the 'exercise of the responsibilities incumbent upon Member States with regard to the maintenance of law and order and the safeguarding of internal security' shall not be affected.[48]

As a consequence, the internal institutional framework within which the fight against terrorism is waged is an exemplary instance of diversity. The differences begin with different ministries responsible for counter-terrorism, a variety of law enforcement bodies involved in counter-terrorism, their competences and position in a hierarchy and the existence or otherwise of special courts or prosecutors. The differences end with the range and competences of security services and intelligence agencies and other potential contributors to internal security, such as borders/customs authorities or financial units that grapple with terrorism. Mechanisms of co-ordination, be they permanent or ad hoc, also vary from country to country as do the existence of special bodies dedicated to co-ordinating counter-terrorism efforts.

---

[46] J. Zielonka 'Enlargement and the Finality of European Integration', in C. Joerges, Y. Meny and J. Weiler eds., *What Kind of Constitution for What Kind of Polity? Responses to Joschka Fischer* (Florence, Robert Schuman Center 2000) pp. 151-162. Also N. Walker, *supra* n.45, p. 28.

[47] On the critique of the unanimity requirement and other practical shortcomings of the third pillar regime, see H. Nilsson, 'Decision-Making in EU Justice and Home Affairs: Current Shortcomings and Reform Possibilities' *Sussex European Institute Working Paper No 57*.

[48] Art. 33 (ex Art. K.5).

Enlargement increases diversity. New Member States bring their own distinct counter-terrorism machinery and are attached to their own procedures and practices. At first glance this diversity might seem to complicate further efficient counter-terrorism co-operation in the EU, as national delegates of one Member State will have to, at least roughly, know the institutional framework of the other Member States, i.e. who they should approach or what the competences of their counterparts are. This problem is sometimes solved by legislation providing a Member State with a fragmentary image of the institutional setting of other Member States, such as the competent authorities to be collaborated with[49] or informal documents prepared by the General Secretariat of the Council.[50] However, all these attempts do not provide national officials with a complete picture of counter-terrorism.

One should not, however, be tempted to view this diversity as a stumbling block. The problem is not diversity as such but, rather, lacking information and inefficient co-ordination, both at national and EU level. As this variety of institutional settings grants a unique opportunity to compare different solutions, stimulate an exchange of views, practices and finally formulate recommendations, it should be perceived as a building block on which all Member States may draw on within the EU framework.

4.3 Trust

Trust has always been an indispensable foundation of co-operation in the JHA policy sphere, both in the TREVI forum and within the Union framework alike.[51] Its shortage is likely to limit the effectiveness of any meaningful co-operation while its total absence may practically annihilate it, whether carried out through bilateral channels or within a multilateral forum. The case of Europol, whose usefulness in the fight against terrorism is closely associated with its appreciation in the Member States, is a good case in point.

The enlargement has evoked among European societies a wide spectrum of feelings from genuine enthusiasm to more or less concealed enmity. It should not thus be a surprise to detect a similar variety of sentiments among European counter-terrorism services, perhaps with a mixture of indifference and distrust having an upper hand on the eve of the enlargement. One could note that the

---

49 See e.g. Council Regulation 2580/2001 of 27 December 2001 on specific restrictive measures directed against certain persons and entities with a view to combating terrorism, *OJ* 2001 L 344/93.

50 Extensive assistance rendered by the Council Secretariat at the stage of the introduction of the European Arrest Warrant is a good case in point.

51 For a stimulating conceptual analysis of the problem of trust and the connections between the idea of trust and JHA policy area, see N. Walker, *supra* n. 45, pp. 19-35, for different perspectives of trust and its relevance for police co-operation, see M. Anderson 'Trust and Police Cooperation', in M. Anderson and J. Apap, *supra* n. 45, pp. 35-46.

arrival of any new country in a successful long-standing club involves a period of adaptation during which mutual trust between the new and old members is forged, and mistrust may steadily fade away. This round of enlargement presents, however, a qualitatively disparate challenge in comparison to the previous round.

First, the overwhelming majority of the new Member States has less experience in counter-terrorism than some of their Western partners that have grappled with terrorist menace for decades. Terrorism, in the meaning offered by the Framework Decision on combating terrorism,[52] did not essentially constitute a major threat in the majority of the new Member States before the fall of the Iron Curtain.[53] To the contrary, the Soviet bloc was more often accused of supporting international terrorism than praised for its vigorous suppression.

The collapse of the bipolar world order and the radical political turnaround that ensued entailed the establishment of new internal security machinery. Discredited secret services had to be significantly rebuilt and adapted to a completely new democratic setting. These are rather young and fledging structures that are in many cases still undergoing institutional transformation. This does not contribute to building confidence in the eyes of their Western colleagues. This is not to say that the counter-terrorism services in the West are not subject to transformation but, rather, that the extent of the changes is usually much more limited and evolutionary.[54] However, the institutional flexibility in the new members gives one undeniable advantage. It greatly facilitates any reorganisations of the internal security machinery as these do not have to overcome strong institutional interests, deep-rooted traditions and customs existent in the old members. It is all the more important given that frequent transformations that are taking place at EU level in the wake of 11/09 and 11/03. In this context Europol officers admitted unofficially that they often received more information from new members than from the old ones.

Third, the reconstruction of new counter-terrorism services posed an important question as to who should be employed in the new structures. Since the dismissal of all old civil servants would have practically annihilated the capabilities of these services for a long time, the new Member States often chose a middle way, i.e. they amalgamated old and newly hired people, albeit in differing proportions. The fact that these services still employ former officers of

---

52 Council Framework Decision 2002/475/JHA of 13 June 2002 on combating terrorism, *OJ* 2002 L 164/3.

53 In fact, what some of those countries experienced, especially in the first years of the communist rule, was a phenomenon called 'state-terrorism', which was coined in the eighteenth century during the French Revolution to label a form of politically motivated violence used by regimes that rule by a fear and intimidation of the populace.. Nowadays, this term has been sometimes utilised to describe the Israelis approach to the Palestinian problem. See *Agence Europe* of 20 April 2004.

54 For example, in the 2002 Portugal established a Unit for Anti-terrorism Coordination called UCAT while Italy created the same year a technical group for prevention and repression of terrorism.

the previous regime as well as the alleged pro-American stance of the Central and Eastern European countries, is for some Western services not conducive to closer co-operation.

Another argument being advanced is that these states are not the most likely targets for Islamic terrorists. Indeed, they do not report significant levels of terrorist activity or terrorist recruitment and their local Muslim communities, let alone their extremist margins, are relatively small. Therefore, the most vulnerable Western countries, namely the United Kingdom, France, Spain and Germany, do not see a pressing need for a closer co-operation with the counter-terrorism services in the new Members States unless required by the need for specific operational data.

All these factors combined with the high sensitivity of the matter under discussion, cultural and linguistic differences, compounded by insufficient knowledge of one another's legal systems might explain to a certain extent the palpable shortage of trust. After the shocking events of 11/03 a special meeting of European secret services, known as G5, was held in Madrid. It is striking that no single delegate from the Ten was invited to that meeting.[55] This exclusion of the entrants from the informal form of enhanced co-operation coupled with a lofty stance bordering on arrogance,[56] provided a gloomy image of mutual trust and an example of negative differentiation by the Fifteen towards the Ten, based on lack of trust. As exclusion inevitably engenders feelings of isolation and rejection, the gap in trust can be expected to widen and to hamper efforts to bridge that gap. Interestingly, not only did this rejection evoke negative feelings among the Ten but it also provoked their attempts to induce Western colleagues to co-operate more closely with them by way of underscoring their readiness to co-operate or highlighting their importance in the fight against international terrorism. To give an example, Polish secret services supposedly tried to increase their importance in the eyes of their western counterparts through an 'over-interpretation', as it was termed by the press, of the so-called 'Norway report', which was to contain and interpret discovered covert Al-Quada declaration and plans on further targets, modes of action etc. Polish secret services were to intercept and then interpret the Al-Quada declaration in such a way as to suggest an immediate terrorist threat to the state authorities, seeking thereby to induce their western colleagues to co-operate more closely with Polish services.[57]

---

55 The Madrid meeting of European secret services dedicated to the Madrid events was to be held on 22 March 2004. 'Solana warns against an over-reaction after Madrid' in *EUobserver*, 22 March 2004, www.euobserver.com.

56 'Manipulacja czy ignorancja' [Manipulation or ignorance] in *Rzeczpospolita*, 13 April 04.

57 *Supra* n. 57.

4.4 Double standard

When the EU embarked upon an ambitious counter-terrorism programme in the aftermath of 11/09, many believed that the lofty political declarations and commitments would soon be turned into reality. In actual fact, the sense of commitment and urgency prevalent immediately after 11/09 soon dissipated among the Member States as the sense of insecurity waned and the concern with national sovereignty re-emerged. As a consequence, the implementation of a number of measures has been disappointing.

The main legal development in counter-terrorism, the Framework Decision on Combating Terrorism of 13 June 2002 setting out the first legal definition of terrorist offences within the framework of the Union, was to be transposed into national legislation by the end of 2002.[58] Apparently, the date of enlargement caught at least two Member States, Greece and the Netherlands, unprepared and in delay. Similarly, three Member States, Denmark, Greece again and Italy, failed to implement the second flag ship – the Framework Decision on the European Arrest Warrant of 13 June 2002. The deadline for transposition of the Decision on Joint Investigation Teams of 13 June 2002 was disregarded by at least five countries, namely Belgium, Greece, Ireland, Italy, and Luxemburg. The problem of the implementation gap by the Fifteen within the Justice and Home Affairs perimeter has been swelling and repeatedly highlighted both by the Commission and more recently by the Counter-Terrorism Co-ordinator. The growing preoccupation with timely implementation of fast-growing JHA *acquis*, together with lacking trust and confidence in the unproven performance of ex-communist countries,[59] had a discernible impact on the conditions of accession required of candidate countries for EU Membership. For the first time in the history of European integration a new form of a safeguard clause concerning JHA *acquis* was added.

Article 39 of the Act of Accession provides that in case of, 'serious shortcomings or any imminent risks of such shortcomings in the transposition, state of implementation, or the application of the framework decisions or any other relevant commitments, instruments of co-operation and decisions relating to mutual recognition in the area of criminal law under Title VI of the EU Treaty, the Commission may, 'take appropriate measures and specify the conditions and modalities under which these measures are put into effect. These measures may take the form of temporary suspension of the application of relevant provisions and decisions in the relations between a new Member State and any other Member State or Member States.'

This safeguard clause provides the Commission with a powerful and broadly defined stick to discipline those new Member States which lag behind or

[58] Council Framework Decision of 13 June 2002 on combating terrorism, *OJ* 2002 L 164, Art. 11.1

[59] K. Inglis, op. cit. n. 22, at p. 971.

inappropriately implement JHA *acquis* adopted pursuant to Title VI. Thus the Commission has been afforded considerable powers at the enforcement phase over new Member States that it clearly does not enjoy with regard to old members. The Fifteen is subject to rules provided for in Title VI of the EU Treaty, which give the Commission very limited authority. Implementation is almost entirely in the hands of Member States and the Commission does not enjoy the power to open an infringement procedure for failure to act, as provided for under Article 226 EC Treaty. The Commission can only basically apply political pressure which appears to have been of limited impact. The difference in treatment is thus even more striking in JHA than in Internal Market area, where a similar safeguard clause applies under Article 38 Act of Accession, since in the former sphere the Commission can only apply largely ineffective political pressure while in the latter the Fifteen is subject to Article 226 EC. The paucity of effective legal measures in JHA may induce the Commission to make use of the safeguard clause to a greater extent than in respect of Internal Market. However, the actual application of Article 39 may place the Commission in a politically difficult position as it can be applied only to new members. What decision would the Commission make if it found both new and old members in breach of their implementation duties remains an open question.

The double standard in the treatment of the Ten compared to the Fifteen at the enforcement stage is all the more acute given the relatively broad scope of the provision. It covers all sorts of commitments, decisions and instruments of co-operation relating to mutual recognition in criminal matters. It is a broad area that covers, *inter alia*, pre-trial orders, sentencing and follow-up post-sentencing decisions and one should not forget that we are only at the beginning of the long road to the full implementation of the principle of mutual recognition.[60]

In view of the fact that it will take many years to fully implement the principle, the time limit of potential measures applied pursuant to Article 39 of the Act of Accession becomes all the more significant. Although it stipulates that these may be taken 'until the period of up to three years after the date of entry into force of this Act [of Accession]' it goes on to say that 'they may however be applied beyond the period specified in the above paragraph [three years] as long as these shortcomings persist.[text in brackets added]'. It thus implies effectively that the existence of two distinct regimes of enforcement does not have a clear end point. The Ten may be treated in the same legal situation differently in comparison to the Fifteen and this unequal treatment may be applied years after the enlargement. Without denying the need and legitimacy for more effective arrangements on enforcement of EU acts adopted under Title VI of the EU Treaty, the diversification of enforcement rules by the cited provisions of the Act of Accession created a questionable double standard.

---

[60] For details see the Commission Programme of measures to implement the principle of mutual recognition of decisions in criminal matters of 15 January 2001, *OJ* 2001 C 12/02.

Finally, the double-standard enforcement introduced by virtue of Article 39 should be viewed in a wider context amongst other, more broadly described in the literature,[61] elements of diversification of the legal status of new Member States. The uncompromising stance of the Commission on the subject of implementation of the massive and dynamic JHA *acquis* required candidate states to adopt it *en bloc* without making any opt-outs according to their own domestic sensibilities.[62] It is all the more surprising as earlier examples of legal differentiation had already been set by the UK, Ireland and Denmark in respect of Schengen *acquis*.

5 Conclusions

New Member States adhered to the EU at a time of profound and far-reaching transformation of EU counter-terrorism. Since the year 2001 an avalanche of measures have been taken, touching on an increasingly broad range of policy areas. The recent Madrid atrocities can be expected to keep up the momentum in policy development. As counter-terrorism activity is set to flourish in the years to come within the Union of twenty-five Member States, the problems of complexity, diversity, double standard and the lack of trust between counter-terrorism services, merit particular attention.

As regards the complexity of the EU legal framework, all signs seem to indicate that the problem will persist, at least in a short term, for a number of reasons. It reflects deep-rooted tensions in the field of JHA, thriving EU counter-terrorism activity that is steadily spilling over into further policy areas, and a fast-growing body of legislation. The problem of complexity might, however, be somewhat alleviated by the introduction of measures which are now in the pipeline. The institutional framework would be streamlined and, to some extent, simplified by the Constitutional Treaty as the pillar division would be abolished. Although a number of specificities of JHA will remain and numerous ambiguities in the text still persist, progress is visible. In the meantime, the Commission's recent proposal to replace the Schengen *acquis* with a comprehensive legal instrument on the crossing of internal and external borders is likely to mitigate the intricacy of those aspects of counter-terrorism linked to border management. As the complexity of the institutional setting is set to remain, it is important for all Member States to counter it by themselves. The establishment of national counter-terrorism co-ordinators linked to their EU counterpart and held responsible for keeping track of EU counter-terrorism developments and their implementation at national level, would be a highly positive development.

---

[61] See especially K. Inglis, op. cit. n. 22 pp. 938-973.

[62] On the JHA acquis, see G. de Kerchove 'Relations extérieures at élargissement', in G. de Kerchove and A. Weyembergh , eds., *L'espace pénal européen: enjeux et perspectives,* (Bruxelles, Editions de l'Université de Bruxelles 2003) pp. 275 – 276.

As regards diversity, every effort should be made to preserve it yet a fine-tuning of those national arrangements that hamper efficient cross-border co-operation seems necessary. This especially concerns the 'crown jewels' of Member States, as the Irish Justice Minister, Michael McDowell, labelled the intelligence sharing, but also to criminal justice co-operation. To this end and in view of enlargement, the pace of the peer review mechanism should be significantly accelerated and its scope broadened to embrace other sensitive areas of counter-terrorism where far-reaching instruments are out of the question. This could help to identify gaps and stumbling blocks, facilitate the sharing of ideas and, finally, permit recommendations to be put forward so as to stamp out obstacles to efficient co-operation.

Improving trust between Member States seems to be the most arduous challenge. The sensitivity of counter-terrorism in such a sophisticated and diversified environment means that a good deal of time will pass before truly efficient co-operation materialises at EU level. The rather shallow reservoir of trust promises to persist if political and legal differentiation between the Ten and Fifteen continues. The examples of the exclusion from the 'Big Five' format, unfair representation in the Situation Centre and the double standard in enforcement stand out. It is sometimes forgotten that headway made in bridging the gap of trust between the Fifteen and the Ten will be hampered if such examples of differentiation are allowed to continue. Furthermore, confidence-building and mutual-learning measures should be more vigorously promoted. Common meetings and conferences among national officials, within European agencies and outside,[63] exchange programmes, common training, also with the use of Commission-funded programmes, should be organised more frequently, as these could assist in creating stronger bonds between national officials and the security community. The proliferation of common threat assessments, now after Solana's plan covering internal threats, could also help to build a common perception of the security challenges, which is a first step to hammering out divergences pertaining to other aspects of counter-terrorism. The introduction of common minimum standards as regards fundamental procedural rights in criminal proceedings should be considered a crucial step towards greater trust across the Union[64] while 'soft approximation' through the proliferation of guidelines and best practices should not in any case be sidelined. The recent idea of disseminating the 'recipe' for the successful Spanish-French co-operation in suppressing ETA[65] is worth noting. Finally, the peer assessment mechanism should be more intensively employed as it proved an effective method of 'new governance' that is capable of improving trust and anti-terrorist capabilities of the Member States through a non-intrusive EU action.

---

63 The Rome conference on counter-terrorism in 2003 is a good example.

64 Proposal for a Council Framework Decision on certain procedural rights in criminal proceedings throughout the European Union, COM(2004) 328 final.

65 'EU co-operation vital in war on terror' in *European Voice*, 18-23 March 2004.

We can foster the hope that the inevitably progressing europeanisation (or perhaps atlantisation) in countering the threat of terrorism and evident common benefits of closer co-operation in the fight against it will be conducive to overcoming deep-rooted tensions and wide-ranging divergences within the enlarged Union. Otherwise, the grim prospect of crossing the five thousand death toll that Europe has witnessed over the past thirty years might materialise faster than we think.

PART 3 – THE EU POLICY OF CONDITIONALITY

CHAPTER 10

EU Enlargement – Membership Conditions Applied to Future and Potential Member States

Kirstyn Inglis

1 Introduction

Nowhere in the Treaties is enlargement set out as an end-goal of the European Union. The Constitutional Treaty,[1] which will enter into force on 1 November 2006[2] provided all twenty-five Member States have ratified it, will not change this fact. However, enlargement as a means to uniting the peoples of Europe, must be seen as a core goal of the Union in order to further peace, prosperity, stability and security on the European continent. This chapter[3] explores current and future pre-accession conditionality as it applies to current and future candidates for accession and is not concerned with the historical evolution of that pre-accession conditionality.[4] The evolving nature of pre-accession conditionality reflects the particular nature and circumstances of both the incoming countries as well as the Union itself. Pre-accession conditionality, the enlargement or membership conditionality (including Art. 49 EU, the Copenhagen criteria, and the instruments of the pre-accession strategy) that applies during a country's preparations for membership of the Union is a distinct category of the conditionality that the Union applies in its external relations with third countries.

This chapter takes a snapshot of the pre-accession conditionality as it stands momentarily and considers the direction that it has taken from the starting point, mostly, of the fifth enlargement. While doing so it is important to bear in mind that enlargement has always been a core aim of the Union. The preamble to the European Coal and Steel Community Treaty, signed in Paris on 18 April 1951, had little to say about coal and steel but, rather, spoke of safeguarding peace, establishing an economic community and substituting for age-old rivalries and bloody conflicts the merging of essential interests.[5] The premise of the later European Economic Community Treaty was that of an ever closer union of the peoples of Europe. Indeed, enlargement was already under consideration not

---

1 The full title of the Constitutional Treaty is 'Treaty establishing a Constitution for Europe' can be found in *OJ* 2004 C 310/1.

2 Art. IV-447 Constitutional Treaty.

3 The content of this chapter is taken from the PhD thesis being drafted by the author under the title 'European Enlargement: an analysis of pre-accession and transitional arrangements with case studies on agri-food and environment law', forthcoming.

4 See F. Hoffmeister, 'Earlier enlargements' and 'Changing requirements for membership', in A.Ott and K. Inglis, eds., *Handbook on European Enlargement. A commentary on the Enlargement process* (The Hague, TMC Asser Press, 2002) at pp. 87-102. See also K. E. Smith 'The Evolution and Application of EU Membership Conditionality' in M. Cremona, ed. *The Enlargement of the European Union* (Oxford New York, Oxford University Press 2003) at pp. 105-139.

5 See W. Nicoll and A. Salmon, eds., *Understanding the European Communities*, (Worcester, Philip Allan, 1990) at p. 7.

6 See Nicoll and Salmon, op. cit. n.5 at pp. 23-24.

even three years after the entry into force of the EEC Treaty on 1 January 1958 with the talk of bringing in Britain, Denmark, Ireland, Norway and Switzerland. The UK first applied for membership on 31 July 1961, while Ireland applied the day before (30 July 1961) and Denmark on 10 August of the same year. The accession negotiations that followed were soon to fail for a variety of reasons but primarily because of what can only be described effectively as a veto by President de Gaulle at a press conference in Rambouillet on 14 January 1963.[6] Early deliberations of the first Member States and the Union institutions in that context clearly show early elements of pre-accession conditionality. Moreover, the summit of 1 and 2 December 1969 in The Hague, commonly known for the launch of the European Political Co-operation, set out a triptych for action[7] completion (to lay down a definitive financial arrangement for the Common Agricultural Policy (CAP)); deepening (or consolidation), and; widening (or enlargement).

Enlargement conditionality includes conditions and incentives and disincentives that apply to aspiring Member States but it also includes a conditionality that applies to the receiving Member States. The current membership conditionality applicable to any country eligible to accede to the European Union officially began in 1993 with the adoption by the June 1993 Copenhagen European Council of the 'Copenhagen criteria'. These were the criteria that applied in the fifth enlargement of the European Union, which took place on 1 May 2004.[8] The Copenhagen criteria read as follows:

The associated countries in Central and Eastern Europe that so desire shall become members of the Union. Accession will take place as soon as a country is able to assume the obligations of membership by satisfying the economic and political conditions. Membership requires:

- that the candidate country has achieved stability of institutions guaranteeing democracy, the rule of law, human rights and respect for and protection of minorities;
- the existence of a functioning market economy, as well as the capacity to cope with competitive pressures and market forces within the Union;
- the ability to take on the obligations of membership, including adhering to the aims of political, economic and monetary union;
- the Union's capacity to absorb new Members, while maintaining the momentum of European integration, is also an important consideration in the general interest of both the Union and the candidate countries.[9]

---

7 See *Bull. EC* 2/70.

8 Treaty concerning the Accession of the Czech Republic, the Republic of Estonia, the Republic of Cyprus, the Republic of Latvia, the Republic of Lithuania, the Republic of Hungary, the Republic of Malta, the Republic of Poland, the Republic of Slovenia and the Slovak Republic to the European Union, Signed in Athens on 16 April 2003, *OJ* 2003 L 236/1, hereafter 'the Accession Treaty'.

9 *Bull. EU* 6/1993, point 13.

This chapter is concerned with pre-accession conditionality, current and future, insofar as it applies to aspiring and candidate countries. Section 1, however, begins by looking at the pre-accession conditionality that applies to the receiving Member States – the fourth set of Copenhagen criteria – and predicts the ways in which this criteria will grow in significance as a pre-condition to membership as the Union enlarges, especially since the fifth enlargement on 1 May 2004. Section 2 explores pre-accession conditionality compared to other forms of conditionality generally, taking as a starting point Article 49 EU on eligibility for membership, which contains the legal basis for enlargement of the Union. The implications of the Constitutional Treaty are explored as is the content of the Copenhagen criteria in practice. Some comments are made on the borders of the Union and the possibility of more enlargements again. Section 3 gives an overview of the instruments of the pre-accession strategy that carry the current pre-accession conditionality. It is broken up into three sub-sections outlining the instruments of the pre-accession strategy insofar as it relates to: those candidates with which accession negotiations have been opened (Bulgaria and Romania); those candidates with which accession negotiations have not been opened (Croatia and Turkey), and; potential candidates (the countries of the Western Balkans).

2 The imperative of the fourth Copenhagen criteria as a precursor to future enlargements?

The fourth set of Copenhagen criteria is not the subject of this paper as such but a few comments thereon are relevant to this introduction. It is after all the Union that enlarges and the candidate that accedes. Each enlargement of the Union has emphasised the dilemma of the strain that widening puts on the deepening of integration efforts; how will the Union function in decision-making and how can such a complex diversity of countries integrate further? So far the Member States have not reverted to the fourth Copenhagen criteria in order to prevent an enlargement from going ahead as planned in political negotiations between the European Council and the candidates. When such a possibility has been tendered, it has been pushed aside by Council, Commission and the European Parliament in particular as an excuse and a disincentive that contradicts the political commitments and promises of the Union and which would ridicule the Union not only before the candidate that has worked so hard in good faith to meet its membership conditionality but also before the international community.[10] But in a Union of twenty-five Member States, will the fourth

[10] See for example the European Parliament resolution of 14 March 1985 on the deadlock in accession negotiations for Spain. Negotiations nearly failed because of an intractable dispute among Member States concerning access of Spanish boats to EC waters. The Parliament pointed out that the failure to agree was 'not enough to justify the failure of the negotiations and postponement of enlargement'

Copenhagen criteria of the Union's capacity to absorb more countries and the matter of maintaining the momentum of European integration continue to take a back seat in pre-accession conditionality compared to the three Copenhagen criteria that are addressed to those aspiring to membership?

It is useful, therefore, to keep in mind the fourth Copenhagen criteria because further enlargements will emphasise and accentuate the problems facing the Union in terms of its capacity to absorb new Members and the continued evolution, implementation and enforcement of the *acquis communautaire*. Indeed, the strain on further deepening integration efforts was prevalent in the Union already prior to the fifth enlargement. This can be seen in the various means and policy tools developed by the Union as a means of allowing integration to proceed in a flexible way so that some Member States have been able to remain out of core Union activities or to enable a majority of willing or able Member States to deepen their integration efforts without the full participation of the remainder of the Member States.[11] It is also the case that the Member States have repeatedly pushed ahead with their widening ambitions in a committed and determined way while holding back – for whatever reason[12] – from undertaking the necessary internal reforms, with all the sacrifices and compromises that those reforms require.

While the incoming ten Member States of the fifth enlargement have been more rigorously prepared for Membership than any previous entrant, the sheer number of Member States that have to be accommodated within unfamiliar (if not inadequate) structures and the multitude of complicating factors, including layers of transitional arrangements introduced with consecutive enlargements and the matter of working languages, demand a far greater effort for deepening integration efforts. Already one of the new Member States, Malta, is struggling to keep up with the language demands of integration,[13] a structural problem that is particularly demanding for any small Member State. In the coming years

and that if this were the outcome, it 'might constitute a mortal blow to the Community's credibility as regards its ability to respect its commitments and negotiate effectively with third countries', *OJ* 1985 C 94/77.

11 Notably in the cases of Schengen and EMU.

12 Of the more recent literature considering the future context of the Constitutional Treaty see G. Bermann and G. de Búrca, 'The Legal Foundations of the Enlarged European Union' in G. A. Bermann and K. Pistor, eds., *Law and Governance in an Enlarged European Union* (Portland Oregon, Hart Publishing 2004) pp. 141-151. See also de Witte, 'The Impact of Enlargement on the Constitution of the European Union' in Cremona, op. cit. n. 4. at pp. 209-252.

13 See Regulation 930/2004, *OJ* 2004 L 169/1. It provides for a temporary derogation to the effect that only Regulations adopted jointly by the Parliament and the Council have to be translated into Maltese. English is the second official language in Malta but according to the Maltese Constitution, should any conflict arise between the Maltese and English language version arise, the Maltese language should prevail. See Nic Shuihbne, 41 *CML Rev.* 2004 at pp. 1093-1111.

the Union has to transform itself further while consecutive accession treaties will enter into force.[14] Even at the time of the signature of the fifth Accession Treaty on 16 April 2004[15] the Union itself was not fully ready; two examples stand out. It is not clear as yet how the European Central bank will continue to function once the new Member States of the fifth enlargement are ready to enter the Eurozone.[16] The fifth Accession Treaty was signed before the full package of reform measures in respect of the Common Agricultural Policy had been agreed,[17] raising certain important (negative) implications for the new Member States which, as a result, they were not able to negotiate in the Accession Treaty.[18]

So has enlargement become an imperative over the Union's capacity to absorb new Members and over deepening? If this is the case, possible scenarios are seemingly unending. If indeed enlargement has become an imperative over deepening, looking to future enlargements, can this continue? Would further enlargements be self-defeating in that they threaten to weaken the fabric of the Union to such an extent that would threaten the very aims of peace, prosperity, stability and security on the European continent that it set out to achieve? Or is it that in order to continue to meet these aims in the context of the European continent, the Union must live with a looser integration? Will the political will be as present in the future among the new Member States in the absence of the incentive that integration provided pre-accession? Should the Union push ahead with flexibility mechanisms among willing Member States, with all the risks of introducing political conflicts or jealousies and further weakening the links between Member States? Or would the extreme alternative of reverting to a more shallow integration generally speaking be the only true alternative if the Union is to function in an harmonious way as it enlarges?

If enlargement cannot be seen as an imperative over the Union's capacity to absorb new Members and deepening of integration, then it will be no surprise to see the fourth Copenhagen criteria being used in future accession negotiations to slow down the pace of negotiations, maybe even to postpone a candi-

---

14 Apart from the ratification and entry into force of the Constitutional Treaty, Bulgaria and Romania have recently signed and ratified their Accession Treaty (see *infra*) and other candidates (actual and potential) are holding the Union to promises of accession, which in turn will require revised decision making procedures and structures.

15 *OJ* 2003 L 236/01.

16 See M. Lelart 'The Eurozone and the Single Currency in an Enlarging Union' in N. Neuwahl, ed., *European Union Enlargement; Law and Socio-Economic Changes*, (Montreal, Les Editions Thémis, 2004) pp. 133-162. See also K. Inglis ' The Union's Fifth Accession Treaty; New Means to Make Enlargement Possible' in 41 *CML Rev.* 2004 at p 948-949.

17 See Commission Press Release 'Enlargement and agriculture: Commission tables amendments to take account of CAP reform', IP/03/1454 of 27 October 2003.

18 It was presented as a sort of fait accompli and as such incited an outcry in the incoming countries, notably in Poland, even before they acceded. See Inglis, op. cit. n. 16 at p. 951.

date's accession or to impose even longer and/or more complicated transitional arrangements and safeguard clauses to the benefit of the receiving Member States.

It is too early, perhaps, to predict the reaction of the Twenty-five to the sixth Accession Treaty for Bulgaria and Romania, which was signed on 25 April 2005[19] and ratified by Bulgaria on 11 May and by Romania on 17 May.[20] Certainly, however, the functioning of the Union will experience considerable pressures to extents that so far have not been experienced in the Union's institutional structures. Bulgaria and Romania are already 'in', to all intents and purposes, albeit in a limited capacity, given their participation in the institutions and decision-making as observers in the European Parliament[21] and in the Council and in its preparatory bodies.[22] As already noted, Bulgaria and Romania, all going to plan, will accede two months after the entry into force of the Constitutional Treaty. Necessarily, the institutional reforms introduced by the Constitutional Treaty that will take effect in November 2009 as concerns the votes of Bulgaria and Romania, will only be a starting point.

Whether the fourth Copenhagen criteria will take on new significance in pre-accession conditionality thereafter can be anticipated to depend on a number of factors. Significant among them will be how smoothly the Union functions in the next few years in terms of decision-making to continue to develop the *acquis communautaire* and of its implementation and enforcement. The new devices of the fifth Accession Treaty to continue pre-accession conditionality in the

---

19 Not yet published in the *OJ*.

20 See 'Bulgaria ratifies EU Accession Treaty' and 'Romania ratifies EU entry', www.EurActiv.com visited on 18 May 2005.

21 Since 26 April 2005 Bulgaria and Romania have sent observers to the European Parliament: eighteen in the case of Bulgaria and 35 in the case of Romania. Such observers can speak but cannot vote. However, see 'EP changes mind over Bulgarian and Romanian observers', www.EurActiv.com, visited on 13 May 2005: 'On 4 May, the European Parliament, led by the two biggest parties, the Socialists (PES) and the Christian Democrats (EPP), had set an earliest date of January 2006 for admission of observers. However, negotiations between the EP groups and Bulgarian and Romanian political parties continued, leading to PES leaders dropping objections to an earlier date. This led to a proposal from EP President Josep Borrell on 12 May that the observers should be welcomed from September or October 2005. The observers will attend Parliament sessions in preparation for the admission of the two countries to the European Union in January 2007. Leaders of all the EP groups agreed. The Parliament's change of mind came the day after the Bulgarian Parliament voted to ratify the country's treaty of accession to the EU.'

22 As of 26 April 2005. See Press Release of the Council of the European Union, Press 100, 8418/05, 25 April 2005. An information and consultation procedure for the adoption of decisions and other measures during the period preceding accessionwhich attaches to the Final Act of the Accession Treaty by means of an exchange of letters. This provides for the acceding states to be kept adequately informed on proposals, communications, recommendations or initiatives that might lead to decisions by the institutions or bodies of the European Union.

first years after the new Member States' accessions, are evidence of the Union's preoccupation with ensuring its capacity to function as well as its ability to continue to deepen its integration efforts as it enlarges. Equally significant will be the matter of maintaining the political commitment to enlarge as well as the outcome of national referendums in the receiving Member States.

3 Pre-accession conditionality as a sophisticated form of conditionality

Pre-accession conditionality is very different from the conditionality that the Union has incorporated into its external relations with third countries generally. The conditionality of the Union in its relations with third countries has grown in intensity and the ends sought by the Union have been supplemented and become increasingly specific, especially since the Treaty on European Union, which gave rise to 'the Union's self-appointed mission to propogate human rights and democracy.'[23] The Union sought to foster development and consolidation of democracy and the rule of law as well as respect for human rights and fundamental freedoms in its development co-operation policy and the Common Foreign and Security Policy. More recently, the Union has been concerned with terrorism and migration under the heading of Justice and Home Affairs to promote its soft-security concerns in third countries.

The conditionality that is prevalent in the Union's external relations with non-candidate countries includes, generally speaking, human rights and democracy, good neighbourliness, democratic institutions, the rule of law, market economy principles, the promotion of sustainable development.[24] The nature and content of conditionality very much depends on its legal basis in the specific bilateral relationship concerned as well as the political and economic context. Thus, 'conditionality' as a concept is hard to describe in exhaustive and in concrete terms. Membership conditionality however is easier to describe because of the range of official documents and legal, political and economic instruments that contain and develop it within the pre-accession strategy.

The main reason for such a different approach to third countries that are 'in pre-accession' or even potentially so, is their future status as a Member State. Accession involves becoming a member of the European Union and Party to the Treaties on which the Union is founded as amended or supplemented.[25] Acced-

---

[23] See E. Lannon, K. Inglis, T. Haenebalcke, 'The many faces of EU conditionality in Pan-Euro-Mediterranean Relations' in M. Maresceau and E. Lannon, eds., *The EU's Enlargement and Mediterranean Strategies: A Comparative Analysis* (New York, Palgrave, 2001) pp. 97-138, at p. 97.

[24] See Lannon, Inglis, Haenebalcke op. cit.n.23. pp. 117-132.

[25] Typically, Art. 1 of an accession treaty.

ing to the Union is to accept, without reserve, the Treaty on European Union and all its objectives, all decisions taken since the entry into force of the Treaties establishing the European Communities and the Treaty on European Union and the options taken in respect of the development and strengthening of those Communities and of the Union.[26] This has always been the case.[27] Moreover, accession necessarily involves recognising that Community law takes precedence over any national provisions that might conflict with it, accession requires that procedures exist for ensuring the uniform interpretation of Community law and, finally, it implies recognition of the binding nature of these rules, observance of which is indispensable to guarantee the effectiveness and unity of Community law.[28]

With the Western Balkans countries, only recognised as potential candidates in 2000, the Copenhagen criteria could be seen from the outset in the Union's approach to the entire region.[29]

3.1 Eligibility for EU membership, admissibility and procedure

Article 49 EU establishes the conditions of eligibility to apply for EU membership as well as the procedure for becoming a member of the Union. Before an accession treaty may be signed, the aspiring country makes a membership application to the Council, which takes a unanimous decision after having received the opinion of the Commission and the assent of the European Parliament acting by absolute majority of its component members (upon each application for membership where there is more than one). Parliamentary assent is not normally necessary for treaty-revision.[30] These documents introduce the Accession Treaty in the preamble to the Treaty of Accession. While no specific reference to the participation of the Community Institutions is made – notably the European Commission – their participation is not excluded.[31] As for the conditions of admission and adjustments to the Treaties which might be required in

[26] See in the case of the fifth enlargement, recital 9 of the Commission Opinion of 19 February 2003 on the applications for accession to the European Union by Czech Republic, the Republic of Estonia, the Republic of Cyprus, the Republic of Latvia, the Republic of Lithuania, the Republic of Hungary, the Republic of Malta, the Republic of Poland, the Republic of Slovenia and the Slovak Republic, *OJ* 2003 L 236/3.

[27] See for example Commission Opinion of 19 January 1972 on the applications for accession to the European Communities by the Kingdom of Denmark, Ireland, the Kingdom of Norway and the United Kingdom of Great Britain and Northern Ireland, *OJ* 1972 L 73/3.

[28] See recital 10 of the Commission Opinion of 19 February 2003 ibid.

[29] Notably with the Stability Pact of South Eastern Europe. See Smith, op. cit. n. 4 at p 136-137.

[30] Art. 48 EU.

[31] See P. J.G. Kapteyn and P. VerLoren van Themaat, *Introduction to the Law of the European Communities*, (The Hague, Kluwer Law International, Third Edition, 1998) at pp. 93-94.

the first years after a new Member's accession, the second paragraph of Article 49 EU leaves this to 'an agreement between the Member States and the applicant State' and provides that such 'agreement be submitted for ratification by all the contracting States in accordance with their respective constitutional requirements'.

None of the receiving Member States in any enlargement have rejected an accession treaty after its signature and no national referendum has been used in the receiving Member States in any of the first five enlargements, whether before or after signature of an accession treaty. Of course, they have ratified the accession treaties in accordance with their own national constitutional requirements, which do not necessarily involve any referendum. As for future enlargements, the possibility of reverting to the use of a national referendum in one or more of the receiving twenty-five Member States, however, is increasing in the popular press. Thus for example, President Chirac has announced that France will hold a referendum on the accession of Turkey[32] – despite the fact that it did not hold a referendum on previous accession treaties, including the fifth and specifically requiring the introduction of amendments to the French Constitution in order to do so. Moreover, as concerns future enlargements, it is also true that the new CEEC Member States have more of a tradition of using referendums and in some cases the 'souverainist' character of their constitutions requires a referendum in respect of any treaty amendment that is of primary relevance to their national constitutional procedures.[33] An accession treaty involves provisions of a fundamentally constitutional nature. In the case of the fifth enlargement, only one of the ten acceding countries – Malta – held a national referendum that was consultative rather than required by its constitution and every referendum was affirmative. For the rest, the result was positive and in some cases overwhelmingly so.

However, for future enlargements, it remains to be seen whether the receiving Member States will revert to national referendums as a pre-condition to ratification of an accession treaty, not only among the CEEC Member States but potentially also the 'old' fifteen Member States. The fact that Denmark, France, Ireland, Luxembourg, the Netherlands, Portugal, Spain and the United Kingdom – in addition to the new Member States of Poland and the Czech Republic – have held or will still hold a referendum on the Constitutional Treaty indicates the political concerns of these countries [except Ireland for which every ratification of a new Treaty has had to be subjected to a referendum according to an explicit clause to this effect in the Irish Constitution]. The political reasons include for example:[34] making a genuine commitment to the Constitutional

[32] See 'Chirac considering referendums on future EU enlargements', www.euobserver.com/?aid=17408, visited 4 October 2004.

[33] See A. Albi, 'Referendums in Eastern Europe', *EUI Working Papers*, RSC 2002/65.

[34] See C. Closa, 'Ratifying the EU Constitution: referendums and their implications' in US- Europe Analysis Series, November 2004, 10 pages, to be found at www.brookings.edu.

Treaty and renewing the expression of its legitimacy; resolving splits between a national parliament and its electorate; to act as arbiter between national political parties of opposing view; to resolve divisions between anti and pro-integrationist groups within one and the same political party.

In terms of eligibility to make an application for membership, Article 49 EU specifies that '[a]ny European State which respects the principles set out in Article 6(1) may apply to become a member of the Union'. In this regard, 'European' remains undefined – neither the Commission nor Council have fixed the geographical boundaries of the Union.[35] With the countries of the European Economic Area for example or Switzerland as a member of the European Free Trade Area, the "Europeanness" was not questioned. In fact it was these countries that chose not to participate for their own reasons.[36] The Union has never withdrawn its extended hand to these countries and if they were able to overcome their own internal wranglings, there is no reason to prevent them from acceding. So the debate continues as to the geographical, historical and cultural elements that constitute 'European'. The fact that the association agreements signed with the CEECs were called 'Europe Agreements' was certainly recognition by the Union of their 'Europeaness'. Although at the time of the first Europe Agreements, eastwards enlargement was not the Union's expressed intention[37] these association agreements did differ from ordinary or qualified trade agreements such as Partnership and Co-operation Agreements concluded with Russia, Ukraine, Belarus and Moldova.[38]

It seems of little use to explore the meaning of 'European' in abstract terms in the context of today's pre-accession strategy. In concrete terms, included among the actual and potential candidates for accession to the Union, are countries that do not fall wholly within the European continent (for example, Turkey) and countries for which the very prospect of accession to the Union had not been contemplated in the early Nineteen-nineties (for example, Albania[39]).

---

[35] See Commission Communication 'Europe and the Challenge of Enlargement', *Bull. EU*, Suppl. 3/92 at p. 11. See M. Maresceau in 'Association, partnership, pre-accession and accession' in Maresceau, ed., *Enlarging the European Union. Relations between the EU and Central and Eastern Europe*, (London and New York, Longman, 1997) at p. 13.

[36] Where national referendums resulted in a rejection of accession for example (Norway and Switzerland). In the case of Lichtenstein, it was so closely bound up with the Switzerland that it had no choice but to follow Switzerland's lead.

[37] See M. Maresceau and I. Montaguti, 'The relations between the European Union and central and eastern Europe: a legal appraisal', *CML Rev.* (1995) at p. 1328.

[38] See P. C. Müller-Graff, 'Legal Framework for Relations between the European Union and Central and Eastern Europe: General Aspects' in M. Maresceau (ed.), *Enlarging the European Union. Relations between the EU and Central and Eastern Europe*, op. cit. n. 35 at pp. 27-40.

[39] The June 2000 Feira European Council stated that all the SAP countries are 'potential candidates' for EU membership and the Thessaloniki Summit of June 2003 reconfirmed this prospect. Albania had

Turkey's inclusion in the pre-accession strategy is now a fact, while Morocco was expressly excluded on the basis of the geographical criterion alone.[40] Also in concrete terms, changes in the geopolitical situation have been accompanied by an inclusion of the Western Balkans as eligible[41] and they are now even officially recognised as 'potential candidates' for accession to the Union, including Albania.[42] The Commission refers to the Western Balkans as having a 'European vocation',[43] and states clearly that the June 2000 European Council's objective of enlargement to the South East 'is a promise which the EU will honour when each country fulfils the criteria'. This seems logical from a geographical viewpoint alone – once Romania and Bulgaria join the Union, these Balkan countries, will be entirely surrounded by Union Member States.

With the certainty of future enlargements, the debate on the geographical limits of the Union seems of minor relevance and it would seem to have been sidelined to the political goal of enlargement. The geographical criterion would seem superfluous in the context of future (potential) applications from Ukraine and Moldova as both of these countries are situated wholly on the continent of Europe. As concerns Ukraine in particular, it is the political and economic

signed a Trade and Co-operation Agreement with the Union in 1992, *OJ* 1992 L 343/1 but still in 1996 the Union's approach was more to foster a regional approach in its co-operation with and amongst the Balkans countries, namely Bosnia-Herzegovina, Croatia, the Federal Republic of Yugoslavia (prior to the launch of the regional approach the Union had no contractual links with these three latter countries), Albania and Macedonia. See two reports from the Commission to the Council and Parliament, the first on "Prospects for the development of regional co-operation for the countries of the former Yugoslavia and what the Community could do to foster such co-operation", SEC(96) 0252 and the second, on "Common principles for future contractual relations with certain countries in South-Eastern Europe", *Bull. EU* 1/2-1996, point 1.4.108. See also the European Parliament Resolution A4-0127/97 on said reports, *OJ* 1997 C 167/143.

40 Morocco's application was made in 1987.

41 See Maresceau in 'Association, partnership, pre-accession and accession', op. cit. n 35, at pp. 4-5. Indeed, in the later 1980's and early 1990's Yugoslavia was 'usually regarded as an impossible applicant', see Nicoll and Salmon , eds., op. cit. n. 5 at p. 36.

42 Namely, Serbia and Montenegro (including Kosovo), the Former Yugoslav Republic of Macedonia, Bosnia-Herzegovina, and Albania. See sections 2.1 and 2.2 further referring to and citing the Presidency Conclusions of the June 2000 Feira European Council and of the December 2002 Copenhagen European Council, the March 2003 Brussels European Council and the June 2003 Thessaloniki European Council. Conclusion 40 of the Presidency Conclusion to the June 2003 Thessaloniki European Council reads: The European Council, recalling its conclusions in Copenhagen (December 2002) and Brussels (March 2003), reiterated its "determination to fully and effectively support the European perspective of the Western Balkan countries, which will become an integral part of the EU, once they meet the established criteria".

43 See Commission Report, *The Stabilisation and Association process for South East Europe*, COM(2004) 202, 30 March 2004, at section 1.1.

factors that militate against tentative approaches made by Ukraine concerning a possible application.[44] Following the dramatic re-run of the presidential elections in Ukraine in December 2004 the matter of whether Ukraine might join the Union has come to prominence and outright exclusion of Ukraine has been carefully avoided by the European Commissioner in charge of the enlargement dossier.[45]

Article 6(1) EU requires that any aspiring Member State respect the principles upon which the Union 'is founded' and 'which are common to the Member States', namely, 'the principles of liberty, democracy, respect for human rights and fundamental freedoms and the rule of law.' But the reference to Article 6(1) EU must be seen as no more than a codification of an unwritten constitutional principle common to all Member States.[46] The full range of principles and rights that make up the fabric of the Union are included and reach out even to the terminology used in the European Convention on Human Rights and its Protocols, for example, or to the 1990 OSCE Copenhagen Declaration concerning minorities.

Under the Constitutional Treaty in Title IX on Union Membership, Article I-58(1) and (2) establishes "Conditions of eligibility and procedure for accession to the Union", which promises to introduce a few changes both in terms of the relevant conditions but also in terms of the procedure. The European Parliament and the Member States' national parliaments will be "notified" of any application for membership and the European Parliament will only have to reach a majority, as opposed to an absolute majority, of its MEPs voting in plenary in order to give its assent on an application. As concerns conditions, Article I-58(1) will, by reference to Article I-2, add to the list of explicit values (no longer referred to as principles) upon which the Union is founded. However, it will also require that the newcomer be 'committed to promoting [these values] together'. The wording of the draft gives a more inclusive vision of the Union based on common values: 'The Union shall be open to *all* European States which respect the values ... and are committed to promoting them together' [emphasis added]. Moreover, the fact that Article I-58(1) uses precisely the same wording as the very first Article of the Constitutional Treaty emphasises this point. The list of values upon which the Union is founded will then include "respect for human dignity, liberty, democracy, equality, the rule of law and respect for human rights, including the rights of persons belonging to minorities. These values are

---

44 See Joost Lagendijk MEP and Marinus Wiersma MEP, "The ultimate borders of the European Union" on www.euobserver.com, visited on 17 December 2001.

45 See for example the words of Enlargement Commission "We should never say never. But first it is better to offer Ukraine economic and political support", speaking to Radio Free Europe/Radio Liberty on 10 December 2004, on the topic 'EU discusses Romania, Turkey, Ukraine' to be found at http://www.isn.ethz.ch/news/sw/details.cfm?id=10340.

46 See F. Hoffmeister, op. cit. n. 4 at pp. 93-96.

common to the Member States in a society of pluralism, non-discrimination, tolerance, justice, solidarity and equality between men and women prevail".

As already noted, subject to ratification by the Member States, the Constitutional Treaty is to enter into force on 1 November 2006 (Art. IV-447 thereof), in advance of the entry into force of the Accession Treaty with Romania and Bulgaria. A new formula for the structure and format will be required for incorporating future accession treaties within the Constitutional Treaty once its enters into force. However, while there will be procedural changes and national referenda on the Constitutional Treaty and even on future enlargements, the Constitutional Treaty will not change the eligibility test of any country aspiring to membership of the European Union.

3.2 The Copenhagen criteria as applied to actual or potential candidates and the pre-accession strategy

The Copenhagen criteria refer specifically to the countries of Central and Eastern Europe but today the Copenhagen criteria are the catch-all phrase for the pre-accession conditionality that applies to any country aspiring to membership of the Union. While the Copenhagen criteria are set out in four brief sentences, their content is vast and all embracing[47] and vague even.[48] An impression of the enormity of the task of meeting the Copenhagen criteria emerges from the legal, financial and policy instruments of the pre-accession strategy dealt with in the next section.

While the core threads of the Copenhagen criteria can be traced back through the first four enlargements of the European Union, the membership conditionality that has evolved since the end of the Cold War has had to be dynamic in order to cope effectively with the diversity of the incoming Member States among themselves as well as compared to the receiving Member States. The incentive of accession has driven vast and wholesale reforms in countries aspiring to membership while other forms of conditionality incentives or conditions, combined with dialogue and interaction, are more effective in specific circumstances or to bring about specific goals.[49] Moreover, it is always understood that an acceding country adheres to the aims of the Union when it accedes.

The evolution of the current membership conditionality must be understood as an extension and working-out of the pre-accession strategy that has grown up since the June 1993 Copenhagen European Council. The European Commission briefly presents the three Copenhagen sets of membership conditions in

---

47 See Hoffmeister, op. cit. n. 4.

48 See Smith 'The Evolution and Application of EU Membership Conditionality' op. cit. n. 4 at p. 137-138.

49 See Smith, op. cit. n.4 at p. 136.

its Opinion on the applications of the Ten new Member States, which Opinion introduces the fifth Accession Treaty.[50]

The Commission's brief description can be supplemented by the so-called Essen and Madrid conditions. The criteria of good neighbourliness, formally established by the December 1994 Essen European Council, had its effect on the CEEC relations under the Europe Agreements and in the pre-accession strategy.[51] In the context of the Stabilisation and Association Process, regional conditionality takes on a whole new dimension in the EU's regional approach. This regional approach to the conditionality is one of the very first building blocks even for meeting the Copenhagen criteria and opening negotiations for bilateral contractual relations as a basis for developing the association between the EU and each country in turn. The December 1995 Madrid European Council requirement could be implied by reference to the Copenhagen criteria that the applicant have the 'ability to take on the obligations of membership, including adhering to the aims of political, economic and monetary union'. The conclusions stated simply that the applicants should "adjust their administrative structures" which was made in the context of the broader reform and modernisation of public administrations that had to be undertaken in the transition economies as they emerged from the entirely different political, judicial and administrative structures of their Communist pasts.[52]

Compliance with the Copenhagen criteria is not only a precondition to membership. While a candidate's efforts to meet the Copenhagen criteria to the very letter typically continue throughout the accession negotiations up until the very moment of accession[53] certain of the Copenhagen criteria must be complied with before accession negotiations can begin. At the time of its decision to endorse Agenda 2000 and open the first round of accession negotiations with the CEECs in December 1997, the Luxembourg European Council stated categorically that:

'Compliance with the Copenhagen political criteria is a prerequisite for the opening of any accession negotiations. Economic criteria and the ability to fulfil the obligations arising from membership have been and must be assessed in a forward-looking, dynamic way.'[54]

---

[50] At recital 3, op. cit. n. 8 at p. 3.

[51] *Bull. EU* 12/94. See Maresceau 'Pre-accession' in Cremona, op. cit. n. 4 at p. 18. See also Smith 'The Evolution and Application of EU Membership Conditionality' in Cremona, op. cit. n. 4 at pp. 121-130.

[52] *Bull. EU* 12-1995.

[53] And even after accession, transitional arrangements in an accession treaty allow limited temporary and exceptional situations where a new Member State has time to fully comply with certain laws.

[54] See Presidency Conclusion 24 *Bull. EU* 11/97.

3.2.1 Pre-conditions to the opening of accession negotiations

If one looks at the Commission 1997 opinions on the ten CEEC applicants as well as Malta and Cyprus, attaching to the European Commission's Agenda 2000 document,[55] the decisive factors in the Commission's recommendation to open accession negotiations were as follows: a candidate may not open accession negotiations:

- in the absence of having free and fair elections;
- without the Opposition party playing a normal part in the operation of the institutions;
- without having stable institutions to enable public authorities to function properly and democracy to be consolidated and to guarantee the rule of law and human rights.[56]

Establishing conditions and attaching incentives conducts the behaviour of the candidate and is in line with the inclusive nature of the Union's approach to candidate countries – all candidates are treated on an equal footing. At the same time membership conditionality has had to be dynamic in order to differentiate between the states of readiness and particular situations and problems or needs of the candidates. The matrix of political, legal and economic tools outlined in the next section devised to prescribe the pre-accession conditionality reflect this inclusive-yet-differentiating approach to the region. The systematic approach adopted is designed to prevent the impression of any arbitrary discrimination between candidates in preparation for the negotiations or during the negotiations. Any perceived arbitrary discrimination would threaten the effectiveness of the pre-accession conditionality in that it threatens to heighten political jealousies between future Members and destabilise their relations between them and with the Member States.

Bulgaria and Romania continue to fulfil the Copenhagen political criteria[57] but it is also that case that they are still pushing on with reforming the judiciary, the fight against organised crime, anti-corruption efforts and discrimination against the Roma persists. Each has their own specific problems.[58] The Copenhagen political criterion includes the respect for and protection of minorities

---

[55] European Commission Communication *Agenda 2000; For a Stronger and Wider Union* of 15 July 1997.

[56] Slovakia failed to meet this political criterion. See Agenda 2000 ibid. part 2 at p. 45.

[57] Commission Communication *Strategy Paper of the European Commission on progress in the enlargement process*, COM(2004) 657, 6 October 2004 at p. 3.

[58] Bulgaria must address libel and defamation by journalists, the trafficking of human beings and prison conditions, the placement of mentally disabled people or inadequacies in child welfare. Romania must improve policy making, the management of court cases and judicial judgements, and introduce standards for child protection services, as well as trafficking in human beings and prison overcrowding.

but lacks in the respect for and protection of minorities were not considered an impediment to opening accession negotiations[59] with the twelve countries of the fifth and sixth enlargement waves.

3.2.2 The Copenhagen political criteria

3.2.2.1 Turkey and the political criteria

Keeping on the theme of actual candidates for the moment, Turkey was refused accession negotiations alongside the CEECs, Malta and Cyprus because of anomalies in the functioning of public authorities, persistent human rights violations and major shortcomings in the treatment of minorities.[60] The lack of civilian control over the army was a cause for concern. The means of taking relations with Turkey forward were dealt with separately in order to take the relationship beyond the customs union in the light of the decision of the April 1997 Association Council.[61] In 1998 the Commission insisted that Turkey make a constructive contribution to the settlement of all disputes with the various neighbouring countries by peaceful means in accordance with international law – good neighbourly relations is dealt with further.

In the case of Turkey, there is now distinction of Turkey compared to other candidates as concerns political reforms. This is due to the different circumstances of Turkey. The political conditionality imposed on Turkey, since December 2004, has become increasingly specific in terms of the actions that Turkey has to take in its own particular context. In its annual report on Turkey's progress towards accession of 6 October 2004, the Commission dedicated thirty-five pages to its evaluation of the political criteria and Turkey's track record in meeting the political criterion since the 1999 Helsinki summit when Turkey was nominated a candidate but was refused accession negotiations.[62] The Commission recommended that negotiations begin with Turkey. It considered that Turkey sufficiently fulfils the political criteria by means of substantially progressing in its political reform process with far reaching constitutional and legislative changes – although certain significant essential laws have still to

---

[59] Hoffmeister, op. cit. n. 4, refers to the minimum standards of Art. 27 of the International Covenant on Civil and Political Rights (1996) and the fact that Arts. 31 and 32 of the OSCE Copenhagen Declaration of 1990 specifies the sort of rights that a minority should enjoy in a candidate country and since OSCE states that wanted to conclude a Partnership Agreement with the EC had to accept these provisions as binding, that same standard must apply a fortiori for all candidate countries. Hoffmeister also refers to the Council of Europe Framework Convention for the Protection of National Minorities, 1995.

[60] See Agenda 2000, op. cit. n. 55, Part 2., pp 67-68.

[61] See COM(1997) 394, 15 July 1997, *Bull. EC* 6-1993, point I.12.

[62] See *Bull. EU* 12/1999, points I.2. to 1.27.

enter into force.[63] There have been talks of projected dates for entry of 2017 or later.[64]

The Commission did also point out that the proper implementation of the reforms would require 'strong efforts'. The Commission's and the Member States' concern is to ensure that these reforms are sustainable and that they are not reversed during the negotiations or after the eventual accession of Turkey. During the course of the pre-accession process after the negotiations are opened, the Commission has proposed to make use of the relevant tools available to it to recommend the suspension of the negotiations in a case of serious and persistent breach of the principles of liberty, democracy, respect for human rights and fundamental freedoms and the rule of law. The decisive December 2004 European Council spoke of a draft safeguard measure – perhaps even a permanent provision – to this effect concerning the movement of Turkish workers and access to regional policy funds, which would be adopted by qualified majority in the Council.[65] However, there are already certain clauses within the legal instruments of the pre-accession strategy that might also provide an additional means of keeping up the pressure on Turkey during the negotiations. Under Article 4 of Regulation 390/2001[66] the Council has a legal basis for suspending assistance. Said Article 4 reads: 'Where an element that is essential for continuing to grant pre-accession assistance is lacking, in particular when the commitments contained in the EC-Turkey Agreements are not respected and/or progress towards fulfilment of the Copenhagen criteria is insufficient, the Council, acting by a qualified majority on a proposal from the Commission, may take appropriate steps with regard to pre-accession assistance granted to Turkey.'

To pick up on the Commission's insistence on Turkey's contribution to the settlement of all disputes with the various neighbouring countries, this is an example of the good neighbourly relations requirement established first by the 1994 Essen European Council but then reiterated in Helsinki in 1999. Turkey has been keen to emphasise its pursuit of a peaceful foreign policy and in its National Plan for the Adoption of the *Acquis* (see further), it was keen to emphasise in the very first introductory paragraphs the significance of the principle of a peaceful foreign policy, how she will to continue to develop her relations

---

63 Law on Associations, the new Penal Code and the Law on Intermediate Courts of Appeal. Other measures have still to be adopted: Code on Criminal Procedure, legislation establishing the judicial police and the law on execution of punishments and measures. See Commission Press Release, *Commission recommends to start negotiations with Turkey under certain conditions*, Press Release IP/04/1180, 6 October 2004.

64 In an interview with President Jacques Chirac of France for the TF1 journal at 8pm on Wednesday 15 December 2004, the interview conducted by Patrick Poivre d'Arvor, President Chirac emphasised that the work to be undertaken by Turkey would take 'certainly no less than ten or fifteen years'.

65 See *Turkey Could face permanent safeguard clause*, www.EurActiv.com visited on 30 November 2004.

66 *OJ* 2001 L 58/1.

with neighbouring countries on the basis of peace-seeking foreign policy and to undertake initiatives and efforts towards settlement of the bilateral problems through dialogue with Greece.[67] However, while the December 2004 Brussels European Council asked Turkey to sign the Protocol enlarging the Customs union with Turkey to the ten new Member States, whether this implies recognition of Cyprus is highly debatable (and foremost a these of Cyprus).[68]

3.2.2.2 The Western Balkans and Copenhagen political criteria

The sort of pre-pre-accession strategy that has been devised with a view to preparing the accession of the Western Balkan countries has added a new dimension of differentiation again to this membership conditionality and the Union's regional approach to its pre-accession conditionality is exceptional and specific to the region. A sort of 'pre-pre-accession' conditionality emerges. The Union insists that the countries of the Stabilisation and Association Process (the SAp) make 'credible headway' in complying with the general political criterion in order to conclude bi-lateral contractual relations with the Union in the form of a Stabilisation and Association Agreement (SAA).[69] A checklist of the elements that the Commission takes into account when examining the level of compliance of SAp countries with the general political criteria is established by the April 1997 General Affairs European Council.[70]

Democratic principles

- Representative government, accountable executive;
- Government and public authorities to act in a manner consistent with the constitution and the law;
- Separation of powers (government, administration, judiciary);

---

67 See the contribution by Ahmet Sözen in Chap. 12.

68 Thanks to Frank Hoffmeister on this point. After all, it is not clear how Turkey can secure resolution of the Cyprus issue. See *'Turkey accession and Cyprus'* of 18 April 2005 to be found at www.EurActiv.com.

69 Take the example of Croatia. It opened negotiations for an SAA with the EU following the positive opinion of the Commission on its application of 24 May 2000 (See *Report of the Commission on the feasibility of negotiation a Stabilisation and Association Agreement with the Republic of Croatia*, COM(2000) 311 of 24 May 2000). The Commission was satisfied in particular with the parliamentary and Presidential elections. Rather than being a rigid pre-condition to opening negotiations on the SAA, the Commission was moved to its favourable opinion because of 'the encouraging steps undertaken by Croatia to fulfil the EU conditionality' and it was convinced Croatia 'has the capacity ultimately to fulfil the obligations of an SAA' The benchmarks are the same as those identified in the Commission's positive opinion for opening accession negotiations on nine of the candidates of the fifth enlargement in its *Agenda 2000* country opinions. Following signature and conclusion of the SAA Croatia it entered into force 1 February 2005. See *OJ* 2005 L 26/3.

70 Council conclusions of 29 April 1997 on the application of conditionality with a view to developing a coherent EU strategy for its relations with the countries in the region, *Bull. EU* 4-1997, point 1.4.67.

- Free and fair elections at reasonable intervals by secret ballot.

Human rights, rule of law
- Freedom of expression, including independent media;
- Right of assembly and demonstration;
- Right of association;
- Right to privacy, family, home and correspondence;
- Right to property;
- Effective means of redress against administrative decisions;
- Access to courts and right to fair trial;
- Equality before the law and equal protection by the law;
- Freedom from inhuman or degrading treatment and arbitrary arrest.

Respect for and protection of minorities
- Right to establish and maintain their own educational, cultural and religious institutions, organisations or associations;
- Adequate opportunities for these minorities to use their own language before courts and public authorities;
- Adequate protection of refugees and displaced persons returning to areas where they represent an ethnic minority.

Market economy reform
- Macroeconomic institutions and policies necessary to ensure a stable economic environment;
- Comprehensive liberalisation of prices, trade and current payments;
- Setting-up of a transparent and stable legal and regulatory framework;
- De-monopolisation and privatisation of State-owned or socially-owned enterprises;
- Establishment of a competitive and prudently managed banking sector.

The opening of accession negotiations is a matter for subsequent discussion. A lower level of compliance is insisted on for the start of negotiations on an SAA than for the conclusion of an SAA. This approach paves the way for reaching a higher level of compliance with the Copenhagen criteria and thus also prepares the way for opening accession negotiations proper. The conclusion of an SAA in turn becomes an incentive for compliance with the Union's pre-accession conditionality and is the bilateral legal instrument of the pre-accession strategy for each country of the Western Balkans. The conditionality attaching to the conclusion of an SAA gives further legal form to pre-accession conditionality.

As was seen recently in the case of Croatia, accession negotiations are not contemplated if a country cannot, for example, guarantee the rule of law. In Croatia's case, the fact that it was unable to deliver an indicted war criminal to the ICTY was fatal to its anticipated date for beginning actual accession negotiations on 17 March 2005. The EU has since set up a special task force to advise the Member States on Croatia's readiness to enter into accession negotiations.[71]

The political conditionality attaching to good neighbourly relations and good neighbourliness takes on new significance in the regional conditionality applied to the Western Balkans. Good neighbourly relations has been established as a general principle in terms of ten universally recognised principles deriving from the Charter of the United Nations, the Helsinki Final Act and the Paris Charter for a New Europe.[72] Good neighbourliness can be said to encompass good neighbourly relations and add in to the equation appropriate means of developing friendly relations among states, of mutual respect, of trust and confidence, of security and peace. While regional co-operation and good neighbourliness were fostered by the Union during the pre-accession of the CEECs, there was less demand of circumstances to develop regional conditionality in comparison with that seen in the context of the SAp.

Good neighbourly relations/good neighbourliness conditionality must be read alongside the Copenhagen-plus criteria for pre-accession insofar as concerns countries of the Balkans. The general political criteria of the Copenhagen criteria specify concerns for democratic principles, human rights and the rule of law, respect and protection of minorities as well as market economy reforms. The Union sets out these conditions 'broken down into operational, verifiable elements' in the Annex to the 1997 Council conclusions (as detailed above).

Certain additional and generally applicable political conditions are also specified for the region. In addition to the right to return for refugees and displaced persons and the readmission of any of their nationals that are illegally present in the Union, the general conditions in the regional approach require the implementation of the Dayton Peace Agreements and 'proven readiness to enter into good neighbourly and co-operative relations with [...] neighbours'.[73] In addition

---

[71] See www.EurActiv.com visited on 24 March 2005.

[72] Sovereign equality, respect for rights inherent in sovereignty, refraining from the threat of use of force, inviolability of frontiers, territorial integrity of States, peaceful settlement of disputes, non-interference in internal affairs, respect for human rights and fundamental freedoms, including freedom of thought, conscience, religion or belief, equal rights and self-determination of peoples, co-operation among states, fulfilment in good faith of obligations under international law.

[73] 35 *ILM* (1996), 75: 1. Credible offer to and a visible implementation of real opportunities for displaced persons (including so called "internal migrants") and refugees to return to their places of origin, and absence of harassment initiated or tolerated by public authorities; 2. Readmission of nationals of the States concerned who are present illegally in the territory of a Member State of the EU; 3. Compliance of the countries which are signatories of the GFAP with the obligations under the peace agreements, including those related to cooperation with the International Tribunal in bringing war criminals to justice; 4. A credible commitment to engage in democratic reforms and to comply with the generally recognised standards of human and minority rights; 5. Holding of free and fair elections at reasonable

to the foregoing general conditions, each country must meet its own specific conditions and these reflect the Union's concern to improve and secure better relations in the region.[74]

The 'potential candidates' covered by the Stabilisation and Association Process have been working towards compliance with the political and economic membership criteria in all relations with the Union, even in advance of establishing contractual relations. Moreover the political and financial conditioning of the work of the SAp countries is far more detailed and rigorously applied than the pre-accession conditionality that applied to the initial technical and financial assistance provided by the PHARE programme.[75] In the case of the SAp countries these criteria have been rigorously specified in general, regional and country specific terms and then prioritised according to the nature of the relationship in order to benefit from assistance, from autonomous trade preferences and in

---

intervals on the basis of universal and equal suffrage of adult citizens by secret ballot, and full and proper implementation of the results of these elections; 6. Absence of generally discriminatory treatment and harassment of minorities by public authorities; 7. Absence of discriminatory treatment and harassment of independent media; 8. Implementation of first steps of economic reform (privatisation programme, abolition of certain price controls); 9. Proven readiness to enter into good neighbourly and cooperative relations with its neighbours; 10. Compatibility of RS/FRY as well as the Federation/Croatia agreements with the Dayton peace agreements.

74 Ibid. Croatia had to 1. Comply with the obligations under the Basic Agreement on eastern Slavonia and co-operation with Untaes and OSCE; 2. Open the customs border between Croatia and Republika Srpska; 3. provide evidence of credible pressure on the Bosnian Croats to dissolve Herceg-Bosna structures and to co-operate in the establishment and functioning of the Federation, as well as evidence of the implementation of a truly unified City Council in Mostar and of effective functioning of the United Police Force of Mostar (UPFM). Evidence that the Government of Croatia is using its influence in bringing Bosnian Croat war criminals to justice before the International Tribunal. Bosnia and Herzegovina had to 1. Establish functioning institutions as provided for in the constitution, and formulation of a foreign trade and customs policy for Bosnia and Herzegovina; 2. Begin a credible process towards free movement of persons, goods and capital within Bosnia and Herzegovina; 3. Co-operate with the High Representative including on Brcko; 4. Provide evidence of the implementation of a truly unified City Council in Mostar and of effective functioning of the UPFM, and co-operation in the establishment and functioning of the Federation. Dismantling of all structures which the OHR judges contrary to the spirit and letter of the GFAP. Evidence of co-operation with the International Tribunal, notably in bringing Bosnian war criminals to justice before the Tribunal. FRY had to 1. Show credible pressure on the Bosnian Serbs to co-operate in the institution building and the implementation of the provisions of the constitution. Evidence that the government of FRY is using its influence in bringing Bosnian Serb war criminals to justice before the International Tribunal; 2. Prove the existence of a real dialogue with the Kosovo Albanians on the status of the Kosovo within the borders of the FRY.

75 The PHARE instrument was only later reoriented under the pre-accession strategy after the 1993 Copenhagen European Council and later again and in a more accession driven manner following the Commission's 1997 *Agenda 2000 document* (op. cit. n. 55).

advance of the establishment of any bi-lateral contractual relations. Thus, the Association Agreement Macedonia underlines in its preamble the importance of the SAp, 'to be further developed by an EU common strategy for the region, in the establishment and consolidation of a stable European order based on co-operation, of which the European Union is a mainstay, as well as the framework of the Stability Pact.'

3.2.3 The Copenhagen economic, legal and administrative capacity criteria

The Copenhagen economic and legal criteria are more flexible than the political criterion in that accession negotiations may begin provided that a candidate has taken first steps in their direction and can be expected to meet the requirements in advance of their accession. There is a political dimension to these criteria as could be seen from above checklist relating to the countries of the SAp. As Hoffmeister points out, a functioning economy can be measured by several indicators:

- trade and prices must be liberalised;
- significant barriers to market entry (establishment of new firms) and exit (bankruptcy) are absent;
- economic rights and contracts are legally enforceable, and;
- macroeconomic stability exists.[76]

These indicators must be present to prove the capacity to cope with competitive pressures and market forces once a Member. Additionally, this sub-clause of the economic criterion requires that:

- infrastructures and the financial climate together with education and research are sufficiently developed, and;
- the role of the state in the economy should be modest and the trade integration with the Union advanced.[77]

Since the fifth enlargement, the candidates must be willing to enter into EMU and adopt Stage II EMU, which requires central bank independence, co-ordination of economic policies and respecting the Stability and Growth Pact. However, it should be noted also that the need to fulfil the Maastricht convergence criteria and the Stability and Growth Pact objectives are not accession conditions.[78] To proceed to Stage III EMU a Member State needs to meet the convergence criteria in order to introduce the EURO single currency and thus

---

76 See Hoffmeister, op. cit. n. 4.

77 See the Commission's Opinions on all applicants contained in part 3 of Agenda 2000, op. cit. n. 55.

78 See Dziechciarz, 'Candidate countries and economic and monetary union', in *Handbook on European Enlargement*, op. cit. n. 4 , at p. 710.

the new Member States were not obliged to completely fulfil their obligations under the EMU acquis upon accession.[79] But this stage cannot be reached until after accession to the Union.

As for the legal criteria, this relates directly to the acceptance of the rights and obligations, actual and potential, of the Community system and its institutional framework as described by the Commission in its preparations for the last enlargement.[80] Typically an association agreement will include a clause providing for the approximation by the partner with the laws of the Union, as was the case in the Europe Agreements and as is also now the case as concerns the SAAs for example.[81] The examples of the fifth and sixth enlargements provide useful templates and experience in approximation for the countries of the Western Balkans and Turkey. But in the end, the transposition and implementation exercise is their own responsibility and must work in their own situations. For the Balkans countries there is singular advantage in the approximation efforts because their whole association is based upon the premise that they may well become candidates and in that optic, their approximation efforts will be accession driven even in advance of any formal declaration by the Union of their actual candidate status.

Nowadays the word *'acquis'* is also used to denote European Union activities outside the EC Treaty proper and falling under the second and third pillars of the Treaty. The obligation of membership extends to the application of the entirety of the acquis as it stands on the date of accession regardless of whether a receiving Member State does not apply the entire acquis. It will be interesting to see how this criterion would be developed in future enlargements should the Member States of the European Union have made use of the various mechanisms for enhanced co-operation. If a majority of the Member States should decide to push ahead with legislative measures, the question arises as to whether such a flexibility measure would be considered an obligation of membership. Leading on from this question is that of whether the flexibility measures would continue to be legitimate if, after an enlargement, there would no longer be a majority of Member States participating.

As for administrative capacity, the ability to take on the obligations of membership necessarily include the ability to correctly transpose, implement and then enforce the acquis communautaire. In practical terms, institution-building involves budgetary implementation, decentralisation of management of

---

79 See F. Amtenbrink, 'Economic and Monetary Policy in the Framework of EMU' in Ott and Inglis, op. cit. at 4 at pp. 701-702.

80 See Europe and the challenge of enlargement, *Bull.EC*, Supplement 3/92 at 12.

81 On the obligations of the associate to approximate, see in particular A. Lazowski "Approximation of Laws" in Ott and Inglis, op. cit. n. 4. pp. 631-639. Lazowski considers the obligations of the candidates to approximate their legal systems to the acquis communautaire, and explored the scope of the approximation work a well as the technical assistance made available to associated countries to this end.

PHARE and other pre-accession funding and long-term secondment of experts from ministries of the Member States.[82] Intimately linked with the Madrid criterion is the matter of trust between Member States. Trust and reciprocity are not specified. Nicolaides points out that the issue of implementation of the acquis, while important to the enlargement process, also has the potential to obstruct it.[83] The Union's approach has been criticised for its approach to capacity building, in the main because it has consistently recommended the accession countries follow the 'M&M solution' - meaning men and money[84] - which fails to account of the willingness of those responsible for applying and enforcing the acquis. Nicolaides advocates an approach of 'credible commitments' in order to establish the core of integration and to do so by means of an institutional approach. Credible commitments involves the accession countries demonstrating to the Union their commitment to apply the acquis and assign the task of implementation to sufficiently empowered and accountable institutions which will both have considerable decision-making independence and be subject to performance obligations. Trust and reciprocity become a 'radical challenge' to the system of co-operative regulatory relations and trust at the heart of the Common Market.[85]

With the fifth enlargement the acceding countries have had both to prove that they have adequate administrative capacity and to guarantee their continued administrative capacity as Member States. The concerns of the Fifteen on this point led to the insertion of the safeguard clauses into the fifth Accession Treaty, so that in the event of the failure by the incoming Member States to maintain their compliance and enforcement of the acquis, 'appropriate measures' may be taken by the Union against the country concerned.[86]

4 An overview of the pre-accession strategy instruments that carry the current pre-accession conditionality

A direct consequence of the Union's eagerness to diffuse the potential political fall out of such a rigourous and demanding conditionality has been the expansion of the role of the executive institution of the Union, the European Commission, in the pre-accession strategy generally. The Commission's role in managing, monitoring and evaluating compliance of the

---

82 See Agenda 2000, op. cit. n. 55, Vol. 2 at pp. A-3 – A-5.

83 See P. Nicolaides, 'Preparing for Accession to the European union: How to Establish Capacity for Effective and Credible Application of EU rules' in Cremona, op. cit. n. 4 at p. 46.

84 See Nicolaides, ibid. at p. 44.

85 See F. Bignami, 'The Challenge of Co-operative Regulatory Relations' in G.A. Bermann and K. Pistor, op. cit. n.12, pp. 97-140 at 99.

86 See Inglis, 'The Union's Fifth Accession Treaty: new means to make enlargement possible', op. cit. n.16.

candidates' pre-accession progress has been dramatically enhanced compared to previous enlargements commensurate with the number of candidates and the complexity of the preparations. The political organs of the Union, the European Parliament and the Council, have of course been heavily involved but the administration of the instruments of pre-accession conditionality have been held firmly in the grip of the European Commission, taking political heat out of the implementation and progress of the pre-accession strategy and bringing structure to the accession negotiations.

4.1 Candidates with which accession negotiations have been opened

Bulgaria and Romania began accession negotiations in February 2000.[87] Of course, these countries have since signed and ratified their Accession Treaty, so this section explores how the pre-accession strategy applied to them in advance of that date. This section does not cover the provisions of the sixth Accession Treaty concerning Bulgaria and Romania in the months leading up to their accession on 1 January 2007. While accession negotiations have already 'closed' with Bulgaria and Romania, as experience in all previous enlargements shows, in the interim between signature of the Accession Treaty and its entry into force, the pre-accession conditionality that applied prior to the signature of the Accession Treaty outlined below will continue to apply as established during the negotiations. Under their Accession Treaty, Bulgaria and Romania fall subject to a new type of safeguard clause which will enable the Union to delay their entry to the Union in the event that they fail to meet the commitments that they made during the negotiations.

The Accession Partnerships set out the short, medium and long term priorities and objectives of the candidate. Contrary to the impression of joint agreement that the word 'partnership' implies, they are unilateral legal instruments of the European Council and take the form of Council Decisions. The legal basis is contained in a 1998 Council Regulation[88] and they are updated annually upon the advice of the European Commission after it has published its annual report[89] on the progress that each candidate has made towards meeting the accession conditions. The candidate responds by adopting its own National Plan for the

---

87 See L. Maurer 'Negotiations in progress' in Ott and Inglis, op. cit. n. 4, pp. 113-129.

88 Council Regulation 622/98 of 16 March 1998 on assistance to the applicant States in the framework of the pre-accession strategy, and in particular on the establishment of Accession Partnerships, *OJ* 1998 L 85/1.

89 The last Progress Report of the Commission for Romania is dated 6 October 2004, SEC(2004)1200 to be found at www.europa.eu.int/comm/enlargement/report_2004/pdf/rr_ro_2004_en.pdf. The last Progress Report of the Commission for Bulgaria is also dated 6 October 2004, SEC(2004) 1199 to be found at www.europa.eu.int/comm/enlargement/report_2004/pdf/rr_bg_2004_en.pdf.

Adoption of the acquis (NPAA) in order to meet the objectives of the Accession Partnership. It is more a mutually complementing and parallel process than one based on a bilateral contractual association.

Typically, an accession partnership will specify, for example, that the candidate must complete trade liberalisation measures under the Europe Agreement or make progress in approximation efforts under the Europe Agreement. However, the Accession Partnerships are more demanding than the Europe Agreements because the Accession Partnerships are purely accession driven, in particular specifying the work to be done in order to implement the acquis. The Accession Partnerships form the basis for programming all pre-accession assistance from Community funds and from International Financing Institutions. The Accession Partnerships will continue to guide Bulgaria and Romania in their activities until the date of their accession. The general objective of this strategy is to offer a coherent programme for preparing these countries for membership of the European Union, and more particularly:

- to bring together the various forms of aid offered by the European Union within a single framework, the accession partnerships;
- to familiarise applicants with the European Union's procedures and policies by offering them the opportunity to participate in Community programmes.

Three financing instruments are used for both Bulgaria and Romania: PHARE,[90] SAPARD,[91] and ISPA.[92] The support provided by the PHARE programme and the other pre-accession instruments focuses on the priorities established in the accession partnership. These countries, as is shown in the Commission's annual Progress Reports for Bulgaria and Romania, are also being included in the decision-making procedures of the EU institutions (not as full Member States as such but as observers) and in the Community and agencies and programmes.[93]

---

90 Regulation 3609/89 of 18 December 1989, as amended.

91 Pre-accession measures for agriculture and rural development through the pre-accession instrument SAPARD Council Regulation 1268/1999, *OJ* 1999 L 161/87.

92 Support for infrastructure projects in the fields of environment and transport through the structural instrument ISPA Council Regulation 1267/1999, *OJ* 1999 L 161/73.

93 Protocols were adopted to the Europe Agreements to this end and the incorporation of both Bulgaria and Romania within Community programmes and agencies is a central component of the pre-accession strategy.

4.2 Candidates with which accession negotiations have not been opened: Croatia and Turkey

Turkey signed an Association Agreement with the Union in 1964 and although negotiations have not been opened with Turkey (at the earliest in October 2005), it is an official candidate for membership of the Union. The pre-accession strategy that applies to the countries with which accession negotiations have been opened is the model for the pre-accession instruments in the case of Turkey. Thus the Association Agreement Turkey is the bilateral legal basis for the association but it is the Accession Partnership Turkey that programmes the work, funding and assistance given to Turkey and determines the actions under the Association Agreement. There is a separate financing instrument for Turkey.

The operative Accession Partnership for Turkey is that of 2003.[94] Turkey's NPAA is available on the Union's Europa site[95] and Turkey is also being included in the Community programmes and agencies. The most recent Commission report on the progress of Turkey in meeting its membership conditions is that of 6 October 2004.[96] In terms of financial assistance, the Pre-accession Facility programme for Turkey was adopted in December 2001[97] and the procedures for programming and implementing it largely follow those of the Phare programme. Significantly, it may also be used to finance activities that the ISPA and SAPARD programmes finance for Bulgaria and Romania. Between 1995 and 2003, EUR 1,098 million has been committed to Turkey while the programme for 2004 had an allocation of EUR 235.6 million.

It is useful to mention Croatia in this section because it has been formally recognised as a candidate but, like Turkey, negotiations Croatia has not yet opened negotiations for the reasons outlined above. The pre-accession strategy instruments for Croatia are dealt with in the next section because the relevant conditionality is applied within the SAp for the countries of the Western Balkans.

4.3 Potential candidates: the countries of the Western Balkans

The potential candidates under the SAp are referred to as such in the body of the SAA once the country has met the conditionality required in order to negotiate an SAA. This is significant. Neither Bulgaria nor Romania had been recognised as a 'potential candidate' until the 1993 Copenhagen Euro-

94 Council Decision 2003/398/EC, *OJ* 2003 L 154/40.

95 www.europa.eu.int/comm/enlargement/turkey/pdf/npaa_full.pdf.

96 SEC(2004)1201, of 6 October 2004.

97 The Commission reports annually on the use of the funds available under this facility. See for example the Commission's *2004 Report on Turkey's progress towards accession*, SEC(2004) 1201 of 6 October 2004.

pean Council reoriented the Europe Agreements. It was only the CEEC partners that had expressed their accession aspirations.[98] Moreover, the SAAs are framed in such a way as to reflect the pre-accession strategy reorientation of the bilateral association. The Stabilisation and Association Process provides a framework that programmes the content and negotiations of the SAAs in a way that was not done for the Europe Agreements. So far SAAs have only been signed and ratified with the Former Yugoslav Republic of Macedonia and Croatia.[99]

Instead of accession partnerships, the Council adopts 'European partnerships'. They are similar in that they provide a single framework for the programming of EU funding and assistance in line with the conditionality set out by the Union but they cannot be thought of as pre-accession instruments in the same way as the accession partnerships. In particular, they are used to programme the work of the countries of the Western Balkans even in advance of the existence of contractual relations. The equivalent of Regulation 622/98[100] is Regulation 533/2004 establishing the European Partnerships for the SAp countries.[101] However, these two Regulations take a different legal basis in the EC Treaty and the SAp Regulation contains no essential elements clause to allow for the suspension of pre-accession assistance in the event that essential elements are missing as is the case in Regulation 322/98.

The European Partnerships are based on Article 181a(2) EC rather than Article 308 EC, which was the legal basis for Regulation 622/98. Article 181a(2) has been used as opposed to Article 179 EC because a number of the beneficiary countries are considered countries in transition. Article 181a is the only provision which is capable of referring to association agreements and agreements concluded with states which are candidates to the Union. Thus, it is appropriate because the SAp countries either have already signed an association agreement or will do so in the future. The focus of the European Partnerships changes according to the country concerned but the purpose is the same. European Partnerships[102] have been adopted for Albania, Bosnia and Herzegovina, the Former Yugoslav Republic of Macedonia, and with Serbia and Montenegro and Croatia. However, as yet only Croatia has been formally recognised as a candidate for membership, and only FYROM and Croatia have concluded SAAs.

---

98 See M. Maresceau, 'Association, Partnership, Pre-accession and Accession' in M. Maresceau, ed., op. cit. n .35, pp. 3-22 at p. 9.

99 See *OJ* 2004 L 84/13 and *OJ* 2005 26/3 respectively.

100 *OJ* 1998 L 85/1.

101 Council Regulation 533/2004 on the establishment of European partnerships in the framework of the stabilisation and association process, *OJ* 2004 L 86/1.

102 See Communication from the Commission to the Council and the European Parliament *The Western Balkans and European Integration*, COM(2003) 285, 21 May 2003 at p. 3-4.

Some EUR 197 million in Community funding to promote regional co-operation in the Balkans is provided under the CARDs programme.[103] The Commission decided on strategic directions of regional financial assistance for the Western Balkans on 15 December 2004 (Multi-annual Indicative Programme (MIP) 2005-2006). The Union is also planning for the incorporation of these countries in Community programmes and agencies.[104]

5 Conclusions

The Union's conditionality in pre-accession is contained within an inclusive-yet-differentiating approach. This is the inclusive-yet-differentiating approach that the Union followed in the case of the fifth enlargement : all candidates within the region are treated on an equal footing but they may progress faster in the negotiations if they have progressed faster in their preparations. To hold back one country that is ready to accede because of another's failure to make the same progress would run against the grain of the Union's pre-accession conditionality. In the fifth Accession Treaty the Twenty-five Member States underscored the 'continuous, inclusive and irreversible enlargement process' in their Joint Declaration *One Europe*,[105] declaring the accessions of Bulgaria and Romania in 2007 an 'objective' and 'welcoming' the next stage in Turkey's candidature.[106]

As with the fifth Accession Treaty, the sixth Accession Treaty with Bulgaria and Romania will also contain the safeguard clauses to protect the functioning of the Internal Market and in the case of the 'Justice and Home Affairs' *acquis*. It will also contain the general economic safeguard clause that has been contained in every Act of Accession so far. The Commission certainly raised doubts as to the readiness of the incoming countries of the fifth enlargement. In its Opinion of February 2003 on the applications for accession,[107] required under Article 49 EU, unlike previous accession treaties, the Commission '[called] on the acceding States to pursue vigorously the improvements that still [need] to be made in the context of the political and economic criteria for membership and in relation to the adoption, implementation and enforcement of the *acquis*; the Commission will continue to monitor the implementation of the commitments and obliga-

---

[103] Council Regulation 2666/2000 of 5 December 2000, *OJ* 2000 L 306/1.

[104] Communication from the Commission to the Council and Parliament *Preparing for the participation of the Western Balkan countries in Community programmes and agencies*, COM(2003) 748, 3 December 2003.

[105] See Declarations adopted by the Plenipotentiaries, annexed to the Final Act of the Accession Treaty, op. cit. n. 8.

[106] This was confirming the decisions taken by the Informal European Council in Athens on the same day as the signature of the fifth Accession Treaty on 16 April 2003.

[107] Commission Opinion of 19 February 2003, *OJ* 2003 L 236/3.

tions taken on by the acceding States, and will assist them with the available instruments'.

The introduction of entirely new forms of safeguard clause in the fifth Accession Treaty are an added conditionality tool and these clauses are to be included in the new Treaty with Bulgaria and Romania. The fifth Accession Treaty also provides an example of how pre-accession conditionality is applied to new Member States in terms of maintaining and improving administrative capacity. For three years beginning 1 May 2004, the new Member States must continue in their efforts (particularly as regards administrative capacity) and two financial instruments to this end have been introduced to this end: the transition facility (Art 34 Act of Accession) and the Schengen facility (Art. 35 Act of Accession). In the cases of Bulgaria and Romania, an additional safeguard clause provides for the postponement of their accession for up to one year 'if there is a serious risk' that either of these countries is 'manifestly unprepared to meet the requirements of membership by the date of accession', the only qualification to this requirement being that it must be so in 'a number of important areas' (Art. 39 Act of Accession). This was because of the number of commitments, undertaken in the course of the negotiations by Bulgaria and Romania, to make progress and the time outstanding for the time of the envisaged date of accession in January 2007, all of which the Commission has to monitor. While Bulgaria has made 'excellent progress', Romania is in a more doubtful circumstance.[108]

The postponement clause on the one hand, is remarkable: it is an indication of the EU's political commitment to enlargement in spite of doubts remaining. This clause enables the Union to meet its political commitment to its planned date of enlargement. There is no further possibility, beyond the one-year postponement clause, if either Bulgaria or Romania fail to demonstrate their ability to fulfil their commitments made in the negotiations, to introduce separate treaties and acts of accession for these two countries. This too would run counter to the inclusive-yet differentiating approach of the pre-accession strategy that still applies to these two countries as it had done in respect of their counterpart CEEC candidates that acceded on 1 May 2004.

The postponement clause is clearly more of a conditionality stick than other accession treaty safeguard clauses. The two safeguard clauses are dubious because of their potential to discriminate between the incoming Member States compared to the receiving Member States and to undermine the solidarity between Member States. The Commission has made clear that it does not intend to make use of them for these and other reasons.[109] The postponement clause

---

[108] See the words of the enlargement Commissioner, Olli Rehn speaking before Members of the European Parliament on 29 March 2005 and reported on in 'MEPs back Bulgaria and Romania to join the EU' www.EurActiv.com visited on 31 March 2005.

[109] See Inglis 'The Union's Fifth Enlargement: New Means to Make Enlargement Possible' op. cit. n. 16 at p. 957.

by comparison is simple and categorical and applicable in any or all areas of the *acquis communautaire*; it continues the pre-accession conditionality even after the signature of the treaty and it is not negotiated with the incoming Member State, being adopted by unanimity in the Council, acting on a proposal of the Commission. In the case of Romania, serious doubts have been raised as to its ability to meet the commitments that it gave in the negotiations in time for its accession and may well face the use of the postponement clause should it fail to make better progress, particularly as concerns its fight against corruption, public procurement legislation, state aid in its outsized steel sector, and the preparedness of its judiciary. [110]

So has enlargement become a political imperative even over candidates' readiness to accede? Has enlargement become a political imperative over the Union's readiness to enlarge? Is enlargement premature? To find answers to these questions, one must take into account the fact that such safeguard clauses in an accession treaty are tangible evidence of the importance that the Union gives to the candidate's ability to meet the Copenhagen criteria both before and after their accession. Also relevant will be how the new Member States continue to meet their obligations as Member States and whether the safeguard clauses contained in the accession treaties are used against new Member States. If the pre-accession conditions applied to the country have no meaning after it becomes a member, the very purpose of EU enlargement would be negated. The thoroughness of the pre-accession strategy and the limited transitional arrangements in the accession treaty certainly limit the possibility of new Members failing in their obligations as Member State.

The tension and uncertainty arising between the project of enlarging and the Union's own functioning and continued deepening has been apparent in all enlargements. However, for the first time in any enlargement incoming Members do not participate in areas such as the CAP, EMU and Schengen on the date of the accession. This accentuates these tensions and uncertainties. It is in addition to the fact that the Union must further revise its decision-making structures and institutions so that it can enlarge again and is a restraint on future enlargements.

While the European Commission has advised that accession negotiations be opened with Turkey,[111] the perspective of Turkey becoming a Member State will of course accentuate again the uncertainties facing the Union. In its Staff Working Document *Issues Arising From Turkey's Membership Perspective*,[112] the Commission highlights the effects of Turkey's integration into the Union. The issues raised are central to the capacity of the Union to absorb new Members –

[110] See www.EUobserver.com visited on 24 January 2005.

[111] Turkey see Commission Communication *Recommendation of the European Commission on Turkey's progress towards accession*, SEC(2004)656, 6 October 2004.

[112] SEC(2004) 1202, 6 October 2004.

the fourth Copenhagen criteria. It is emphasised that the 'considerations in the present paper do not constitute additional criteria or conditions to be fulfilled'[113] by Turkey but it is also clear that it is too early to reliably predict the problems likely to arise during the negotiations. Not least among the uncertainties is the possibility of earlier accessions of countries in the Western Balkans, further EU policy development, the special arrangements made for Turkey (including transitional arrangements) and the fact that the current financial perspective will change. The ability of the Union to go on deepening integration among the Member States and even to continue with what has already been achieved is brought into question. The negative referendums on the Constitutional Treaty in France and the Netherlands are like red lights to both the deepening and widening ambitions of the Union. How the Union functions, how it sees itself as much as the vision for an enlarging Union – such questions are becoming urgent. In this context, with every new candidate, enlargement become less a question of the ability of a candidate to meet the membership conditions set down by the Union and more one of the fourth Copenhagen criteria: the capacity of the Union to absorb new members, in terms of its functioning and its future vision for the European Union.

[113] Ibid. at p. 1.

CHAPTER II

Minority Protection in the EU – Challenges Ahead

Peter Van Elsuwege

1 Introduction

The collapse of the communist regimes in Central and Eastern Europe, the dissolution of the Soviet Union and, foremost, the violent disintegration of the Federal Republic of Yugoslavia have placed the issue of minority protection on the agenda of the European Union. An important indication of this evolution was a declaration proclaimed during the European Council of Luxembourg in June 1991. On this occasion, the European Community and its Member States described the protection of human rights as a corner stone of European co-operation as well of their relations with third countries. Significantly, the European Council stressed 'the need to protect human rights whether or not the persons concerned belong to minorities'.[1] This first reference to minority rights, as an inclusive part of a general human rights protection policy, has later been reiterated in several other documents. Minority protection even became a specific aspect of the EU's emerging conditionality approach in relations with third countries.[2] In this regard, conditionality – i.e. the linking of benefits to the fulfilment of certain conditions – is essentially used by the EU as a foreign policy instrument to influence the minority protection policies of third states.[3]

In December 1991, for instance, the EC Member States decided to link the recognition of new states in Eastern Europe and in the Soviet Union to 'guarantees for the rights of ethnic and national groups and minorities in accordance with the commitments subscribed to in the framework of the CSCE'.[4] The June 1993 Copenhagen European Council further highlighted the importance of minority rights and established the 'respect for and protection of minorities' as a precondition for accession.[5] Meanwhile, a Council statement of 11 May 1992 had established the rule that all Co-operation and Association Agreements between the EC and its CSCE partners would contain provisions on respect for human rights.[6] Accordingly, the second generation of Europe Agreements[7] all

---

1 Presidency Conclusions Luxembourg European Council, Annex V, Declaration on Human Rights, 6 *Bull. EC*, 1991, I.45.

2 On conditionality, see contribution of K. Inglis in Chapter 10.

3 K.E. Smith, 'The Evolution and Application of EU Membership Conditionality', in M. Cremona, ed., *The Enlargement of the European Union* (Oxford, Oxford University Press 2003) p. 108.

4 Guidelines on the recognition of new States in Eastern Europe and in the Soviet Union, 12 *Bull. EC.*, 1991,1.4.5. [CSCE stands for Conference on Security and Co-operation in Europe]

5 Presidency Conclusions Copenhagen European Council, 6 *Bull. EC*, 1993, 1.13.

6 Council statement on respect for democratic principles, human rights and principles of the market economy, 5 *Bull. EC*, 1992, 1.2.13.

7 The 'second generation' refers to Europe Agreements with the Czech and Slovak Republics, Bulgaria, Romania, Slovenia and the Baltic States. For an analysis of the differences between the 'first' and 'second' generation of Europe Agreements, see: K. Inglis, 'The Europe Agreements compared in the light of their pre-accession reorientation', 37 *CMLRev.* (2000) pp. 1173-1210.

defined democratic principles and respect for human rights – as established by the Helsinki Final Act and in the Charter of Paris for a New Europe – as an essential element of the agreement. Although minority rights are not explicitly mentioned in these so-called 'essential element clauses', the preamble to the agreements referred to 'human rights, including those persons belonging to minorities.' Moreover, the two OSCE documents mentioned (Helsinki Final Act and Charter of Paris) both contain references to minorities and, thus, indirectly confirmed the EU's commitment to minority protection.[8]

The explicit reference to external OSCE documents is not a coincidence but reflects the virtual absence of a well-designed internal EU policy in the field of minority protection. The main reason for this weakly developed *acquis* is related to a lack of normative competence. Due to the principle of enumerated powers, the European Community can only intervene on the basis of a particular article in the EC Treaty. Only after the entry into force of the Amsterdam Treaty, which inscribed a reference to 'ethnic discrimination' in Article 13 EC, the legal basis for EU action has been improved. Nevertheless, the existing non-discrimination provisions seem to be rather limited in comparison to the focus on minority rights in the EU's external relations. In this regard, Bruno De Witte concluded that 'for the European Union, concern for minorities is primarily an export product and not one for domestic consumption.'[9] The logical consequence of this phenomenon is that the EU has been subject to the allegation of applying 'double standards' on minority rights, which necessarily weakens the credibility and legitimacy of the EU's monitoring activities.[10] The aim of this paper is, first, to assess to what extend these allegations are justified and, second, whether the process of EU enlargement and the debate on the future of the European Union have changed the basis for minority protection in the EU.

2 Minority protection and political conditionality in the EU's external relations.

2.1 A growing commitment to human and minority rights

General concern for human rights in the external policies of the EC/EU started at the end of the 1970s, against the background of flagrant violations of human rights in African countries which were party to the Lomé

---

8 F. Van Den Berghe, 'The European Union and the Protection of Minorities: How Real is the Alleged Double Standard?', 22 *YBEL* (2003) p. 166.

9 B. de Witte., 'Politics Versus Law in the EU's Approach to Ethnic Minorities', *EUI Working Papers*, 2000, 4, p. .3.

10 G. Amato, J. Batt, 'Minority Rights and EU Enlargement to the East', *RSC Policy Paper* 98/5, available at: http://www.iue.it/RSCAS/WP-Texts/98_05p. htm.

I Convention. In 1977, the European Parliament, the Council and the Commission issued a joint statement in which they stressed their commitment to the protection of fundamental rights 'in the exercise of their powers and in the pursuance of the aims of the EEC'.[11] In a subsequent report on the negotiations for the new Lomé Convention, the European Parliament argued in favour of the inclusion of clear references to human rights in the new agreement.[12] The EEC, however, was not ready to establish a genuine human rights policy. As a result, the Lomé II Convention did not even include a single reference to human rights.

The quest for binding human rights clauses in the EEC's external agreements returned to the fore on the eve of the negotiations for the Lomé III Convention. Due to legal and political constraints, no human rights clause was included in the body of this agreement.[13] The Convention only contained some vague and ambiguous references to 'human dignity'. Several reports of the European Parliament invited the Commission to draw up proposals aimed at the incorporation of more specific provisions to human rights into agreements with third countries. In the absence of a clear legal basis for a comprehensive external human rights policy, the Commission proposed the inclusion of a human rights clause in the Lomé IV Convention.[14] This provision, contained in Article 5 of the agreement, affirmed the parties' commitment to human rights but did not contain a suspension provision to be applied in the event of serious human rights violations. The agreement, therefore, reflected a first application of the EU's conditionality approach providing only for incentive measures without the possibility of eventual sanctions.

Conditionality is not an unequivocal concept.[15] After the Lomé IV Convention, several other types of human rights clauses, varying in context as well as in enforcement, have been developed.[16] Significantly, the end of the Cold War induced increased attention to minority protection as a specific element of a human rights policy *vis à vis* third countries. This concern for minorities

---

11 Joint Declaration of the European Parliament, the Council and the Commission, *OJ* 1977 C 103/1.

12 Report of the European Parliament 'On the negotiations for a new Lomé Convention', Working Documents 1978-1979, Doc. 478/78.

13 E. Fierro, *The EU's Approach to Human Rights Conditionality in Practice* (The Hague, Martinus Nijhoff, 2003), pp. 55-59.

14 Ibid., pp. 66-70.

15 See: E. Lannon, K. Inglis and T. Haenebalcke, "The Many Faces of EU Conditionality in Pan-Euro-Mediterranean Relations", in M. Maresceau, and E. Lannon, eds., *The EU's Enlargement and Mediterranean Stategies. A Comparative Analysis* (Houndmills, Palgrave 2001), pp. 97-138.

16 See e.g. D.C. Horng, 'The Human Rights Clause in the European Union's External Trade and Development Agreements', 9 *ELJ* (2003), pp. 677-701; K. Pollet, 'Human Rights Clauses in Agreements between the European Union and Central and Eastern European Countries', 7 *RAE-LEA*, (1997), pp. 290-301; V. Millar, 'The Human Rights Clause in the EU's External Relations', House of Commons Research Paper 04/33, available at www.parliament.uk/commons/lib/research/rp2004/rp04-033.pdf.

became obvious during the negotiations of Trade and Co-operation Agreements with former communist countries. In 1989, the negotiations of such an agreement with Bulgaria were suspended because of violations of the rights of the Turkish minority and in 1991 the Community suspended the Co-operation Agreement with Yugoslavia.[17] These events inspired the Council declaration of 11 May 1992, which declared that from then on all Co-operation and Association Agreements between the Community and its CSCE partners would contain clear political conditionality provisions.[18] A first application of this principle was made in the Trade and Co-operation Agreements with the Baltic states, which contained the provision that a serious violation of democratic principles and human rights could lead to the suspension of the agreement. Significantly, the preamble to these agreements referred to 'the importance of guaranteeing the rights of ethnic and national groups and minorities, in accordance with the undertakings made within the context of the CSCE'.[19] In combination with references to the Helsinki Final Act and the Charter of Paris for a New Europe in the body of the agreement, the Community's commitment to minority protection as an inclusive part of the human rights conditionality approach became obvious.[20] The explicit suspension provision, or 'Baltic clause', has since been replaced by a more general non-execution provision, known as the 'Bulgarian clause', which has been included for the first time in the Europe Agreement with Bulgaria[21] and has become a standard formula for the EC's external agreements.[22]

Apart from the inclusion of human rights clauses in bilateral agreements, the EC/EU also launched diplomatic initiatives to encourage the solution of minority problems in Central and Eastern Europe. On the initiative of the French Prime Minister Eduard Balladur, the Community supported a process

---

17 Van Den Berghe, op. cit. n. 8, at. p. 165.

18 Council statement on respect for democratic principles, human rights and principles of the market economy, 5 *Bull. EC*, 1992, 1.2.13.

19 Agreement between the European Economic Community and the Republic of Estonia on Trade and Commercial and Economic Co-operation., *OJ* 1992, L 403/2. An identical provision is included in the TCAs with Latvia, *OJ* 1992, L 403/11 and Lithuania , *OJ* 1992, L 403/20.

20 However, the absence of clear provisions on minority protection in the body of these agreements and the later Europe Agreements may seem surprising, taking into account the presence of large minorities within the borders of the respective countries.

21 *OJ* 1994 L 358.

22 When comparing the two clauses, it is obvious that this so-called 'Bulgarian clause' is drafted more diplomatically. Whereas the old 'Baltic clause' only allowed for an immediate suspension of the agreement in case of a serious breach of the essential provisions, the Bulgarian clause provides for a process of prior consultation in an attempt to reach a solution between the parties. Only in 'cases of special urgency' it is possible to take direct action. For an analysis of the human rights clauses in bilateral agreements, see: Fierro, op. cit. n.13, at pp. 211-244. See also: Communication from the Commission 'on the inclusion of respect for democratic principles and human rights in agreements between the Community and third countries', COM (95) 216 final, Brussels, 23 May 1995.

leading to a Pact on Stability in Europe. The original plan, which entered into the EU's institutional framework as a result of the June 1993 Copenhagen European Council, revealed the two faces of the EU's conditionality approach. On the one hand, the Community promised to 'provide specific assistance to countries taking particular care to solve their problems relating to minorities' whereas, on the other hand, it threatened to 'cut off all co-operation ties with a country flagrantly violating the rights of minorities.'[23] In other words, the EU tried to influence the system of minority protection in these states without direct intervention in the national policies towards minorities. A similar method, aimed at the political stabilisation of the region, characterised the inclusion of minority protection as a pre-condition for accession.

2.2 Minority protection as a condition for accession

2.2.1 An additional criterion for membership?

The inclusion of political criteria for membership has a long tradition in the EC/EU's enlargement history. Already in 1978, the European Council declared that 'respect for and maintenance of representative democracy and human rights in each Member State are essential elements of membership in the European Communities'[24] and in a report to the 1992 Lisbon European Council, the Commission stressed the importance of democratic status and respect of human rights as basic conditions for membership.[25] The 1993 Copenhagen political criteria, which required that a candidate country has achieved 'stability of institutions guaranteeing democracy, the rule of law, human rights and respect for and protection of minorities',[26] thus codified an existing practice. The specific reference to 'respect for and protection of minorities', however, formed an important innovation that can be attributed to the ethnic composition of many Central and Eastern European countries and which has to be seen against the background of the outbreak of ethnic violence in ex-Yugoslavia.

An essential question is whether the protection of minorities forms a separate criterion, or, whether it is covered under a general protection of human rights? Whereas it could be argued that 'respect for human rights' necessarily includes 'respect for minorities' – a point of view reflected in the Presidency Conclusions of the 1992 Lisbon European Council[27] – there is a general

---

[23] T. Ueta, 'The Stability Pact: from the Balladur Initiative to the joint EU Action', in M. Holland, ed., *Common Foreign and Security Policy. The Record and Reforms* (London-Washington, Pinter 1997) p. 93.

[24] Copenhagen European Council (7-8 April 1978), 'Declaration on Democracy', 3 *Bull. EC.*, 1978, 6.

[25] European Commission, 'Europe and the Challenge of Enlargement', 24 June 1992, *Bull. EC*, 1992, Suppl. 3, p. 8.

[26] Emphasis added. Copenhagen European Council (21-22 June 1993). Presidency Conclusions. *Bull. EC*, 1993, 6, 1.13.

[27] Lisbon European Council (26-27 June 1992). Presidency Conclusions. 12 *Bull. EC*. 1992, I.17.

tendency to regard minority rights as a (quasi) autonomous set of rules. In this regard, a distinction can be drawn between 'non-discrimination' on the one hand and 'special minority rights' on the other.[28] Non-discrimination is a general human rights principle which can be applied to people belonging to minority groups. It is an individual human right, aimed at the removal of all obstacles to guarantee the enjoyment of equal rights for these persons. Special minority rights are group specific, including positive measures in order to preserve the identity of the minority group. They can conceptually be divided into individual and collective minority protection rights.[29] A comprehensive minority protection policy is based on a combination of both elements. In other words, minority protection *sensu strictu* encompasses anti-discrimination measures whereas minority protection *sensu latu* also includes positive measures designed to protect and promote the separate identity of minority groups.[30]

The 1993 Copenhagen European Council did not elaborate the membership conditions. This was the task of the European Commission. A first explanation on the actual content of the membership criteria could be found in Agenda 2000 of July 1997.[31] In this comprehensive document on enlargement, the Commission placed 'respect for minorities' under a separate heading.[32] Reference was made to texts adopted by the Council of Europe, in particular the Framework Convention for the Protection of National Minorities and Recommendation 1201 of the Council of Europe's Parliamentary Assembly. These documents adopt a rather broad interpretation of minority protection, including both the recognition of collective rights and the safeguarding of individual rights of persons belonging to minority groups. The Framework Convention, for instance, includes a number of specific minority rights, which cannot easily be reduced to the traditional list of general human rights.[33] Furthermore, the Commission revealed that the formal recognition of minority rights would not be sufficient to pass the conditionality test.[34] Finally, the Commission avoided

28 See: A. Wiener and G. Schwellnus, 'Contested Norms in the Process of EU Enlargement: Non-Discrimination and Minority Rights' in: G. Bermann and K. Pistor, eds., *Law and Governance in an Enlarged European Union* (Oxfort, Hart 2004), p. 458.

29 Ibid., p. 459.

30 K. Henrard, 'The impact of the enlargement process on the development of a minority protection policy within the EU: Another aspect of responsibility/burden sharing?', 9 *MJ* (2002) p. 370.

31 Smith, op. cit. n.3, at. p. 115.

32 Agenda 2000. For a Stronger and Wider Union. COM(97) 2000 final, p. 44.

33 Bruno De Witte refers to 'a qualified right for individual members of a minority to use their language in dealing with courts, public authorities and in the public service media, and a right to receive instruction in that language in the public education system'. De Witte, op. cit. n.9, at. p. 10.

34 The focus on the effective implementation of minority rights was most obvious with regard to the situation in Slovakia. Here, the Commission observed that 'where such rights are in principle recognised, the Hungarian minority faces a number of *problems in exercising its rights.*' Emphasis added. Agenda 2000, op. cit. n.32, at p. 45.

a rigid definition of minorities. In its Opinions on the Estonian and Latvian membership applications, the Commission made clear that it would take into account the situation of all the ethnic and cultural communities residing in these countries, irrespective of the nationality of the people concerned.[35] In this respect, the definition of the concept of minority adopted by Estonia in a declaration to the Council of Europe Framework Convention,[36] was called to be irrelevant. Hence, the Commission clearly preferred a rather broad interpretation of minority protection and defined the integration of minority populations into society as an essential prerequisite for democratic stability.[37] Hence, specific attention has been devoted to the question of minority protection in the framework of the pre-accession process. The Commission Opinions on the applications for membership and the regular reports on the progress towards accession contained a – sometimes rather moderate – chapter on 'minority rights and the protection of minorities'[38] and, on the basis of these reports, the Council adopted Accession Partnerships to lay down a number of priorities related to minority issues.[39] In line with the enhanced pre-accession strategy, launched after the December 1997 Luxembourg European Council, financial assistance to the candidate countries was targeted on the priorities of the Accession Partnerships. The entire strategy was based on the principle of conditionality: the 'carrot' of financial assistance could only be granted if certain conditions were satisfied,

---

35 Commission Opinion on Latvia's Application for Membership of the European Union, COM (97) 2005, pp. 15-16; Commission Opinion on Latvia's Application for Membership of the European Union, COM (97) 2006, p. 13.

36 The Republic of Estonia understands the term 'national minorities', which is not defined in the Framework Convention for the Protection of National Minorities, as follows: are considered as "national minority" those citizens of Estonia who
- reside on the territory of Estonia;
- maintain longstanding, firm and lasting ties with Estonia;
- are distinct from Estonians on the basis of their ethnic, cultural, religious or linguistic characteristics;
- are motivated by a concern to preserve together their cultural traditions, their religion or their language, which constitute the basis of their common identity.
See, List of Declaration made with respect to Treaty no. 157, available at conventions.coe.int/treaty/Commun/ListeDeclarations.asp.

37 *Agenda 2000, For a Stronger and Wider Union*, op. cit. n. 32 at p. 45.

38 Remarkably, the European Commission's 2003 comprehensive monitoring reports on the ten acceding countries did not contain a specific chapter on minority issues, which contributes to the perception that the minority questions are settled as far as the EU is concerned.

39 For instance, the 1999 Accession Partnership with Slovakia called for strengthened implementation of the Roma integration strategy, measures aimed at the fighting against discrimination and implementation of the minority language legislation. Council Decision of 6 December 1999 on the principles, priorities, intermediate objectives and conditions contained in the Accession Partnership with the Slovak Republic, *OJ* 1999 L 335/22.

whereas Regulation 622/98 on the establishment of Accession Partnerships contained the 'stick' of eventual sanctions.[40]

2.2.2 Impact of the EU conditionality approach

The prospect of accession and the mechanism of financial conditionality have brought the EU into a privileged position to monitor and influence the minority situation in the applicant countries. The proclaimed impact of the EU's conditionality policy remains very controversial. Whereas certain observers subscribe to the official stance that the prospect of accession contributed to significant improvements, for instance with regard to the situation of the Russian-speaking minorities in Estonia and Latvia,[41] others have criticised the EU's conditionality approach for being too lenient, stressing the positive developments and ignoring the remaining problems.[42] The main reason for this inefficiency is generally attributed to the lack of clear internal standards, which is in turn related to the absence of clear legal competences to develop a comprehensive minority rights policy at EU level. As a result, the Commission assessments essentially relied on documents of external bodies, such as the OSCE and the Council of Europe. For instance, all Commission reports refer to the Council of Europe Framework Convention on National Minorities. The observation that several EU Member States have not ratified this Convention,[43] in combination with the weakly developed *acquis* in the field of minority protection, necessarily undermines the legitimacy of the Commission's work.

---

40 Council Regulation (EC) No 622/98 of 16 March 1998 on assistance to the applicant States in the framework of the pre-accession strategy, and in particular on the establishment of Accession Partnerships, *OJ* 1998 L 085/1.

41 See e.g. M. A. Jubulis, "The External Dimension of Democratization in Latvia: the Impact of European Institutions," 13 *International Relations* (1996), pp. 59-73; N. M. Gelazis, "The Effects of EU Conditionality on Citizenship Policies and Protection of National Minorities in the Baltic States", in V. Pettai and J. Zielonka, *The Road to the European Union (Vol. 2). Estonia, Latvia and Lithuania* (Manchester, Manchester University Press 2003), pp. 46-74.; J. Dorodnova, 'EU Concerns in Estonia and Latvia: Implications of Enlargement for Russia's Behaviour Towards the Russian-speaking Minorities', *EUI Working Papers* 2000/40, p. 45.

42 J. Hughes and G. Sasse, 'Monitoring the Monitors: EU Enlargement Conditionality and Minority Protection in the CEECs', *JEMIE* (2003), at www.ecmi.de/jemie/download/Focus1-2003_Hughes_Sasse.pdf, pp. 1-36; M. Maresceau, 'Quelques réflexions sur l'origine et l'application de principes fondamentaux dans la stratégie d'adhésion de l'UE', to be published in Liber Amicorum Jean Raux (Rennes, 2004).

43 Of the 'old' Member States, Belgium, Greece, Luxembourg and the Netherlands had not ratified this Convention on 1 May 2004 whereas France had not even signed the document. Of the acceding countries, only Latvia had failed to ratify the Convention. See: http://www.coe.int/T/E/human_rights/minorities/.

A comparative analysis of different progress reports clearly illustrates that the Commission failed to produce clear-cut and consistent recommendations. According to the 2003 monitoring report on Latvia's preparations for EU membership, for instance, Latvia is expected 'to ensure sufficient flexibility regarding transition to bilingual education in minority schools'.[44] This rather general and unclear provision exemplifies the European Commission's reluctance of active engagement in the discussion on Russian-language minority education in Latvia.[45] This observation can be surprising in the light of the attention paid to the use of minority languages in other Progress Reports and Accession Partnerships.[46] It also departs from the unambiguous statement of the 1997 Commission Opinion on Estonia's application for EU Membership that state-funded education in the Russian language 'should be maintained without time limit in the future.'[47] These obvious differences provoked allegations that the EU is using 'double standards' in the field of minority protection, not only between the EU Member States and the applicant countries but also among the applicant countries. At the least, it seems obvious that the Commission's analyses of the minority issues lacked consistency and profundity to produce more tangible results.

The rather limited capacity of the European Commission to monitor the minority situation in the candidate countries more thoroughly does not imply that the EU is completely irrelevant with regard to minority questions. Subsequent Treaty revisions have gradually enhanced the scope for direct and indirect actions in the field of minority protection. Hence, the question arises as to what extent the EU has developed an internal policy in this field as well as whether and how the forthcoming Constitutional Treaty will further modify the legal basis for the development of a more consistent approach to minority protection.

---

44 Emphasis added. European Commission, Comprehensive Monitoring Report on Latvia's Preparations for Membership, at www.europa.eu.int/comm/enlargement/report_2003/pdf/cmr_lv_final.pdf.

45 P. van Elsuwege, 'Russian-speaking Minorities in Estonia and Latvia: Problems of Integration at the Threshold of the European Union', *ECMI Working Paper* 20 (2004), p. 22.

46 For instance, the 1999 Accession Partnership on Slovakia referred to the necessity of protecting 'the use of minority languages in the fields of education, culture and the media...' (*OJ* 1998 C202/85). For a comparative analysis of the Commission reports on Slovakia and the Baltic states, see: Maresceau, op. cit. n. 42.

47 Opinion on Estonia, op. cit. n.35, at p. 15.

3 Minority protection as an internal EU policy

3.1 From Maastricht to Nice: small steps forward

In the pre-Maastricht period, the European integration process was primarily an economic project. For this reason, the original Treaties did not contain any direct or indirect legal references to the issue of minority protection. As a result, the European Economic Community showed little interest in minority issues. Only the European Parliament, 'in conformity with its value-oriented role' and as a promoter of human rights clauses in the Community's external agreements (cf. *supra*), initiated several motions for resolutions dealing with the situation of minorities.[48] These resolutions, which mainly focused on the linguistic dimension of the minority question, are non-binding from a legal point of view and, therefore, failed to produce real, tangible results.[49] Due to the lack of legal competence in the field of minority protection, it was impossible to adopt binding normative acts such as directives or regulations.

The adoption of the Maastricht Treaty significantly changed the legal framework of European integration. The introduction of the three-pillar structure implied that this process received a clear political dimension, which – at least potentially – opened new perspectives for the development of an EU minority protection policy. However, as the ECJ observed in Opinion 2/94, 'no Treaty provision confers on the Community institutions any general power to enact rules on human rights or to conclude international conventions in this field'.[50] Assuming that minority rights form a specific part of general human rights, it is obvious that the absence of a clear legal basis constitutes the main obstacle for a comprehensive minority rights policy. This observation does not imply that the EC Treaty is totally irrelevant with regard to minority issues. For instance, it has been argued that references in Article 128 EC Treaty (Article 151 EC) to 'the flowering of the cultures of the Member States' and respect for their 'national and regional diversity' provide a legitimate basis for specific EU actions aiming at the preservation of minority identities and cultures.[51] In practice, the cultural programmes based on these provisions are not specifically aimed at minority protection.[52] Notwithstanding their potential for the adoption of incentive

---

[48] For an overview, see: G. von Toggenburg, 'A Rough Orientation Through A Delicate Relationship: The European Union's Endeavours for its Minorities', in S. Trifunovska and F. De Varennes, *Minority Rights in Europe: European Minorities and Languages* (The Hague, Asser 2001) pp. 208-213.

[49] The most visible results include the establishment of the European Bureau for Lesser Uses Languages (EBLUL) and the financing of programmes supporting the promotion of lesser used regional or minority languages.

[50] ECJ, Opinion 2/94 *on Accession by the Community to the ECHR* [1996] *ECR* I-1759, para. 27 at I-1787.

[51] G. Amato, J. Batt, 'Minority Rights and EU Enlargement to the East', *RSC Policy Paper* 98/5, available at: www.iue.it/RSCAS/WP-Texts/98_05p. htm.

[52] K. Henrard, 'The impact of the enlargement process on the development of a minority protection policy within the EU: Another aspect of responsibility/burden sharing?', 9 *MJ* (2002) p. 382.

measures and recommendations, it is obvious that they are an insufficient first step in the direction of a minority protection policy. Article 151 EC does not give a clear-cut competence for the adoption of specific minority rights but only allows for additional measures.

The amendments introduced by the Treaty of Amsterdam further improved the scope for Community actions affecting the fate of minorities without establishing a general EU minority protection policy. First, the Treaty of Amsterdam amended the scope of former Article F (Art. 6 EU), by stating unequivocally that the Union is founded on the principles of liberty, democracy, respect for human rights and fundamental freedoms, and the rule of law. The absence of a reference to minority rights in this transposition of the Copenhagen political criteria into primary law raised doubts about the EU's commitment to give minority protection a clear internal dimension.[53] It could, however, be argued that minority rights are included in the expression 'human rights and fundamental freedoms'.[54] In this regard, reference can also be made to Article 6 (2), which defines respect for fundamental rights, as guaranteed by the European Convention for the Protection of Human Rights and Fundamental Freedoms (ECHR) and deriving from the constitutional traditions common to the Member States, as general principles of Community law. Article 14 ECHR is particularly important because this article prohibits discrimination, *inter alia*, on the basis of 'association with a national minority'. This principle of non-discrimination is, therefore, a general principle of Community law. Notwithstanding the legal limits of this interpretation,[55] it is noteworthy that the Treaty of Amsterdam also amended Article 46 EU (ex Art. L). Consequently, the ECJ was granted jurisdiction to guarantee the observance of Article 6 EU. In practical terms, this implies that a member of a national minority who feels discriminated on the basis of his minority status is able to challenge that discrimination against an action of the EU institutions and against actions by the Member States when acting in the context of Community law. It is, however, impossible to invoke Article 6 EU against a Member State that would infringe fundamental rights as such.

---

53 Gabriel von Toggenburg, for instance, argued that 'the fact that the minority issue was kept separate appears to indicate that its inclusion – whereby it would have assumed a clear binding force and an internal dimension – was not desired. Von Toggenburg, op. cit. n.48, at p. 225.

54 F. Hoffmeister, 'Enlargement. Changing Requirements for Membership', in A. Ott and K. Inglis, *Handbook on EU Enlargement. A Commentary on the Enlargement Process* (The Hague, Asser Press 2002) pp. 94-95.

55 First, the application of the non-discrimination principle under Art. 14 ECHR is subject to 'the enjoyment of the rights and freedoms set forth in this Convention'. Second, the general principles of Community law do not incorporate the provisions of the ECHR, as such, in EU law. See: C. Hillion, 'Enlargement of the European Union – The Discrepancy between Membership Obligations and Accession Conditions as Regards the Protection of Minorities', 27 *Fordham International Law Journal* (2004) 2 p. 719.

In other words, the amended Article 6 EU provides only for a limited remedy against the beach of the principle of non-discrimination based on 'association with a national minority'.[56]

Second, the Treaty of Amsterdam established under Article 7 EU a new procedure to suspend the rights of a Member State as a result of a 'serious and persistent' breach of the principles mentioned in Article 6(1) EU by this State. If minority rights are included under the notion 'human rights and fundamental freedoms', political action could thus be possible against a Member State disrespecting the rights of its minority population. The rather extensive procedural requirements, including unanimity in the Council and the assent of the Parliament before the suspension mechanism could be started, reveals the exceptional nature of this procedure. Moreover, attempts to invoke Article 7 EU against Austria after the coming to power of the extreme right Freedom Party in 1999 illustrated the limits of this provision. In order to anticipate against potential breaches of fundamental rights, amendments to Article 7 EU were written into the Nice Treaty. It is now possible to determine that there is a clear risk of a serious breach of principles mentioned in Article 6 (1) and there is a requirement of prior consultation. In essence, however, the procedure of Article 7 EU remains a rather exceptional path to guarantee minority protection in the EU.

Of more significant importance has been the introduction of Article 13 EC, which grants to the Community the power 'to take appropriate action to combat discrimination based on sex, racial or ethnic origin, religion or belief, disability, age or sexual orientation.' Notwithstanding the limits of this Article, such as the requirement of unanimity in the Council and the absence of direct effect or specific references to national minorities, this provision offers a basis for adopting measures which help to protect the rights of minorities. In this regard, the Council adopted a Directive in June 2000 'implementing the principle of equal treatment between persons irrespective of racial or ethnic origin'.[57] Whereas the Directive is not explicitly aimed at minority protection, it contributes to the development of a basic framework for protection against ethnic discrimination in the EU. The Directive established a far-reaching scope of application, covering not only direct and indirect discrimination but also 'harassment'.[58] This prohibition of discrimination applies to a wide range of areas, including employment, vocational training, social protection, education and access to goods and

---

56 Ibid., pp. 721-722.

57 Council Directive 2000/43 EC of 29 June 2000 implementing the principle of equal treatment between persons irrespective of racial or ethnic origin, *OJ* 2000 L 180/22. For a commentary, see: Toggenburg, 'The Race Equality Directive: A New Dimension in the Fight against Ethnic Discrimination in Europe', 2 *European Yearbook of Minority Issues* (2001/2) pp. 231-244.

58 According to Art. 2.3 harassment shall be deemed to be discrimination when *'an unwanted conduct related to racial or ethnic origin takes place with purpose or effect of violating the dignity of a person and of creating an intimidating, hostile, degrading, humiliating or offensive environment.'*

services.[59] Significantly, the Directive also applies to third-country nationals. However, it does not cover difference in treatment based on nationality and is without prejudice to provisions and conditions relating to the entry into and residence of third-country nationals or stateless persons on the territory of Member States. In addition, the Directive does not apply to 'any treatment which arises from the legal status of the third-country nationals and stateless persons'.[60] Notwithstanding these important restrictions, the Directive lays down minimum requirements aimed at combating discrimination against ethnic minorities. Member States are under an obligation to ensure effective defence of individual rights.[61] Victims of discrimination must have the right of redress through an administrative or judicial procedure. Once a plaintiff has established facts on the basis of which it can be presumed that there has been discrimination, the burden of proof shifts to the respondent.[62] Plaintiffs are to be protected against victimisation and in particular against dismissal.[63] Finally, Member States have an obligation to disseminate information on their anti-discrimination legislation in co-operation with non-governmental organisations,[64] to establish a specialised body for the promotion of equal treatment[65] and provide for 'effective, proportionate and dissuasive sanctions' in case of breaches of the anti-discrimination legislation.[66]

The anti-discrimination measures contained in the Race Equality Directive represent an important point of reference for the protection of ethnic minorities living in the territory of the European Union. It, therefore, constitutes a significant step forward in the development of an *acquis communautaire* with minority protection effects. But, due to the absence of minority related provisions in the Treaties, a binding legal framework for minority protection in all Member States is not available. The drafting of the EU Charter of Fundamental Rights (hereafter 'the Charter') did not fundamentally alter this situation. Notwithstanding several proposals urging for the inclusion of a separate minority clause in the Charter, the document is characterised by a relative absence of clear provisions on minority rights.[67] Only in Article 21 of the Charter is 'membership of a national minority' identified as a ground on which discrimination is prohibited. Whereas the explicit reference to national minorities is a major innovation, it

---

59 Art. 3.1 of Directive 2000/43, *OJ* 2000, L 180/24.

60 Art. 3.2 of Directive 2000/43, *OJ* 2000, L 180/24.

61 Art. 7 of Directive 2000/43, *OJ* 2000, L 180/25.

62 Art. 8 of Directive 2000/43, *OJ* 2000, L 180/25.

63 Art. 9 of Directive 2000/43, *OJ* 2000, L 180/25.

64 Art. 10-12 of Directive 2000/43, *OJ* 2000, L 180/25.

65 Art. 13 of Directive 2000/43, *OJ* 2000, L 180/25.

66 Art. 15 of Directive 2000/43, *OJ* 2000, L 180/26.

67 G. Schwellnus, 'Much ado about nothing? Minority Protection and the EU Charter of Fundamental Rights', *Constitutionalism Web-Papers, ConWEB* 5/2001, available at les1.man.ac.uk/conweb.

cannot in itself be considered a breakthrough in the Member States' commitment to minority rights. First, Article 21 of the Charter resembles the wording of Article 14 and Protocol 12 of the European Convention on Human Rights and, thus, reflects the principles laid down in Article 6(2) EC and the ECJ case-law.[68] Second, non-discrimination is only one element of minority protection but is, generally, not in itself regarded as a sufficient basis for an efficient and comprehensive minority protection policy (cf. *supra*).[69]

Finally, the absence of a clear enforcement mechanism has been identified as a major flaw of the Charter of Fundamental Rights. Nonetheless, it has been argued that the inclusion of 'membership of a national minority' as a basis for non-discrimination 'opens up opportunities for norm entrepreneurs to argue more convincingly in favour of a substantial minority standard than ever before, as well as a point of reference for the ECJ to extend its recognition of national minority protection and maybe even establish minority protection as a general principle of Community law.'[70] Under the present situation, the ECJ has never excluded this possibility and already defined the protection of minority rights as 'a legitimate aim' for state behaviour.[71] The Court, thus, seems to accept that minority protection is a ground for the justification of an infringement on the principle of non-discrimination on the basis of nationality.

The remarks of the ECJ, new Treaty provisions on the diversity of cultures and non-discrimination on the basis of ethnic origin in the Treaties of Maastricht and Amsterdam respectively, in combination with the inclusion of a reference to national minorities in the Charter of Fundamental Rights, reveal a piecemeal and indirect progress towards the recognition of the importance of minority protection in the EU's internal legal order. This observation does not imply that the EU has established a common European standard or a clear set of binding commitments to minority rights nor has there been a clear transfer of competences from the Member States to the EU level. It can be argued that the reasoning of Opinion 2/94 is still valid: the EU is not legally competent to adopt a comprehensive minority policy since the Member States have retained this power. This observation highlights a discrepancy between EU pre-accession conditionality required of candidates and the post-accession membership obligations of the same countries.[72] In this regard, the absence of any specific reference to the protection of minority rights in the Treaty on European Union has

68 Ibid., p. 19.

69 See e.g. Open Society Institute, *Monitoring the EU Accession Process: Minority Protection in the EU Accession Process*, (Budapest, OSI 2001) p. 16 and 'The Bolzano Declaration on the Protection of Minorities in the Enlarged European Union, available at www.eurac.edu/Org/Minorities/ELD/Projects/Pecede/Policy_Recommendations.htm.

70 Schwellnus, op. cit. n.67, at p. 20.

71 ECJ, Case C-274/96 *Bickel/Franz v.Italy* [1998] *ECR* I-7637, para.29.

72 See C. Hillion, 'Enlargement of the European Union – The Discrepancy between Membership Obligations and Accession Conditions as Regards the Protection of Minorities', 27 *Fordham International Law Journal* (2004) 2 pp. 715-740.

been heavily criticised. While it can be argued that minority rights are covered by the broad notion of 'human rights and fundamental freedoms' mentioned in Article 6(1) EU (cf. *supra*), the omission of any specific reference to minority rights is surprising in the light of the Copenhagen criteria. Moreover, the Accession Treaty is completely silent on minority issues. In contrast to other parts of the *acquis*, the EU did not provide for safeguard clauses or transitional arrangements to deal with the remaining deficiencies in the new Member States, which means that the EU will no longer be able to apply its political conditionality in respect to these countries. Of course, Article 7 EU contains a procedure to suspend the rights of a Member State in case of 'a serious and persistent breach' of the Union's foundation principles but the stringent procedural requirements reveal that this Article may only be invoked as a last resort. In other words, the Union does not seem to have adequate legal tools to monitor the minority integration efforts of the new Member States after enlargement. The question therefore arises to what extend the new 'Treaty establishing a Constitution for Europe' will affect the existing situation.

3.2 The Treaty establishing a Constitution for Europe – further progress in the field of minority protection?

The quest for a more consistent approach to minority protection has – amongst many other issues – provoked discussion in the European Convention and the subsequent Intergovernmental Conference (IGC).[73] The Hungarian representatives, having in mind the presence of considerable Hungarian minorities in its neighbouring countries, actively promoted the inclusion of a reference to minority rights in Article I-2 of the Constitutional Treaty.[74] Mr. Peter Balázs, a Hungarian member of the European Convention and later the first Hungarian Commissioner, referred to the necessary addition of 'the missing element of the Copenhagen criteria, which makes an important part of the *acquis*.'[75] Notwithstanding the fact that several other Convention members supported the proposal to replace the expression 'respect for human rights' into 'respect for and protection of human rights and those of minorities',[76] this

---

[73] The most far-reaching and provocative proposal came from the Hungarian Convention Member Jozsef Szajer, who suggested the creation of a 'Committee of National and Ethnic Minorities' (CONEM) in the institutional structure of the EU. See: 'Unity in diversity – Proposal for the representation of national and ethnic minorities in the institutional system of the European Union, Committee of National and Ethnic Minorities (CONEM)' CONV580/03 26 February 2003.

[74] For an overview of the proposals and initiatives of the Hungarian government regarding the rights of national minorities at EU level, see: http://www.hhfr.org/htmh/background/prop_eu.htm.

[75] Suggestion for amendment of Article 2 by Mr. Peter Balázs, available at european-convention.eu.int/Docs/Treaty/pdf/2/Art%202%20Balázs.pdf.

amendment was not accepted. Accordingly, the 'Draft Treaty establishing a Constitution for Europe' did not contain any reference to the protection of minorities in Article I-2.[77] The issue returned on the table of the IGC.[78] On the initiative of the Hungarian delegation, the Italian Presidency submitted an amended version of Article I-2 of the Draft Treaty, including a reference to 'the rights of persons belonging to minority groups'.[79] Notwithstanding the opposition of new Member States such as Latvia and the Slovak Republic, not unsurprisingly countries with a significant minority population, this amendment has been included in the final version of the Treaty establishing a Constitution for Europe as agreed during the Brussels summit of 18 June 2004 and officially signed by the 25 Member States on 29 October. Article I-2, which replaces Article 6(1) EC, now proclaims that:

'[t]he Union is founded on the values of respect for human dignity, freedom, democracy, equality, the rule of law and respect for human rights, including the rights of persons belonging to minorities. These values are common to the Member States in a society in which pluralism, non-discrimination, tolerance, justice, solidarity and equality between women and men prevail.'

In contrast to Article 6(1) EU, this new provision introduces 'human dignity' and 'equality' in the list of Union values whereas the expression 'fundamental freedoms' has been removed. In addition, a completely new sentence has been introduced. It is arguable that the concepts 'pluralism', 'tolerance' and 'non-discrimination' indirectly relate to the objective of minority protection.[80] Last but not least, Article I-2 explicitly refers to minority rights as an inclusive part of human rights. In other words, this provision merely codifies the broad interpretation of Article 6(1) EU, according to which the notion 'human rights and fundamental freedoms' already included minority rights. From this perspective, the supplemented expression 'including the rights of persons belonging to minorities' does not represent a revolutionary change. It is, however, an

---

76 Suggestion for amendment of Article I-2 by Mr Péter Balázs, Mr József Szájer, Mr Pál Vastagh, Mr. Hannes Farnleitner, Mr Alain Lamassoure, Mr Jens-Peter Bonde, Mr Kimo Kiljunen Mr Evripidis S. Styliandis, Mr Péter Gottfried, Mr István Szent-Iványi, Mr António Nazaré Pereira, Mr Jürgen Meyer, available at european-convention.eu.int/Docs/Treaty/pdf/2/2_Art%20I%202%20Balázs%20EN.pdf.

77 Draft Treaty establishing a Constitution for Europe, *OJ* 2003 C 169/8.

78 Already at the June 2003 European Council, the Hungarian Prime Minister Peter Medgyessy called for the inclusion of a reference to 'the national and ethnic minorities' collective rights'. See n.74.

79 IGC 2003 – Non-institutional issues, Brussels, CIG 37/03 PRESID 3 24 Oct. 2003, p. 3. This compromise text changed two important aspects of the Hungarian proposal. First, it restricted the reference on minorities to individual rather than collective rights. Second, it omitted the words 'national and ethnic' and only retained the qualification of 'minority rights' in general.

80 Hillion, op. cit. n. 72 at p. 733.

important signal of the EU's commitment to minority rights which provides more consistency between the Copenhagen criteria for accession and the EU's foundational principles. For instance, it will now be very clear that the EU could sanction a state for infringements of minority rights on the basis of Article I-59 of the Constitutional Treaty, which basically replaces Article 7 EU.[81]

Whereas respect to minority rights is now defined as a foundational value of the EU, it is not expressly mentioned as a Union objective as laid down in Article I-3. It was, not unsurprisingly, the Hungarian Convention member Pál Vastagh who claimed for the insertion of a clear reference to 'respect for and protection of minorities' in this Article.[82] Other Convention members proposed the introduction of the more general term 'human rights' or argued for the introduction of a reference to non-discrimination on the basis of racial or ethnic origin.[83] Eventually, the Constitutional Treaty only refers to the objective to 'combat social exclusion and discrimination' in general and specifically mentions the protection of the rights of the child. In addition, Article I-3 also proclaims that the Union 'shall respect its rich cultural and linguistic diversity' and thus contains only indirect links with the issue of minority protection.

Apart from Article I-2, the only other direct reference to minority rights is included in Article II-81, which incorporates Article 21 of the Charter of Fundamental Rights and thus defines 'membership of a national minority' as a ground for discrimination. Article II-81 also identifies 'language' as one of the grounds on which discrimination is prohibited. Remarkably, no reference to minorities or language can be found in Articles III-118 and III-124, which retain the more limited grounds for discrimination mentioned in Article 13 EC (sex, racial or ethnic origin, religion or belief, disability, age or sexual orientation). In addition, the unanimity requirement for the adoption of measures combating discrimination shall also apply after the entry into force of the Constitution.[84]

Given the limits to the scope of application of Article II-81, the Constitutional Treaty does not seem to extend the Union's competences with regard to the adoption of measures against discrimination of minorities. First, Article II-111 proclaims that the Charter of Fundamental Rights 'does not extend the field of application of Union law beyond the powers of the Union or establish any new power or task for the Union or modify powers and tasks defined in the other Parts of the Constitution.' In combination with the principle of conferral of powers, which is explicitly included in Article III-124, it is therefore clear

81 Arguably, this is already possible under the current provisions. The Constitutional Treaty will only contribute to the objective of more transparency and clearness.

82 Suggestion for amendment of Art. 3, paragraph 3 by Mr. Pál Vastagh (HUN), available at: http://european-convention.eu.int/Docs/Treaty/pdf/3/Art3Vastagh.pdf.

83 See: european-convention.eu.int/amendments.asp.

84 Without harmonising national laws and regulations, incentive measures can be taken on the basis of qualified majority voting (Art. III-124 (2) Constitutional Treaty).

that the Union will not be more competent to undertake actions in the field of non-discrimination as under Article 13 EC. Second, the Charter's binding force is based on so-called explanations that were added to each Charter article and explain their background and limitations. According to this explanation, Article II-81 'does not create any power to enact anti-discrimination laws in these areas of Member State or private action, nor does it lay down a sweeping ban of discrimination in such wide-ranging areas. Instead, it only addresses discriminations by the institutions and bodies of the Union themselves, when exercising powers conferred under other articles of Parts I and III of the Constitution, and by Member States only when they are implementing Union law...therefore [Article II-82] does not alter the extent of powers granted under Article III-124 nor the interpretation given to that Article.'[85] From this perspective, the impact of the newly incorporated Article II-81 will be rather limited and is clearly not sufficient to speak about a significant evolution in the EU's minority protection framework.

4 Conclusion

The above analysis of the 'Treaty establishing a Constitution for Europe' reveals that in the field of minority protection no revolutionary changes have taken place. The inclusion of a reference to minority rights in Article I-2 is to be welcomed because it provides more consistency between the Copenhagen criteria and the EU's foundational principles. In itself, however, this is insufficient to develop a comprehensive EU minority rights policy. This would require the transfer of powers and the attribution of legal competences to adopt measures pertaining to the protection of minorities. The absence of any references to minorities in the EU's objectives (Art. I-3) and the non-discrimination provisions of Articles III-118 and III-124 reveal that the EU institutions will not be legally competent to adopt measures exclusively aimed at the protection of minority rights. This, of course, does not exclude that other Treaty provisions might have important minority protection effects, as is already clearly illustrated by Article 13 EC (Art. III-124 of the Constitutional Treaty) and the adoption of the Race Equality Directive. The inclusion of the Charter of Fundamental Rights in a specific part of the Constitution further improves the visibility of the EU's commitment to human rights and contains a specific non-discrimination provision for people belonging to minority groups. However, the limited applicability of the Charter, which prevents any extension of the Union's competence, excludes the possibility to enact specific measures to combat discrimination based on membership of a national minority. A similar horizontal provision is

85 Declaration concerning the explanations relating to the Charter of Fundamental Rights, CIG 84/04, ADD 2, p. 37.

included in the protocol related to the accession of the Union to the European Convention on the Protection of Human Rights (ECHR), as provided for in Article I-9(2). Hence, it can be argued that the Constitutional Treaty does not imply a revolutionary shift with regard to the Union's competences in the field of minority protection. On the other hand, the explicit recognition of minority rights in Article I-2, the incorporation of the Charter of Fundamental Rights and the prospective accession to the ECHR confirm the growing recognition of minority issues in the EU's internal sphere. As has been argued, this evolution is not a natural process reflecting the common constitutional traditions of the Member States but is 'rather constructed *'post hoc'* after the issue entered the Union's agenda in the context of Eastern enlargement.'[86]

The slowly progressing internalisation of minority protection in the system of the EU does not provide a comprehensive binding legal framework for minority protection. It is merely limited to a non-discrimination provision and there seems to be hardly any political will among the Member States to go much further.[87] It is therefore unlikely that minority issues will gain a very prominent place in the EU's internal policies. As a result, the long-standing discrepancy between the rather limited provisions on minority protection in the EU's internal framework and the rather extensive demands in the field of external relations might continue to exist. On the other hand, it may be difficult to ignore the existence of minority problems in several Member States. The most probable scenario might therefore be that, in the absence of clear common standards, minority questions will be dealt with in a pragmatic way.[88] In this regard, close co-operation with the Council of Europe might be an option, particularly after the EU's accession to the ECHR. In addition, internal monitoring procedures could be enhanced, for instance by including a separate subheading on minority rights into the European Parliament's regular reports on human rights in the Member States.[89] Improved internal monitoring and increased attention to minority issues in the Member States are a prerequisite to strengthen the legitimacy of the EU's focus on minority rights in its external relations policy in general and enlargement policy in particular. This exercise is highly relevant in the light of the prospective EU accession of countries with a history of ethnic tensions such as Turkey and the countries of the Western Balkans that are included in the Stabilisation and Association Process. Furthermore, minority protection can be expected to become an essential element of the EU's emerging Neighbourhood Policy.[90] Consequently, the combined challenge of minority

---

86 Schwellnus, op. cit. n.67, at. p. 2.

87 Van Den Berge, op. cit. n.8, at p. 185.

88 Ibid., p. 194.

89 The Bolzano Declaration on the Protection of Minorities in the Enlarged European Union, available at www.eurac.edu/Org/Minorities/ELD/Projects/Pecede/Policy_Recommendations.htm.

issues inside and outside the enlarged EU will necessarily enhance the need for a more consistent EU policy on minority protection, notwithstanding the legal limits characterising the European integration process.

90 The Commission *Strategy Paper on the European Neighbourhood Policy* proclaimed that '[t]he privileged relationship with neighbours will build on mutual commitment to common values principally within the fields of the rule of law, good governance, the respect *for human rights, including minority rights*, the promotion of good neighbourly relations and the principles of market economy and sustainable development.' [emphasis added] COM (2004) 373 final, Brussels, 12 May 2004, p. 3.

CHAPTER 12

Turkey's Democratisation in Light of its EU Candidate Status

EU Enlargement at a Crossroads

Ahmet Sözen

1 Introduction

Turkey's relations with the European Union (EU) date back to 1959 when Turkey applied for associate membership to the then European Economic Community (EEC). It took 30 years until Turkey was officially declared a candidate country for final membership at the EU Helsinki Summit in December 1999.

Turkey – EU relations has an important impact not only on Turkey and the EU but also, on a far larger scale. The future nature of this relationship will help to shape the nature of the relations between the EU and its neighboring Muslim countries. Both Turkey and the EU are now at a crossroads where the course they plot will have important implications and impact on world politics in the post-9/11 era.

1. The EU must decide whether it is a Christian club and that the clash of civilizations is inevitable, or that it is based on certain norms (with respect for human rights, democracy and superiority of the rule of law as the starting point) which, if fulfilled by a European Country, determine its membership – thus, it can be an example of consensus of different civilizations. The intention of the EU to further the accession negotiations with Turkey (to be finalized by accession based on the decision of the EU Council on 17 December 2004 to start the accession negotiations with Turkey on 3 October 2005, as recommended by the EU Commission on 6 October 2004[1]) will probably be the most crucial milestone in the Turkey – EU relations.

2. Turkey must decide whether it wants to be a fully democratic state or remain a semi-democracy with the possibility to become a more Middle Eastern and more authoritarian state – thus, failing to be a model[2] of a democratic country with a Muslim population for the Central Asian and Middle Eastern states. It seems that the steady reforms in Turkey since the early 2000s show that Turkey has already crossed the critical threshold and that a clear promise of accession by the EU will help Turkey to maintain its progress and momentum.

It is the observation of the author that the democratisation reforms through purely internal dynamics in Turkey have progressed very slowly. It was only recently, in the late 1990s, that the democratisation attempts increased in Turkey mainly due to Turkey's aspirations towards EU membership – an external dynamic. In other words, the EU's conditionality tool is working in the

---

1 See Commission Communication to the Council and the European Parliament, Recommendation of the European Commission on Turkey's progress towards accession, COM(2004) 656, 6 October 2004.

2 Turkey was seen as the only secular democratic country with a predominantly Muslim population. In that regard, after the end of the Cold War, lots of articles were written suggesting that Turkey could be a model for the newly independent states of Central Asia and the Middle Eastern states which have predominantly Muslim populations.

background of Turkey's internal democratisation reforms. Hence, the EU plays a very important role in Turkey's democratisation.

This chapter analyzes democratisation in Turkey through the EU criteria, which in turn holds important implications for world politics – at least directly involving Europe, the Middle East, Central Asia and the United States (US).

In order to understand the conditionality impact of the EU on democratisation in Turkey, one has to look at the Turkey – EEC (later the European Community (EC), and then European Union (EU) relations in their historical context and in more detail.

2 Turkey – EEC relations

2.1 The Association Agreement

Greece initiated a contractual association with the EEC in June 1959, Turkey also did so, in July 1959. While Greece signed an Association agreement in July 1961, Turkey signed the Ankara Agreement with the EEC in September 1963. The Association Agreement came into force on 1 December 1964. The Agreement aimed at establishing a customs union between the Community and Turkey and made reference to Turkish membership of the Community.[3] The Agreement has three stages:

1. *Preliminary Stage*: During this stage, which was to be from 1964 to 1973, the EEC would give some direct financial aid to Turkey and establish preferential trade conditions with Turkey.
2. *Transition Stage*: This stage was to cover twenty-two years where the Community and Turkey would eliminate all tariffs and trade barriers in order to establish a customs union between Turkey and the Community.
3. *Final Stage*: Should the necessary progress be observed, the Community would examine the possibility of Turkey's accession to the Community as a full member.

The main driving force behind the Turkish application for the Associate Membership was mostly political rather than economic.

International recognition as a member of the Western community of nations had been an objective of Turkish leaders since the days of the Tanzimat (1839),

[3] See Art. 28 of the Agreement establishing an Association between the European Economic Community and Turkey ('the Ankara Agreement'); 'As soon as the operation of this Agreement has advanced far enough to justify envisaging full acceptance by Turkey of the obligations arising out of the Treaty establishing the Community, the Contracting Parties shall examine the possibility of the accession of Turkey to the Community.' First published *JO* 1964 217 (French language version), *OJ* 1973 C 113/2 (English language version).

and was seen as a logical extension of Turkey's membership of NATO and other Western organizations. The need to avoid being outflanked by Greece was also an important motive, and almost certainly hastened the Turkish decision. The economic objective of gaining easier market access to the EEC, which already accounted for about 35 per cent of Turkey's exports, added to the incentive.

However, though ironic, due to mainly political reasons Turkey signed an Agreement the content of which was purely economic. The first stage of the Agreement proceeded rather smoothly where the EEC extended preferential trading conditions to Turkey together with direct financial aid. However, the second stage experienced its ups and downs, mainly due to the conditions in Turkey, and partly due to EEC policies.

Neither Turkey nor the EU had been enthusiastic in implementing the conditions of the Agreement. While Turkey was adamant to eliminate tariffs and other trade barriers in the 1970s, the EC, especially in the 1980s, started to put forward political conditions on Turkey. The military coup of 1980 in Turkey resulted in a freeze in the Turkey – EC relations for at least three years until the first elections took place in Turkey in 1983. In addition, the economic (oil) crisis in 1973 and the 1987 Single European Act were the major concerns of the Community and made the Community very cautious in eliminating tariffs and other trade barriers with Turkey, especially in textile and agricultural products.

In 1987 Turkey shocked the EC by submitting its official application for full membership to the EC. This was a premature application. However, the Community did not want to alienate Turkey. Hence, the Commission prepared its official Opinion and issued it in December 1989.[4] 'In essence, the Commission's Opinion was a polite rebuff of the Turkish application.'[5]

The Opinion is divided into four parts. The first part is about the Community's difficulties in the integration process due to the Single European Act. The following two parts were about Turkey's problematic economic and political contexts that pose difficulties for the EC to open negotiations for accession of Turkey. The last part of the report suggests areas of focus in the relations between Turkey and the Community.

The Commission's Opinion on Turkey's membership of the EC was clear that Turkey was not ready economically for accession to the EC, although Turkey had many sectors ready to compete with the European products, such as textiles and agricultural products.

---

4 See Commission Opinion, SEC(89) 2290, 22 December 1989.

5 Hale, op. cit. n. 4, at p. 178.

In the political sphere, the Commission claims that Turkey had two major political problems: human rights with respect to the ethnic minorities (the report intended to address the matter of the Kurds) and the Cyprus problem.

According to the Turkish Constitution, Turkey is a unitary state and the only minorities in Turkey are the non-Muslims, such as the Jews, Greeks, Armenians and so forth. Kurds are Muslims and according to the Constitution they are Turkish citizens with equal rights just like every other Turkish citizen. In order to recognize the Kurds as a separate political community, Turkey would have to change its Constitution. Some of the Kurds, with the pressure of the PKK,[6] in the southeast of Turkey want to establish a Kurdish state (or at least a federal or autonomous Kurdish state). Turkey's war against the PKK, until the late Nineteen-nineties, delayed the reforms regarding the cultural rights of the Kurdish population. However, very important critical reforms were made in the recent past, which included education and broadcasting in Kurdish.

As for the Cyprus Problem, Turkey claimed that it was the two communities in the island who should come together to decide their own destiny. In fact, the leaders of the Turkish Cypriot and Greek Cypriot communities agreed, in 1977 and 1979, in High Level Summits in order to reach a solution based on the establishment of a bi-zonal, bi-communal federation, comprising two equal partners, similar to the Republic of Cyprus[8] that had been established in 1960. Turkey's aim in the Cyprus issue has been to find a solution that will guarantee the safety and survival of the two communities, with which not only the communities in Cyprus but also Turkey and Greece would be satisfied since the two motherland countries have strong interests in the region. The current trend is in that direction, although there is disagreement on a few, but fundamental, issues such as security and property.

2.2 Customs union: catching the train?

After the Commission's Opinion on the Turkish application, such external factors as the end of the Cold War and the breakdown of the socialist regimes in the Soviet Union and Central and Eastern Europe influenced the Community's vision for the future.

First, the Central and Eastern European states were gaining their independence, ridding themselves of socialist regimes and endorsing democratic parliamentary regimes and building market economies similar to the Western European states. They saw their future within the bigger system of European

---

6 An internationally accepted terrorist Kurdish movement (supposedly Marxist) having as its aim is to establish a Kurdish state on the territory of southeastern Turkey and northern Iraq; however it represents only a minority of the Kurdish people.

7 After the British left Cyprus in 1960, the two communities established a state comprising of two politically equal partners, which worked only until 1963.

states – hence, within the Community. Secondly, the Community was moving towards a political union in parallel with economic union. The Maastricht treaty was transforming the Community into a political union where, in 1992, the Community changed its name from 'EC' to 'EU.' Thirdly, such values as respect for human rights, democracy, rule of law and protection of minorities were finding more and more supporters and becoming more important in shaping the foreign policies of the European states.

It was against this background that Community membership became more and more important in Turkey. According to the Ankara Agreement, Turkey should have established a customs union with the Community by 1995.

1. As mentioned before, the requirements of the Ankara Agreement, especially of the second phase (transition phase to customs union) were not dealt with enthusiastically neither by Turkey nor by the Community. In that regard, during the first years of the 1990s, Turkey was faced with a Community in the process of deepening its integration and becoming more inward looking. In addition, Turkey felt the time restraint for establishing the customs union and became aware that it had not done its homework properly with regard to preparing the Turkish economy for the customs union. On top of everything, at this time Turkey was faced with a Greek veto. Greece announced that, due to Turkey's poor human rights record, it would veto the customs union between Turkey and the Community. Thus, Greece put forward certain conditions to be satisfied by Turkey: Turkey should take the conflict over the Aegean with Greece (such as the continental shelf and territorial waters) to the International Court of Justice (ICJ).

2. No financial aid through the EU's Financial Protocol should be given to Turkey until its human rights record was 'clean'.

3. Turkey should lift its opposition to the EU's opening of the accession negotiations with the (Greek) Republic of Cyprus.

In short, Turkey was faced with a dilemma: catching the European train with a seat in the third class wagon or missing the European train either indefinitely or for a very long time. In other words, Turkey should either sign up to a customs union with the acceptance of the above mentioned conditions or completely give up the idea of becoming a full member of the EU. There was of course a third option for Turkey, which was to insist on more negotiations on the above-mentioned conditions. However, Prime Minister Tansu Çiller insisted on customs union with the EU at all costs. In that regard, Turkey, under Tansu Çiller's premiership, chose the first option. With a badly negotiated deal, a customs union with the EU came into effect on 1 January 1996. Turkey made a few important concessions, which later became a heavy burden for Turkey in its relations with the EU:

1. Turkey remained silent, up to the start of the accession negotiations of the EU with (Greek) Republic of Cyprus, on the Cyprus accession.

2. Turkey accepted a customs union without receiving financial aid, which had been Turkey's right deriving from the Association Agreement.
3. Turkey agreed to take the conflicting issues of the Aegean with Greece to the ICJ.
4. Turkey accepted the EU's demand that there would be no free movement of Turkish workers in the EU which was envisaged in the Additional Protocol.[8]

Although the customs union was a badly negotiated deal for Turkey, it nonetheless provided closer economic ties between Turkey and the EU. For Prime Minister Çiller and many Turks, the customs union symbolized Turkey's future full membership of the EU. For the EU, the customs union did not automatically mean guaranteed future membership for Turkey. As a matter of fact, the EU was very keen on proceeding with the customs union through an association relationship and the EU had never provided a perspective of full membership to Turkey during the customs union negotiations.

2.3 The Luxembourg Summit: worsening of relations

After the signing of the customs union, relations between the EU and Turkey started to go sour due to certain key developments in Turkey and froze at their peak with 1997 Luxembourg Summit.

In December 1995 and January 1996 a serious crisis took place between Turkey and Greece regarding the Kardak/Imia islets. Both sides claimed sovereignty over the islets, which brought the two sides to the brink of an armed clash. US diplomatic intervention that cooled the situation down and have the EU sided with the Greeks, pointing to the ICJ for the solution of problems in the Aegean. Once again, Greece had successfully carried its problems with Turkey onto the EU platform and strained the relations between Turkey and the EU.

The Islamist Refah Party won the parliamentary elections on 24 December 1995 and received 21% of the votes. However, it had to wait two short-lived coalition governments under the premiership of Çiller and Yılmaz, respectively, before it formed its coalition government on 8 July 1996 with Çiller's DYP. This coalition government shocked the European capitals because Çiller threatened the EU, during the customs union negotiations, that if the customs union had not been established between the EU and Turkey that would have strengthened the Islamists who were known to be anti-EU. The EU Member States started to lose faith in Turkish politics upon seeing the same Çiller form a

[8] Article 36 of the Additional Protocol: 'Freedom of movement for workers between Member States of the Community and Turkey shall be secured by progressive stages in accordance with the principles set out in Article 12 of the Agreement of Association between the end of the twelfth and the twenty-second year after the entry into force of that Agreement.' , *OJ* 1972 L 293.

coalition government with the Islamist Refah Party. Therefore, the EU officials would summarize Çiller's and, hence also, Turkey's EU policy as 'the EU being cheated.'[9]

In 1996 and 1997 serious crises took place regarding Cyprus that involved Turkey, which made the Turkish – EU relations more tense:

1. Greek Cypriot motorcyclists announced that they would hold a demonstration and cross the UN buffer zone to the Turkish Cypriot side, claiming that they would protest the 'Turkish occupation of the north Cyprus.' During the demonstration on 11 August 1996, one Greek Cypriot, Tasos Isaak, who was caught up in the barbwire in the UN buffer zone, was beaten by the extreme right wing Turkish demonstrators and died in hospital the same day.
2. During Tasos Isaak's funeral on 15 August 1996, a Greek Cypriot demonstrator, Solomon Solomonu, crossed the barbwire in the buffer zone and climbed up the Turkish flag post in order to bring down the Turkish flag. He was shot down by a gunfire, opened from the Turkish side.
3. On 18 December 1996, the European Court of Human Rights (ECHR) took a decision on the Loizidu case (1989) finding Turkey (and not the Turkish Cypriot authorities) guilty of obstructing Titania Loizidu from returning her property in north Cyprus (Turkish Republic of Northern Cyprus). That decision, in a way, implied that Turkey is an 'occupational force' in Cyprus.
4. The decision of the Greek Cypriot government to purchase Russian S 300 missiles to be installed in Cyprus as a defense/offense mechanism against Turkey, brought very strong opposition from Turkey only to be intervened by the US and the UK. Finally, the missiles were installed on the Greek island of Crete.

In addition, the *post-modern* military intervention on 28 February 1997 in Turkey to topple the Islamist Refah Party – DYP coalition, raised many concerns in the EU regarding the role of the military in Turkish politics.

All these factors, coupled with the debates within the EU that the 'EU is a Christian club in which Turkey has no place', put EU – Turkey relations in a very difficult situation. The 1997 Luxembourg Summit was the last drop that brought the EU-Turkey relations to a complete freeze.

During the Luxembourg Summit, Turkey was excluded from the list of candidate countries for EU membership. The EU followed the Commission's vision of an enlarged EU contained in its Communication of 15 July 1997, *Agenda 2000*.[10] Here, the Commission foresaw the accession of the Central

---

9 T. Çerçi, *Avrupa Yalanı: Avrupa Birligi Virajında Türkiye* [The EU Lie: Turkey in the EU Turn] (Istanbul, Tez Yayınları 2002) p. 47.

10 See Commission of the European Communities, *Agenda 2000* for a stronger and wider Union, COM(97) 2000, 15 July 1997.

and Eastern European countries together with the 'Republic of Cyprus' in the 2000s. This enlargement would take place in two waves. Six countries would be in the first wave (Poland, Hungary, Czech Republic, Slovenia, Estonia and Republic of Cyprus), while the second wave would include five more (Slovakia, Latvia, Lithuania, Bulgaria and Romania). Turkey was not included in either of the two enlargement waves. In addition, during the 1997 Luxembourg Summit the EU decided to open accession talks with the Republic of Cyprus on behalf of the whole island, completely disregarding the opinion of the Turkish Cypriot people. The Turkish reaction to the Luxembourg decision was immediate, clear and strong.

First, Turkey declared that it would not accept the EU as a legitimate party for negotiating any issue other than Turkey's Community membership procedures. In other words, Turkey implied that it would not accept EU's involvement as a third party in such issues as the Cyprus conflict and Turkish – Greek disputes. Secondly, the Turkish government announced that it would start integrating Turkish Republic of Northern Cyprus with Turkey in the same way the EU proposed to integrate the Republic of Cyprus. Finally, Turkey declared that it would not communicate with any EU official until the EU changed its attitude towards Turkey – meaning until it declared Turkey a candidate country for EU membership.

2.4 The Helsinki Summit: the beginning of the end?

After the Luxembourg Summit, EU – Turkey relations deteriorated for two years until the EU Commission issued its 1999 *Regular Report,*[11] where it recommended that Turkey be included as a candidate country in the enlargement process of the EU. However, the Commission did not set any definite date for the start of the accession negotiations with Turkey. According to the 1999 *Regular Report*:

'Turkey continues to comply with most of its obligations under the Customs Union. Additional efforts should be made in order to reach full compliance with the acquis notably in the completion and customs fields. In most of the areas identified in the European strategy, alignment efforts have continued. The administrative capacity to apply the acquis in the context of the Customs Union remains very satisfactory. However, Turkey needs to further modernize its administrative structures and increase staff training.'[12]

According to the Commission, Turkey must fulfill the political criteria laid down by the June 1993 Copenhagen European Council Summit (discussed below)

[11] See European Commission Regular Report on Turkey's progress towards accession, 13 October 1999.

[12] See Commission of the European Communities, op. cit. n.12, at Annex 1.

in order to start accession negotiations. The EU Council followed the Commission's recommendations and invited Turkey together with the other candidate countries to the Helsinki Summit in December 1999. In order to lift the traditional Greek veto on Turkey's candidacy, Turkey agreed to solve its disputes with Greece through peaceful means (including taking the matters to the ICJ) and to support the efforts of the UN Secretary General and his mission of good offices to solve the Cyprus problem.

After the Helsinki Summit, the EU Commission prepared the Accession Partnership for Turkey in November 2000, where the Commission identified conditions that Turkey has to meet in the short run (within one year) and in the medium run (one to four years time) in order for the accession negotiations to start with the EU.

Now, Turkey is faced with the challenge of fulfilling the political Copenhagen criteria, which means that Turkey should establish a fully democratic regime.

3 Democratisation in Turkey according to the Copenhagen criteria

3.1 The role of the Turkish military and the legacy of Atatürk in Turkish politics

Turkey is a unique case among other Muslim states in that it has always been a Western oriented modern state since its establishment. The Turkish military has played the role of a guardian in keeping Turkey in the Western oriented track.

The military in Turkey has always played a role in shaping politics even when the army is thought to be in the barracks. They have usually played a moderator role having veto power in the National Security Council (since 1961) meetings, which were held once a month. This consists of the President, the Prime-Minister and a few other ministers, such as the ministers of Defense, Interior, Foreign Affairs, the Chief of Staff and the Deputy Chiefs of Staff of the military. The most recent intervention of the military as a moderator was on 28 February 1997 where a 'semi'-intervention of the praetorian military to demand stronger adherence to secularism (laicism), democracy and Atatürk's reforms, took place in the National Security Council meeting.

The Turkish military also played a role which was closer to moderator but more intense in that it bore similarities with a guardian type role, and in 1971 imposed a civilian government of its liking, without actually physically coming to power. In 1960 (until 1961) and in 1980 (until 1983), the military coups actually toppled the civilian governments and the military ruled the country with technocrats for brief periods. They even discarded the old constitutions (of

1924 and 1961) and designed new constitutions (of 1961 and 1982). However, the Turkish military's role in the 1960 and 1980 coups could not be regarded as 'rulers.' Their role was more like *guardians* who came to *save* the country from going into chaos. Having done so, they would withdraw to their barracks again. They promised this after the coups and always followed their promises after each coup. Therefore, since the establishment of the Turkish Republic, the Turkish military have mostly been moderator praetorians.

In order to understand the Turkish military's mindset in detail and have a more complete picture of the Turkish military interventions into politics, one has also to talk about Atatürk's legacy on the Turkish military.

Atatürk's[13] revolutions/reforms of Nineteen-twenties and Nineteen-thirties took place in Turkey, which greatly shaped and, in certain cases, re-made the Turkish political culture. In terms of political transformation, the some six hundred years old semi-theocratic monarchy of the Ottoman Empire was replaced by the French model nation-state. Atatürk thought that changing the structure of the country (i.e., changing the old institutions, laws, and replacing them with the new Western ones), would also lead to the change of the political culture, which would in turn support the changes, i.e., the revolutions/reforms.

Atatürk proposed six tenets as the guidelines for his revolutions for the young Turkish Republic: Nationalism, Republicanism, Statism (Etatism), Secularism (Laicism), Populism and Revolutionism. Atatürk pointed to Europe, which he identified with civilization, democratic systems and liberal economy, as an example for the Turkish Republic. He started with the basics; a reformed language;[14] a new system of law,[15] and; a new sense of national identity, based on a newly invented[16] (or created) tradition and culture excluding Islamic and Arabic elements (i.e., the Ottoman heritage).

The key to keep in mind is that Atatürk prepared the Turkish military as a *guardian* of the reforms/revolutions – his six tenets and his efforts to Westernize the Turkish state. Since the establishment of the Turkish republic, the military have been the most powerful and vigorous supporter of the reforms/revolutions, and since Atatürk's death (1938) they have been the strongest guardians of the Atatürk legacy.

The Turkish military officers regard themselves as the followers of Atatürkism and the guardians of its principles. Hence, this implies that the Turkish army should not deal with or should not be involved in, the day-to-day of

---

[13] Mustafa Kemal Atatürk was founder of the Turkish Republic and its first president (1881-1938).

[14] Adoption of the Latin alphabet.

[15] A code of penal law from Italy and a civil code from Switzerland.

[16] Eric Hobsbawm's argument that national identity is in fact an assortment of invented traditions engineered by political elites to control mass political mobilization during periods of rapid socio-economic change. See, E. J. Hobsbawm, *Nations and Nationalism Since 1780* (Cambridge, Cambridge University Press 1990).

government policies but, rather, should be a depoliticized institution, helping to guard the reforms/revolutions from such movements as ethnic separatism and religious fundamentalism both within and outside Turkey. So far, the training of the young cadets has uncompromisingly been conducted in that direction, and it seems this will continue in that same direction for some time.

It is no surprise that one can see a strong opposition from the Turkish army to the democratisation steps in the areas related to ethnicity and religion. The Turkish military announces very clearly that it regards issues such as ethnicity and religion, as very sensitive and closely related to national security. In that regard, for example, the military might see freedom of expression as a separatist threat by the PKK or as a threat by the religious fundamentalists to transform the country into a theocracy. Whether true or an illusion, the military look at the democratisation through the Copenhagen criteria (discussed in more detail below) with great caution.

3.2 The lost years: the Nineteen-eighties and nineties

As discussed in the previous section, such political standards as democracy, rule of law, respect for human rights and protection of minorities rose in importance globally in the early Nineteen-nineties – coinciding with the end of the Cold War. It was clear that Turkey felt the need to adopt such norms during the customs union negotiations with the EU. It was precisely then that Turkey slowly started to take important democratisation steps due to the EU pressures (an external dynamic).

Since the 1980 military coup, and especially with Turgut Özal's coming to power in 1983, Turkey has been liberalizing its economy in order to integrate it with global financial markets. However, due to a few internal factors, political liberalization (democratisation) has been rather slow until 2000:

1. Since the mid Nineteen-eighties, Turkey had been fighting the PKK separatism militarily. This war had cost more than 30,000 casualties, a state of emergency rule in some parts of the Southeast Anatolia and billions of dollars on military spending.
2. From the late Nineteen-eighties until today, Turkey has been poisoned by political instability where Turkey has witnessed thirteen different governments and fifteen different Foreign Ministers since November 1989.

Serious democratisation reforms started in Turkey after the Helsinki Summit in December 1999 where Turkey was declared as a candidate country for EU membership.

3.3 EU criteria for Membership

Article 237 of the Treaty of Rome stated that any 'European' country could apply to become a member of the EEC. So, the membership requirements were:

1. being European;
2. having a developed economy comparable to the Member States' economies (i.e., not being an economic burden on the member countries). The Birkelbach Report (1962) adopted by the European Parliamentary Assembly, tried to set more specific and detailed standards for membership:

'[Only] states which guarantee on their territories truly democratic practices and respect for fundamental human rights and freedoms can become members of our Union.'[17]

But only in 1978 did the European Council adopt a Declaration insisting on the respect for and maintenance of a parliamentary democracy and human rights as an essential pre-condition to EU membership.

With the Maastricht Treaty in 1992, Article 237 of the Treaty of Rome was repealed and replaced by Article 49 EU. Being a 'European' country with a developed economy only does not say anything about the post-Cold War values, such as democracy and respect for human rights. Also, the Member States sought more flexibility. The criteria of 'Europeanness,' for example, were debatable for such countries as Turkey, Malta, Cyprus and the Baltic states during the Cold War. In addition, keeping Article 237 of the Treaty of Rome would definitely create problems for the Eastern and Central European countries' membership process in terms of their poor economics and human rights records (if not in terms of their Europeanness).

The Maastricht Treaty itself offered only a very general account about the conditions of membership in the EU, without explicit mention of the membership requirements or criteria.[18]

---

[17] Quotation taken from D. Ethier, 'Is Democracy Promotion Effective? Comparing Conditionality and Incentives', 10 *Democratisation* (2003) p. 101.

[18] This was covered in Article o under the Final Provisions (Title VII) in the Maastricht Treaty: 'Any European State may apply to become a Member of the Union. It shall address its application to the Council, which shall act unanimously after consulting the Commission and after receiving the assent of the European Parliament, which shall act by an absolute majority of its component members. The condition of admission and the adjustments to the Treaties on which the Union is founded which such admission entails shall be the subject of an agreement between the Member States and the applicant State. This agreement shall be submitted for ratification by all the contracting States in accordance with their respective constitutional requirements'.

The established criteria countries aspiring to EU membership, although not written, included:

1. being European,
2. having comparable economies to those of the Member States and
3. to have political stability in their territories, Parliamentary democracy and respect for human rights as well as the rule of law and respect for and protection of minorities.

The EU tries to improve its relations/ties with non-member states by various means of contractual relations in the form of bi-lateral association agreements. These provide a framework for economic and technical assistance and improving trade relations in specific commodity categories. Certain association agreements prepare non-member countries for eventual membership in the EU or they suggest creation of a customs union between the non-member states and the Union. Cyprus (1973), Malta (1971), and Turkey (1964) are in this category.

Today, the criteria for EU membership are very clear. The EU established the necessary criteria for membership in the Copenhagen Summit in 1993:

1. *Political Criteria*: The candidate country has to achieve stability in its institutions, to guaranteeing democracy, the superiority of rule of law, respect for human rights and respect for and protection of minorities;
2. *Economic Criteria*: The candidate country has to have a functioning market economy and the capacity to cope with competitive pressures and market forces within the Union;
3. *Acquis Communautaire*: The candidate country has to have the capacity to approximate its administrative structures to the European Community legislation, so that all the Community legislation and provisions under the Community treaties are adopted by the candidate country. In addition, the candidate country should be able to take on the obligations of membership, such as adopting the aims of political, economic and monetary union of the Community.

3.4 Democratisation in Turkey as a result of the Copenhagen criteria

After the Helsinki Summit, the EU Commission prepared the Accession Partnership for Turkey (AP Turkey)[19] on 8 November 2000 where the EU put forward the conditions that Turkey has to satisfy in the short run (within one year) and in the medium run (within four years). In response to the AP Turkey, Turkey prepared its National Programme for the Adoption of the Acquis

[19] See the document at the website of the Commission's Delegation to Turkey, www.deltur.cec.eu.int/english/turkey2000ap. rtf. The AP Turkey was adopted by Council Decision of 8 March 2001. See *OJ* 2001 L 85.

(NPAA)[20] on 19 March 2001 where it committed to meeting the conditions in the AP Turkey in the short and the medium run.

3.4.1 Accession Partnership Turkey

Although the AP Turkey is very detailed covering areas ranging from human rights to fisheries, Turkish politics have been programmed to address only a very small portion of the APD: the Cyprus issue, Greek-Turkish disputes and the rights of the Kurdish population. The AP Turkey, in addition to the Copenhagen criteria, included these issues as pre-conditions to opening accession negotiations.

According to the liberal critics, Turkey was trying to mask its unwillingness to fulfill the reform requirements of the EU with these 'national' issues where the general public is very sensitive. Many liberals argued that Greek – Turkish, Cyprus and the Kurdish issues were minor issues and Turkey should be more flexible on these issues in order to join the EU. According to this view, Turkey did not want to fulfill the economic criteria (such as passing competition laws, reforming the market to be more open) and that the army did not want to lose power. Hence, the Turkish government hid behind these sensitive issues.

The critics of the AP Turkey, however, claimed that it would be foolish to see the latest developments as a coincidence:

1. The issue of the Armenian genocide had recently come to the attention of many European parliaments and was recognized by the European Parliament (EP).
2. The Cyprus issue entered the AP Turkey among the short-term criteria that Turkey had to solve according to the UN Secretary General's proposals. Interestingly, Kofi Annan made a verbal proposal to the two sides in dispute after the end of the fifth round of Cyprus talks. The proposal did not include elements of a confederation, which had been put forward by the Turkish Cypriot side in the five rounds of talks.
3. Turkish Foreign Minister Ismail Cem was interrupted and harassed during his speech at the EP's Foreign Relations Committee by two left-wing demonstrators. The Turkish government saw this as an action that had been planned by some Members of the European Parliament since there should have been tighter security.
4. A letter written by Alain Servantie, the Head of the Turkish Desk at the EU Commission, to the 'Presidential Council of PKK' was discovered. It was regarded as a scandal that the EU Commission had even exchanged a letter from the terrorist organization, which tried to divide Turkey. The incident was regarded as a 'shameful mistake' by the Commission President Romano Prodi, who apologized to Turkey.

---

[20] EU General Secretariat, Turkey's National Program (Official Publication of Turkish Prime Ministry 2001).

These incidents gave legitimacy to the critics of the AP Turkey to claim that the EU was not sincere in its consideration of Turkey in its pre- accession process.

Turkish domestic reactions in the political parties, the army and non-governmental organizations to the AP Turkey had dominated the Turkish media and pushed the other problems facing Turkey (such as the economic crisis in the stock market, the rise of interest rates, the country-wide strike of civil servants and so forth) to the lower priority level.

Initially, the Turkish government and the army adopted a very hard position towards the AP Turkey. President of the Turkish Republic of Northern Cyprus Rauf Denktas was invited to the National Security Council meeting in Ankara. There, the National Security Council supported Denktas' decision to not participating to the sixth round of the Cyprus talks. This was a very clear reaction to the AP Turkey.

The army and the government in general, and Bülent Ecevit's DSP and Devlet Bahçeli's MHP in particular, are the most vocal supporters of the NSC's support to Denktas. Tansu Çiller's opposition party DYP also adopted a very nationalistic policy towards the AP Turkey. They claimed that the AP Turkey includes elements that might prove a threat to the 'unitary state structure' of Turkey. The religious FP however criticized the government's policy (for the sake of criticizing!). However, there were a few important incidents involving some members of the government worth mentioning here, which were different from the government's policy.

Mesut Yilmaz (ANAP) (the Deputy Prime Minister and the State Minister Responsible for the EU Affairs), Ismail Cem (DSP) (the Foreign Minister) and Hikmet Sami Türk(the Minister of Justice) tried to smooth over the NSC's decision:

1. Mesut Yilmaz was known for his press briefings where he advocated Kurdish TV. He claimed that the AP Turkey had a few rough areas but that they were "fixable".
2. Ismail Cem claimed that Turkey should not rush to quick decisions and that Turkey should wait (and not make an irreversible decision on Cyprus) until the end of the EU's Nice Summit (in December 2002) to see the changes on the AP Turkey.
3. Hikmet Sami Türk argued that Turkey had indicated its reservations at the EU's Helsinki Summit and that the AP Turkey would not create a problem.

After the AP Turkey was declared, a heated and significant debate started in Turkey on the country's aspirations for EU membership. A good development was that the NGOs and leading intellectuals were also positively contributing to this debate. The heavy economic crisis of 2001 also raised lots of criticism of corrupt and undemocratic practices in Turkey. At this juncture, reforms in Turkey were seen as necessary and inevitable. According to many liberals and businessmen, the AP Turkey and the NPAA would be a good start for Turkey to reform itself and join the club of the 'civilized states.'

The type of discourse that the EU adopted towards Turkey especially after the Helsinki Summit also softened the atmosphere in Turkey towards the EU. In the past, the Community, usually bluntly, had condemned Turkey for its poor record on human rights and democratic practices. However, since the late Nineteen-nineties (especially with the Helsinki Summit in 1999), the EU has adopted a more constructive and smooth discourse towards Turkey. In all the Regular Reports of the Commission (1999 - 2004), Turkey was praised for its democratic reforms and politely encouraged to take further steps towards democratisation and improve in the areas of human rights and so forth.

3.4.2 Turkey's National Programme for the Adoption of the Acquis

The preparation of the NPAA has been one of the most important progresses that the Turkish Government has made since the EU's Helsinki Summit. Following the Helsinki Summit, the Turkish Government established an institution called the European Union General Secretariat (EUGS), which has been regulating the EU affairs in coordination with the Ministry of Foreign Affairs. It was also the EUGS who prepared the NPAA. Here, it is very important to note that the EUGS had been headed by Ambassador Volkan Vural[21] under the deputy-Prime-Ministry of Mesut Yilmaz who has proved a vocal, pro-EU politician.

The NPAA was prepared, as a response to the AP Turkey where the EU specified its demands from Turkey before the accession negotiations could begin (2004).

The actual NPAA was about 500 pages in length. Together with addendums, it reaches to around 1000 pages. The political and economic criteria occupied about 20 pages, while the remaining 500 pages included articles that would be harmonized with the EU's *acquis communautaire*.

According to the NPAA, Turkey would implement 4000 administrative changes, modify 94 laws and pass 89 new laws in order to comply with the EU's *acquis communautaire*. The crucial question here is how close the Turkish NPAA was to the EU's AP Turkey? In other words, to what extent did the Turkish NPAA satisfy the demands put forward in the AP Turkey? The above question can be answered in two ways:

1. The NPAA, although proposing to harmonize the Turkish legal system and economic and political structures and laws with the EU, used very general and vague terms on very important areas: the death penalty; the role of the National Security Council; cultural rights, including radio and TV broadcasting and education for minorities in languages other than Turkish. The reaction of some of the foreign media and a very small

[21] Ambassador Volkan Vural is a pro-Europe former Ambassador to Germany and a very skilled diplomat.

number of extreme pro-EU Turkish elite was that with the current NPAA Turkey was losing its chance to be a EU member. In other words, the above-mentioned areas, which were left vague, were so important that the current NPAA did not satisfy the demands of the EU put forward in the AP Turkey.

2. The NPAA, although it used very general and vague terms in some important areas, was, nonetheless, a promise of radical reform. Once the NPAA was implemented, Turkey would have new rules and laws covering a vast range of fields, such as how fishing will be carried out; the conditions of child labour; what one can sell in the streets; to the quality of food packaging; job security, and so forth. Such changes would dramatically change and transform Turkey from being a 'developing country' to a country that belongs to the group of the 'civilized nations.' In that sense, the NPAA should be seen as a huge step forward and should be supported by everybody who wants to see Turkey as a EU member.

When one looks at the NPAA objectively, it can be said that it was a major development given the serious constraints in Turkey:

1. Turkey was being ruled by a coalition government of three ideologically different parties (a soft-left of Bület Ecevit, an extreme right of Devlet Bahçeli and a conservative-liberal party of Mesut Yılmaz). It is very normal that all the decisions were taken through consensus which made any dramatic change or reform difficult.
2. The military was still very strong in Turkey and was very sensitive on issues regarding the 18 year-old fight with the PKK (since 1984) and Islamic Fundamentalist movements. The army thought that some democratisation moves would provide platforms for the PKK and the Islamic fundamentalists to increase their strength.
3. Corruption was very widespread in Turkey. Moreover, it reached and spread to very high positions. Such places exerted implicit pressures to the change of the status quo (i.e., the corrupt system). In that sense, the NPAA promised a transparent system where corruption would not be tolerated.

As the domestic constraints explicitly show, the Turkish NPAA can be regarded as a big step forward for the completion of Turkish modernisation.[22] The crucial question here is whether Turkey had the necessary political will to implement

[22] It is a funny coincidence that the other (economic) 'National Programme' of Turkey, which was designed by the World Bank veteran, the then Minister responsible for Economy Kemal Dervis for the Turkish economic crisis, came out at the same time. It seems like that these two 'National Programmes' should be treated as parts of a whole. While the NP for the EU promised to transform Turkey mostly politically and legally into a democracy, the NP for the economy intended to transform Turkey into a liberal economy.

the NPAA, or rather, did Turkey have the politicians with the political courage to risk their political careers for the implementation of the NPAA? Before answering this question lets look at the following table, which gives a summary of the EU's political demands inthe AP Turkey, and whether the NPAA is compatible with the EU's demands in the AP Turkey.

A comparison of the National Programme for the Adoption of the Acquis (NPAA) with the Accession Partnership for Turkey according to the Copenhagen Political Criteria.

1.1 SHORT TERM	
1.2 AP Turkey	NPAA
1. In accordance with the Helsinki conclusions, in the context of the political dialogue, strongly support the UN Secretary General's efforts to bring to a successful conclusion the process of finding a comprehensive settlement of the Cyprus problem, as referred to in point 9(a) of the Helsinki conclusions.	Partly compatible in the short term. Conditional support is given in the introduction of the NPAA, but not within the political criteria.
2. Strengthen legal and constitutional guarantees for the right to freedom of expression in line with Article 10 of the European Convention of Human Rights. Address in that context the situation of those persons in prison sentenced for expressing non-violent opinions.	Compatible in the short term.
3. Strengthen legal and constitutional guarantees of the right to freedom of association and peaceful assembly and encourage development of civil society.	Compatible in the short term.
4. Strengthen legal provisions and undertake all necessary measures to reinforce the fight against torture practices, and ensure compliance with the European Convention for the Prevention of Torture.	Compatible in the short term/ medium term.
5. Further align legal procedures concerning pre-trial detention with the provisions of the European Convention on Human Rights and with recommendations of the Committee for the Prevention of Torture.	Compatible in the medium term.
6. Strengthen opportunities for legal redress against all violations of human rights.	Compatible in the medium term.
7. Intensify training on human rights issues for law enforcement officials in mutual co-operation with individual countries and international organizations.	Compatible in the short term.
8. Improve the functioning and efficiency of the judiciary, including the State security court in line with inter-national standards. Strengthen in particular training of judges and prosecutors on European Union legislation, including in the field of human rights.	Compatible in the short term.
9. Maintain the de facto moratorium on capital punishment.	Compatible in the short term. The Turkish Parliament's decisions would be respected.

10. Remove any legal provisions forbidding the use by Turkish citizens of their mother tongue in TV/radio broadcasting.	Not compatible.
11. Develop a comprehensive approach to reduce regional disparities, and in particular to improve the situation in the south-east, with a view to enhancing economic, social and cultural opportunities for all citizens.	Compatible in the medium term.

1.3 MEDIUM TERM	
1.4 AP Turkey	NPAA
1. In accordance with the Helsinki conclusions, in the context of the political dialogue, under the principle of peaceful settlement of disputes in accordance with the UN Charter, make every effort to resolve any outstanding border disputes and other related issues, as referred to in point 4 of the Helsinki conclusions.	Partly compatible. NPAA stresses resolution of conflicts through political dialogue.
2. Guarantee full enjoyment by all individuals without any discrimination and irrespective of their language, race, color, sex, political opinion, philosophical belief or religion of all human rights and fundamental freedoms. Further develop conditions for the enjoyment of freedom of thought, conscience and religion.	Compatible in the short term/ medium term.
3. Review of the Turkish Constitution and other relevant legislation with a view to guaranteeing rights and freedoms of all Turkish citizens as set forth in the European Convention for the Protection of Human Rights; ensure the implementation of such legal reforms and conformity with practices in EU Member States.	Compatible in the short term/ medium term.
4. Abolish the death penalty, sign and ratify Protocol 6 of the European Convention of Human Rights.	Partly compatible. The Turkish Parliament would discuss the issue in the near future.
5. Ratify the International Covenant on Civil and Political Rights and its optional Protocol and the International Covenant on Economic, Social and Cultural Rights.	Compatible. No time frame has been indicated in the NPAA.
6. Adjust detention conditions in prisons to bring them into line with the UN Standard Minimum Rules for the Treatment of Prisoners and other international norms.	Compatible in the short term.
7. Align the constitutional role of the National Security Council as an advisory body to the Government in accordance with the practice of EU Member States.	Compatible in the medium term.
8. Lift the remaining state of emergency in the south- east.	Compatible in the medium term.
9. Ensure cultural diversity and guarantee cultural rights for all citizens irrespective of their origin. Any legal provisions preventing the enjoyment of these rights should be abolished, including in the field of education.	Not compatible.

Source: Accession Partnership with Turkey (Council Decision of 8 March 2001 – OJ 2001 L 85); Turkey's National Programme (Turkish Prime Ministry EU General Secretariat of 19 March 2001); B. Oran, Türk Dis Politikasi, Cilt II, [Turkish Foreign Policy, Vol. II] (Istanbul, Iletisim Yayinlari 2001) p. 363.

As can be seen from the above comparison between the AP Turkey and the NPAA, the NPAA, although not fully compatible with the AP Turkey in certain issues such as 'education in mother tongue,' was a major step forward in democratisation for Turkey. The NPAA looks good on paper and changes several laws towards more democratization.

3.4.3 The reform packages

On 19 June 2003 the Turkish Grand National Assembly voted in favour of the sixth EU Harmonization Package that included laws permitting broadcasting of languages other than Turkish in public and private radio and TV stations. Beside other democratisation steps, the package also included a modification in the Law Against Terrorism (Terörle Mücadele Yasası).[23] A more substantive reform package, known as the seventh EU Harmonization Package, was adopted by the Turkish Ground National Assembly on 30 July 2003. According to this package:

1. Competences of the National Security Council (NSC) were restricted. The decisions of the NSC were no longer binding on the government. Hence, the Council became an advisory organ, the secretary general of which could be a civilian.
2. Government Accounting Bureau (Sayistay) would be able to audit the spending of all institutions (including the army) using public resources and finances.
3. Civilians would not be tried in the military courts.
4. The legal age of a child was changed from 15 to 18.
5. Restrictions on the right to demonstrate and the right of assembly were eased.
6. Restrictions on the foreign foundations were eased.[24]

Considering the fact that during these reforms Turkey was governed by a difficult coalition government of DSP (a nationalist soft left), MHP (extreme right wing nationalist) and ANAP (conservative liberal), these packages were truly important reforms and can be seen as a major step in fulfilling the Copenhagen political criteria.

The EU Commission, in its 2003 Regular Report on Turkey, applauded the sixth and seventh EU Harmonization Packages and stated that Turkey was very close to having its laws in line with the Copenhagen political criteria.[25] The Commission encouraged Turkey to take the necessary steps to adopt the rest of

---

[23] See daily *Milliyet* (20 June 2003) for more details.

[24] See daily *Radikal* (31 July 2003) for more details.

[25] See Commission of the European Communities, *Regular Report on Turkey's progress towards accession 2003*, at p. 134.

the laws that would satisfy the Copenhagen political criteria and recommended Turkey to put the newly adopted laws into implementation without delay. The Table below is a summary of the state of the Copenhagen political criteria in Turkey as analyzed by the Commission in its 2003 Regular Report on Turkey:

1a) The state of the Copenhagen Political Criteria in Turkey according to the 2003 Regular Report

1.5 Targets of Priority	1.6 Regular Progress Report (2003)
To strongly support UN Secretary-General's efforts on the resolution of the Cyprus problem.	Implemented to a great extent through the 'political dialogue' framework.
In accordance with the Helsinki Summit conclusions, steps should be taken in line with the relevant provisions of the UN Charter for the peaceful settlement of disputes in order to resolve existing border disputes and all other related problems.	Implemented to a great extent.
- The ratification of international agreements and protocols on civil and political rights, and on social, economic and cultural rights. - The ratification of the 6th Protocol to the European Convention on Human Rights. - To act in accordance with the provisions of the European Convention on Human Rights and Fundamental Freedoms, and implement the decisions of the European Court of Human Rights (The II. Part of the Convention).	The laws are compatible. There are problems concerning implementation.
Steps should be taken in accordance with the recommendations of the European Committee on the Prevention of Torture and with the Art. 3 of the European Convention on Human Rights to prevent torture and inhuman and degrading treatment. The judicial system should be reformed so as to enable the effective investigation of torture cases and the punishment the perpetrators.	The laws are compatible. There are problems concerning implementation.
In accordance with the European Convention on Human Rights, to guarantee (in practice) for the detainees and those under police custody access to a lawyer (and right to meet in private with their lawyers), and to promptly inform the families of those under custody of their situation.	The laws are compatible. There are problems concerning implementation.
- Regarding freedom of expression, and especially concerning the freedom of the press, reforms should be undertaken and implemented. The legal restrictions regarding Articles 10, 17 and 18 should be abolished. - The situation of those detained or under investigation for the expression of non-violent views should be reformed. - In accordance with the decisions of the European Court of Human Rights the legal framework necessary for the proper implementation of the right to retrial needs to be established.	The laws are compatible to a great extent. There are problems concerning implementation.

- Reforms in the field of peaceful assembly and association should be undertaken and implemented. - Especially the restrictions concerning the trade unions should be abolished and reformed in accordance with Articles 11, 17 and 18 of the European Convention on Human Rights. - The development of civil society should be encouraged.	There are shortages concerning legal harmonization. There are serious problems with implementation.
- In law and in practice, the fundamental rights of all, irrespective of their language, race, sex, political thought, religion and belief should be ensured without being discriminated on the grounds cited above, and in accordance with the international and European conventions to which Turkey is a party. - In accordance with Art. 9 of the European Convention on Human Rights, the freedom of conscience and religion of all individuals and groups should be ensured in law and in practice. - In accordance with the current practice in the EU, conditions for the proper functioning of religious groups should be provided. In this framework, the property rights of these groups, their education, the appointment and education of the clergy should be ensured (legally and judicially) in accordance with the First Protocol to the European Convention on Human Rights. - Irrespective of their origin the diversity and cultural rights of all should be ensured. The existing reforms should be implemented and the remaining restrictions lifted, so that the rights of radio and TV broadcasting in languages other than Turkish can be effectively enjoyed.	There are shortages concerning legal harmonization. There are serious problems with implementation.
The military should be put under civilian control and the structure and working method of the NSC should be rearranged in line with practices in EU countries.	The laws are not completely compatible. There is need for more civilian control.
- The independence and efficiency of the judiciary should be strengthened. The legal reforms concerning fundamental rights and freedoms need to be interpreted in line with the European Convention on Human Rights. - Measures need to be taken so that all the judicial authorities fulfill their obligation of acting in accordance with the case law of the European Court of Human Rights. - The functioning of the State Security Courts should be harmonized with existing European standards. Preparation should be done for the establishment of appellate courts.	There are shortages concerning legal harmonization. There are problems with implementation.
The current state of Turkish prisons needs to improved and reformed in line with European standards.	The laws are compatible. There are problems concerning implementation.

- In the framework of the fight against torture and ill-treatment, the security personnel should be trained on modern interrogation techniques. - The training of judges and prosecutors needs to strengthened so that they will be able to implement the European Convention on Human Rights and its case law.	The laws are compatible. Implementation is carried out successfully.
With the aim of increasing the economic, social, and cultural opportunities, especially concerning the improvement of conditions in the South East of Turkey, in the framework of reducing regional disparities, a general strategy needs to designed and implemented.	The laws are compatible. There is both success and failure in implementation.

Source: 'Targets of Priority' column was modified and translated from TUSIAD's report 'Midium-Term Targets in the Modified APD and the regular report on Turkey – 2003' ['Yenilestirilmis KOB'da Orta Vadeli Hedefler ve AB'nin Türkiye Ilerleme Raporu – 2003'] (10 November 2003 TS/BXL/03-43). (The modified parts according to the previous APD are shown in bold).

3.4.4 The AKP government and the struggle to start the accession negotiations

The November 2003 parliamentary election resulted in the AKP coming to power with two-thirds of the seats. It was after 12 years of coalition governments (1991-2003) that Turkey was once again ruled by one party government of the AKP. The AKP government came to power with a party programme that called for more democratisation and Turkey's EU membership. Unlike many previous governments, the AKP government has successfully showed its commitment to democratisation and Turkey's EU membership process by measurable deeds. During the AKP government, more than 200 new laws were adopted in line with the Copenhagen criteria. After the latest constitutional changes in 10 Articles on 7 May 2004, known as the eighth EU Harmonisation Package, one third of the 1982 Constitution has been modified. With the eighth Package, Turkey has fulfilled the Copenhagen political criteria in its Constitution and laws. It includes the following important topics:

1. Gender equality was guaranteed by the constitution.
2. The State Security Courts were abolished.
3. There will be no member from the military in the Higher Education Council.
4. Military spending will be audited by the Government Accounting Bureau (Sayıstay).
5. International treaties and coventions on fundamental rights and freedoms will have priority over national laws.
6. The Statute of the International Criminal Court is recognised.
7. The death penalty in any situation was completely abolished in the Constitution.
8. Freedom of press is guaranteed by the Constitution.[26]

[26] See daily *Radikal* (8 May 2004) for more details.

In addition, the Turkish Grand National Assembly, after a hot debate on 'adultery' orchestrated by the AKP, voted in support of the new Turkish Civil Law on 27 September 2004.[27] This was the last requirement of the EU Commission from Turkey before the Commission's decision on the start of the accession talks with Turkey. Hence, the EU Commission, on 6 October 2004, published its annual Regular Report on Turkey, together with a communication to the EU Council where the Commission indicated that Turkey had fulfilled the Copenhagen political criteria and recommended that the Council open accession negotiations with Turkey.[28] After tough negotiations at the EU Council Summit on 17 December 2004, the Council decided to start the accession negotiations with Turkey on 3 October 2005. Though, the accession negotiations with Turkey would be 'open-ended'[29] it was a historic decision of the EU to take the first step towards the consensus of civilizations.

4 Conclusion: the future of Turkey's EU process

As the analysis above shows, Turkey has taken enormous steps in democratisation as a direct result of the Copenhagen political criteria since the 1999 EU Helsinki summit, when Turkey was officially declared a candidate for EU membership. It is obvious that this EU conditionality tool played a key role in the recent transformations in democracy in Turkey. Especially through the sixth, the seventh, the eighth EU Harmonization Packages and the new Civil Law, Turkey has not only fulfilled the Copenhagen political criteria on paper but has proved it is committed to the EU process.

The democratisation steps in the domestic domain reflect also on traditional Turkish foreign policy. Certain important changes in traditional Turkish foreign policy in the last few years are also significant indications for Turkey's commitment to the EU process. Since the 1999 Helsinki Summit, Turkey has behaved as an ideal EU member – committed to solving its foreign policy conflicts through dialogue and peaceful diplomacy. The rapprochement with Greece since the 1999 Helsinki summit was the beginning of the new orientations in the Turkish foreign policy. Turkey carefully refrained from its traditional verbal threats and nationalistic discourse towards Greece and in a way brought Greece to the resolution of its bilateral conflicts with Turkey through political dialogue

[27] The New Civil Law which replaced the 78 years old Italian model Civil Law was approved by the Turkish President on 12 October 2004. See daily *Sabah* (28 September 2004) for the details on the New Civil Law.

[28] See Commission of the European Communities, op. cit. n. 1.

[29] See Arts. 17-23 and specifically Art. 23 for the framework for negotiations in Presidency Conclusions, Brussels, 16/17 December 2004.

and diplomacy. Turkey also showed its goodwill and co-operation in the Cyprus negotiations in New York, Nicosia and Bürgenstock (Switzerland) during February and March 2004. The result of the April 2004 referenda in Cyprus, where the Cyprus peace plan (known as the Annan Plan) which called for the unification of Cyprus in a loose federal structure and the membership of the unified island in the EU, was supported by 65 per cent of Turkish Cypriot votes while it was rejected by 76 per cent of Greek Cypriot votes, showed Turkey's capacity for compromise and its commitment to the EU. Furthermore, on 1 March 2003, the rejection of the Turkish Parliament (the Grand National Assembly) of a resolution that would authorize the US military forces to enter Turkey en route to Iraq was a clear message from the Turkish MPs that Turkey would not be a part of the controversial war in Iraq. This was a significant departure from the traditional Turkey-US relations where Turkey had mostly been very co-operative with the US in security matters. Hence, one can clearly see significant signals in Turkish foreign policy that Turkey is strongly committed to its EU process both domestically and also in its foreign policy.